Canadian Cataloguing in Publication Data
Germano Celant
The European Iceberg
Creativity in Germany and Italy Today
Based on an exhibition held at the Art Gallery of Ontario,
Toronto, Ontario, February 8-April 7, 1985
Includes bibliographical references and index

First published in the United States of America in 1985 by
RIZZOLI INTERNATIONAL PUBLICATIONS, Inc.
597 Fifth Avenue, New York, NY 10017

ISBN 0-8478-0657-X
LC 85-43051

Printed and bound in Italy

The European Iceberg

Creativity in Germany and Italy Today

by

Germano Celant

The European Iceberg
Creativity in Germany and Italy Today
curated by Germano Celant
foreward by Roald Nasgaard

The Art Gallery of Ontario is funded by the Province of Ontario, the Ministry of Citizenship and Culture of Canada, the Government of Canada through the National Museums Corporation and the Canada Council, and the Municipality of Metropolitan Toronto.

Sponsored by Mr. and Mrs. Roger Davidson and family, with the support of Crownx Inc., Alitalia, the Goethe Institute Toronto, Istituto Italiano di Cultura, Auswaürtiges Amt, Bonn, Currier & Smith Limited, and the Volunteer Committee of the Art Gallery of Ontario.

Lenders to the Exhibition

Salvatore Ala Gallery, New York
Acerbis International S.p.A., Bergamo
Alessi, Crusinallo
Giovanni Anselmo, Torino
Gae Aulenti, Milano
Banca Commerciale Italiana, New York
Giuseppe Bartolucci, Roma
Lothar Baumgarten, Düsseldorf
Galerie Jean Bernier, Athens
Galerie Bruno Bischofberger, Zürich
Gottfried Böhm, Köln
Mary Boone/Michael Werner Gallery, New York
Braun AG, Kronberg
Cassina S.p.A., Milano
Vincenzo Castella, Roma
Leo Castelli Gallery, New York
Pierluigi Cerri, Milano
Clark Equipment Company, Benton Harbor
Contempora Designs International Inc., Toronto
Minsa Craig, Los Angeles
Nicola De Maria, Torino
Liliane & Michel Durand-Dessert, Paris
Luciano Fabro, Milano
Flos S.p.A., Brescia
A.G. Fronzoni, Milano
Verena von Gagern, München
Luigi Ghirri, Modena
Marian Goodman Gallery, New York
Gregotti Associati, Milano
Hans Hollein, Wien
Rebecca Horn, Zell Bad König
Mimmo Jodice, Napoli
Galerie Johnen & Schöttle, Köln
Klaus Kinold, München
Michael Klar, Schwäbisch Gmünd
Josef Paul Kleihues, Berlin
Knoedler, Zürich
Sammlung Crex, Zürich
Karl Heinz Krug, Leichlingen
Herbert Lindinger, Hannover
Italo Lupi, Milano
Gerhard Merz, München
Mario Merz, Torino
Nino Migliori, Bologna
Reinhard Mucha, Düsseldorf
Art Gallery of Ontario, Toronto
Galerie Peter Pakesch, Wien
Giulio Paolini, Torino
Giuseppe Penone, Torino
Galleria Giorgio Persano, Torino
Renzo Piano - Building Workshop S.R.L., Genova
Mario Pieroni, Roma
Galerie Raab, Berlin
Salomé, Berlin
Remo Salvadori, Milano
Lutz Schirmer, München
Galerie Schmela, Düsseldorf
Philipp Scholz Rittermann, San Diego
Wilhelm Schurmann, Herzogenrath
Sonnabend Gallery, New York
Ettore Sottsass jr., Milano
Ettore Spalletti, Pescara
Galerie Thomas, München
Galerie Gamile Weber, Zürich
Sperone Westwater Gallery, New York
Edwin L. Stringer, Q.C., Toronto
Gino Valle, Udine
Emilio Vedova, Venezia
Vignelli Associates, New York
Waddington Galleries, London
Wadsworth Atheneum, Hartford
Ycami Collection S.R.L., Milano

The achievement of an exhibition and a catalogue calls for the collaboration of a large number of people, particularly when, as in this case, two countries (Germany and Italy) are involved in all their complexity. The help and encouragement I have received during the course of my work for this event have been most heartening. It is impossible to mention all the names, but I should at least like to express my thanks to the most important.
Working out a project of this sort would have been unthinkable without Roald Nasgaard's stimulus. With remarkable enthusiasm and courage he has accepted and backed up what is really a mammoth undertaking.
I am also grateful to the artists, architects, filmmakers, actors, directors, graphic designers, photographers and designers tout court, both for their advice and for the material they have come up with.
I should also like to thank Giovanni Anceschi, Giuseppe Bartolucci, Vittorio Boarini, Nicoletta and Andrea Branzi, Bazon Brock, Tilmann Buddensieg, Bruno Corà, Francesco Dal Co, Gillo Dorfles, Johannes Gachnang, Vittorio Gregotti, Peter Iden, Arturo Carlo Quintavalle and Wolfram Schütte for their help in finding facts and information for the show and for their theoretical contributions contained in the catalogue.
Ida Gianelli with her admirable meticulousness and tireless research has given the catalogue its scientific framework as well as dealing with the infinite problems involved in the European organization.
I am grateful to Massimo Vignelli for the wealth and flexibility of his ideas and suggestions that have lent so much to layout of both exhibition and catalogue. And I would also like to thank Robert Sckolnick for all he has done to overcome problems in design and image.
I have also been lucky enough to be able to rely on the help of Salvatore Ala, Heiner Bastian, Gianfranco Benedetti, Jean Bernier, Marie Puck Broodthaers, Ginestra Calzolari, Leo Castelli, Mary Boone, Andrea Cibic, Cineteca di Bologna, Ester Cohen, Michelle Coudray, Minsa Craig, Elena Cumani, Liliane and Michel Durand-Dessert, Didi Gayer, Marian Goodman, Konrad Fischer, Shunji Ishida, Kasper König, Madeleine Jenewein, Elisabeth Kaufmann, Helen van der Meij, Giorgio Persano, Mario Pieroni , Massimo Scheurer, Anna Serra, Ileana Sonnabend, Monika and Ulrike Schmela, Johnen & Schöttle, Robert Smith, Christian Stein, Hartmut Stroht, Pierluigi Tazzi, Michael Werner, Angela Westwater and Marco Zardini, who have added invaluable documents and information to our undertaking.
The English edition of the catalogue would have been impossible without the tirelessly professional collaboration of Leslie Strickland and Joachim Neugroschel who put energy and experience into the difficult task of translating from the German and the Italian. My heartfelt thanks also go to Bianca Franchetti and Carlo Giani of Mazzotta, as well as to Domenico Pertocoli of A&P Editing for all their publishing knowhow and effort.
Last but certainly not least I should like to thank all those who have lent works, and the entire staff of the Art Gallery of Ontario whose support have made this event possible.
Many thanks.

Germano Celant

Catalogue edited by Ida Gianelli

Cover by Massimo Vignelli

Translation from Italian: Joachim Neugroschel, New York
Translation from German: Leslie Strickland, Bremen
Editing: A&P Editing, Milan
Printing: Arti Grafiche Leva A&G, Sesto S. Giovanni, Milan
Publisher: Nuove Edizioni Gabriele Mazzotta, Milan

Contents

The European Iceberg: Creativity in Germany and Italy Today

Roald Nasgaard
Chief Curator
Art Gallery of Ontario

Foreword

During the eighties in Canada, as well as in the United States, we have increasingly become aware of the significance of contemporary development in European art. In the seventies when we spoke of international art, we were usually thinking about American art, or more specifically about New York art. European art, and that of the rest of the Western world, with some exceptions of course, figured minimally in our discourse, and was largely assumed to be provincial. With surprising rapidity we have had to reassess that view and learn to look as avidly across the North Atlantic as we used to gaze on New York.

The relative insularity of the North American perspective was partially explained by the increased self-absorption of New York during the seventies, as it had consolidated itself as the center of the international art world and of the art information distribution system, at least in the English language. Because of the amount of major American art continually being produced in New York itself, the overload of information to be absorbed and processed made it difficult to look elsewhere. Meanwhile, of course, equally serious and independent art was being produced in Los Angeles (and Toronto, as never before, although no one outside Canada seemed to notice), and for Europeans, also in Paris, London, Turin, Amsterdam, Düsseldorf, Berlin, etc. In other words, what was often too facilely assumed to be a centralized situation was in reality quite pluralistic, although perhaps much international art production was governed by minimalist and conceptualist aesthetics that somehow could be subsumed with a New York value system. In our own decade decentralized internationalism has not only become accepted as a fact but is also understood on new terms whereby specific geographical and historial contexts play as important a role as do the aesthetic universals. As if to force this reassessment European art has cast a broad shadow across the North American continent, to the extent that some Europeans have not been adverse to suggest that the action has quite entirely shifted to Europe.

However that may be, in North America we have perhaps, even in 1985, only sighted the very tip of the vast European iceberg of creativity, its breadth and depth still unexplored. In the first and most ambitious exhibition of its kind in Canada and indeed on this continent, the Art Gallery of Ontario in "The European Iceberg" takes a major step toward correcting that. Feeling that the occasion demanded a strong, but balanced European viewpoint, as well as a truly interrogatory approach, the Gallery invited Germano Celant to act as guest curator for the exhibition, in order to draw from his long and active engagement in European (and American) art as a critic, historian and curator.

From the first discussions between Germano and myself about the exhibition, we envisaged it on a large scale. This had to do with Germano's own ideas on how to address so big a problem, which he discusses in his introductory essay, and also with my notions of what was needed for the Art Gallery of Ontario and Toronto.

Although by now we have had the opportunity to see a good variety of recent European art here, and several of the artists' names are familiarly bandied about, our knowledge of the European scene remains fragmentary and largely secondhand. Certainly, speaking of North America in general, current European art has not yet been seen in any larger meaningful context. When it first appeared it was through the auspices of a number of New York dealers. But as has often been pointed out, they quite naturally concentrated their energies on a small number of artists, with much reiteration and reputation building, leaving North Americans with an imbalanced perspective and largely ignorant of the careers of many other equally significant artists. Valuable viewpoints were provided by several important museum exhibitions such as "German Drawings of the Sixties" at the Yale University Art Gallery and the Art Gallery of Ontario in 1982, "Italian Art Now: An American Perspective" at the Solomon R. Guggenheim Museum in 1982, and "Expressions: New Art from Germany" in 1983, organized and circulated by the St. Louis Art Museum. But on this continent we have not had the advantage that Europeans regularly have of large-scale international surveys, whether they are recurring such as Documenta or the Venice Biennale, or one-time events such as "Westkunst" (Cologne, 1981) and "Zeitgeist" (Berlin, 1982), exhibitions which readily keep Europeans amply informed not only about their own developments but also those in North America. In the absence of such forums for broad and in-depth coverage here, and with the consequent dearth of knowledge, it seemed necessary, if the Art Gallery of Ontario's first contemporary international survey exhibition in the eighties were to be a significant intervention into our consciousness, that it must also be grand and comprehensive.

Even so, to consider covering the whole of Europe, given its divers and multiform cultural make-up would be too complex a task for one exhibition to undertake. We chose instead to scale down the problem and to calve the iceberg, splitting off for closer scrutiny the creative work of only two countries, Germany and Italy. An examination of their cultures from out of the entire European spectrum, we felt, would most forcefully underscore the significance, independence and historical lineage of the European achievement. (It was also the so-called German and Italian "invasions" of New York, beginning in 1979-80, which precipitated the reappraisal of what constitutes international art.)

As Germano Celant envisaged the exhibition, the exploration of German and Italian creativity would be both more potent and provocative if it were conducted, not only from the perspective of painting and sculpture, but also within the broader visual fabric of such disciplines as design, architecture, fashion, photography, cinema and theatre. The exhibition consequently presents each of these disciplines in its own right, indicating the respective national contributions, while at the same time it tries to uncover their mutual correspondences without, however, wanting thereby to diminish the cultural complexity they arise from.

Two other aspects about the exhibition may be quickly noted. The exhibition concentrates on work of the eighties and will present several new faces. Nevertheless it is important to remember that many of the artists that we in North America recently took to be new when we first encountered them at the dealers or in the magazines, in fact, have substantial careers behind them. In other words, the vitality of the recent development which has hit North America with such force, is not new to European art, but something that was going on all along even if very little news of it reached us during the seventies. As Elizabeth Baker pointed out in an editorial in *Art in America* in its September 1982 issue, the magazine's first occasion to devote itself fully to new developments in Europe: "Consider such major figures from the pre-'new painting' generation as Sigmar Polke, Gerhard Richter or Marcel Broodthaers, whose complex, prolonged and (in Europe) influential œuvres, if better known here, would change our ideas about the 'invisible' European seventies." (Her call for full museum coverage of the three artists in North America remains unfilled.) There appears indeed to be a kind of asynchronism in the two continents' respective awareness and understanding of one another's art.

A second interesting aspect of "The European Iceberg" is that, rather than being hesitant to present art under national labels (German and Italian) — lest its real purposes somehow be construed as extra-artistic — the exhibition has found it essential to do so. Contrary to our more Platonic internationalist assumptions during the puristic years of Minimal and Conceptual Art, the achievements of contemporary European art seem increasingly to be outcomes of specific geographical and historical contexts. To deny as much would be to misread and misunderstand. In the words of Edy de Wilde, musing about the future from a Dutch perspective, in his introduction to the exhibition "Sixties-eighties Attitudes/Concepts/Images", the Stedelijk Museum's (Amsterdam) 1982 survey of the two preceding decades: "In Western Europe, the divergences and similarities become increasingly evident. It looks as if the 'Europe of the fatherlands' (Charles de Gaulle), is going to materialize in the visual arts. In its subjective emotive approach to reality, the young art in Germany, Italy and the Netherlands has a common denominator. It is true that the poignant expressionism of Kiefer or Baselitz stands wide apart from the light-footed lyricism of Cucchi and Chia, also from the earnestness of Van Hoek in his endeavor to subject emotion to the classical laws in painting. Art proves to be deeply rooted in the cultural environment in which it is born."

The national identifications of the newer European art (and for that matter, can the work of Joseph Beuys or the Arte Povera artists escape such identification?) have not unexpectedly been viewed with some (on occasion frankly chauvinistic) consternation by a number of critics in North America as simplistic, even perniciously parochial reactions to the long-standing dominance of American art. The polarized positions in this kind of argument can be illustrated as follows. On the one hand, Kynaston McShine's introduction to the Museum of Modern Art's 1984 "An International Survey of Recent Painting and Sculpture," an exhibition which enthusiastically embraced contemporary art from around the western world in its many local forms, nevertheless repeatedly insisted on its internationalism, and its purpose to demonstrate "some of the concerns that are 'basic, universal,' " and "that transcend international boundaries." On the other hand, American critics in a discussion recently published in the Swiss periodical *Parkett* (no. 2, 1984) worried that the North American fascination with the new German and Italian painters seen here was based on a "complete miscomprehension of what German (and Italian) culture is about after the war." So obscure is the regionalism of artists like Kiefer, one of the speakers proposed, that even people from other parts of Germany cannot understand him.

Controversy over the relevance of geographical and historical contexts, and critical anxiety about the accompanying political and ideological implications of the new painting and sculpture need not, of course, be demonstrated only in terms of intercontinental rivalries. These are issues argued as heatedly between modernists, who espouse incontrovertible universal aesthetic values, and the postmodernists, who throughout the disciplines represented in the exhibition refer to notions of roots, identity, place and culture. It is, of course, not coincidence that the advent of postmodernism should be accompanied by an attack within art history on the hegemony of French modernism in our understanding of nineteenth-century art, and by a discovery that serious, investigative, if not avant-garde art, was possible on its own terms in other European countries, including an area as geographically peripheral as Scandinavia. I refer to the latter because the viewpoint of the present text is from another peripheral country (in art world terms), namely Canada, which, not because of any inferiority of its recent art, but rather because of an ingrained attitude of condescension from the centres of power toward what occurs beyond, finds it difficult to be heard outside its own borders.

Canada may not possess the depth of artistic history of the Scandinavian countries but will nevertheless have a keen ear for the ironies of Pontus Hulten's analysis of the rules of how history is formulated (proposed in his introduction to "Sleeping Beauty-Art Now", an exhibition of contemporary Scandinavian art held at the Solomon R. Guggenheim Museum during the "Scandinavian invasion" of New York in 1982):

"It is axiomatic that the less known art from peripheral countries always imitates the better known art from the center. It is of no importance if dates and documents presented prove the contrary. Even the attempt to prove the contrary is regarded as regional busybodiness or, in the best cases, as touching wishful thinking."

From such a perspective a country like Canada must look with some interest at changing international attitudes in the eighties, in which, in the art world, the notion of regionalism (perhaps a more apt as well as politically neutral term than nationalism), for better or worse has become a positive factor. It may be argued that the present exhibition merely celebrates two "new" powers, Germany and Italy, and certainly their presence in the market place would seem to underscore that they are. And yet, at the same time, the decentralization of geographical focus in the eighties concomitant with postmodernism's cultivation of the specifics of locale and history are also a reality. The parallels are hardly exact, but postmodernism's desertion of visual and intellectual abstraction in favour of renewed contact with the world of more immediate experience, whatever its form, has bred a regionalist orientation similar to that which arose over a century earlier with naturalism's new discovery of the observable world. The latter precipitated the growth of significant schools of national painting which have recently suddenly aroused both popular and specialist interest. The fate of artists from other countries who in the 1870s and 1880s flocked to Paris to learn their lessons in naturalism, is well, if a little sentimentally described (to continue the Scandinavian model) by the late nineteenth-century Norwegian painter, Erik Werenskiold: "... with naturalism a national art *had* by necessity to come... It is love of nature that brought naturalism into the world, love and good sense. And love of nature must of necessity lead artists back to their own land; because they cannot possibly understand and consequently cannot to the same degree care for foreign lands as their own."

Perhaps we should leave the last word on this unruly problem to another late nineteenth-century Norwegian naturalist, Christian Krogh, who neither swerved from his regionalist commitments in his art, nor even doubted his international importance. He proposed a resolution in terms of a simple paradox: "All national art is bad, all good art is national."

The organization of an exhibition as ambitious as "The European Iceberg" is a large and complex task calling for the dedicated work of many people whose input in many cases will not even have begun by the time acknowledgements need to be compiled in order to meet publication deadlines. Contemporary exhibitions, much more so interdisciplinary ones, pose special problems because they involve as much the organization of a host of personalities, as they do the bringing together of a group of objects. Deadlines become a special problem because of the eagerness of both the participating artists and the organizers to include as much new, significant, and heretofore unexposed work as possible. In several instances artists are best represented by work especially constructed *in situ* during the short installation period prior to the day of the opening. The many uncertainties which result may give a special air of excitement to the project for the participating curators, but they impose real burdens on other museum staff who have to cope with them in the midst of already busy on-going regular demands on their time. For this reason I begin with my thanks to all the members, too numerous to name individually, of the various departments of Art Gallery of Ontario who have both patiently and enthusiastically given of their skills and talents to realize this exhibition. I must, however, express my special gratefulness to William J. Withrow, Director of the Art Gallery of Ontario, who has supported me through the many stages of this venture; and to Peter Gale, Deputy Head of Education, Catherine Jonasson, Head of Audio Visual Services, and Marie Fleming, Associate Curator of Contemporary Art, for their indispensable contributions in developing and organizing key aspects of the exhibition and the accompanying program.

Both William J. Withrow and I want to express our thanks to all the people outside the Art Gallery of Ontario who in their respective ways have played crucial roles in making the exhibition a reality: to Germano Celant for his work in conceiving and curating this tremendous undertaking, and to Ida Gianelli who with Germano co-edited the catalogue and organized the flow of so much of the information that had to be assembled for the exhibition; to the artists and designers in each of the several sections without whose co-operation and contributions none of this could have been possible; to the lenders on both sides of the Atlantic; to the authors of the catalogue essays; and to Gabriele Mazzotta for our congenial collaboration in the production of the catalogue. It was exciting to have as distinguished a designer as Massimo Vignelli, not only participating in the exhibition, but acting as its over-all designer.

In Toronto special thanks go out to Carmen Lamanna who in the exhibition's preconception stage acted as a trans-Atlantic curatorial match-maker and thus played an initial role in bringing the project to fruition. In the actual planning and production of the exhibition the Gallery finally owes a great debt to several representatives of Germany and Italy in Toronto, for their advice, their hard work, their assistance with financial support, and for direct program support: to Giancarlo Boccotti, Vice-Consul of Italy for Cultural Affairs, Italian Cultural Institute, Toronto; Dr. Ernst-Günther Koch, Consul General of the Federal Republic of Germany; and Dr. Helmut Liede, Director, and Doina Popescu, Program Co-ordinator of the Goethe Institut, Toronto.

The European Concert and the Festival of the Arts

Germano Celant

European culture is a blend of heterogeneous elements in the most heterogeneous cultures (German, French, Spanish, Italian, Dutch, Swiss, Polish, Russian, Finnish, Yugoslav, Austrian, Greek, etc.), which, in their coexistence, demonstrate the possibility of a relationship based on osmosis and on conflict as mainsprings of history. Europe does not have a single, harmonious culture. Instead, it has a mosaic and a precariousness of encounters and engagements, creating an extraordinary voyage across the complex and chaotic territory of individual countries and languages. In order to deal with this situation, we would have to outline the infinite fronts of conflict, the places where the transformation is in continual progress.

As a convergence and arrangement of diverse forces, which cannot be summed up from a single viewpoint without being neutralized, European culture must be accepted as a multiple organism. If we nevertheless decide to navigate through it, we risk going astray in a series of areas subject to the ebbs and flows of time. And if we hope to find our bearings, we have to draw fragmentary and dynamic coordinates that systematically shatter on both manifest and hidden variables, we have to determine contours and peripheral zones, we have to list known and unknown parts — and yet fully realize that the result is a partial and sketchy map. Based on relationships between fragments, our chart is a nucleus of intersections, a crisscross of languages and media running into and against one another in order to establish new relationships. We cannot mediate this culture or compose its concatenations in order to render it monolithic and monumental, or push it into a dominant area. As a complex and changing organism, it defies definition and it is completely independent of any transcription in space or time.

If we want to have a glimpse of European culture, would a bird's-eye view allow us to perceive the geography of a few parts?

The image of a "European Iceberg" has several functions. It serves to indicate the enormous complex of European culture, which cannot be shown in its totality. And the metaphor also emphasizes that the visible part here — Italy and Germany — leaves all the other countries hidden underwater. Furthermore, the portion surfacing in Canada is the one now emerging in the territory of the arts, and it could not exist without the portion that is still concealed. We must always bear this in mind because of its profound influence on the visible situation.

This awareness, in the form of a question, has led to our exhibition. Because of the elusive and intricate nature of European culture, we have avoided an overall presentation of all countries and territories. Such a project would have required an enormous deployment of means and space — not to mention an impossible synthesis and density. Instead, we have opted for a concentration, albeit partial, on several lines of tension — Germany and Italy. The social and historical identities of these countries, their creative and philosophical characters bear witness to and shed light on the virtually indefinable European quintessence, which is nevertheless intense and present.

Our subject and our program were neither restricted nor unequivocal, but, rather, heterogeneous and all-encompassing: they involve the presence of a system — Europe — which subdivides into several subsystems. We had to work with several partial factors, which instead of operating in a regular and homogeneous way, exist in collisions and frictions — as we can see in the cultural nuclei of Germany and Italy.

The development of European culture lacerates and

fragments any homogeneity, it slides along the parallel and yet differentiated paths of identities. In both our exhibition and our catalogue, we therefore considered it useful to indicate several presences and languages, passing from the specific to the general, from Art to the arts, from Culture to cultures, and emphasizing the ways in which they interweave and interact. We wanted to find an overall relationship that brings out the cultural practice of all the arts, which are arranged in such a way as to show networks of articulation and to extend their borders and expand their territories.

Beyond its analogy with the subject of "Europe," this cardinal vision is imbued with the conviction that there are no such things as central and peripheral media. What we really have is nothing but a communication involved in a historical process. This is why the various media have to view one another; within the "European Iceberg" they are cited as parallel systems. Rather than staging a monologue (characteristic of a separate and schizophrenic thinking), we opted for a dialogue. All these media have to know and recognize themselves in one another as parts of an articulate production that, in order to reflect the society (societies), live on synthesis and dialectics instead of analysis and linearity.
The resulting exhibition may be called "undisciplined" because it not only glorifies the artistic discipline (as required by the very name of the museum), it also discusses and verifies artistic discipline within the climate of its relationship to architecture, cinema, theater, design, fashion, and photography.

The reinsertion of the artifact (literally: the object made, *factum*, into art) within overall communication removes its economic connotation and restores its true denotation. No longer a luxury and fetish, and now the equivalent of all the other signs, the artifact once again becomes a highly informative and critical instrument for a society of real and possible facts.

Our current situation forces us to adopt a methodology based on the pluralism of linguistic and cultural territories. Today, we see our environment as conditioned and surrounded by forces that no longer distinguish between "high" and "low" culture; instead, they struggle for an equivalence in diversity. This equalization is due to the historical development of the mode of cultural production, which has created an increasingly rich and diversified system of communication with a much vaster audience than ever before. This massification has leveled the media and their specific products; it has placed the creative and communicational value of paintings and comics, novels and advertisements, poetry and architecture, design and fiction, on the same level. Our plurality ultimately derives from the futility of delimiting within cultural matters the trends and movements that translate the appropriation of research by an ego that tends to replace scientific investigation with the facility of a shallow definition, preening itself on every knee-high "neo" adapted to all consumers and all times.

G.T. Hopfer, *Emblem*, 1680.

An event like "The European Iceberg, Creativity in Germany and Italy Today," representing national cultures and a continental culture, appears to be located between the extreme terms of chauvinism and cosmopolitanism. It exalts the creative products of ethnographic and anthropological individualities, yet tries to place them beyond any differences and peculiarities in order to demonstrate their internationality.
Such confusion between chauvinism and cosmopolitanism is not new — indeed, it is age-old. Recently, from 1945 through the seventies, cosmopolitan culture was identified with the United States, whose cultural sway involved an extreme chauvinism toward other cultures. This domination was then challenged with the war in Viet Nam, the Yom Kippur War, and the accompanying loss of international identity. Now, it again seems to be Europe's turn to proclaim itself the bearer of values; yet such an act would likewise have a chauvinist overtone. How can we smash this perverse mechanism?

North America has followed a straight line and fallen in love with the cube. These geometric notions indicate distance or the perimeter from the beginning to the end. Europe, in contrast, is attracted by crazy vectors that go in unprogrammed directions and take chaotic courses, upsetting any expectations and assumptions about confines. Drawn to the explosion of closed and rigid visions, knowledge proceeds not by construction but by destruction. Indeed, every new discovery consists of shattered elements and historical collapses that are imbued with memory and tradition and filled with fissures left by human and natural cataclysms. Although projecting into the future, European culture remains aware of the enormous complexity of history; it also senses that it is moving forward and inward in order to find itself at the crossroads of eras, areas and languages. This spiraling back and forth between the past and the present has guided us in selecting the elements of a jam session of the arts — histories within History.

Instead of abdicating from one day to the next, Europe has created the legend of defeat and decomposition. It has resigned itself to enduring the invasion of the "new worlds," though inculcating a morbid enthusiasm for weakness and tragedy. It has made up for its lacerations by celebrating the necessity of disaggregation and crisis as instruments of development and evolution. Europe's ruins and devastations over thousands of years have thus become ecstatic visions and descriptions of the future. Unlike America, Europe is not a mental or physical factory regulated by a coherent apparatus, whose machines are systematically inspected and kept up to date, in the latest state-of-the-art technology. Instead, Europe is a stockpile of age-old repertoires and advanced mechanisms that reciprocally compensate for one another's lacks. Often damaged and corrupted by poor conservation, these gears are made of a stupefying mixture of spoiled and ancient materials that are recycled from the past in terms of an intuitive and illogical vision of progress. Any manifestation of their existence seems generated and dominated by an oneiric and metaphysical perspective that sees universes upside-down, so that life arises from death, renewal from war, and organization from the explosion of disorder.
Thus, culture seems to come from a spoiled flesh and a deteriorated spirit. It lives on damnation and on the nightmare of a death that is unceasingly expiated and purged. Hence the importance of expelling and evacuating impurities. It is in this light that we must understand the works of Pasolini and Fassbinder, Kounellis or Kiefer, all of whom recirculate historical ruins and nightmares. Their labors are therapeutic activities, a metaphor of thought and action, describing from the past until today a wicked and repugnant contamination that

Piranesi, *Carceri*, 1745.

has to be exorcised. Drawing energy from the black and murky humors of a feverish society tormented by centuries of nightmare, war and pestilence, these artists seek revivification.
Fashion, design and architecture work in the same therapeutic direction. These areas are in quest of some mind-boggling secret recipe — the key to a protected existence that is neither toilsome nor corroded by evil. The refined objects of Sottsass or the architectural rituals of Rossi and Hollein are scaled to this negromantic and alchemical dimension. They are instruments for purifying the eye and the touch, and they display pleasure and joy, almost as if they had managed to flee a tragic destiny. They all seem to be working against the system of disasters and catastrophes, forever in search of magical ways of escaping the hallucinations of history. Thus, any gestures of theirs connotes negative salvation. It is a means for interpreting contemporary events; but, as in Beuys, Horn and Merz, or in Kleihues and De Lucchi, it tragically insinuates the constant presence of obsessions to be free or to materialize the inconceivable.
European culture could be likened to an enormous house of dreams in which day and night are confused. It daily consumes surreal mythologies whose shadows and figures seem to be made up of soot and mercury, fat and spoiled materials, black inks and burned oils. Here, as we can observe in Böhm and Aulenti, in Castiglioni and Fronzoni, in Vedova and Baselitz, in Wenders and Taviani. The lines between real and unreal, between possible and impossible, between sacred and profane, between abstract and concrete, between holy and accursed, between pure and filthy are vague and shifting. One might almost say that the structural ambiguity is intrinsic to all cultural products that try to free themselves from the eternal seesawing of creation and corruption, birth and decay, to clutch at the materialization of the impossible and fantastic. The idea of welding creativity to disaster is the European weapon for linking up with contemporary life and making it triumph over history, while keeping both the past and the present tightly clasped in an indivisible dialectical relationship. It is through familiarity with devastations and with social death, through coexistence with fragments of history that the drama of shades and nightmares has been dissolving in Europe, making them seem perfectly congruent with the ingredients of a present-day life projected into the future. It is the experienced, narrated, and theoretical frequentation of the products and derivates of a destruction that brings the new European idols to life.

If the cleft is the central motif in European culture, the most widespread image of Germany is that of a mediator between East and West and Italy as a mediator between North and South. These polarities hold the reciprocal mechanisms of production together in that all works aspire to fixing the real or imaginary, symbolic or fantastic clefts that separate the two hemispheres.
The disjunction in German culture obviously acquires the meaning of a tragic opposition. It is absolute and dramatic, and it signifies loss and lack. Thus, within the creative space of art and cinema, theater and architecture, the fission of the poles of East and West is never healed; it remains a source of extreme anxiety and disquiet. The two Germanies are involved in a status quo that produces disorderly and hallucinatory visions such as death and war, disasters and tragic sagas. Every event is marked by the separation induced by an external trauma. Routes are interrupted and creativity is used up to recompose the disunited parts (just think of the films of Wenders of Fassbinder). Consequently, forms are not compact and materials are opaque, with disjoint strokes and compound colors, as in Kiefer's paintings or Beuys's sculptures. They involve an interchange between a positive and a negative side, and the possibility — or hope — of an internal equilibrium. Thus, the whole of German culture is projected upon the singularity of its disjunction between the "real" term and the "fantastic" term, its hallucinatory pole, whether in the East of in the West. Its archetypes plunge into meanders and mazes, into forests and plains traversed by imaginary figures that pass through the mirage of unity. The whole is marked by an absence of the festive and by a hybrid quality that turns the elements into dry, colorless materials. Traversing it means cutting through gardens of stone and mire.
In Italy, the fracture is more subtle, almost subterranean. It is not projected upon national equilibriums for which the division is neither absolute, nor rigid, nor catastrophic, but internal and social. The instability exists between the opposite polarities of economic and political levels, the collective order with extremes of living conditions between rich and poor, North and South.
If German culture is characterized by excess and transcendence, Italian culture is conditioned by temperance and internal reformism. It emphasizes

its interests in tones and equilibriums. It works on impalpableness and on the enigmatic density of objects and media, as we can see in Paolini and De Maria, in Cerri and Vignelli, in Piano and Burri in Migliori and Ghirri. It believes in the consistency of compact masses and the wealth of their functions within the contexts of the past and the present. The quality of consistency and measured unity can be seen in all media, even when they contain ruins and memory fragments as cultural aliment. In contrast to the dry hardness of the German division, Italian culture offers the tactility and sensuality of thick, homogeneous bodies, in which hardness has become fluid and seductive. The reference is always to: continuity.

The process of considering oneself a victim is a method of research.

The premise of the new cultural condition in Germany and Italy was established in the forties after the caesura of World War II. This new condition developed through the social convulsions and rebellions of 1967 and 1976, which were unconscious mechanisms that marked the creative energy with explosive charges.
Our exhibition includes three generations of artists, designers, architects, photographers, filmmakers and graphic artists who gained body and submerged impulses from war and revolt. Their statements (from Lüpertz to Syberberg, from Taviani to Bertolucci, from Valle to Gregotti) identified and concretely responded to historical anxieties and social paranoias from fascism to nazism. There have been obvious moments of return to past and primitive cultures — from Pistoletto to Penck, from Jodice to von Gagern, who have produced critiques of a country or a city, from East Berlin to Naples, or the schizophrenic conditions of history, from classicism to industrialism, whose existence can develop only through dramatic splits and clefts resulting from political wars or natural catastrophes such as earthquakes or cholera. And intellectuals like Fo and Wenders, Moravia and Grass, touched by the drama of postwar Europe and by the false utopia of post-industrialism have offered realistic retorts to the past, even if their discourses, spoken or shouted, have been viewed by the ruling culture as attacks on "ideal" values. These intellectuals have rejected the affirmation of a flat, monolithic culture that is both perfect and immobile. Instead, they have opted for iconoclastic behaviors and procedures that take into account the horrors and errors of an ill-omened history from nineteenth-century liberalism to the imperialism of enemy blocs.
Thus, in 1943, then 1967, then 1976, they looked first to North America, then to South America, then to China, and finally to ethnic and sexual minorities. The seeming absence of stimuli was translated into reconstructive hypotheses and social explosions that helped to revamp society. In 1967, a year crucial to most of the people represented in this exhibition, Europe began to define creativity as something "concretely" meaningful in counterpoint and in relation to the social, in order to view that creativity as a determined historical action tied to the events of aesthetic, artistic and non-artistic thinking. The attitude of the fifties, i.e., that a creative person was an isolated worker almost cut off from the social process, was now replaced by the premise of a "critical" creativity. Rather than accepting facts as ultimate and impenetrable elements, this creativity presupposes a vision of culture that lays bare its assumption and necessities and develops an awareness of the difference between "seeming" (*Schein*) and "being" (*Sein*).
Artists from Fabro to Darboven, from Cerri to Krug, from Deganello to Hess, from Scholz Rittermann to Paladino, from Böhm to Stein, have been inspired by philosophy and the eperience of creativity as developed within the German and Italian contexts from 1966 until today. In fact, the principle of their activities in the contradiction between image and social structure, and rather than trying to reconcile them, they have studied the differences between them. The result is a "critique" of research in the field of visions — a critique that makes itself a self-critique. The impulse is toward self-liberation, which definitively abandons the semblance of a "neutral" procedure in order to move in terms of social antagonisms; hence, the abolition of the mystical vision of creativity as a superior and hegemonic entity in favor of a concrete criticism of internal and external systems.
In order to work out a schema of social-historical references that enables us to identify the relevance assumed by this "critical" creativity, we ought to recall the convulsive and lacerated situation of the world during the mid-sixties, concomitant with the crisis of traditional aesthetic work such as painting and decoration, household and family.
1967 brought a new critical "subject" that tends to mark the road of social changes: the repoliticization of Western Europe. This demand was made by a

new generation that wants to — utopianly — abolish all stratification and hierarchy. These young people felt an imperious and unnegotiable need to break loose and fight for an equivalence and equality between similar things and beings. They made this demand chiefly in Southern Europe, from Italy to France and from France to Germany; their goal was to annul the moral and ideological legacies, and to create a true cultural transformation. Thus, the new generation focused on an ethical vindication of social relationships; and the challenge was made in both Paris and Berlin, Rome and Turin, with the all-out revolt of university students. These young masses, impelled by events in Eastern and Latin-American countries, were willing to go to any extremes of action. Their sometimes simplistic and illusory thrust was to shake off all traditions, the full weight of the past. They scrutinized every mechanism "critically," in order to verify the defects in its control, the rigidity and complexity of the structure and its use. A huge tempest brought to the surface anything hidden in the age-old foundations of the system. The radical critique of society, in its most advanced industrial phenomena, brought out a model of operative extremism, based chiefly on poor and marginal values. The results were: Arte Povera, Street Theater, Radical Architecture, things that traditionally belonged to the masses, who were still highly creative and spontaneous. And these were the sources that many creative people turned to for inspiration and energy, ultimately blowing up the reasons and the current fantasies on which their fragments took vengeance with the reversal and poetic transformation of culture and society.

And this attempt was made during 1967 and 1968: the rebellion on the campuses and in the industrial towns, although expressed in primitive and dissociated forms, tried to define the disquiet of a generation that rejected work and esploitation and demanded pleasure — a request impossible both yesterday and today.

The illusion was enormous, virtually a mirage. Nevertheless, this destabilization of constituted order and the resulting malaise contaminated the entire productive and cultural processes, including art, which was also affected by the fundamental revolt — that of the creators. The efforts of art were now caught in the same crisis of concrete awareness. Artists no longer wished to delegate their procedures to others (critics or dealers, curators or collectors), and they rejected the hierarchy of media and materials. For centuries, artists had based their discourse on a logic that had become more and more repressive. They now had to make some statement about this and repoliticize their research if they wished to preserve its strength. There were various approaches to redefining its specific role. Since it was believed that the malaise and crisis of culture depended on maintaining bonds with history and the past along with an indifference to the desires and precariousness of life, the new artistic works broke out of the suffocating embrace of memory to submerge into the present. The value of this break is as yet uncertain. Nevertheless, the awareness of the contingent and the existential had an "alternative" character, which had repercussions on the mentality, the customs and the practical conduct of art. For the first time, Europe witnessed a large-scale if not massive emergence of the critic-creator, who managed to discuss the entire sphere of his activity, philosophy and behavior. What does this mean? More than anything, artists began to deal with the effects produced by the private and social context of their work; and they began to study behavior as part of their research. This manner of seeing and thinking defined the classical mode of the conceptualization of art. Yet at the same time,

Ca' d'Oro, Venice.

artists realized that the relationship between the internal and external spheres was a specific form of the individual and the environment. On the one hand, there was the world of the idea and its "dematerialization," i.e. the realm of pure theory.

On the other hand, there was the world of nature and the person, with their materialization of sensorial and sensible perceptions. This dualism, which kept alive the impossibility of a total explanation (typical of the metaphysical religions, among which painting and sculpture had been renewed for centuries), contained the goal of Arte Povera, as Conceptual Art and Body Art.
The creative events of 1967-68 thus marked a historical watershed: the dogma of neutrality was rooted out, since there is no way of separating the object from the aesthetic act, from the awareness of and participation in its reasons and technical input. Art is no longer a virginal nature; it is a form of knowing and seeking, both activities being conditioned by ideology and practice. Previously, its cognitive and political values had been non-existent because its paradigms had never been discussed or tested. Now, the discussion has commenced.

History has demonstrated that cultural revolutions have never altered the autonomy of the social or private structure; they have changed only the modes of governing the collective and the personal. Thus, the supremacy of the political factor in European creativity during the sixties brought an autonomy not of decision or movement, but of self-awareness as a mundane territory. This decade did not construct a real situation for which creativity could establish a different and free condition. We only learned that the human being will never give up existing as a social and private "whole."

The vindication of "totality," which, in art, was translated into overall intervention (from Body Art to Land Art, from Radical Design to Radical Architecture), very nearly became an abstract method applicable to any sort of objective, but hard to link to the reality of the individual. During the seventies, the hypothesized totality was impossible and inadmissible because it failed to apply change to the fragment of private life. Thus, the ideologies proved to be frail, and human frailty became an ideology.

The 1968 exasperation about unrealizable utopias made the seventies schizophrenic. In order to react to the abstract ideological paternities determined by the Cold War and maintained by the "post-ideological" thinking of the youth culture, this decade clutched at the ecstasy of the private. Thus, after a historical period in which Europe remained submerged by a political surplus in the form of armed struggle and social uprising, we witnessed the rejection of ideologies and the exaltation of individualism. Under the concentric attacks of diversity and deviance, feminism and ecological awareness, the false securities dissolved — i.e., the family, sex, Marxism, normality, the male/female relationship, internationalism and modernism. A wave of skepticism brought the exhaustion of the ideas of progress and ultimate values, which proved fantastic and fictitious with respect to the real substance of things. And while revolution no longer excited people, they felt abstracted from a strong sensitivity to human presuppositions. This was why the thrust of this era was the quest for an identity that could reawaken the desire for autonomy of both the person and the culture.
The early eighties wiped out the last doubts about the simulacra of universality and objective rationality, administered only by a country or by a father-socius, in favor of events and torments distinguished from individual wholes, whether ethnic or social entities or beings. This is a period in which cultures are trying to rediscover their own roots, which are buried in both memory and history. We are now once again obeying feelings and inner forces, with a consequent return to religion and tradition.

Schloss Pillnitz, Dresden.

Berlin Wall.

Thus, after the catastrophe caused by the revolts and rebellions that shook Europe, a need was felt for fideistic reassurance in devotion to the hero and the flag.
The same development occurred in the art world. Again, we heard the conservative demand for a strong individual, a strong medium, a strong image; it was almost a revival of the thirties. Art was depoliticized, and artists returned to the aristocratic and individualistic spirit of the Nietzschean superman, with the consequent appearance of stars and celebrities hungry for the frantic consumption of creative and decorative goods.
This hero, whose only goal seems to be the total marketing of the self, placed himself between the idea-creator and the consumer. He became an artmaker, that is, a professional and a technician of art, rather than an artist. As a showman able to hold together the medium, the stage, and the auditorium, he designs the artifact, well aware of the tastes and desires of the public. In this light, we can understand why creativity has asserted itself as a "social fact" since 1980. It has coopted the covers of our magazines and the headlines of our newspapers; it has entered banks and stock markets as the prey of Kitsch and consumerism. Although transformed from a mechanism of consumers and markets into a means of banal ostentatiousness, creativity nevertheless did not want to lose its progressive character. So art has returned to the expressionistic and romantic bombast of the *créateur maudit*, while design and architecture have gone back to the surprising and conciliatory figures of history and archeology. Paintings and sculptures convey a pattern that is pseudo-hostile to society; they seem vaguely dangerous and anxiety-filled, exemplifying the introverted nature of artistic efforts, the ascetic and self-flagellating procedure within the studio, and making the "excessive" effort of creative living sensual and palatable. This was a way of making the crisis and the personal drama acceptable, allowing them to be acquired and consumed.
In contrast, the designer or artist or architect has reappropriated historical figures and is citing them. He attacks them in order to possess them and to create a neo-iconography based on the redesign of history. Thus, after demolishing any sign of effervescence and alteration and wiping out formalistic linearism, the creative voyage feels the demand for an iconic indemnification and is once again sating itself on the exceptionality of images and materials. Artists are working on the surplus and excess, on the luxury and obesity of processes and figures. Thus, since 1979, we have been witnessing a development between the tradition of the avant-garde and the avant-garde of tradition. We have seen the birth of the academism of experimentation, which involves the experimentation of the Academy.
This excursion into the images of the past, from Palladio to Kokoschka, from Cabiria to Art Déco, from Gaudí to Tiffany, involved the construction and de-signification of modern aesthetics, opening up new cognitive perspectives of history. Performed with highly refined and precise instruments, this reanalysis could be used to explain and revisit the archetypes. Instead, using a mattock and a rake, a burin and a plumb-line, the creators of Neo-Expressionism and Neo-Fauvism and the implementors of New Design and Post-Modern Architecture have merely achieved a simple remixing of the historical humus, almost a banal raid into the land of memory. Their collapse in ecstatic dreams about the past is excluded from our exhibition because it exemplifies a conservative retrogression. Nevertheless, if the quest for intensity about oneself and about the past can lead to the quicksand of frantic romanticism and national craft, it can also give positive shakes to the rigid and abstract edifices of the sixties.
Above all, it helps the creators to leave the arid

Alberto Moravia and Pier Paolo Pasolini.

conceptual path and again enjoy the visual and tactile pleasure derived from the new explosion of colors and materials that are both delightful and mellow. Painting and decoration are dominating the scene again, abundance has won out over penury and personalism over collective exercises. We are witnessing the reversal of the preceding decades. Creativity is giving up social action and exalting the heroic grandeur of traditional media and movements linked to a cynical, ruthless and amoral protagonist who is blessed by mass consumption. Hounded by the desire for protagonism, the creators of the eighties are imbued with a pathological passion that impels us only to perceive success and narcissistic immobility. This is a desire for self-consumption that can easily turn into something one-sided and immature, offering no other solutions than self-immolation on the altar of solitude and the market. What leaves us perplexed in accepting this void is the generic quality of a perpetual and monotonous existence, which finds a procedural solution only in the reconciliation and overlapping of the self and the style, the self and history.

The affirmation of creativity as a personal and immutable, a perfect and obscure instrument moving within the reassuring delimitations of the sacred personality or consolidated academicism is opposed by an iconoclastic conduct and procedure exemplified by artists such as De Maria or Bagnoli, Mucha or Schütte, Castella or Schurmann, who perceive the problems of real existence and move in relation with the multiplicity of times and contexts. For this reason, we have to reject any absolute definition and remain on the level of attention in order to acknowledge that creativity has the function of mediation and not rigid definition. What counts is the indeterminate and latent character of a procedure that, rather than attaching itself to its data, discusses them, confronts them and deconstructs them to look for an existence within the discontinuity of comprehension and self-understanding. Rejecting univocal vision, this iconoclastic process prefers multiple viewpoints, and it replaces the binding law of memory with the various circumstances in which constructions and representations are applied. The openness to the risk of existence creates an ability to find a correspondence in the dynamics between oneself and the world and to plunge into the surrounding vertigo with Spalletti and Salvadori, with Gerdes and Hollein, in order to establish unprecedented profiles and relationships between oneself and others.

The idea is to run across the entire keyboard and to grasp the entire series of all aspects of reality, in an attempt to introduce sounds and echoes of an alterable consciousness that is acquiring historical weight. Hence the absence of fideistic and religious reassurances about one's own being-there (*Dasein*) in order continually to appropriate whatever depends on things and facts. The serenity of a seemingly calm world that phagocytizes and wipes out all dramas is disrupted by an ever-changeable plan of action, of uncertain and unknown hesitations, whereby creativity is regarded as capable of shifting the gravitational center of communication in any and all directions.

Architecture

Gae Aulenti
Gottfried Böhm
Vittorio Gregotti
Hans Hollein
Josef Paul Kleihues
Renzo Piano
Aldo Rossi
Gino Valle

It's All in the Proportions...
The City and the "New Architecture"

Tilmann Buddensieg

"As long as the main lines are undisturbed... the impression will remain basically the same. It's all in the proportions." (Theodor Fontane, *From Twenty to Thirty*, 1898)

"Il faut tuer la 'rue-corridor'" (" Death to the street as corridor") wrote Le Corbusier in 1929, referring to the most important structural element of the historic city. In its place he set the ruling concept of New Architecture, open space: free-standing residential towers in an unbroken park landscape, the open city with unbounded freedom of movement. The chaos and disorder of the nineteenth-century metropolis were to give way to the ordered, shining, functional city of the future. Like Le Corbusier, Bruno Taut wanted to liberate Berlin from its despised tenements by blasting them to bits. Van Esteren, a Dutchman, Hilbersheimer, Mies van der Rohe, Gropius and even Hugo Häring placed solitary towers, rows or screens of glass in open spaces that promised liberation from the matrix of the historic city and its social conditions. This kind of planning involved modern construction, rigorous replacement of the old or expansion into the unrestricted spaces surrounding and facing away from the old city. In all of his urban models, Le Corbusier was not concerned with improving the existing city but with a new, completely different kind of city that would pay exquisite attention to the slightest modulations of hills and dales and riverbeds while thoroughly disregarding the historic reality of the already existing, inhabited city. Wherever extant, a mostly unpopulated, untouched *centro storico* would be left standing for the viewing.

The leading German architects of the Weimar period shared this contempt for the cities of the previous century. Denied public contracts in the city and defeated in large-scale competitions for inner-city projects, the social democratic neighborhoods could not become integrated components, as in Amsterdam-South, but appeared as fragments of a city of the future that was to replace, not augment the old city.

In 1945 the utopian dreams of the architectural avant-garde were unintentionally fulfilled, with apocalyptic suffering: the reputedly ugliest tenament city in the world had been largely incinerated and obliterated. What social utopians and revolutionaries had been unable to accomplish, the war had — "son sol est rendu libre; son sol est disponible," shouted Le Corbusier on seeing Berlin in ruins in 1957. The ground seemed to have become free, open at last for the realization of modern town planning on a scale that had remained a utopian dream for forty years, achieving an isolated *Gestalt* only as individual structures, public squares or neighborhood settlements.

The aging protagonists of New Architecture did not see in the ruins of Berlin a terrible loss but a freshly plowed field in which the new seeds of the "wide open" city would surely thrive. At most, the totally new organization of the city would have to defer to the underground transit system, sewers and mains, it was thought, but no longer to the historically defined constellation of streets, squares and residential sections. With the fall of the Third Reich one had also "gotten rid of a terribly over-built cityscape" whose mistakes were to be avoided in the future. A new city was to arise, "full of light and air and gardens" (Max Taut, 1946).

Walter Gropius, in 1947, wanted to avoid the "preservation of antiquated sections of the city within the destroyed city." In a letter to Richard Scheibe on 11 May 1948 he wrote: "A new organization of communities such as I have worked out in theory [is not] possible under present conditions." Gropius believed "that it was nevertheless most necessary, especially in Germany, to initiate reconstruction along rational lines that would preclude foreclosing better

options for the future" (Kolbe-Museum, Berlin). Thus spoke — alongside the light-and-air utopians — the rational pragmatist Gropius, a voice of reason which surely did not garner its arguments from the *misère* of old relics. Hans Scharoun, too, saw in the aftermath of destruction by bombs and street battles "the possibility of shaping a cityscape out of the [ruins]" — i.e., as with Le Corbusier, the liturgy of the avant-garde of obliterated history, of fertile Nature, of a hygenic order that would be able to restore life-giving light, air and freedom of movement to the urban dweller. The new vision resisted becoming part of the history of urban renewal projects which, however radical and extensive, were never total and the sum of which added up to *the City*. One could totally replace the old, destroyed city. The relics that had remained standing after the inferno could be abandoned to the fate of all ruins, since mere chance had preserved them in the first place. For the twenty-one-year old Jeanneret/Le Corbusier — fresh from a reading of *Zarathustra* in 1908 — all architecture of the past, with the exception of Greek architecture and cathedrals, was just the dead weight of history that killed everything new and must therefore be swept away. The old architecture of the cities became for him Hegel's "charnel houses" left over from an age concerned with a world that no longer exists (*Introduction to the History of Philosophy*). Le Corbusier wanted to "connect [architecture] with the things I love about our times." Did this purest product of his reading of Nietzsche apply to Berlin in ruins in 1957 too? Was it necessary to use a bulldozer to fulfill the "first obligation of architecture..., the revision of accepted values" (*Vers une Architecture*, 1922), i.e., Nietzsche's "transvaluation of all values" ("Umwertung aller Werte")? The young Jeanneret underlined the last sentence of the introduction to *Zarathustra* about the "breaker" as "creator."
The totalitarian rule of the Nazis justified a return to the battle positions of the Weimar avant-garde. It augmented the pathos of new beginnings with the sufferings of the German people in the catastrophes of their history. Max Taut's *Berlin under Construction* (*Berlin im Aufbau*) of 1946 is an expression of this introverted return to the family garden plot, this regression to the tamed residential communities of the Weimar period. Sunflowers were blooming everywhere on the levelled ruins. The Reuter-Village in Bonn, built in 1948, can still give us an impression about this ideal of the postwar Berlin idyll-amidst-the-rubble. These German visions of the city, then, with their tormented urgency to purify, forget, obliterate, have nothing of the intellectuality of Le Corbusier's Napoleonic gesture of conquest. The freedom of the avant-garde quickly turned into the freedom of unconscious negation — tear down, isolate, replace, expose, sweep clean. The depressing continuation of wartime destruction by peaceful means leaves a bitter aftertaste, as if all the devastation had been a good thing after all.
Four major town-planning proposals can be distinguished. First, one could bring back from Harvard Martin Wagner, City Building Commissioner for Berlin until 1933, respected champion of the unions, administrative strategist, outstanding architect and, not least of all, friend of the right architects; invite him to take up the thread of his extraordinary accomplishments within an intellectual and political milieu that was ravaged by the Nazi era.
Secondly, one could have considered Le Corbusier's latest plan, dated 1957, for new construction. Incorporating decades of hope, it would have totally subordinated the entire historical city of Berlin south of the Linden and the remote remnants of the old city from around the Lustgarten to the Mehringplatz to the geometric grid which was to provide the new ordering principle for the residential towers. The handful of historic monuments in the southern part of Friedrichstadt, today's Berlin-Museum, or the Mendelsohn Trade Union building might perhaps have been preserved, but only as *objets trouvés* to be incorporated as construction materials for the New City. If nothing was done with them, these relics would fare even worse, ending up on left-over spaces between widened streets, belonging neither to the old nor the new order. A community and citizen-oriented concept of the city was thus reduced to a caricature of Hilbersheimer's "airspace between buildings," or to Gropius's "open-air facilities" idea (1930), or a distortion of the concept of historic continuity as exemplified by the Mehringplatz today.
Thirdly, the Bonatz Plan gave in to the historically understandable West German desire for improvement and reparations through greater German town planning, which to Scharoun's distress the proponents of the plan arrogated to themselves.

Fourthly, decisions were put into the hands of one of the most outspoken defenders of the anti-historical stance of New Architecture: Hans Scharoun laid claim to the devastated open spaces of the city as anchorages for his enormous modern structures. In effect, this was just an ornamental variation on Le Corbusier's essentially identical notion of the total disposability of the historic city. Whether it was ships at anchor and dinosaurs or cut crystals, transparent cubes, rectangles and glass screens on open green fields, both concepts thrived on the absence of the historic city, and both had the pathos of historic justification on their side, as well. Le Corbusier liked to talk in terms of an analogy between the physical shape and function of the New City, on the one hand, and the political, economic and technological structure of society with its confidence in boundless growth and dreams of machine-made happiness in the future, on the other. And the idealistic humanism expressed in the passionate plea for universal access to light, air and freedom of movement in endless expanses of greenery was quite capable of harmonizing with the interests of Michelin, Citroen and Voison with its utopian vision of a transparent city without walls.
No one, not even the critics, can resist the interiority of Scharoun's psychogrammatic interior spaces, an interiority that wants to see the communality of public life develop only in interior spaces — a difficult concept, though, when it comes to having such externally brittle structures accomodate a street without putting a new bend in it or taking some cognizance of their neighbors or predecessors on the same spot.
Because of the hiatus created by the Nazi period, what had been a radical new departure following World War I became, after World War II, an inner contradiction, a restoration of the avant-garde as the enemy of the historic city. The new buildings forgot the historic and thus differentiated structures of the cities. The speed with which the new construction sites were planned and built up led at first to a legitimate uniformity among these emergency structures but later resulted in universal abuse of urban spaces as purely utilitarian material and in the terrible uniformity of German cities since 1945. It is obvious in Falkenhagener Feld, for instance, but everywhere else too, that the freedom enjoyed by the planners turned into wanton misuse of spaces declared or rendered open, with no one bothering to distinguish good from bad intervention. Max Taut's, Hans Scharoun's and Le Corbusier's hopes for the rise of the New City out of the mega-ruins of Berlin collapsed more dramatically by far than the countermodels of the Weimar avant-garde in the Gropius-Stadt and Märkischer Viertel, for instance, since the latter had been formulated as a potential alternative at a time when the functioning Reichskapital of Berlin was still a visible stimulus.
The walls of the old city had crumbled neither under the trumpets of the New Jerusalem prophets nor under the Nazis' pseudo-folksong version of the village-idyll qua urban refuge; they had crumbled instead under the screeching bombs of the Allies, a second-hand legacy. Thus the beautiful Hansa district built in 1957 has absolutely no connection to the old city and the sense of illegal usurpation here is as impossible to eradicate as are the shadows of the past.
The ongoing criticism of these dilapidated avant-garde positions over the last twenty years has had no need to point an accusing finger at the toal failure of this philosophy in the work of imitators, however beautiful or ugly it may have turned out to be. And the polemics of the late fifties — over whether Berlin was better off as the Garden City of the West à la Hansa district or as the collective community, socialist realist style, of the East — were after all just the work of cold and old warriors. What is at issue now is the inevitable conclusion that architectural and urban planning will have to re-establish their visible connection with the changed structures of social consciousness if they wish to lay legitimate claim to more than just private construction projects and to the support of political power brokers; furthermore, if they wish to cut through the verbal criticism, the impotence of juried prizes, the empty victories in architectural journals and isolated mini-solutions to get at a substantive formulation of the alternatives.
The work of the IBA represents such an attempt. Josef Paul Kleihues's overall plan for dealing with the extensive urban blight between Kreuzberg, south Friedrichstadt and the Tiergarten from Zoo to Moabit is the first comprehensive concept for such renewal. In 1965 Scharoun could still lead the cavalry attack of the youth movement with the battle cry: "We stand at the beginning of a stylistic era and in the middle of the development of a new kind of art." Kleihues and the IBA

architects no longer feel they're at the beginning of a stylistic period. They are pulling together the conclusions of an era of avant-garde experience and the entire history of the city of Berlin, testing the validity of this accumulated architectural vocabulary and attempting to open the taboos of an historic period that experienced the year zero (1945) at the moment of its own greatest creativity. These architects believe in the continuity and evolutionary potential of the forms of human life and their architectural expressions; in their repeatability and metamorphosis, rather than in the Musée Imaginaire of supposedly original creations, or the rummage rooms of the epigones.

Kleihues's plan rejects the idea of growth and mobility that has dominated every town-planning concept of modern times — and presumably since Babylon. City planners for Berlin have always, with complete confidence, defined the city as the greater metropolitan area of Berlin with, conservatively, a population of two million and, optimistically, of twenty million. Martin Wagner thought in terms of residential housing of a "short lifespan" — since the population of Berlin was in the habit of moving every four or five years anyway. We can no longer speak of this kind of mobility and growth. For this reason Kleihues and Haemer intend to anchor their new construction in the pre-existing spatial constellations of the city and to reclaim old buildings. The obvious impossibility of expanding the city and the lack of an intact historical hub are forcing the IBA to pay attention to the remaining segments and fragments.

A fundamental change in the assessment of the beauty and attractiveness of Berlin underlies these intentions. One would have to stand in the middle of the Mehringplatz as it is today to understand Paul Ferdinand Schmidt's 1929 indictment of Berlin as a city "that gives pleasure to no one... [and] whose inhabitants can find no place where they feel at home." Contrast this with Reyner Banham's view of Berlin as the Florence of the twentieth century.

Kleihues's conception of the city distances itself from the defamation of the nineteenth-century city and its fragments as much as from the ideas of the sixties, which saw the city as a modifiable system of technical elements whose neutral structures could be assembled into large frameworks and whose parts were interchangeable. He casts aside the low-and high-rise Garden City as well as the sci-fi notion of the "plug-in city," the "cluster in the air," the total city.

Kleihues has declared his intention of unconditionally preserving almost all of the remaining architectural structures that recall the dimensions and boundaries of the streets and blocks of the Friedrichstadt, regardless of their architectural quality and with no thought of placing these isolated fragments into an ambience that copies the past again. Thus begins the dialogue with field after field of rubble which in many instances were only in small measure created by the bombs and remained heaps of rubble even after being built over again, for these "open spaces" were plastered with new construction without any regard for the history of the site.

Among the relics, which include the Parey Villa, "there is still room for shadows," whose presence was felt so keenly by Alexander von Humboldt among the ruins of Rome in 1804. And hasn't it always been the "ruins" and "fragments" that have inspired the creative architects of all epochs in their assimilation, metamorphosis and variation of forms? In designing one of the city blocks for south Friedrichstadt, the Swiss architects Reichlin and Reinhart chose a building of no particular consequence as the baseline for variations that transform its banality into rhythms of an entirely new composition, much as a composer would treat a popular melody, a writer, a literary topos or a visual artist a motif.

In the adjacent block, Aldo Rossi achieved a level of critical examination of the relevance today of architecture in Berlin between Schinkel and Mies van der Rohe unequalled by any other contemporary Berlin architect.

In Peter Eisenman's architectural reflections on history in the shadow of the Wall, O.M. Ungers' variations on the theme of the Berlin apartment house at Lützowplatz or James Stirling's experimental use of historical quotation to visualize architectural functions in a new way, there is not a hint of Marx's disparaging "fearful conjuring up of the ghosts of the past." All of the IBA plans mirror the experiences of Modernism, but also seek to anchor them in the soil of the historic city. They want to use them in a way that makes sense up close, between the boundary posts of ruins and fragments, rather than employ them in the creation of large-scale, open-spaced mega-

arrangements that can only be appreciated from a bird's-eye view.
The architects' creations must once again learn to subordinate themselves to the "external pressures" (Colin Rowe) of history. These pressures mobilize architecture to use the artifacts of the past with new subjective freedom, a freedom that increases and becomes communicable not only when it participates in restoring what has been destroyed, but also when it intervenes to repair the web torn in two by the Wall or to replace outgrown functions — a shut-down train station, for instance — with new ones.
This is not the place to elucidate Kleihues's blueprint in any detail, but there are a number of features of the plan that will undoubtedly interest all lovers of Berlin. The old block and street system of the Friedrichstadt will be revived for new residential building; thoroughfares will be avoided, for instance by cutting a new intersection through the Kochstrasse, and a large inner-city park created on the former grounds of the Prince Albrecht Palace in the process. The Lindenstrasse will connect Kreuzberg to the Friedrichstadt by way of reconstructed cross streets.
Stresemannstrasse and the streets on the banks of the Landwehrkanal will open up the route westward. This will maintain the old orientation of the Linden toward and crossing the Wall, while at the same time an urgently needed connection to the West will be created. The open space at the Anhalter-Bahnhof will become an inner-city park and the sandy fields at the Potsdamer-Bahnhof a residential section. According to an older plan, Kreuzberg, the Friedrichstadt and Tiergarten were to have been connected to the northern and western sectors of the city, Zoo and Moabit, by an inner-city freeway. This would have resulted in an irreparable isolation of the Cultural Center at Kemperplatz. Yet one more example of those brutal clear cuts through city neighborhoods such as have proliferated in the middle of Cologne, Hamburg, Berlin, etc. for expediting unrestrained traffic flow. The new street as planned by Kleihues is once again embedded in the neighborhood, framed by apartments, trees, parkways, and it betokens his faith in the revival of the boulevard, where car traffic is slowed and adjusted to the other functions of the street, which future estimates of traffic flow are no longer allowed to obliterate.
Most importantly, this plan achieves a careful integration of the large, solitary structures of the Cultural Center with residential streets which can maintain their old connections to Potsdamer Platz and Leipziger Strasse while being sufficiently dovetailed with Kreuzberg and the Tiergarten. By taking the pressure off Potsdamer Strasse and connecting both the National Library and Philharmonic Hall to the new North-South Boulevard, the Cultural Center will be turned into a reduced traffic zone. It will be anchored down by buildings along its perimeter and by virtue of its location in a neighborhood of reconstruction-style city villas, adjacent to the Parey Villa, will not be completely "blacked out" after business hours.
This is the first town-planning effort since the sixties to use the totally changed presuppositions a new cityscape to advantage. It is without doubt the most comprehensive manifestation of international collaboration within a generation of architects who have the power to remold the new and old living spaces of a metropolis to the benefit of its residents. The plan is sufficiently open-ended to guarantee residents and other interest groups a say in the process.
This collaboration was initiated by IBA, which has thereby made Berlin once again a center of new architectural ideas and given it back *one* of the "metropolitan functions" the city has always exercized in the twentieth century with shorter or longer hiatuses.
The CDU leadership in Berlin today would do well to recall the one and only noteworthy town-and residential-planning project a city administration of the centrist party has devised, namely Cologne under Mayor Adenauer, as well as the internationally acclaimed city-planning fantasy of his colleagues in Frankfurt should they be contemplating the chokehold of economy measures. It's up to the CDU to decide whether the Social Democrats are to continue to go down in history as the sole supporters of community-oriented German architecture in the twentieth century. One could of course once again surrender the field to those "experienced, reasonable realists" who discard any architectural idea that's not perched atop an underground garage. But that would mean repeating the fatal mistake committed by Munich's timid city administration following World War I, which has condemned it to a complete void in the tradition of twentieth-century architecture.
Neighborhoods in Berlin planned by Martin

Wagner, the Siemenstadt and various sections of Frankfurt planned by City Building Commissioner May all demonstrate that collaboration by the best architects has resulted in superior town-planning solutions that continue to be attractive for residents and rewarding from a historical point of view. As Hedebrand reported in 1956, Gustav Oelzner's greatly underrated projects in Hamburg, 1924-1933, "gave financial support to good modern architects more readily than to others"; and probably the most daring building commission of the twentieth century, that of Amsterdam, proceeded in exactly the same manner. Here, then, lies the proof for all those timid neighborhood and city councils that the residents and the city benefit whenever imaginative architects are given a free hand, constrained only by a pre-existing system of streets and proportions. City Building Commissioner Wibaut, Mayor Tellegen — known for his interest in town planning — and Commissioner of Housing Keppler performed "the miracle" (Bruno Taut) of Amsterdam: a synthesis of artistic imagination, formal and technological contemporaneity, sensitivity to the less well-off and preservation of the communal and historical physiognomy of the city.

One could name half a dozen more Dutch cities where town-planning projects very different, say, from the Rotterdam model were repeatedly underwritten by City Building Commissioners who accomplished many a community-oriented mission in their role as architects of the New Architecture. Achievements of this order have remained mostly on the drawing board for Holland's European friends, however, most of whom lack comparable room to grow.

And the drawing board is just where the IBA plans would stay if it went according to the wishes of the professional Establishment. The German architectural scene today is far too lively though to cast blanket judgments or cast itself as the defender of the Holy Grail "of the ultramoderns of yesterday" or to use the sheer quantity of built-up space as an argument for alternatives. But continued criticism of lasting avant-garde achievements in residential and town planning under the topos "artistic clique" has always — as in Hegemann's censure of Martin Wagner's work — tended to inspire greater creativity and precision.

1945-1985: Italian Architecture between Innovation and Tradition

Francesco Dal Co

In the sixties, a profound change occurred among the leaders in Italian architecture. The old masters, most of whom were born around the turn of the century, gradually gave way to a generation of younger pupils. Figures like Mario Ridolfi, Giuseppe Samonà, Ludovico Quaroni, Franco Albini, Adalberto Libera, Giovanni Michelucci, Gio Ponti, Pier Luigi Nervi, and the eccentric Carlo Scarpa had begun to work during the thirties. They were able to take part in one of the most exciting periods of contemporary Italian architecture, the era between the late twenties and 1940. The cultural climate, not always favorable, ruled by fascism, was characterized by the works of G. Terragni, Figini and Pollini, G. Pagano, L. Baldessari, the BPR Group, I. Gardella, and many other architects all of whom were committed to dealing with the most advanced international experiences.

For this generation, the collapse of fascism and the disastrous results of World War II led to an overall rethinking of previous positions. However, their revision did not break the continuity of the developmental lines followed by Italian architecture during the past fifty years. Despite the wrenching traumas and despite the radical political change wrought in 1946 by the formation of the Italian Republic, the new routes taken within architecture were more shadow (and, I might say, basically ideological) than substance. The next fifteen years, until the end of the fifties, involved the entire country in a vast reconstruction process. An important role was assumed here by architects, who were certainly active in debating their diversity as well as agreeing on the most pressing demands presented by the drastic conditions in which Italy found itself.

The atmosphere recorded by such neo-realistic filmmakers as Rossellini or De Sica was that of Italy immediately after the war, notwithstanding the most important experiences involving the best of Italian architecture. The national rebirth was celebrated by architecture in its quest for genuine values, which were rooted in the history of a people compactly united in the labor of reconstruction after the wartime disasters. Architects had to give up the magniloquence that fascism demanded in order to illustrate itself; and they also renounced the most radical experiments of the thirties, conducted under the direct influence of other cultures, especially France and Germany.

Thus, Italian architecture of the forties and fifties was deeply criss-crossed by populist veins. We witnessed the efforts of architecture to identify with the collective labour of the Italian people as it overcame the tragedies of dictatorship and war. The professional opportunities offered to architects were quite consistent with these developments. The construction programs launched by the Italian government had several major aims: huge neighborhoods for low-income social classes on the outskirts of big cities; large-scale revitalization of depressed areas in the southernmost part of the Italian peninsula; and public-service buildings in the hearts of the principal urban concentrations. Then there were competitions for the design of the new railroad terminal in Rome (1947); edge-of-the-city neighborhoods such as Tiburtino, Rome (1949-54, by L. Quaroni and M. Ridolfi) or Falchera, Torino (1950-51, by A. Astengo); model installations like the village of La Martella in Matera (1949, by L. Quaroni and others). All these projects induced architects to rework cultural references, which had already been experimented with, but were now stringently verified on both an operative and a

formal, linguistic level. And it was in the linguistic area that these experiments revealed their originality. A common denominator was a quasi-celebration of the dignity of poverty; hence, the rejection of any ostentation, whether technological and structural or with respect to the canons of the modern tradition. The spirit of community, which was supposed to be interpreted by residential constructions right after the war, was also reflected in the formal and typological choices made by the architects.
The ideology was thus expressed in the forms, while linguistic options followed the hopes, including the political ones, that unite the "educated class."
Still, despite all appearances, this too confirmed that the break with the tensions tried during the thirties had more to do with form than with substance. In fact, we can note major similarities between postwar architectural populism and certain aspects of "corporation culture" of the thirties or the so-called "left-wing" fascism. Nor is it hard to see that important features of the postwar reformist ideology were anticipated by Adriano Olivetti's experiments during the thirties. Guiding his mechanical industry with an illuminated mind, Adriano Olivetti played a key role in promoting the most advanced architectural efforts in fascist Italy. He also helped bring about the birth of modern industrial design in our country. Because of his fusion of patronage and a perceptive entrepreneurial spirit, the leaders of rationalist architecture were called upon to collaborate in various ways with the Ivrea project. Starting in 1934, Figini and Pollini began constructing the industrial buildings of the ICO, a cultural center, residential complexes (Castellamonte district, 1938-56, with L. Piccinato, G.M. Olivieri, and M. Nizzoli). L. Belgiojoso, P. Bottoni, the BPR group (G.L. Banfi, E. Peressutti, E.N. Rogers); Figini and Pollini did major urban planning for the areas adjacent to Ivrea (e.g., the Regulatory Plan of Aosta by BPR, 1936), and in 1942, C. Cattaneo designed a hotel center for Ivrea. The postwar period confirmed Adriano Olivetti's role. The Piedmontese entrepreneur took on institutional tasks in the administration of governmental measures for underdeveloped areas in southern Italy. At the same time, he continued his private work of fostering modern architecture. We must recall other projects: Ridolfi (asylum in Ivrea, 1955 ff.); Quaroni and Piccinato (Bellavista neighborhood in Ivrea, 1952 ff.); Nizzoli and L. Cosenza (Olivetti factory in Pozzuoli, Naples, 1954); M. Zanuso, et al. These and other architects helped implement Olivetti's programs, which were meant to demonstrate the entrepreneurial involvement in Italy's social problems and to create a particular public image of Olivetti's industrial activities.
The fact that this activism was to lead to an intelligent image policy is indicated by Olivetti's architectural choices during the late fifties. A few of Olivetti's stores and sales agencies were designed by either C. Scarpa (Venice, 1957-58), BBPR (New York , 1954 and Barcelona, 1960-64), or G. Aulenti (Paris, 1967 and Buenos Aires, 1968) — along with the projects entrusted to prestigious architects from Le Corbusier (electronic laboratory in Rho, Milano, 1962) to Bakema, from Tange to Kahn, from Stirling to Meier and Hollsin. This wide range was consistent with the policies initiated by Adriano Olivetti during the thirties. Under the Olivetti patronage, the generational and regional differences were strengthened, while the entrepreneurial fortunes of the Ivrea factory were confirmed by the projects generously distributed among the principal contemporary architects.
Adriano Olivetti's work shows unique features in its emblematic character. The Ivrea factory contains a basic pole of coalescence for Italian architecture; but other factors also decisively contributed to preparing the generational change that came during the early sixties.
In Venice, the University Institute of Architecture became one of the most important academic centers thanks to Giuseppe Samonà, who took charge of the school right after the war.
Scarpa, Gardella, Albini, Astengo, B. Zevi, L. Benevolo, and then Aymonino, Tafuri, Rossi, Valle, Gregotti, et al. were summoned by Samonà and his successors to become part of the Venetian academic community. Starting in 1953-54, the review *Casabella*, published by Rogers, became an organ of cultural development and indispensable orientation for the younger Italian architects.
A new generation started out by collaborating on and developing the refined and curious problems stirred up by Rogers. The masthead of *Casabella*, or sometimes just a few pages of the magazine, sported the names of Rossi, Gregotti, Gae Aulenti, Tentori, Semerani, Tintori, and others. Ultimately, both Samonà's cultural provocations and the investigations fostered by *Casabella* accelerated

the process of critical revision that Italian architects felt they had to apply to their predecessors. Yet, not surprisingly, this network of experiences produced a lively debate on the problems of redefining in theoretical terms both the cultural procedures of architectural design and the social role of the architect. Even more emphatically than in the past, the basic topic of discussion was the relationship with history and tradition. Architects became more and more explicit about questioning the fairness of the "loyalty oath" sworn by the generation of old masters in their fealty to the orthodox tradition and modern architecture.
This rejection, long anticipated by such exponents of Roman culture as Ridolfi, Quaroni, or Libera, crystallized in other areas as well — and with original markings. It appeared not only on the pages of *Casabella*, which remained the top research organ of the Milanese architects, but also in the discussion organized during the summer session of the CIAM, which took place, not coincidentally, in Venice. Confronting the limits of modern orthodoxy linked to the rationalist experiments, Italian architects were ultimately involved in remodeling the very body of the historical tradition that they felt they had inherited. This confrontation with history was the central subject of architectural discussion as of the late fifties. This was confirmed by the subsequent development of the discussion until the early eighties. Starting in the late fifties, the rediscovery of a different modern tradition animated the works of such designers as Babetti and Isola or the Gregotti-Meneghetti-Stoppino studio. Gabetti and Isola's Bottega d'Erasmo (Turin, 1953), the design objects and constructions of the latter studio during the same years were the most important examples of an attempt at cultural and linguistic revision, which was eventually summed up in the term "neo-liberty." The intellectual concerns that were thus expressed were not just the province of the architects who interpreted this stylistic rediscovery. Not coincidentally, Paolo Portoghesi, who was active in the Rome area, came out in defense of his Milan and Turin colleagues in 1959, while his designs revealed a bold thrust towards history (cf. the Chiesa della Santa Famiglia, Salerno, 1968) as well as an unhesitating commitment to the linguistic experiments of post-modernism.
The experience of neo-liberty was thus the most obvious utterance of a rather widespread malaise,whose symptoms can be pinpointed in various works of the fifties and early sixties. The Velasca Tower in Milan (designed by L. Belgjoioso, E. Peressutti, E.N. Rogers, 1950-58) is the most significant example of this situation. Making itself the interpreters, with an exceptional typology,of the now imminent overcoming of the troubled years of national reconstruction, the BPR developed a style that fused the typically Italian tradition of experimental construction with an obvious goal of historical evocation. By intensifying the image of a medieval tower on a gigantic scale, the Milanese skyscraper is supposed to illustrate both the structural effort and the artisan-like attention to every constructional detail. In the very act of offering itself as a linguistic innovation, the Velasca Tower is thus meant to demonstrate that all progress can only be based on the renewed values of history and the goal of realizing an overall control of the making of form.
A similar attitude during those same years seemed to inspire the lyrical museum designs (Museum of the Palazzo Bianco, Tesoro di San Lorenzo, Genoa, 1950-51 and 1952-56) and the projects (cf. "La Rinascente", Rome, 1957, etc.) of F. Albini or works such as the Casa sulle Zattere, Venice (1954-58) by Gardella. The revision of tradition was accompanied by a lesser verification during the decade after the end of the war. And the younger architects were not the only ones who had to deal with the consequence. This was shown both by the now remembered works and the coherent procedures of such figures as Ridolfi, Michelucci, or Quaroni. Indeed, during the late fifties, Quaroni, a tireless agitator of problems and a keen originator of doubts and uncertainties, understood the demonstrable inadequacy of the "small utopias" with which the architects had tried to lend form to the hopes of the era of national reconstruction.
Guiding a large group of designers, Quaroni worked out a project for a residential neighborhood on the lagoon periphery facing Venice (the CEP district, San Giuliano, 1959). The methodological indication was clear. Strengthened by its openess to formal experiments, Italian architecture now moved toward new design scales and focused on the overall problem of redefining urban form. The Quaroni project thus inaugurated a new era of experimentation, with many

architects working out large-scale projects. They wanted to deal both with the structures of historic cities and with the formal implications of the planning processes, which demanded rational approaches to the developmental trends of Italian society, which had just emerged from its postwar condition.
In this altered situation, there were new possibilities for the architects who had been trained in the wake of the now remembered experiences. From this point of view, the work of a designer like G. De Carlo is symptomatic. Influenced by the cultural climate generated by the final meetings of the CIAM, and active in promoting the international debate of Team Ten, De Carlo had the unique chance to experiment with the *Città universitaria* of Urbino as of 1960, the realization of a series of works open to more contemporary international experiments. A lively animator of the debate during the sixties, De Carlo also interpreted the variously expressed goal of consolidating theories on the diverse levels of urban and architectural planning. Employing an original approach, he dealt with the issues of town design and advocacy planning (cf. the housing development of the Matteotti Village in Terni, 1970-75).
The linguistic revision adopted by De Carlo in Urbino was then interpreted in various ways by other architects while the meaning of urban design became the subject of the theoretical investigations conducted by a group led by G. Samonà for the Vajont area (1964) or the various experiments done for new administrative centers (cf. the designs for the Administrative Center of Turin, 1962, by G. Samonà's group and by G. Polesello and A. Rossi; and the Studio Asse plans for Rome, 1967-70).
Along these lines, the works of an architect like Gino Valle are very important. His office block in Porcio (Udine, 1959-61) for Zanussi Industries demonstrated his ability to deal with the ferment animating the experiments of the New Brutalism on an international level. While Valle's immediately subsequent works attest to his professional efficiency and solid constructional practice, his projects during the seventies and eighties have been less incisive; he has been expressing himself in worn-out stylemes, and the results are sometimes animated by a Brutalism that is purely gestural. Along with his coherent professional practice in his early works, we can look at his distinguished experiments in Milan during the early sixties and seventies, such as Gae Aulenti,V. Magistretti, V.Viganò and, above all, M. Zanuso, involved, like other Milanese architects, in working out the meanings proposed by industrial design.
While this may not be the place to discuss the major contributions made by this generation of Italian architects to the growth of industrial design, we cannot forget that the "school" formed in this area best expresses the heritage of the work done since the thirties. Designers such as E. Sottsass, M. Bellini, A. Castiglioni, Gae Aulenti, M. Zanuso, G. Colombo, T. Scarpa developed their own styles during the second half of the sixties. They dealt with the concomitant provocations offered by the leading figures of the more radical research groups, such as the Florentine Archizoom and Superstudio; the results were then developed by such original people as A. Mendini, R. Dalisi, and A. Branzi.
The change wrought among these diverse types of experiences proved to be highly productive. A good example is the work of Tobia Scarpa, who was responsible for some of the best designs of the seventies, but who can also implement original architectural projects, e.g., the building that the automated store constructed for the Benetton company in Treviso (1980-84).
Having said this, we should now turn to the sixties. Many problems that ripened during that decade were submittted to a radical verification between 1968 and 1970. The difficult social transformations that began in 1968 ultimately influenced both the lives of academic institutions and the future of professional practice. This situation intensified the revisionist trend that had already emerged in architecture during the sixties. The tensions and uncertainties were keenest when architects were given one of their most significant opportunities during the second half of the decade; the competition for the design of the new office project of the Chamber of Deputies in Rome (1967). The importance of the choice was obvious. However, the proposals of Quaroni rather than De Feo, of Aymonino rather than Sacripanti or Polesello expressed a common retreat to the terrain of linguistic intimacy rather than faith in the power of propositions and the transformation of architecture. This retreat led to an inquiry about a freer relationship with the tradition of modern architecture and the most significant

demonstration of the projects designed for this occasion — that of G. Samonà. In paying final tribute to the Le Corbusier models, Samonà, operating with quotations and formal reductions, emptied out the ideological implications. Although their motives may be different, two other works seem to move in this same direction: C. Aymonino's housing project in the Gallaratese area of Milan (1967) and V. De Feo's engineering school in Terni (1969). Aymonino's complex narrative, which also draws on Aldo Rossi, is a final homage to the neo-realist tradition; in a dynamic volumetric interplay, he tries to imitate the realization of an urban metaphor — sometimes with surprising results; the programmatic disorder of the metaphor can only be redeemed by the continuous evocation of norm and tradition. The excited montages of Aymonino encounter the games of subtraction and the apparatuses of quotations utilized by De Feo in his threefold work, which constitutes the necessary prelude to his gradually reductive research on a linguistic level as conducted in the Roman architect's original projects during the seventies and eighties. There is great diversity among the approaches taken by the architects who were trained in the *Casabella* entourage. The "programmatic ugliness" that G. Canella polemically pursued in his early works seems to carry some of Rogers's intuitions to extreme consequences. Filled with historical merits, as are the simultaneous works of G. Michelucci (e.g. the church of San Giovanni Battista near Florence, 1960-64), and yet differently, in the dense realizations of the Florentine architects L. Ricci and L. Savioli, Canella's constructions have gradually shaken off the excesses of their original poetics of anti-grace, achieving a tidier and more deliberate monumentalism (cf. the residential district in Bollate, Milan, 1974, and the Municipio di Pioltello, Milan, 1976).

Different but no less characteristic is the evolution in the work of V. Gregotti. When the experiences of the Gregotti-Meneghetti-Stoppino studio were exhausted, the Milanese architect tried to radically renew the foundations of his own professional practice. In the seventies, the new studio he established as Gregotti and Associates became one of the liveliest sources of Italian architecture. With the valuable help of colleagues, Gregotti led his own work in an important new direction. Proof of this can be seen in several of his ambitious projects during the seventies, starting with his designs for the Zen district in Palermo (1968, etc.) or the university campuses for the cities of Florence (1971) and Cosenza (1975, etc.). One of the designers who collaborated on these works was a young, gifted architect named F. Purini. Indeed, these projects were the premise for one of the most original of Gregotti's designs: the housing development in Cefalù (1976). This project focused Gregotti's great interest in verifying the relationship between the work and its context, between specific formal options and the geographic and territorial givens. Thus, the themes of relationship, rejection of certain forms and hence modification became constant factors in Gregotti's works, which had to confront more and more complex situations. The vast scope and implications of the professional opportunities that Gregotti seems to prefer involve the use of various combinations of disciplinary contributions, which the architect, as their formal coordinator, must organize. While he may sometimes act to the detriment of the precision and accuracy of architectural definitions, there is no doubt that Gregotti's professional practice allows him to properly grasp interesting and topical problems and opportunities. Gregotti seems attracted less to the solitude of forms than to their interrelationships. He is interested not so much in defining a specific language as in understanding the possible interactions of diverse languages; in this way, he has to discount the risk of preferring the programmatic declaration to the constructional verification.

Once the experiments of his youth were past, Gregotti seemed intent on experimenting with the reality, the verification of his own investigations. Diametrically opposed to this is the attitude of A. Rossi. Rossi was one of the most coherent Italian architects in the theoretical revision of the foundations of the modern architectural tradition. Having an intelligent interest in the works of Loos rather than the architecture of Illuminism, in neo-classicism rather than the cities of Veneto, he penned a number of significant texts during the sixties and seventies, expressing a sincere need for renewing the foundations of theory. On the basis of such premises, Rossi codified an original approach to the problems of architectural design and an extremely individual linguistic hypothesis. He obstinately developed his own style, programmatically limiting himself to a restricted

range of situations and formal elements, and translating them into a restrained but not limited language. Initiating an intricate dialogue with history and private memories, Rossi succeeded in defining a poetics that ultimately brought him wide recognition. Indifferent to their own contingent purposes, Rossi's forms have the captivating quality of simplicity without harming the vocation for abstraction. This vocation is revealed in the deliberate nonchalance with which Rossi treats, on the one hand, the implications of the relationship between the project definitions and the historical time and, on the other hand, the accidental nature of reality.
From this point of view, the cemetery Rossi built in Modena (1971, etc.) sums up the peculiarity of his work. As an example of obstinacy applied to a vocabulary of primary forms and dedication to the work of abstraction operated upon the linguistic figures, the cemetery also constitutes a problematic point of passage if viewed in the light of Rossi's most recent designs (cf. the Teatro Carlo Felice, Genoa, with I. Gardella, 1984, and the tertiary house, Buenos Aires, 1984). After constantly demonstrating his perseverance during the seventies, Rossi began to veer toward a mannerist practice, apparently replacing stubbornness with repetition — although we cannot exclude the possibility that this development may be a prelude to new experimental hypotheses.
The panorama described above shows the broken limits of the references that Italian architects can use. To confirm this, we can cite a huge number of contrasting examples. For clarity's sake, we ought to consider the work of such diverse individuals as A. Cantafora or M. Scolari and R. Piano. It would be counter-productive to regard Scolari's or Cantafora's efforts as artistic experiences beyond the pale of architecture.
A nominalist reduction of the complexity of phenomena could easily distort their meaning. Cantafora's and Scolari's paintings actually express both the uncertainties and the crises that have characterized — albeit in a general process of maturation — the developments in Italian architecture during the past decade. Both the surreal, metaphysical vein of Scolari's watercolors and the accurate perspective constructions of Cantafora's oils originated in a meditation on nature and the architectural *modus operandi*. Cantafora's continual *depiction of depiction* focuses on meanings typical of the project that are now in danger of distortion. Indeed, his paintings reveal a desire to recall that architecture is always a composite of experiences that are sometimes uncommunicable, sometimes unutterable, but always destined to interfere with the configuration of every space, every site and form.
In this sense, this modality of expression does not contain a rejection. Cantafora's paintings reveal an attempt at living up to the means of depiction and alluding to all the meanings that architecture must be able to transmit. Thus, the architectural projects depicted by Scolari and Cantafora trace the opposite limit of a conception that the work of a constructor such as R. Piano can fully illustrate. Abandoning the avant-garde bombast that made the Pompidou Center in Paris (1971-77) a noisy but belated utterance, Piano, with his most recent projects, from the museum for the De Menil Collection in Houston (1981-83) to his diverse urban designs of the seventies, seems to be deliberately experimenting with an efficient and rational use of technology devoid of any formal bombast. As unostentatious "machines," Piano's projects have the merit of adhering to an extreme functionality even when their specific purposes could stimulate narcissistic exhibitionism. Witness his Calder exhibition in Turin in 1983 or the stage designs for L. Nono's *Prometeo* in Venice in 1984.
Among barely remembered opposite possibilities, several young architects conducted extremely personal experiments that we should not ignore. We have already indicated the work F. Purini did with V. Gregotti. After the projects on which he collaborated with the older Milanese architect, Purini was unable to have his own designs adequately implemented. Still some of them (e.g., the housing development for Naples in 1984) must be viewed as promises that are waiting to be carried out. A similar statement could be made about several other Roman architects, especially those who gave life to the stimulating projects of the GRAU group during the seventies. Among the various figures trained in avant-garde groups or the late sixties and early seventies, we find the Florentine A. Natalini. In such works as the bank building in Alzate Brianza (Como, 1978, etc.) or in the project for the Technological Museum of Mannheim (1982), he showed that he had overcome the foolish avant-garde wishes shared during his training at the Superstudio. He had decidedly

moved toward coherent and elegant linguistic simplifications. This direction is more salient in the well-characterized efforts of an architect like Francesco Venezia. Trained in the special environment of Naples with such constructions as the Museum of Gibellina in Sicily (1980, etc.) or the design for San Leucio in Caserta (1984), Venezia managed to define a lean, but original language, capable of creating a sincere lyrical touch with a sure architectural sense.

The picture sketched after these digressions should leave no doubts about the impossibility of reducing the Italian architectural panorama of the eighties to common denominators. The disappearance of the masters who had begun working during the thirties opened the way definitively to the process of revising the links with the modern tradition. This process now seems to be terminated once and for all. Hence, it is not surprising that after the disturbances and uncertainties of the seventies, the best Italian architects seem interested in recovering a specific dimension of architectural technique, less determined by ideological options pertaining to the past, and characterized by a tendency to re-establish the role of constructional practice, which is the ultimate verification of any abstract formal approach or linguistic experiment.

On the other hand, in the space marked by the coherence of the consolidated, but not immutable rules of the architectural project, we find that the most brillant Italian architect of this century, Carlo Scarpa, has devoted himself with unique restraint, working in isolation, never turning down even marginal projects. During a career spanning some fifty years, he has produced a substantially limited number of works. Yet he has embodied a lesson that provides much food for thought. Scarpa's mastery is revealed in his architectural imagination; he expertly uses the most diverse materials, reinventing building traditions, drawing new life from old constructions. He has proven his intelligence, his curious and refined knowledge, his ability to look at things and understand them. All this adds up to a unique method of work, craftsmanship, a non-nostalgic revitalization of the secrets of which the architect must continue to be the custodian, and the enigmas that he is called upon to resuscitate or to solve. Starting in the thirties and then with his almost mannerist gems of the fifties (cf. the project for the Villa Zoppas in Conegliano, 1953, or the Villa Veritti, Udine, 1955, etc.), Scarpa established the premises for the lively if belated youth of his old age. His miraculous restorations of Castelvecchio, Verona (1956, etc.), of the Fondazione Querini Stampalia, Venice (1961-63), his most famous efforts right after the war constitute several stages in the history of contemporary Italian architecture.

However, it was his final projects and constructions — Piazza della Loggia, Brescia (1974), a villa in Ryadh (1978), or the Banca Popolare, Verona (1973, etc.), that gave the measure of Carlo Scarpa's stature as an architect. The ultimate demonstration of his genius was the monumental Brion tomb at the cemetery of San Vito d'Altivole (Treviso, 1969, etc.).

This masterpiece distilled all the complex meanings of his investigations. Scarpa's work has the merit and courage of taking for granted the fact that it is not "up to date." It once again confronts the eyes and minds of contemporary culture with figures that allude to the perennial values of architecture, to its mythical origins and its deepest meanings.

As we know, the history of postwar Italian architecture is marked by more or less successful efforts, more or less rigorous and generous attempts to continually renew the relationship between the project and its time and, therefore, with tradition and history. And in Scarpa's works, time, history, and tradition are the materials for constructing the development of the ancient craft of architecture.

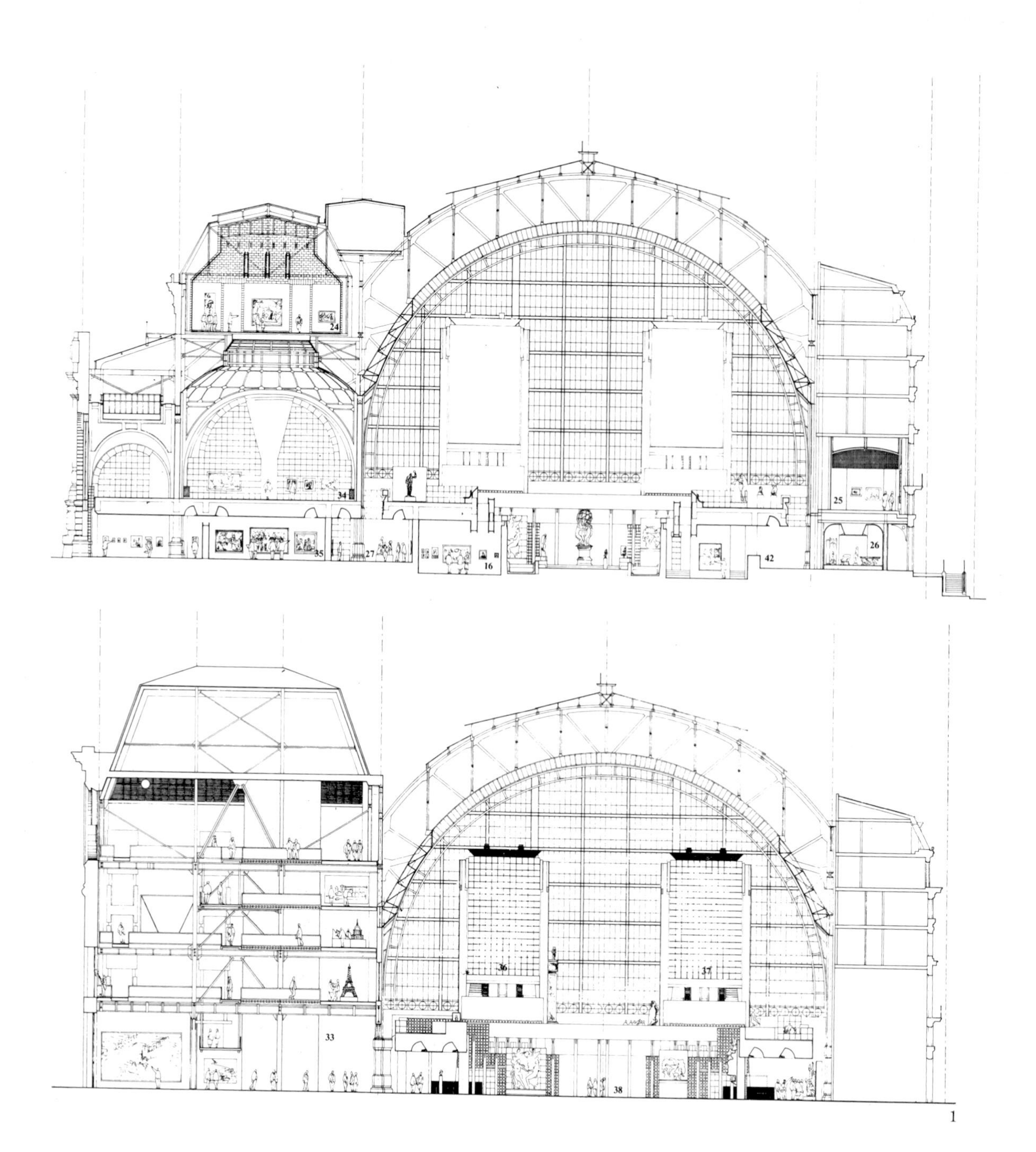

Musée d'Orsay, Paris, 1980-1986
Transformation of the Gare d'Orsay into a Museum of French Art, 1849-1914.

1. Longitudinal sections of the museum.
2. The nave with the arcade of the "Salons Ovales" to the left.

2

1

Administrative Building of the Züblin Company, 1982-1984.

1. Plan, 1981.
2. Inside and outside views of the building.

2
3
4
5

Vittorio Gregotti

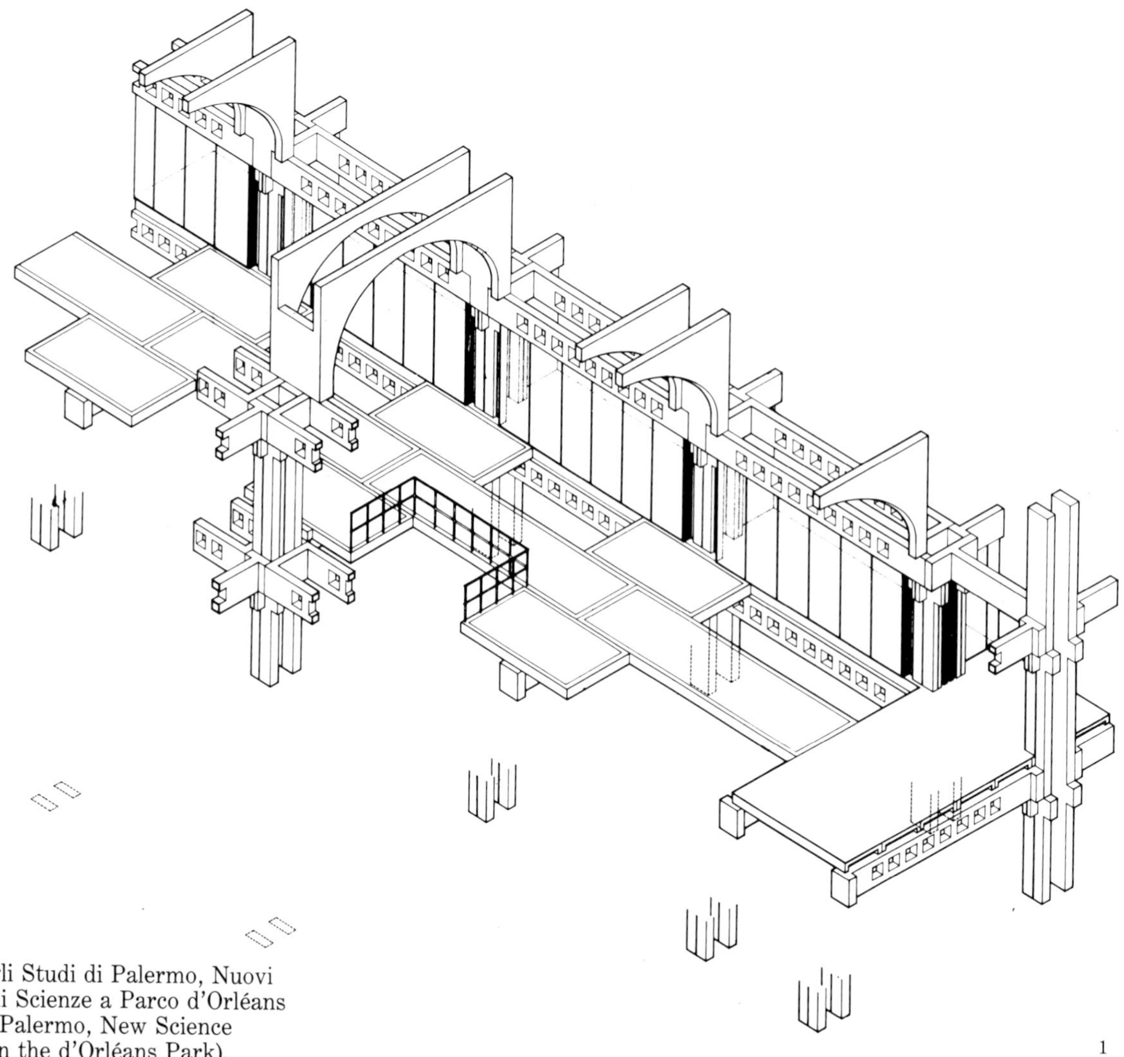

1

Università degli Studi di Palermo, Nuovi Dipartimenti di Scienze a Parco d'Orléans (University of Palermo, New Science Departments in the d'Orléans Park), 1969-1984.

1. Axonometrical view of central way through Chemistry Department.
2. Open theater and Chemistry Department.
3. View of inner courtyard and roofing of Chemistry Department.
4. Central way through Chemistry Department.
5. View of a department interior.

2 3 4 5

Hans Hollein

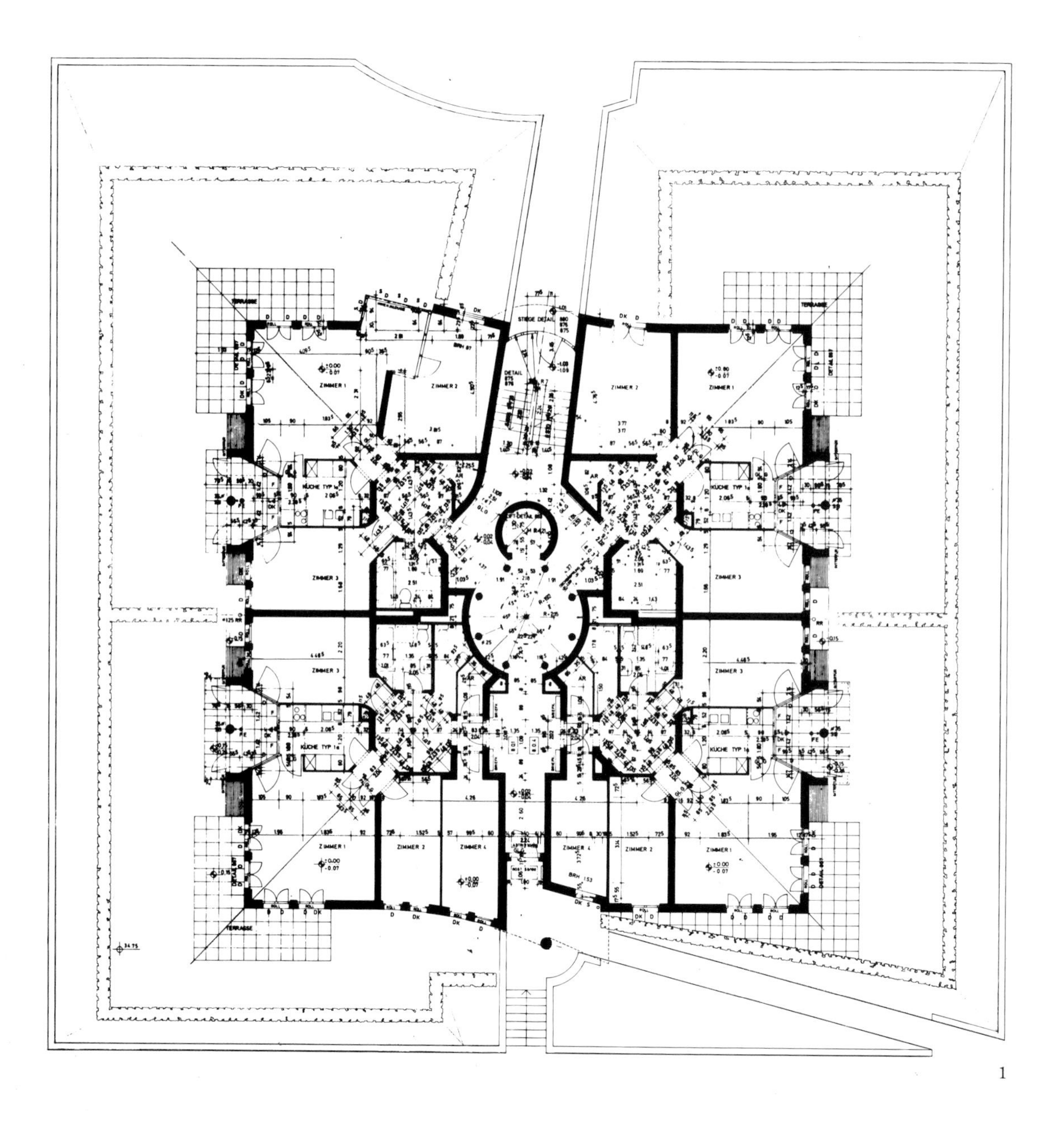

1

Haus 8, Rauchstrasse, Berlin, 1984-1985.

1. Plan.
2. The model.

2

Josef Paul Kleihues

1

2

3

Maasprospekt, Rotterdam, 1982.

1. The model.
2. The harbor.
3. The model of the plan.
4. The prospect of the harbour.
5. General plan.

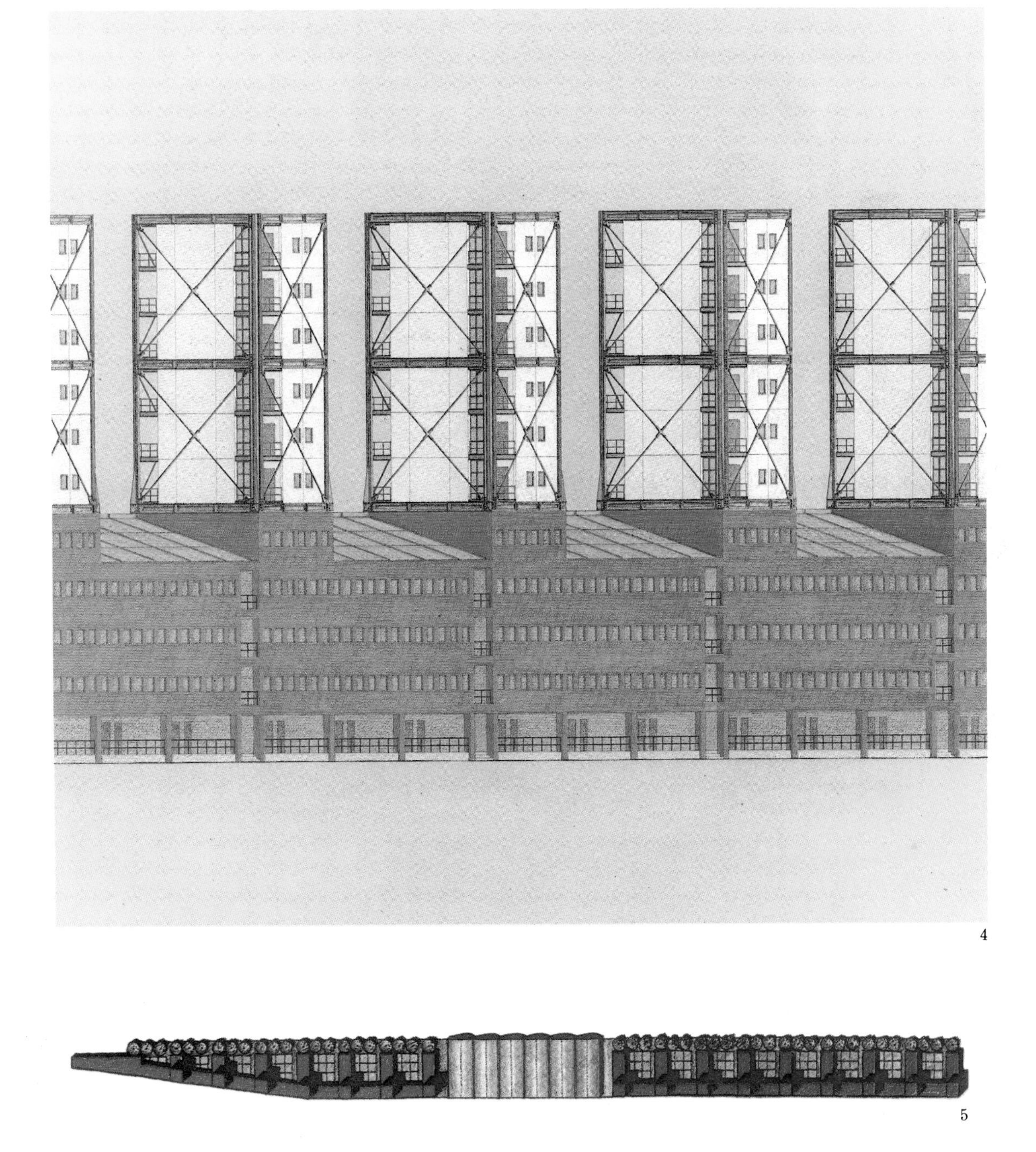

4

5

Renzo Piano

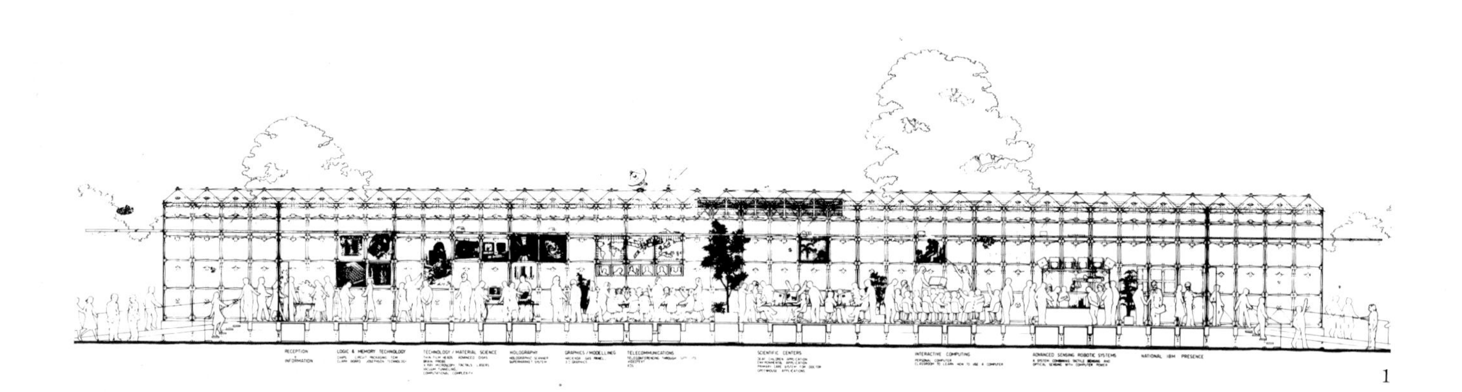

IBM Traveling Exhibition, 1982-1984.

1. Longitudinal section of the building.
2. Interior of pavilion.
3. Pavilion in the Trocadéro gardens, Paris.

2

3

1. *Teatro del mondo (World's Theater)*, Venice, 1979.

Bacino di San Marco, Venice, 1979.

1

Gino Valle

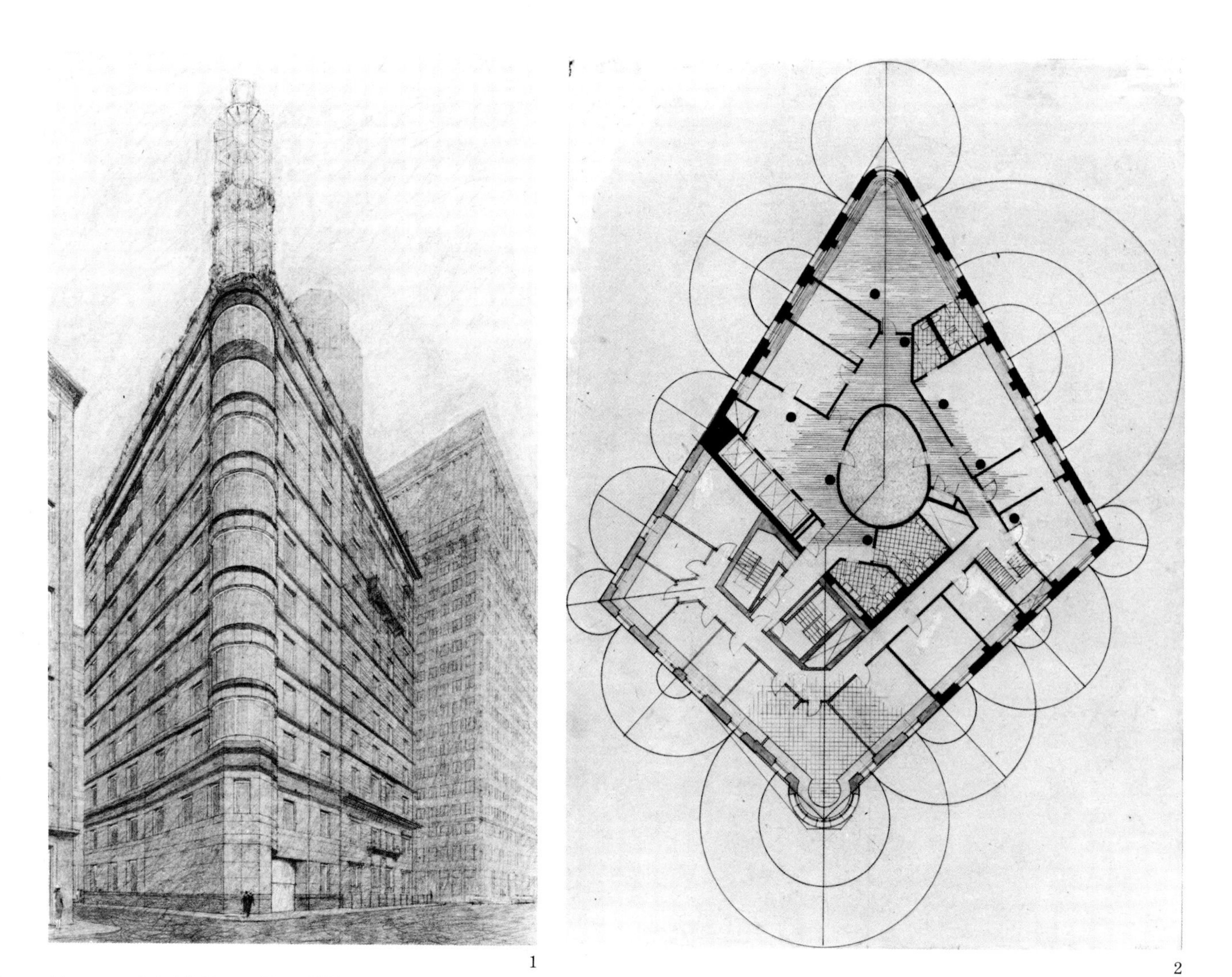

1 2

Banca Commerciale Italiana, One William Street, New York, 1981-1983.

1. Perspective of Mill Lane - Stone St.
2. Plan of seventh floor with indication of generative elements that bisect the opposite corners and overturn the window axes.
3. View from Stone Street. The bird cage is still not up, October 1984.
4. Detail of entrance to Stone Street garage, October 1984.
5. View of the building from South William Street.

3

4

5

Art

Giovanni Anselmo
Marco Bagnoli
Georg Baselitz
Lothar Baumgarten
Joseph Beuys
Alberto Burri
Pier Paolo Calzolari
Enzo Cucchi
Hanne Darboven
Nicola De Maria
Luciano Fabro
Ludger Gerdes
Rebecca Horn
Jörg Immendorff
Anselm Kiefer
Jannis Kounellis
Markus Lüpertz
Gerhard Merz
Mario Merz
Reinhard Mucha
Mimmo Paladino
Giulio Paolini
A.R. Penck
Giuseppe Penone
Michelangelo Pistoletto
Sigmar Polke
Gerhard Richter
Salomé
Remo Salvadori
Thomas Schütte
Ettore Spalletti
Emilio Vedova

Iceberg Europe — The Crystal Faces of the Italian Face

Bruno Corà

To paraphrase the Communist Manifesto — the specter of an iceberg is haunting the immense stretches of the oceans of art. The eye has a hard time measuring the size of this iceberg. And it is even more difficult to gauge how much of it has surfaced and how much is still hidden in the water. Such is the situation of European art at this point in history.

However, we can make out the forms of two groups among the Italian and German artists focused on by Germano Celant's observatory: the peaks and pinnacles of this iceberg are certainly the individual utterances and the crystalline works produced by them.

In regard to Italy, the events taking place on our peninsula, the state of our seas and mountains and the extraordinary quality of our "navigators," I have (with respect to foreign seas and sailors) repeatedly indicated what I feel are the conditions of "navigation" at the given moment. This information is to be found in two "bulletins", published in *AEIUO* and *De Appel* magazines, entitled *Notice for Navigators* and aimed at navigating both local and foreign coasts. In these verbal maps, I deemed it useful to furnish the elements of my sightings, the coordinates, the visions, the things illuminated by the beacon of my gaze. Anyone venturing out into the sea of art was informed of anything related to his own positions. Not coincidentally, one of the greatest navigators of twentieth-century art, Alberto Burri, needed to look up at the sky of painting in order to depict (almost as a universal sign) the constellations that all artists must sight if they want to reach the prodigious light of their colors. Just think of his huge compositions and the sculpture of *Sextant* (1982, berthing in Venice, queen of the sea) and the synthesis paintings of *Voyage* (1980, for Munich). Almost as vast profane cycles, these works convey the grace of planetary gardens and skies surrounding and dominating stormy seas and the self-assurance of the nomadic artist plying these waters. The effect is as vivid as that produced by younger artists, so that we may connect and compare them. Or take Emilio Vedova, who set sail from his native Venice some fifty years ago. Today, in that same city, we see links with his art: the precociousness of voyages with many false and tardy gestures — so frequent in the tides of painting, the coherence of the routes in the restless and fragmented archipelago of signals, the complex and yet precise circumnavigations within the steadiness of unchanged orientation.

After Burri and Vedova, certain leading figures in the Italian art world distinguished themselves by the quality of their explorations. I am thinking of Jannis Kounellis, Giulio Paolini, Luciano Fabro, Michelangelo Pistoletto and Mario Merz.

In various ways, these artists sent out signals of implacable agitation and sometimes real calls for help. SOS's from boats drifting like Rimbaud's and from "rafts" or "arks" — settings for linguistic dramas not unlike that of Géricault's *Méduse*.

For these and other artists present here — Giovanni Anselmo, Giuseppe Penone, and Pier Paolo Calzolari — who began and evolved during the sixties up to the frontier of 1968, the problems inherent in the risk of large-scale navigation became obvious in three ways. Artists had to create and adopt a linguistic vessel that could traverse the entire ocean of earlier art history. They were forced to realize the total lack of a structure necessary for helping a ship in distress (after Futurism, Italy had no harbor, no lighthouse, no lifeboat, no provisions, no saints!). And finally, they had no foundation for choices and behavior in any conditions, since in art, as at

sea, one cannot turn back in vain. The hawsers were gone, and the artists had to push on through these years. They had to reach the most arduous latitudes of the relationship between the artist and the work and between the artist and society — even when the lack of all support instruments made them feel that they would never be able to overcome the difficulties.
Ultimately they reached the open sea and could navigate freely. And today, we can perhaps acknowledge the significance of shipwrecks in comparison with boating on a lake or along the local coast; today, we can recognize the scope and value of the entire artistic enterprise. Among these figures and among the younger ones who ventured out to the high seas, some were inspired by the miraculous achievements of their antecedents, and some by an open-minded recruitment campaign waged by the merchant marine. On the Italian side of the iceberg sighted by Celant, several new peaks could be made out between 1970 and today. These include the works of Ettore Spalletti, Marco Bagnoli and Remo Salvadori, and, contemporary with one another, Enzo Cucchi, Mimmo Paladino and Nicola De Maria who, despite their diversity, were all critically identified and involved in the great call for a return to the painterly and the picturesque style. Each of these artists was concerned with the birth and individual development of his own artistic dimension. Their evolutions took place despite an almost complete absence of any structural reference to such public institutions as museums, to any ruling or cultural class formed within Italy and operating as a resonant interlocutor of their artistic "predication."
Thus, the works of Italian artists participate in, denounce and reflect the features of — not so much the homogeneous and organic cultural pattern of a social history — as a structural "lack" thereof. In practice, the artists themselves, from 1945 until today, have constituted themselves as "facts" and as "histories" of a single Italian culture engaged in a dialogue with the other European cultures. For years, this situation has involved the assumption of a moral and ideological responsibility; and this responsibility is engaged in a direct dialectic with the development of the other visual cultures, which elsewhere, however, especially in Germany, have a reference and a reflection in the social classes that dominate the culture. Thus, a twofold autonomy distinguishes the art of these Italian artists, both in terms of an internal linguistic constitution and in terms of their necessarily solitary and self-aware activity with respect to social history. These are the reasons why various Italian artists represented in this exhibition have calibrated their own expressive modes to the work of one or more earlier artists, whose achievements thus constituted a legacy of reflection, as a direct relationship between artists. These bonds of kinship or comparison, taken from a deep meditation on the syntactical constructions of the vision and conception of space, were nevertheless not sought or recognized only between the lines of a national tradition. They ripened in a vast verification with regard to the finest and most advanced achievement of visual culture in our century and sometimes in previous centuries, both in Europe and elsewhere. These optics lead us, I believe, to the distinct quality of Italian works and to the sometimes opposed if not antagonistic methodologies that each artist has adopted in the course of his own labors. Now just what are the intrinsic features and peculiar qualities of each single "discourse"?
After the events of World War II, a dramatic existential condition decisively marked the efforts of art. Reflecting upon the inertia of material and its initial formless state, artists demonstrated its objective qualities. The epic of complexity in

E. Prampolini, *Béguinage*, 1914.

U. Boccioni, *Forme uniche della continuità nello spazio*, 1913.

instruments and multiple materials for the visual methods had characterized Futurism from Boccioni to Prampolini. Now, it reached the fertile soil of Burri, whose rages have nevertheless always included the calm and supreme measure of his Umbrian forebears from the thirteenth to the fifteenth centuries. The tension of this bow of experience releases the arrow of Burri's work. Together with Fontana, Burri is certainly the most commanding leader in this recovery or resurrection of contemporary Italian art, which is still in a process of renewal. Burri's works include non-painterly materials that he was the first to raise to the nobility of painting. Thus we have *Molds* and *Tars* (1948), *Sacks*, *Humps*, *Combustions*, *Woods*, *Irons*, *Plastics*, *Cracks*, *Cellotexes* and finally the polychrome backgrounds of *Gardens* during those years and the iron sculptures. With these solutions, Burri indited *the poem of matter*. On the other hand, Emilio Vedova's solution, deriving almost entirely from the pictorial gesture of uninterrupted propulsion, reveals an unrivalled capital gained from Action Painting. His recent shows in Venice confirm that even Vedova had an ancient heavenly constellation to gaze at while navigating, and that by means of a constant dialogue with baroque lights or Plastic Dynamism, he was able to fashion the wedges for docking his powerful ship. Few artists have so forcefully managed to stir up the waters of contemporary painting with a legacy of disquiet from Tintoretto, Goya and Boccioni. The beneficial effects of his seismic action have been felt not only today but immediately after the war, as documented by his most committed works.

For some time now, Jannis Kounellis has been modeling his linguistic repertoire on the following factors: the persistence of ideology in history, the values renewed by Burri's art, the steady ghostlike haunting of the concept of "classical" in modern and contemporary bourgeois culture from David to de Chirico, the artist's moral and ideological commitment and the necessity of internationalism in the codices of vision. Kounellis's work frequently exalts a basic "musical score" that never eludes the need for a strong structure for the image, a spatial construction of classical and formally rigid tension with, nevertheless, a fluid sign or figure, often freely moving "to the quick." This internal antithesis of the structuring and destructuring of the image evinces the nervous modality of the artist, who has been active in Rome since 1959.

On the other hand, Michelangelo Pistoletto, in Turin, gave a great deal of thought to the possibility of restoring an adequate future and a new spatiality to figuration after Mondrian and Duchamp had brought perspective back to square one. Pistoletto also aimed at a new existential integrity for figuration after the dramatic mutilations and cancellations in Bacon's figures. Ultimately, Pistoletto produced an œuvre whose "mirroring" quality made possible, for the first time, an integration of the virtual image and the real image.

The phenomenological device that Pistoletto perfected with his *Mirror Paintings* (1962) permits the frequency of a new spatiality that can reverse and open up to a new perspective several exits of modern art that were dramatically turned into cul-de-sacs (Mondrian, Duchamp, Bacon). The spatial opening of Pistoletto's mirror like works gave him free access to the continuous stylistic mutation that gradually generated such pieces as *Objects in Minus* (1965), the theatrical arena of *Zoo*, and a notable number of subsequent works, including his sculptures in polychrome and marble. In all these works, the reflection space is chiefly the space of reality experienced creatively even before the space of pictorial representation; and this includes real existence in all its manifestations, as long as it is interpreted by the conscious and creative mind.

Dizzying and yet under the illuministic control of the *ratio*, the works of Giulio Paolini never forego the tension of surprising the object of the profound dilemma inherent in vision. The reality to be defined after another twenty years is still there, unaltered, in the intuition of *Squaring* (1960), a true confirmation of his crystalline theorem about the impossible delimitation of any image. Since that Paolini drawing, however, that map of the beginning and end of any possible visual composition, all visual instruments have been investigated by him, all the perfect geometries of the complex prism of visual thinking have been measured, all the paths in the labyrinthine process of visualizing the imaginary have been taken — and today, the artist has arrived at the magical *House of Lucretius* (1982-84). His work thus proves to be the product of a state of grace in one of the most lucid visual minds in contemporary art.

Since 1963, Luciano Fabro has been planning and constructing an œuvre as an adequate and suitable habitat for the expectations of his own sensibility. Initially, he conducted a dialogue with the works of Fontana and thus defined the qualities of his own concept of space. Next, he impelled form through the sensitive knowledge of materials toward the epilogue of the formation of the image. Fabro's form is a thorough perusal of "things" by way of the direct experience of artistic labor. Explicitly in his works and articulately in his theoretical writings, Fabro describes a need to define and establish a culture of artistic labor that would permit a cognitive approach to experience. The formation of Fabro's œuvre is simultaneous with the creation of the environment and what he defines as the *ratio civitatis*.

"Desirous of being architecture" of the space of time, all of Mario Merz's works, all his paintings, like a galactic spiral, involve the whole universe of matter and material in their construction. The artist who initially sailed across the waters of formal painting, has navigated the sea of Arte Povera and reached seas and ports where the secular languages of an anti-representational factuality interact with the words of the ancient sacrality of painting. All these factors make Merz's works a passage from the imaginary of the prehistorical and proto-iconographic to the dissolution of representation in the era of relativity. As the agitator of a bucolic but also cosmic myth, Merz uses neon lights as heavenly thunderbolts, but also as concrete segments of light. He builds a stone igloo on a river as if it were a meteorite precipitated from goodness knows what space, and he shows that this construction can be inhabitable both inside and outside. He paints a race of naked legs supporting the crypticness of an automobile's horsepower. He fascinatingly squeezes together fruits and stones in a painting that could be infinitely expanded. Then, using the Fibonacci series and activating it numerically, he constructs a work as a factual continuum — a proliferating artistic action.

The works of Pierpaolo Calzolari deliberately and unequivocally subdivide into two periods perhaps with an equal passion. As of 1967, they were part of Arte Povera; then, as of 1977, they burst out in a pictorial ascension. Calzolari's early works were made of ephemeral but intimate materials such as rose petals, leaves, feathers, moss, hoar frost, ice

G. de Chirico, *La malinconia della partenza*, 1916.

or the feeble flame of a candle. Other works emanated the icy hostility of standardized technological products: lead, brass, neon. When we study these pieces, we realize that the artist employs his elements discreetly; he is trying to produce that "state of not unexpected poetry which defines the nearness of things to one's own daily life" (Calzolari). In his recent paintings on large canvases he has been seeking the same contiguity between psychological introspection and environmental relation with an equivalency between the magnitude and intensity of the color field, which sometimes, as in Monet's *Water Lilies*, is extended so greatly that any overall and instantaneous perception becomes impossible.

A manifestation and containment of energy, a heaviness and lightness of materials: these are the statuary aspects of the plastic paradigm of Giovanni Anselmo. He is a lonesome navigator around the "ultramarine" of a small surface above which the clouds of gray granite are suspended by iron wires attached to a hook. Anselmo lends body to the invisible tensions that his sensibility makes macroscopically evident.

His compass needles, like the hearts of stones, point not only to the north. They also indicate the constant pulsation of the planet's density, the here and elsewhere (both present) of all the concreteness of the perceptions that have weight, color, time, and unlimited space. Anselmo tells about the silent macro- and micro-processes of living, the way they bring the "situations of energy;" he shows their anything but negligible reality and "the will not to crystallize such situations but, rather, to keep them open and alive in terms of our living" (Anselmo).

Paying equal attention to both himself and the world, and, above all, to deducing from regulated nature the qualities, forces, the warp and woof, the various aspects of the multiform varieties of life, Giuseppe Penone has developed a sculptural alphabet with an utterly original organic existence. Employing the ancient practices of wood-carving and sculpture, Penone excavates and uncovers large wooden planks from the outside toward the inside, ultimately attaining the still intact cylindrical shape of a tree. He is virtually seeking the soul of that vegetal and fibrous material or X-raying its identity. And the soul of the wood, as in a cyclical proposition, is the tree. The external imprint of the human skin is like the imprint of the bark, the plastic impress of the body parts is like

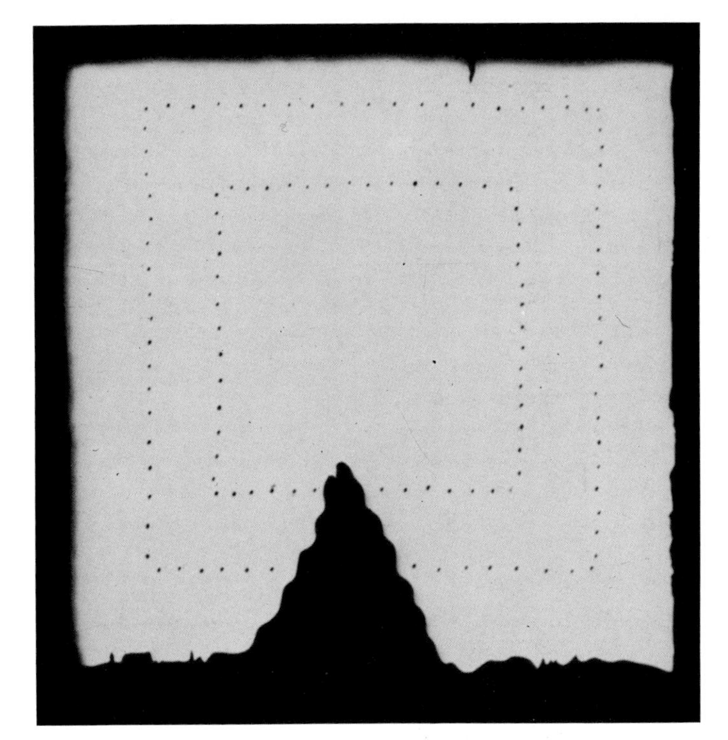

L. Fontana, *Concetto spaziale. Teatrino*, 1965.

the impress of portions of a trunk. Such resemblances evoke the subjectivity of the artist as conscious of the natural link, they manifest its absolute singularity; and yet they are also particulars of a common anthropological dimension. A body, like a tree, lives internally from a sap, a lymph, from a vital breath that always determines its particular aspect, its appearance. Thus, Penone's *Breaths* (1978) manages to offer a successful and synthetic plastic expression of this mimetic exercise between man and nature. We may state that the works of Penone and other artists of the Arte Povera area have fully concluded the intense decade of linguistic maturation from 1960 to 1970, and that the character of several of the younger artists included in this exhibition was already defined and active by the mid-seventies.

One of these artists is Ettore Spalletti, whose early works deserve special attention. Humid in quality, luminously chromatic yet opaque, powdery and smooth to the touch, much of his work, made up of "thicknesses" of pigment, literally submerges into white. Indeed, white is the basis of all his painting-sculpture, which looks chromatically uniform. On closer inspection,

however, it reveals a soft, delicately agitated polychrome. This polychrome emerges from the abrasion of the surface of the chromatic thickness, which is produced by means of successive layers of paint; the technique, equivalent to breathing, consists of adding and subtracting painterly material. By means of this diurnal exercise of color application, his solitary and traditional cohabitation with the devices of painting, and his invention of a "structure color" in painting, Spalletti achieves formal autonomy. He evokes the everyday condition of the artist as a witness to the dawn, the day, the twilight. He uses an ancient method: by uninterruptedly observing the shapes and colors of the world, he extracts the rule for the shapes and colors of his work. In the intact *Collection* of his works, we can sense a desire for airiness, the anxious contact of tints, which, in touching one another, determine the powdered silence of color fields and the perfect fadeouts of curves, solid forms changing from circles to ellipses. Thus, his work is an art of dematerialization and timelessness of painting toward a subtly metaphysical quality that we discern in the penetrating, yet chromatically dreamy gaze of an angel of Piero della Francesca.
The premises are altogether different in the œuvre of Marco Bagnoli, whose singularity I have emphasized elsewhere. Several years ago, in a text I wrote for *Domus* (it was never published), I stated the following: "At this moment in Italy, [I do not feel that there is] any other well-known formulation that opens, as this one does, the constant interrogation about the possibility of ascertaining the metabolism that transforms the materiality of the object into a conceptual quality... In arranging the signs, the artist keeps his eye on the processes of the changes of substances, he separates the derived metaphysical cipher, he attempts and works up the emergence of an *integral* whose constitutive manifestation aims at disarming, once and for all, the powers of psychology in the induction of form... The profiles of form are moved toward the condensation of a body that cannot manifest itself determinately, but, instead, appears with no possibility of defining itself."
An important result of this method of definition and experimental resolution of the image and the work is Bagnoli's recent group of wooden sculptures, *Plastic Conversation* (1964). These works seem to offer him yet another opportunity

P. Manzoni, *Merda d'artista*, 1961.

and possibility of achieving formalization by way of procedures such as scientific verification of the aesthetic, artistic phenomenon. The impulses behind Bagnoli's artistic action are provokingly utopian; they are pushed futurewards, in the space/time dimension, that presumes it can observe the formativity of the work instantaneuosly and ubiquitously.
A latent sculptural attitude, a versatility in translating into images the processes involving the

perceptual aesthetic speculation of the infinite dimensions of reality — these features characterize the modes of Remo Salvadori's œuvre. With decisive shifts in the interpretation of appearances — virtual segues — the artist brings life to a work that is made ambiguously physical and yet maintains a high visionary level. In a chain transformation, a box tree becomes a dog, the layout plan of an experienced site becomes a four-dimensional ceramic body, the drawing of an environment is ideally hoisted with its spatiality on the tripod of a profiled sculpture, almost like a camera that photographs itself. This operation of Salvadori's metamorphic intuition makes his work seem esoteric. However, what I perceive is a lucid faculty for penetrating the poetic sense of the entire essence of appearance when the artist works on it, transforming it into language.
Finally, through the works of artists like Enzo Cucchi, Mimmo Paladino and Nicola De Maria, we find different approaches to a recent phenomenon that is part of Italian painting: primacy of individual emotion seems to prevaricate, in the motivational intensity, every more general reason for the workmanship of the work.
Starting in 1977, Enzo Cucchi's figural program became explosive. His work demanded its own existence as a sanctuary of memory and desire, and its representation was articulated in "an ideography... in which impulses and tensions of the sacred are amalgamated in the unique text of Painting" (Diacono). In Cucchi's canvases, a euphoric melancholy, yearning for the abnormal, the reality of impossible associations that, nevertheless, live in the imaginary, summons the recognized aspects of the most wide-open natures reified in figural archetypes: mountains, ocean, tree, arid fields where skulls blossom in human embraces, the home, fire, the sky laden with cloud masses, farm animals, the barbaric rooster and the dog. Nevertheless, I would say that the enormous number of these recurrent figurations makes us feel that the artist refuses to allow his self-analytical vision to plunge into the whirlpool of mythography. The painter is the visionary/saint/demon, he narrates his own *Season in Hell*, he is well aware that there can be no heroic frontier beyond this descent into the abyss of the self. At the center of every Cucchi image, we seem to find his dominating interest in the ancient enigma of truth, of which the body, as the place for transcribing all human history, is both the object and the narrating ego. The atmosphere of Cucchi's paintings is pneumatic and derealized.
Mimmo Paladino regards the canvas as a reference and surface from which he must distance himself and to which he must then return, for it is the medium of a rite.
Perhaps a few of his paintings do without this traditional support, as some works demonstrate, for this liturgical celebration.
Strongly objectified, his color takes shape and form in ways that are physically different. From time to time, his pictorial energy is concentrated in "wall fragments, spatial situations, ephemeral works" (Paladino).
Yet the marked departure of the painting *Silent* (1977) included Fauve-like equilibriums, that is, still calibrated and balanced within delimited and uniform color fields.
Paladino's desire then expressed itself in other economies; and his iconography, made up half of sign elements and half of expressionistic figurations, seems to include linguistic and cultural conventions in the compositions. The movement of the figures in *Among the Olives* (1982) can be compared dialectically to the movement of the color-shapes in Cucchi's *Brazil, It Is Known*

F. Lo Savio, *Model of "Maison au Soleil"*, 1962.

P. Pascali, *Strumenti bellici*, 1965.

(1978). The freedom of expressive formulation for this artist does not seem to involve registers in which the recurrent qualities of his works can be adjusted. The structural parts of a painting, the architecture of the image, the decorated areas and the jutting and sculptural areas, the use of colors in dry consistencies and blended spreads interact with no apparent preordained functions. The "festival" of the shapes and figurations, cheerful or dark and heavy, reveals all the states of rituals with suggestions of ethnic magic.

In the works of Nicola De Maria, the sign-trace and the color field go beyond the narrative meanings of the titles; they assume their immediate and internal pregnancy, which owes its surprise and wonder to the epiphany of the color. The eruptive happiness of the thin, transparent adjacency of myths and resolute polychromes, the spreading veil of the mural colors, the conception of a room or a sheet of paper as a nest for the irrepressible need for coaction with the color — these aspects place De Maria among artists who are able to affirm that painting is the well-being of the difference discovered within colors. Some years ago, I visited the small room decorated by De Maria in the Torre dello Scoppio in Spoleto. And I can still remember it clearly. It was like a prayer of space, recalling the precious intimacy desired by Federico da Montefeltro in his Ducal Palace in Urbino: he wanted a special place for study and meditation. The decoration of this virtually neo-Platonic Quattrocentesque inlay produced a time of relief for the sensitivity of thought. Similarly, I like to think of De Maria's enchanted shell of colors as the pilot's house, from which we have sighted the huge iceberg that has surfaced during the past few years.

German Paintings: Manifestos of a New Self-Confidence

Johannes Gachnang

For many years art history took 1945 as the starting point for its description of modern art, be it in anthologies and lexicons, in the first "Documenta" in Kassel (1955), or in new museum collections like those of the Moderna Museet in Stockholm and the Louisiana in Humlebaek near Copenhagen (both 1958). By contrast, the organizers of the large retrospective "Westkunst" (Art in the West) in Cologne (1981) chose 1939 as the point of departure for their historical overview, which they, regrettably, terminated over-hastily with the events of 1968. The outbreak and end of World War II were pivotal dates — caesuras that carried their own justification regardless of differing interpretative tacks. Today, at some distance, these dates could perhaps be viewed and evaluated differently; above all, they might well be assigned a different role in history. This point recurs with growing frequency in my observations during the period around 1960, a decisive turning point, I believe, especially for evaluating the development of a younger generation of artists who were born shortly before the outbreak of World War II. At the same time, I observe a kind of gap or break that was first interpreted and adopted as a theme by this generation of artists at that time, a good ten years before it was registered in the economy and politics, spheres which had proved unshakable until the seventies and that only then first began to reflect serious doubts about the order of things and the course of history.

At the beginning of the sixties in various places throughout Europe a new generation of artists awoke who in their way of thinking and seeing from the outset were diametrically opposed to the efforts of two generations and three styles (Action Painting, Informel, Pop Art and Minimal Art) to catch the attention of New York and the world — that is to say, they opposed the international style and the challenge from America. At first European artists responded to this enormous pressure from the New World in small, private circles, without public posture. However varied the directions and interconnections in the work of these artists may have been from city to city — the phrase "mental spaces" was popular at the time — today one can see in this work a consensus, as yet little noted, that bridges the most divergent ideologies. It is expressed both in the effort, in this or that form, to represent the worldwide catastrophes and changes brought on by the various wars and economic crises that followed — understood as a form of discontinuity — as well as in the questioning of the old institutions (museums). There was no such thing as an encompassing aesthetic education for the younger generation any more, especially in German-speaking countries: the old lineage of classical culture had been interrupted for too long, by then, and appeared irreparably broken.

The first decisive and pace-setting responses to this situation came, on the one hand, from Vienna, Berlin and Düsseldorf and, on the other, from Milan, Rome and Turin, in other words from two richly endowed cultural spheres — forming a dualistic entity — which had suffered tremendously under the sad restoration of fascism and which were deprived for many long years of a continuous cultural development. In all areas of life especially that of the mind, the destruction by the war and the Holocaust and the consequent division of the world and of Europe left behind enormous gaps and deficiencies that necessarily struck hard at this generation. It was forced as a result to create and shape its own world with a prodigious output of intellectual energy. It was forced to redefine itself against the American

challenge and the American aesthetics, which attempted, naively and seductively, to conquer and claim for itself all outposts of the avant-garde in the name of progress and freedom, whether in the political, economic or cultural sphere.
This intellectual energy was denied for a long time and the aesthetic force to which it gave rise was undervalued. Its spontaneous and necessary appearance but also the specifics of the situation within which this eruption occurred made the chosen program radical. This new direction was to be defined in the decade that followed and approached a full unfolding only at the start of the eighties, being for the first time, if only provisionally, outlined in an exhibit like "Documenta 7" in Kassel (1982) by artists who continue to break new ground in surprising and pace-setting ways. These observations are confirmed by studio visits — surely a hopeful sign for the coming generation.

All national art is bad,
all good art is national.
Christian Krohg (1852-1925)

All good art is national,
not all national art is good.
Harald Giersing (1881-1927)

A continuing, intrinsic problem for German art and artists seems to be how to penetrate the predominance of gray in order to get to light and color. The origins of this problem lie perhaps in the aesthetic doctrine that was imposed on us and which for so long took its orientation from the historical and cultural events of the Mediterranean world and, later more decisively, from occurrences in France, especially since the Revolution of 1789. These impulses are documented over and over again in the arts, both in our libraries and in the permanent collections of our museums, despite the strong Anglo-Saxon influence that has been parading about at least our, western, part of the world since the end of World War II. By contrast, a rare and at the same time excellent example of balance, it seems to me, is the collection that was assembled by Hugo von Tschudi around the turn of the century for the Nationalgalerie in Berlin. This farsighted museum director gave himself free rein to present the artists of German romanticism on an equal footing with the dominant aesthetics of his time, that of the French Impressionists. This balanced constellation can be viewed again today, namely in the installation of this collection in the Neue Nationalgalerie, built at the the end of the sixties by Mies van der Rohe in the western sector of the city.

A comparable insistence on a new, wider historical perspective — the image, the vision of the New World — was successfully carried out by the experts and historians responsible for the recent reopening of the Museum of Modern Art in New York, though, it seems to me, staged in a very isolated setting.
Exogenous influences have been, as is well known, severely restricted and re-evaluated in recent years, especially as a result of the astonishing output of the European revival at the beginning of the sixties. The fact that decisive impulses emanated from Germany — let me call to mind the two most important centers of art, namely Berlin and Düsseldorf, not to forget Vienna — amazed and alarmed many at first, but was later seen as the logical consequence of historical and cultural facts. An examination of these events will show that the development of the new imagery once again and inevitably had to emerge from the deformation of objects and of the human figure. It was of course easy for the New World, molded exclusively by Anglo-Saxon thought patterns, to renew its talk of "ugly pictures." New World critics didn't tire of assigning these images to a so-called aesthetics of conquest, forgetting thereby that a style such as Gothic, which sprang from and was shaped by this landscape and the German language, may possibly be, to the present day, a co-determinant of the chosen path. It should be noted, in passing, that the 119 photographs of

G. Baselitz, *Die grossen Freunde*, 1965.

sculptures included by the writer Carl Einstein in his book *Negerplastik* (*Negro Sculpture*, published in 1915 in Verlag der Weissen Bücher in Leipzig) continue to inform the aesthetics of this discipline today.

The fact that in the sixties we were verging on a new beginning that was to be decisive for our times was first publicized in statements, manifestos and pamphlets. The new ideas and their expression in art were not understood in a larger context until a good ten years later, and are only today being properly acknowledged and evaluated. What was emerging at that time in cities like Berlin, Düsseldorf or Vienna were an unequivocal counter-image to and rejection of the strivings of the Academy (Informel) and of pressures from the new capital of the art world, New York (Action Painting, Pop Art, Minimal Art). A similar movement also found expression in other European cities such as Milan, Rome and Turin, as well as Copenhagen, Brussels and London. Even Paris no longer wished to stand at the sidelines and, with its Cartesian questions and strategies, awakened new hopes of achieving a fresh self-awareness through a slowly developing dialogue. A development, by the way, that was marked by neither harmony nor logical argument, but by sharp intellectual controversies and ideological demarcations, by frictions that the best minds in the two mainstreams of French thought exploited with cunning to spur their own creative energies, the consequences and by-products of which continue to provide the most important impulses in France today and to define the task at hand. The tremendous American challenge of the fifties and sixties was afflicted with all the signs of a juvenile attack, emanating from a land without a real history and directed against the bastions of a largely shattered occidental culture in the old European centers. To remove oneself from the pressure of this attack cost enormous strength; it cost many their artistic identity. On the other hand, the young artists of Europe were thereby forced to find a direct and unequivocal response that would of necessity be radical in both content and form of presentation — a calm, logical reaction was impossible. From our side a response to the image-worlds of a Pollock, Newman or Still, and later to Warhol and Judd, seemed urgently necessary, while what the American side expected as a matter of course was an unquestioning assimilation of the proposed international style.

In 1959, on the occasion of "Documenta 2" in Kassel, that is, exactly twenty-five years ago, the art world celebrated the emergence of a broadly defined international style, the so-called Informel, as a further step on the path to abstraction, conceived as the program of the future, a program that, five years later, was to be consecrated on the same spot. One last time, Paris, traditional center of the art world, set the tone here, failing to note that its time was up. For with the selection of Robert Rauschenberg for the grand prize in painting at the Venice Biennale that same year, a significant bulwark of the old art world fell into the hands of the Americans. It was several years back that Leo Castelli, eloquent as ever, told the story in the *New Yorker* of his conquest of the city of the lagoons. I would like to suggest that this story marks the beginning of a development that both shaped our generation and also repeatedly served as an occasion for us to show our strength and fight the current in our struggle to formulate the other, European standpoint all the more clearly and to find an adequate *gestalt* for it in our work. The first results of these independent European efforts were highly unusual and left the other side behind, staring in incredulity but also disapproval. Let me call to mind the cross-currents among the ranks of *Fluxus* (Beuys, Brown, Koepke, Kirkeby), *Wiener Aktionismus* (Viennese Actionism) (Mühl, Nitsch, Brus, Schwarzkogler) or *Arte Povera* (Merz, Pascali, Kounellis, Fabro); then, to cite a number of German events, the "Erstes" and "Zweites Pandämonium" (First and Second Pandemonium) (Schönbeck, Baselitz), *Kapitalistischer Realismus* (Richter, Polke, Lueg), *Lidl* (Reinecke, Immendorff), *Dithyrambe* (Lüpertz) and *Stardart* (Penck).

The isolation embarked upon was understandable, for the dominant scenario of the sixties, American Pop Art, was open to widespread use and abuse as well and issued as a result in modes of thought and production that, despite multi-levelled miscarriages, haven't shaken loose even today — to wit, the Harvard Business School or Shakespeare for the man in the street, as in the television series *Dallas* and *Dinasty*.

In Berlin, Vienna, Basel we paid close attention to the first exhibitions of works by Pollock and other young American painters around 1960. Multiple visits to such shows was *de rigueur* at the time. Alongside this, some of our attention was also focused on European artists like Klein, Hains or

Tinguely; also on Jorn, Constant and the *Gruppe Cobra*; in Italy, on Fontana, Burri and Vedova; in Germany, perhaps on Nay and Uhlmann, for the teachers of our just emerging generation came from their ranks. In 1964, coming this time from Berlin, we traveled to Paris, to Ileana and Michael Sonnabend's gallery — still at that time on the Quai des Grands Augustins — where for the first time we experienced the works of Robert Rauschenberg in the original, but also the range of possibilities that were already appearing on the international horizon. By contrast, our visit to the opening exhibition of Galerie Werner & Katz a year earlier in Berlin, an exhibition of the unusual and surprising paintings of a certain Baselitz, had an almost private character to it — despite the energetic intervention of the local prosecuting attorney and the alarm it set off, judging by contemporary reports in the press al least, in the art world.

On the other hand, I must admit that we looked at things in Berlin in the sixties not only with open curiosity but also with skepticism — news about the coyotes (Beuys) that René Block kept presenting at his small gallery, beginning with the mysterious "This way Brouwn" through Beuys' happenings, to paintings and other works by Richter, Polke and *Kapitalistischer Realismus*: news, as it were, from the Rhine, or more precisely, from Düsseldorf and the circle of artists at the Academy there. Here too, as nearly always in these cases, the public was all but absent. To these reports was added news of Rainer and Twombly: they, too, seemed to us to be of some importance and elicited our respect.

A.R. Penck, *Grosses Weltbild*, 1965.

In looking more closely at movements of this sort, we will have to focus in particular on those that were further intensified by the division of the city of Berlin, of Germany and of all of Europe into two antagonistic camps. Once the heart of the Old World, both of the aged, traditional capitals of the German-speaking world, Berlin and Vienna, found themselves abruptly and harshly abandoned on the borders of one of the camps in this newly reshuffled world. The capitals of the two victor-states rose up in the distance, the one far to the east near the Urals, the other on the so-called new continent, claiming to represent the Western world.

In Western Europe after World War II, then, and particularly in the western sector of the Central Europe of old, not only had the Jews vanished but the Slavs as well. From the eastern regions of Germany, for instance Saxony, came Baselitz, Schönebeck and Penck, as well as Richter, Palermo and Knoebel; from Silesia, Polke; from Bohemia, Lüpertz. Cities like Berlin and Düsseldorf served as initial stations on their route to the West. Very few of this generation of artists were born in the West. One came from the Lower Rhine, home of Seghers and Goltzius, namely Beuys, artist and teacher and integrating force at the Academy of Art in Düsseldorf, which was primarily concerned with analytic painting and assimilating the images and influences from the New World, albeit in its own way. The art scene in Berlin was characterized by a number of artists going their own way who focused on a search for the archaic image and the attempt to draw new life from their own native well, however blocked it was the debris of World War II. Thus at the end of the sixties Lüpertz recommended that his German colleagues paint German themes and introduced steel helmets, police caps and other German motifs from the field into his paintings. German and international critics alike and the art world as a whole lay a curse on him for many years for his provocation and disobedience. Times have changed, meanwhile — as many times in the past — and the images generated in the sixties and their aesthetics, situated between Beuys and Immendorff, have become the object of increasingly serious attention for the last ten years, especially in the new heart of the western world on the other side of the Atlantic.

On the other hand, it should be noted that

J. Immendorff, *Tov I*, 1980.

European artists valued and accepted the challenges of artists like Judd and Andre or LeWitt, in dialogues that led to being able to maintain the priority of feelings and passions without having to pay short shrift to the real artistic work of image-making, painting itself, understood as an abstract category. The intensity of the dialogue led, in my opinion, to an even clearer statement of what needs to be accomplished in painting and with its techniques today, as, at the same time, the task of painting was being defined clearly and most unmistakably by Baselitz and Penck.

The development described above is rooted, in my interpretation, in the work and life of two men who have shared a similar fate: the artist Schwitters and the architect Scharoun. Both nurtured the deep wish throughout their lives of being recognized as modern, international artists and both have remained German artists to this day. This might mean that their visions were drowned out by the concerns of the *Zeitgeist* of their times or the voices of the international style — more precisely, of the Bauhaus and Charter of Athens. I see their visions as a first attempt to grasp anew the world that was broken apart in the aftermath of World War II, in visual and spatial terms, even though it was already recognized that significant pieces and transitional passages necessary for a unified vision were missing. The material means developed in the process corresponded to an astonishing degree to the pre-existent givens of the postwar world, or — to use Baselitz' phrase: "Die grosse Nacht im Eimer" ("The grandeur of the night gone to pot"). This direction was deepened with critical intelligence by the generation of artists emerging around 1960 and was to define, two decades later and augmented with new self-awareness, the new imagery. Important paintings like *Die grossen Freunde* (Great Friends) by Baselitz and *Grosses Weltbild* (Grand View of the World) by Penck, both of which date from the mid-sixties, announce early on, through their visual and manifesto-like character, a strong determination not only to create a new imagery, a German imagery, but also to fuse the broken pieces of the world together again one last time. The generation that followed, already in possession of the new aesthetics, has rejected such a bold enterprise in its first works and proclamations. It works with quotations and simultaneously builds segments of its own world amidst fragments of history or within the present constellation of things without giving the future much of a chance. Penck spoke of this type of devaluation theory ten years ago already, when he was still living and working in Dresden. But in the last analysis it is Polke who for a good twenty years has intensely, systematically and with great intelligence pursued decomposition, in the context of our times as well as in art history in general, in order to rediscover painting, to discover a new imagery in his own work and also for a whole generation. This route was surprising to many, but repeatedly and energetically every effort at idealizing a style was rejected in the tireless search for an imagery without a style.

In reflections of this sort regarding my generation, I am forced to ask myself — looking over the road traveled thus far — to what extent the part of the world described here was really shaped by the ideas of the Jewish tent and the Greek temple; whether the little known, passionate forces of the Nordic landscape haven't in reality had a greater influence on our thoughts and actions, and on the *gestalt* we have yet to develop, than we are generally inclined to admit.

Giovanni Anselmo

1. *Il paesaggio con mano che lo indica mentre verso oltremare i grigi si alleggeriscono (The Landscape with Hand Pointing toward It while in the Direction of Oltremare the Grays Gradually Fade Away)*, 1982.*

2. *Il paesaggio con mano che lo indica mentre verso oltremare i grigi si alleggeriscono (The Landscape with Hand Pointing toward It while in the Direction of Oltremare the Grays Gradually Fade Away)*, detail, 1982.

3. *Grigi che si alleggeriscono verso oltremare (Grays Gradually Fade Away in the Direction of Oltremare)*, 1982-84.

1

2

3

Marco Bagnoli

1. *Metrica e Mantrica (Metrics and Mantrics)*, 1982-1984.

2. *Albe of Zonsopgagen*, 1984.

3. *Anti-Hertz*, 1979.

1

2

3

Georg Baselitz

1

1. *Ohne Titel (Untitled)*, 1982.

2. *Deutsche Schule (German School)*, 1979-80.*

3. *Das Atelier (The Atelier)*, 1980.*

4. *Die Familie (The Family)*, 1980.*

2

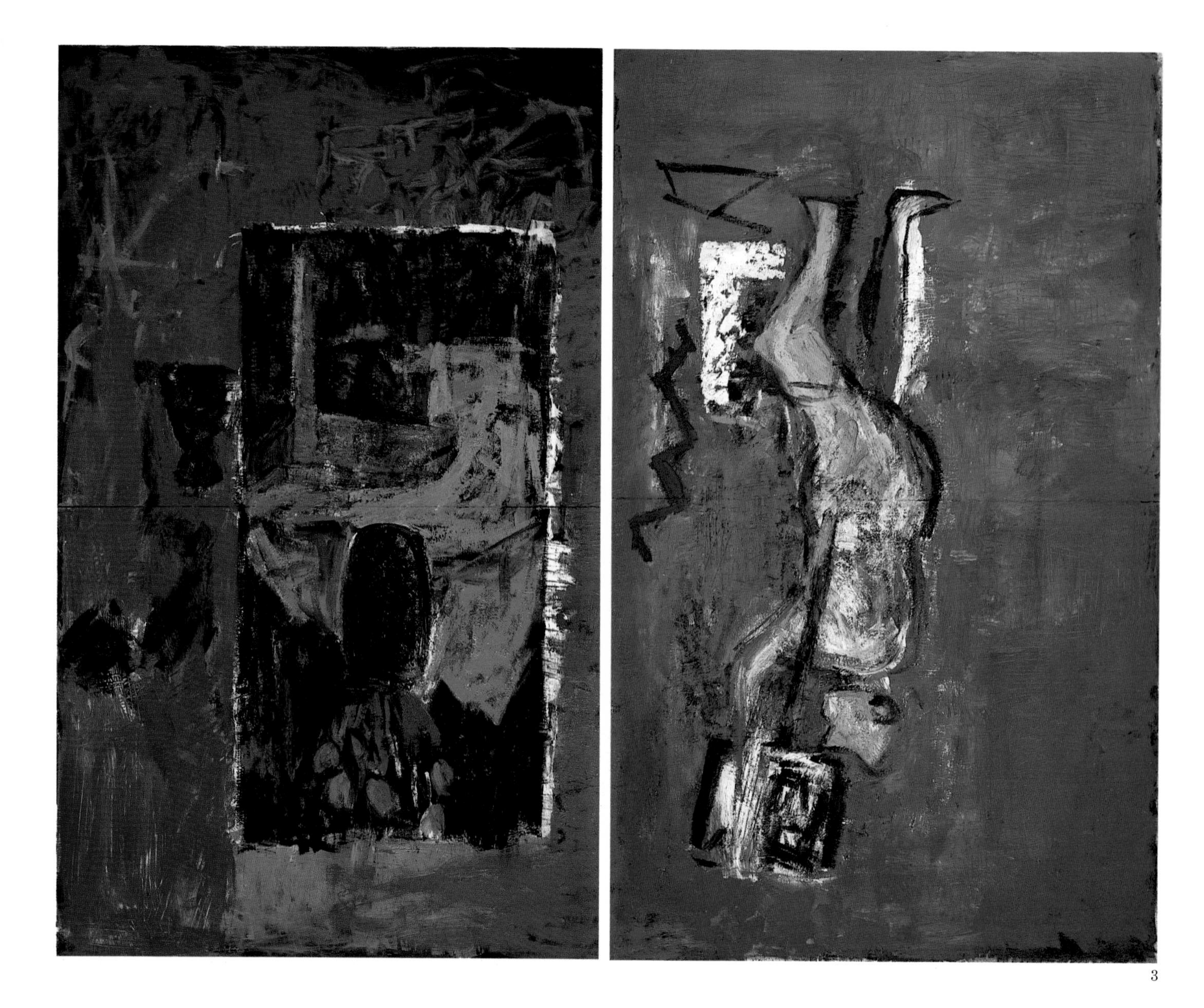

3

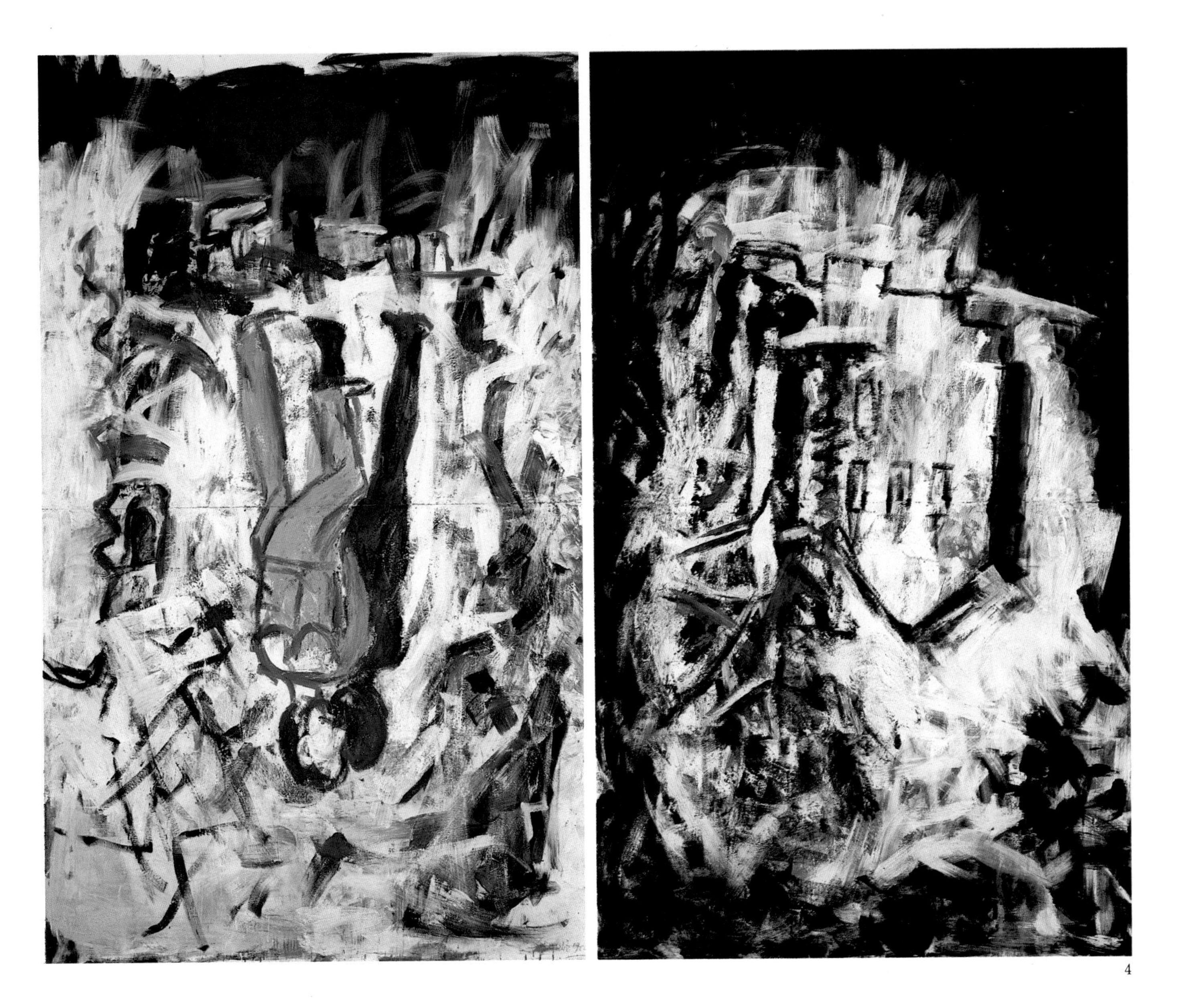

4

Lothar Baumgarten

1. *Monument für die indianischen Nationen Südamerikas (Monument to the Indian Nations of South America)*, 1978-82.

2. *America*, 1983-84.

1

ORINOCO
AMAZ
AME

2

Joseph Beuys

1

1. *Einschmelzaktion (Smelting Action)*, 1982.

2. *Das Ende des 20. Jahrhunderts (The End of the Twentieth Century)*, 1983.

3. *Hinter den Knochen wird gezählt- Schmerzraum (Behind the Bones Will Be Counted - Space of Pain)*, 1983.

2

3

Alberto Burri

1

1. *Cellotex C 1*, 1981.*

2. *Cellotex C 3*, 1981.*

3. *Cellotex C 2*, 1981.*

4. *Cellotex*, 1976.

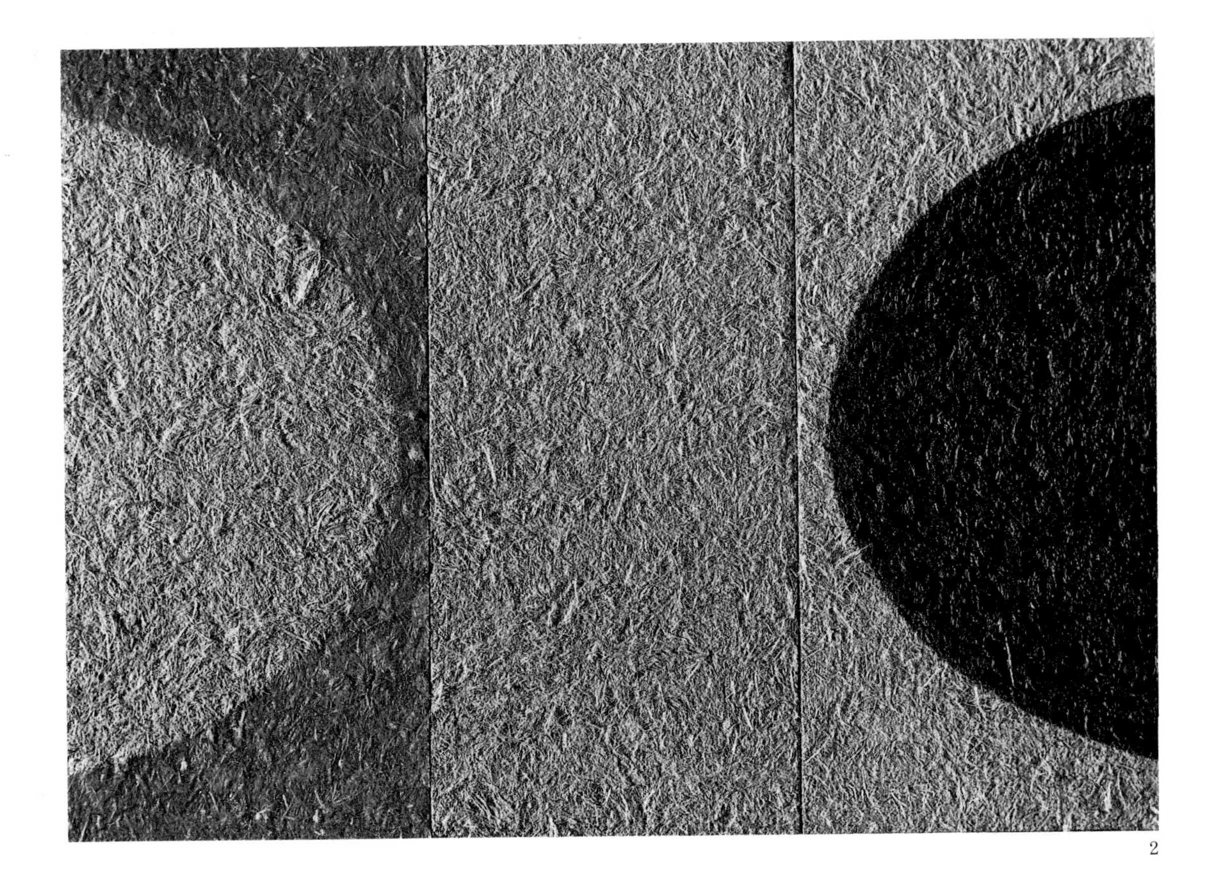

2

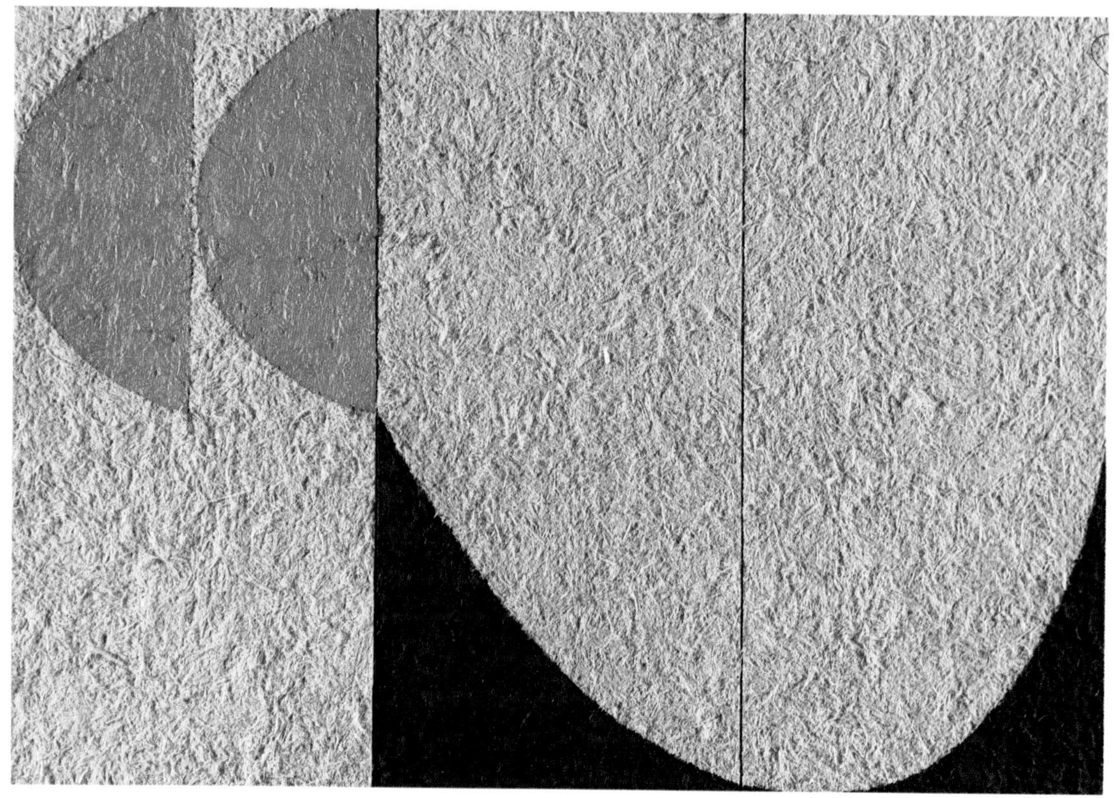

3

4

Pier Paolo Calzolari

1

1. *Senza titolo (Untitled)*, 1984.

2. *Senza titolo (Untitled)*, 1984.

3. *Rideau V (Curtain V)*, 1984.*

2

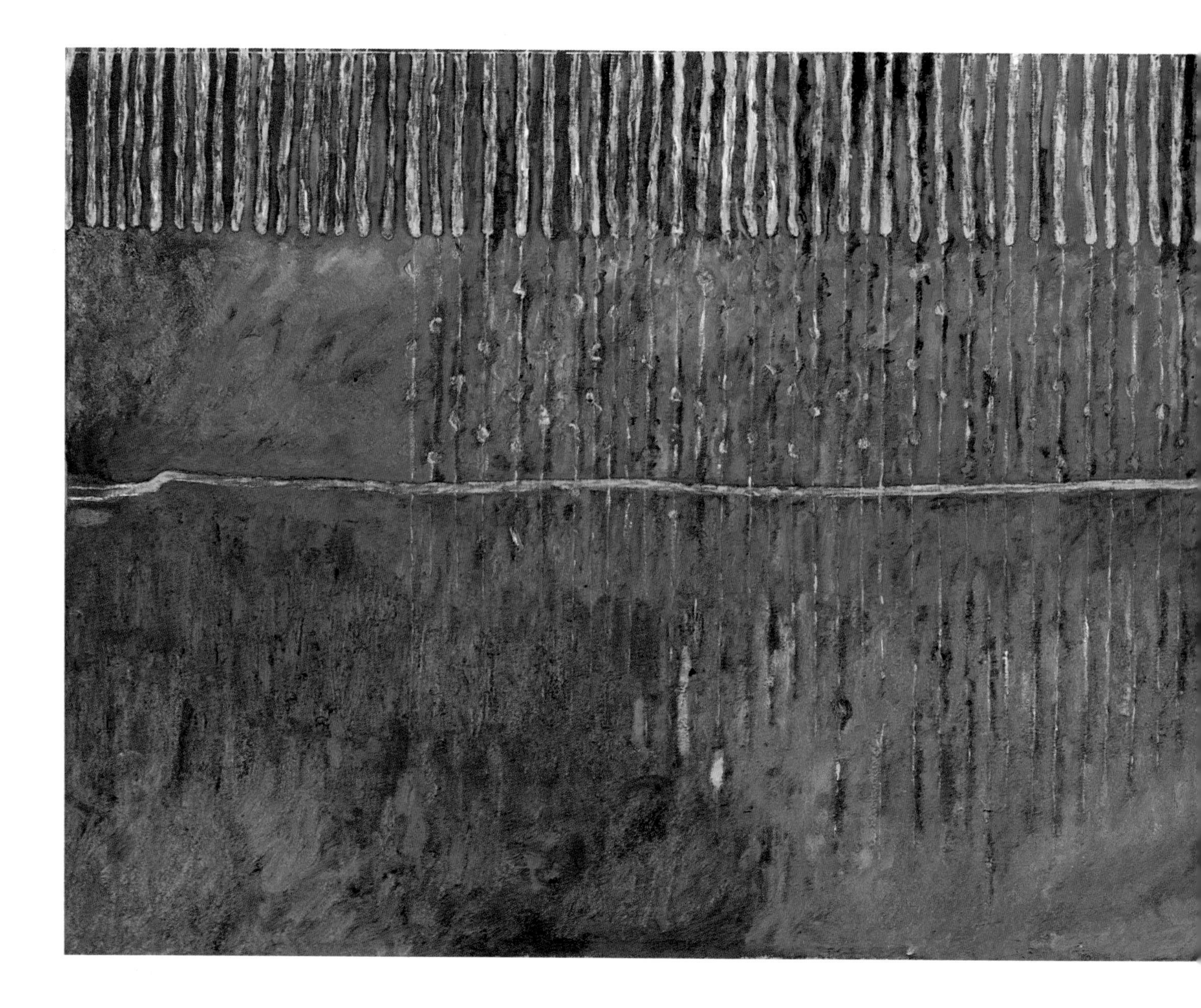

3

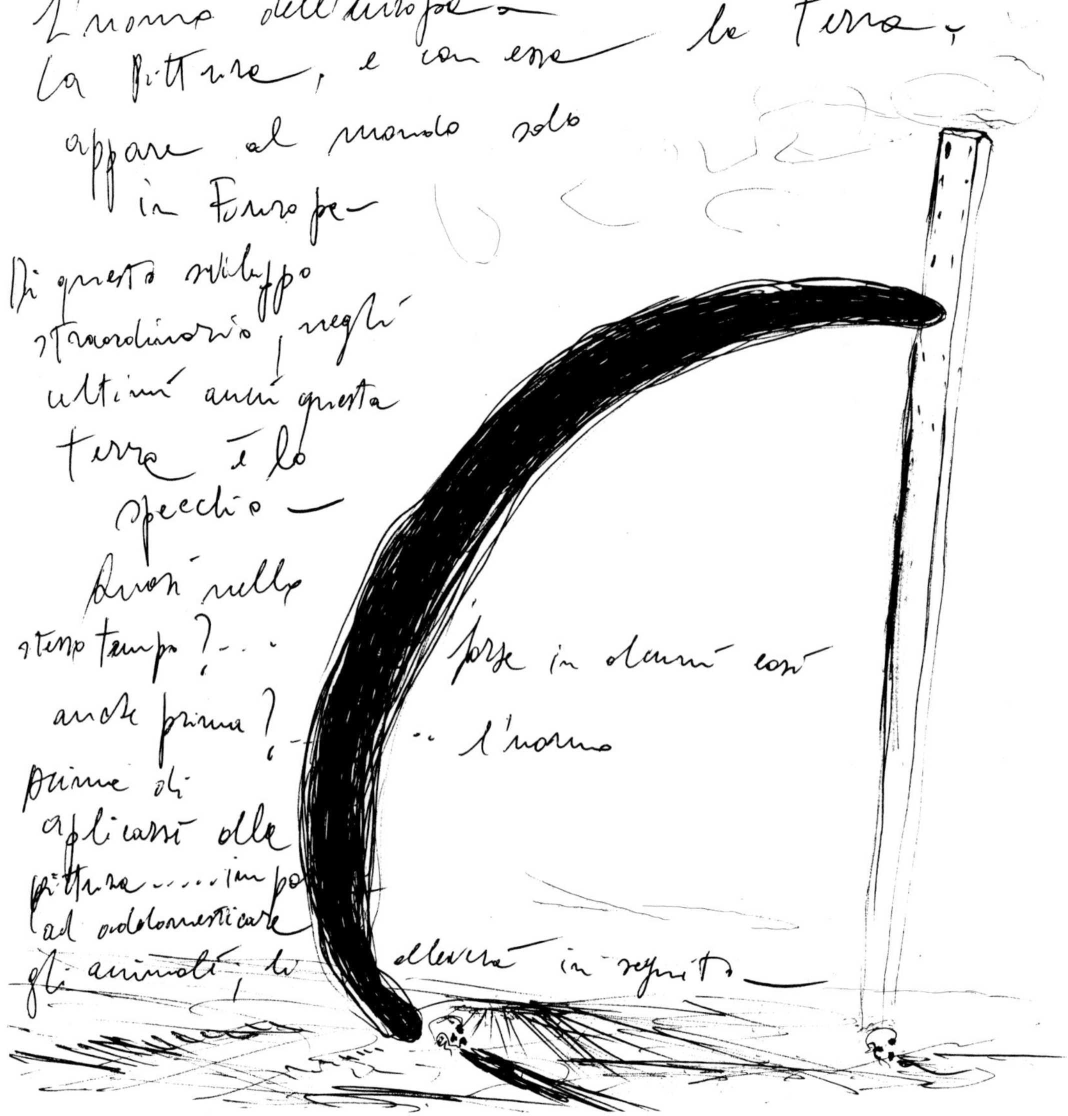

Enzo Cucchi

1

1.2. *L'uomo europeo... (European man...)*, 1984.

3. *Un millenario trasporto comincia a muoversi attraverso la preistoria (A Thousand Year Transport Begins Moving across Prehistory)*, 1984.*

4. *Succede ai pianoforti di fiamme nere (It Happens to Pianos with Black Flames)*, 1983.*

2

3

4

Hanne Darboven

1. From left to right:
12 Months with Postcards from Today of Flowers, 1982; *12 Months with Postcards from Today of Dogs*, 1982; *12 Months with Postcards from Today of Kittens*, 1982; *12 Months with Postcards from Today of Horses*, 1982*.

2. *12 Months with Postcards from Today of Horses*, 1982.

3. *12. Month with Postcards from today of Horses*, detail, 1982.

1

2

Dezember 1982

1
2
3
4
5
6
7
8
9
10
11
12
13
14
15

Dezember 1982

16
17
18
19
20
21
22
23
24
25
26
27
28
29
30
31

3

Nicola De Maria

1. *L'angelo del 1983 (The Angel of 1983)*, 1983.

2. *Sorridi faccia 2 fiori 2 occhi (Smile Face! 2 Flowers 2 Eyes)*, 1980-82.

3. *Tu (You)*, 1983.

1

2

3

Luciano Fabro

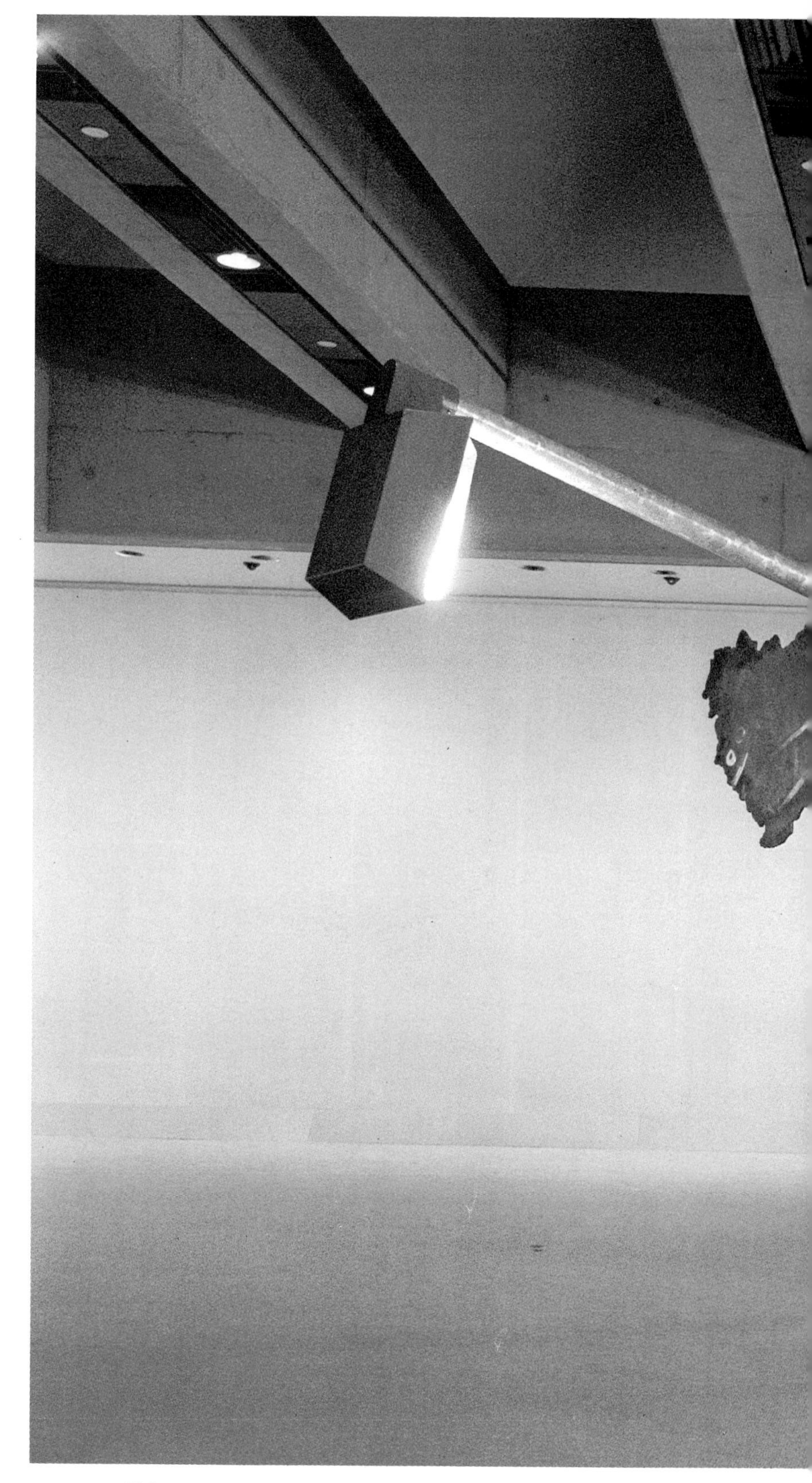

1. *La Germania (Germany)*, 1984.*

2. *Habitat di Aachen (Habitat of Aachen)*, 1983.

3. *Esprit de finesse, esprit de géométrie (Spirit of Finesse, Spirit of Geometry)*, 1984.

1

2

3

Ludger Gerdes

1. *Zwei Vorhangwände. Allegorie der Freundschaft - Künstler und Architekt und drei Freundinnen (Two Curtainwalls. Allegory of Friendship - Artist and Architect and Three Girls)*, 1982.*

2. *Ohne Titel (Untitled)*, 1983.

3. *Ohne Titel (Untitled)*, 1984.

I

2

3

Rebecca Horn

1. *Kopfextension (Headextension)*, 1972.*

2. *Der Pendel (Pendulum)*, 1984.*

3. *Das Quecksilber Bad (Quicksilver Bath)*, 1984.

1

2

3

Jörg Immendorff

1

1. *C.D. beben/heben (Quaking/Lifting)*, 1984.

2. *Hü*, 1984.*

3. *Akademie Ost - Aufgabe Hans Albers (Academy East - Task Hans Albers)*, 1984.*

4. *Akademie Mitte - Aufgabe Städte der Bewegung (Academy Middle - Task Towns in Movement)*, 1984.*

2

3

4

Anselm Kiefer

1

1. *Der Ölberg (Mount Olivet)*, 1980.*

2. *Landschaft mit Flügel (Landscape with Wing)*, 1981.

3. *Des Malers Atelier (The Painter's Studio)*, 1983.*

4. *Untitled*, 1984.*

2

3

4

Jannis Kounellis

1. *Metamorfosi (Metamorphosis)*, 1958-84.

2. *Metamorfosi (Metamorphosis)*, 1975-84.

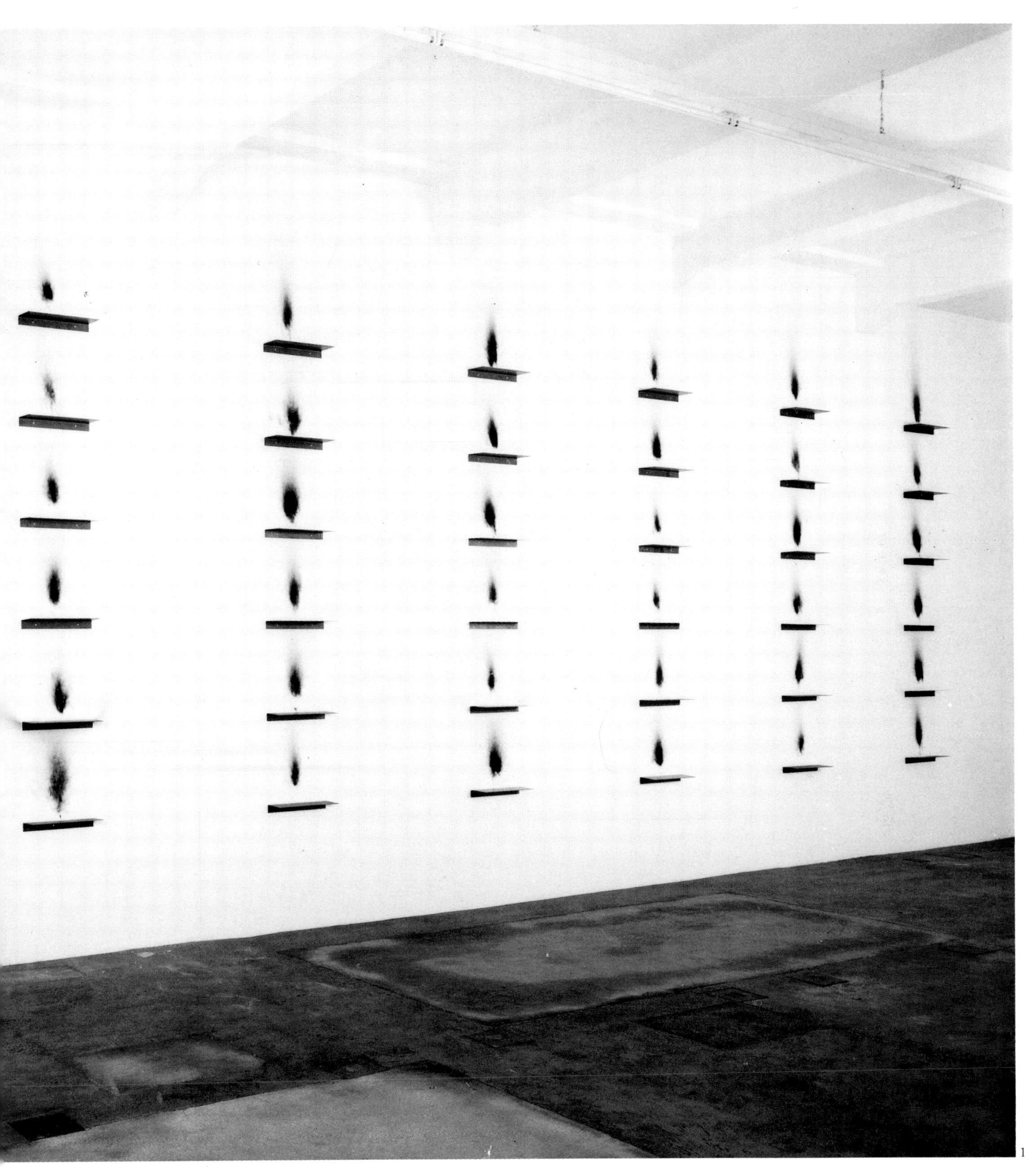

1

2

Markus Lüpertz

1

1. *Il principe (The Prince)*, 1983.*

2. *B.C.*, 1983.*

3. *Der Mohr (The Moor)*, 1983.*

4. *Tourist (Tourist)*, 1983.*

2

3

4

Gerhard Merz

1

1. *Nude Woman*, 1984.

2. *Juan Gris*, 1982.

3. *All'Italia (To Italy)*, 1984.*

4. *All'Italia (To Italy)*, 1984.*

2

3

4

Mario Merz

1. *Senza titolo (Untitled)*, 1979.

2. *Crescite senza fine (Endless Growths)*, 1984.

1

1
2
1
3

2

Reinhard Mucha

1

1. *Lampe (Lamp)*, 1981.

2. *Astron-Taurus* (two details), 1981.

3. *o.T. (Untitled)*, 1982.

4. *Hagen-Vorhalle*, 1983.

2

3

4

Mimmo Paladino

1

1. *Cordoba*, 1984.*

2. *Viandante (Wayfarer)*, 1983.*

3. *Camera in tempesta (Room in Storm)*, 1984.

2

le idee non vengono si nascondono sono il
Le opere compiute sono relitti di GUERRA

3

Giulio Paolini

1

1. *Delfo*, 1965.

2. *Giovane che guarda Lorenzo Lotto (Young Man Looking at Lorenzo Lotto)*, 1967.

3. *Caleidoscopio (Kaleidoscope)*, 1976.

4. *Casa di Lucrezio (Lucretius's House)*, 1981-82.

2

3

4

A.R. Penck

1

1. *Was ist Gravitation? II (What is Gravitation? II)*, 1984.*

2. *Wechseln, verwechseln (To Change, to Exchange)*, 1983.*

3. *Wichtige Begegnung 2 (Important Meeting 2)*, 1982.*

4. *Standard 6*, 1983.

2

3

4

Giuseppe Penone

1. Vegetal gesture, trace, distance, virtual adherence, gesture fossil, static action, expectation, vegetal structure. Finger traces as channels, bundles of fibers traversed by bronze. The leaf on the hero's back, point of death, point of life. The hero as a tree trunk, dragon's blood as a wound, the leaf as a suture. Dragon's blood as non-corruption, the leaf as the life cycle, corruption and death. The leaf has the strength to strike down the hero, it possesses the secret of his life, it protects the natural cycle of things, it gives order to exception, it inhabits the attempt to subvert the true duty of things to death. The vegetal gesture fills up with leaves, a natural vessel of the transience of a form.

2. *Quattro paesaggi (Four Landscapes)*, 1984.*

3. From left to right:
Paesaggio verticale (Vertical Landscape), 1984.
Verde del bosco (Wood Green), 1984.

-so, aderenza virtuale, sensib-

-tera, struttura vegetale.

-anali, fasci di fibre percorre

-ulla schiena dell'eroe punto di

-roe come tronco d'albero,

foglia come sutura, sangue

-riene, foglia come acido vitale,

foglia ha la forza di

il segreto della sua

-aturale delle cose,

imbisce il tentativo

davanti delle cose alla

si riempie di foglie

caducità di una forma

1

2

3

Michelangelo Pistoletto

1. *Leoncini (Little Lions)*, 1984.

2. *Figura che si guarda (Figure Looking at Itself)*, 1983.

3. *Figure che guardano nel pozzo (Figures Looking down a Well)*, 1983.*
From left to right:
Figura che guarda nel pozzo (Figure Looking down a Well), 1983.
Seconda figura rossa (Second Red Figure), 1983.
Prima figura rossa (First Red Figure), 1983.

1

2

3

Sigmar Polke

1

1. *Schnee und Hagel (Snow and Hail)*, 1983.*

2. *Filmschleife (Film Ribbon)*, 1984.*

3. *Regenbogen (Rainbow)*, 1983.*

4. *Tafel: Vermessung der Steine im Bauch des Wolfes und das anschliessende Zermahlen der Steine zu Kulturschutt*, 1980.*

2

3

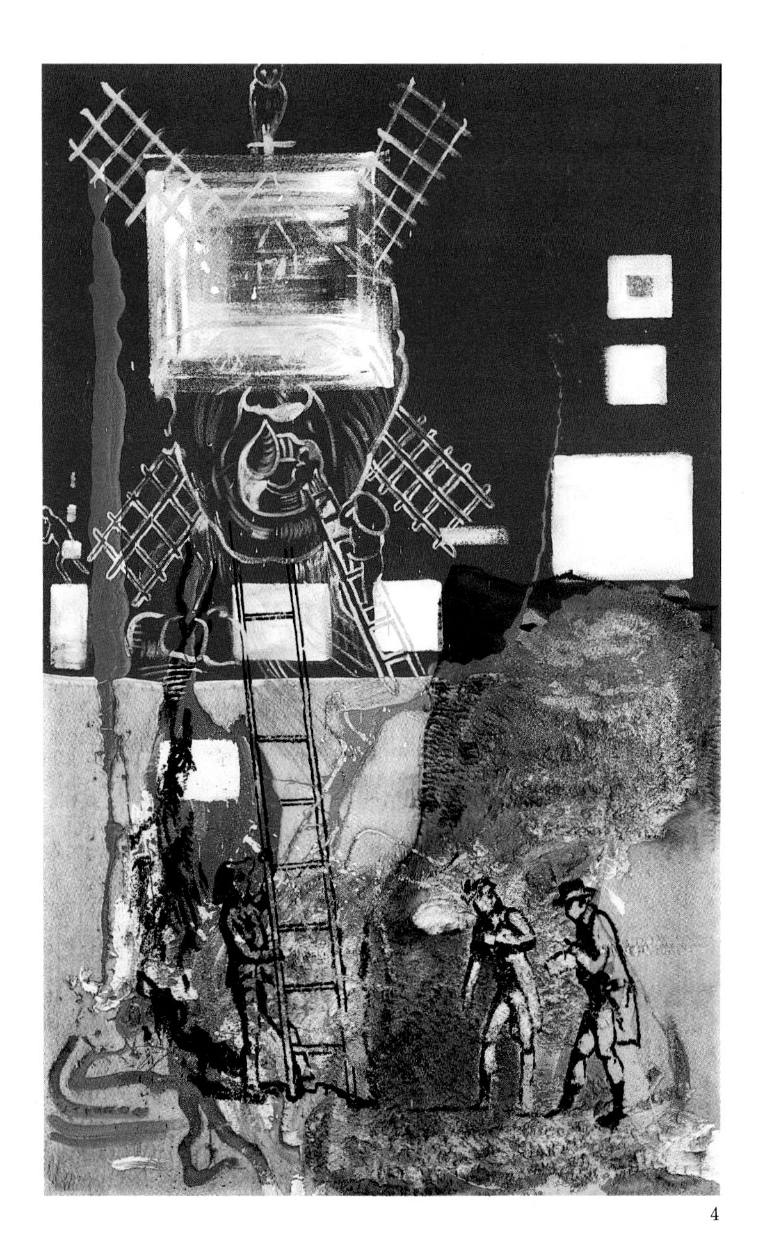

4

Gerhard Richter

1

1. *Lilak (Lilac)*, 1982.*

2. *Abstraktes Bild (Abstract Painting)*, 1984.

3. *Tisch (Table)*, 1982.*

4. *Tor (Gate)*, 1982.*

2

3

4

Salomé

1

1. *Ultramarin (Ultramarine)*, 1982.*

2. *Im Morgenlicht (Light of Dawn)*, 1982.*

3. *Zeitgeist VII (Spirit of Time VII)*, 1982.*

4. *Im Abendlicht (Twilight)*, 1982.*

2

3

4

Remo Salvadori

1

1. *Aim*, 1984.

2. *Modello (Model)*, 1979-83.*

3. *L'attenzione divisa (Divided Attention)*, 1982-83.*

2

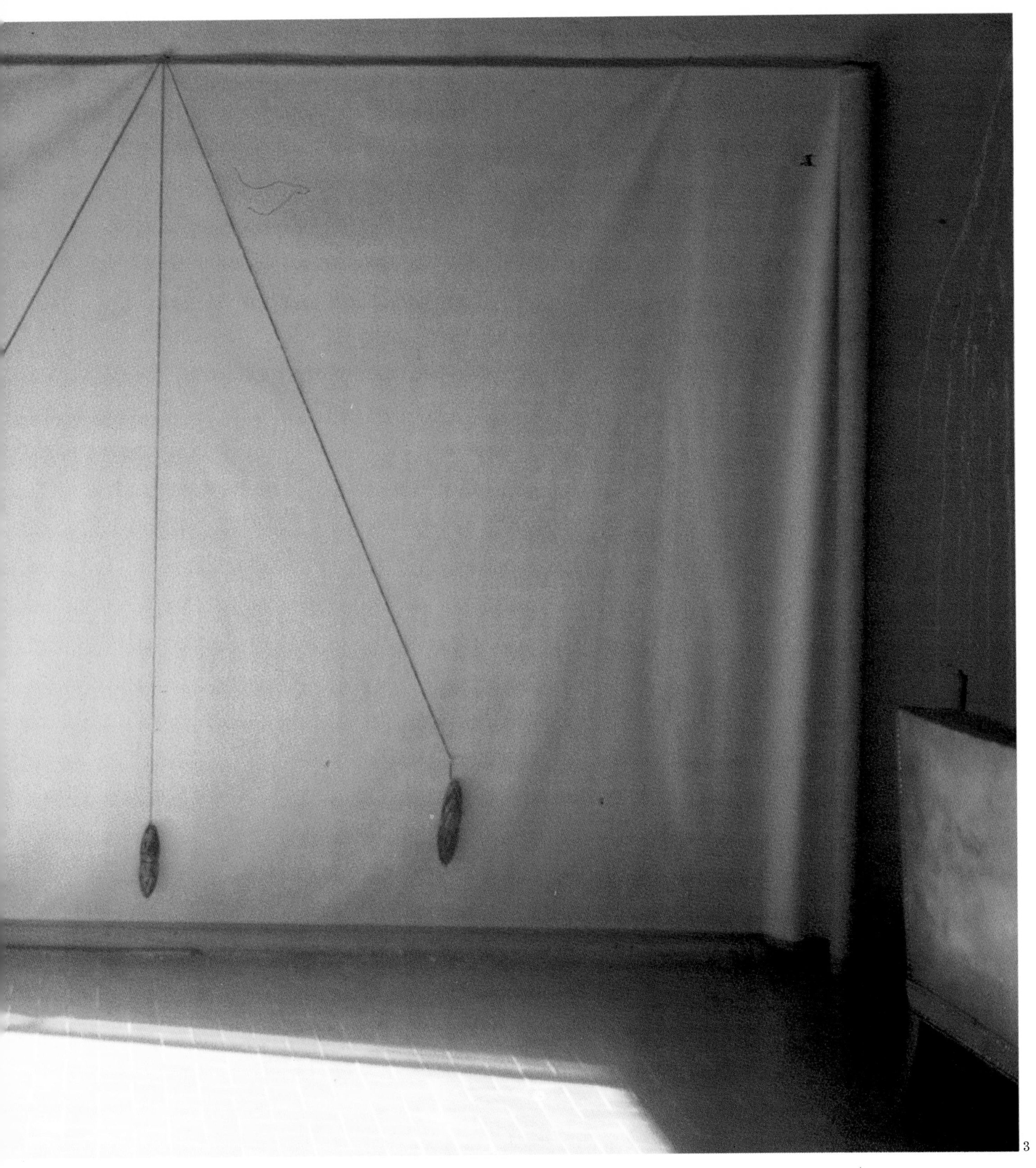

3

Thomas Schütte

1. *Studio I*, 1982-83.

2. *Studio II*, 1982-83.*

3. *Beckmann Building*, 1982.

4. *Haus für zwei Freunde (House for Two Friends)*, 1983.*

2

3

4

Ettore Spalletti

Le radiazioni azzurre e violette, quando
l'atmosfera è attraversata dall'intensità
della luce, producono nei giorni di sereno,
la colorazione azzurra del cielo.

1. *When the atmosphere is pierced by the intensity of light on days of calm, the blue and violet radiations produce the azure coloring of the sky*, 1982.

2. *Anfora, bacile, vasi (Amphora, bowl, vases)*, 1982.*

2

Emilio Vedova

1

1. *Rosso '83-IV- (Red '83-IV-)*, 1983.*

2. *Omaggio a Dada Berlin (Homage to Dada Berlin)*, 1964-65.*

3. *Rosso '83-VI- (Red '83-VI-)*, 1983.*

4. *Rosso '83-VII- (Red '83-VII-)*, 1983.*

2

3

4

Cinema & Film

Robert Van Ackerens
Gianni Amelio
Michelangelo Antonioni
Marco Bellocchio
Carmelo Bene
Bernardo Bertolucci
Jutta Bruckner
Liliana Cavani
Doris Doerrie
Rainer Werner Fassbinder
Federico Fellini
Marco Ferreri
Werner Herzog
Lothar Lambert
Ermanno Olmi
Ulrike Ottinger
Pier Paolo Pasolini
Marianne Rosenbaum
Francesco Rosi
Helma Sanders
Ettore Scola
Hans Jürgen Syberberg
Paolo and Vittorio Taviani
Wim Wenders
Lina Wertmüller

Italian Cinema

Vittorio Boarini

A survey of Italian cinema during the past fifteen years allows me to voice several general observations on a period that still awaits an overall systematic critique.
With so few efforts made in this direction, we might find it helpful to look at Paolo Bertetto's recent book, which is significantly entitled *Il più brutto del mondo* — the Ugliest in the World. His book is interesting not only because of its explicit contents or provocative intentions. Altogether, it manages to draw — though indirectly — an overall picture of the Italian film. Incidentally, when reviewing Francis Coppola's *One from the Heart (Il bagno del neon,* no. 44, January 1983), the same author managed to wax enthusiastic about this movie and about the movies of the New Hollywood in general. Beyond Bertetto's evaluations — often stimulating if not convincing — his two texts are undoubtedly useful in that they inspire a paradoxical question: Why are American movies better than Italian movies? Actually, in going through the map of his Hollywood likes and his Italian dislikes, Bertetto, perhaps unwittingly, accuses the Italian cinema of not being like the American cinema: not so much (not only) for the quality of the movies or the talents of the filmmakers, as for the internal structures and overall organization.
Well, Bertetto is certainly correct. Italian movies are not like American movies. Indeed, we may add, Italian cinema is probably like no other cinema in the world.
European filmmakers have always eyed Hollywood with envy and disdain. Envy because America succeeded in transforming a carnival attraction, a technological marvel, an individual talent into a flourishing industry supported by ironbound production structures, an assembly-line output of high quality. And disdain for the very same reason: the rigorous structures destroy creativity and free artistic expression. For, as everyone knows, or ought to know, movies are an art; and when we speak of *art*, as the term is understood in the modern world, we are speaking of its European origins. Viewed schematically, this was (and for some people, still is) the approach taken for many years by European film critics.
Actually, such a position implies the notion that the artist needs only himself, and thus the cinema, being an art, needs only directors. That is probably why Italians have never given much thought to the film industry as a whole; they never think of a film as the final result of a vast network of production relationships all aiming at the single goal of supplying products for the movie market. However, this is not all that the industry means. It also means creating a series of professions and professionalisms. And that is what Hollywood has been doing from the very outset. What's more, a large part of the Hollywood mythology is based on the gap between the artist and the professional (Stroheim's conflicts with the major studios, Hemingway's and Fitzgerald's failures as scriptwriters, Stravinsky's film scores being rejected by producers, etc.). Beyond all myth and anecdote, the Hollywood story is the history of an industry that, in order to become an industry, has constantly tried to produce professionals: directors, actors, cameramen, scriptwriters, etc. In a word, Hollywood has always worked toward producing a *set,* even if Europeans only discovered this a few short years ago.
From the very start of moviemaking, Italian directors have always worked like painters in the time of Giotto. Each painter saw his master's paintings, went to study in his workshop, manufactured his own pigments, then became a master in turn and painted on his own. If he found

a patron willing to supply his daily bread, then the artist had made it.
In Italy, the film industry has always remained on the level of craft, an art in the medieval sense of "arts and crafts." In America, movies are made with actors, scriptwriters, directors, etc.; in Italy, they are made on themes, they have "messages," and they use actors specializing in certain kinds of parts.
The history of Italian cinema was nothing but a progression toward the professionalism of self-taught talents. This was the case during neo-realism, the great era of Italian filmmaking. And it is also true of Fellini, Antonioni, Risi, Scola, et al. These are self-taught artisans of the highest quality and they acquired their craft by themselves, without assistance, without structures — without anything.
Italian cinema is the cinema *d'auteur*. These are artists who, precisely because they *are* artists, can tell only about themselves, sometimes very artistically, but not professionally in the technical sense; they do not have an industry specialized in simply "telling, narrating," per se. Needless to say, I am talking about professional status, not quality.

P. & V. Taviani, *Padre Padrone* (O. Antonutti).

Hence, in order to talk about Italian cinema during the past fifteen years, we have to begin by establishing this virtually congenital phenomenon. We are dealing with a cinema of auteurs, cineasts, who are not supported by an industry, a cinema without a school, a cinema that is frequently

E. Petri, *La classe operaia va in paradiso* (G.M. Volonté).

improvised (e.g., the films of Pupi Avati).
We might add that the late sixties were emblematic of this situation. And when we say "late sixties," we are referring, of course, to the post-1968 era, the cinema that imposed a revision and completion (a "revolution") of cinematic language.
If we briefly review the years between the late fifties and the early sixties, we find a development that was both unwonted and traditional. New talents emerged in Italy, and the cinema arduously tried to free itself from the oppressive ties of the mannerism to which neo-realism had dwindled. This liberation was a premise for any innovative effort. France — to note the most famous example — produced the now historic phenomenon known as the Nouvelle Vague, the New Wave. This movement was due to several simultaneous and decisive factors. These included the critical and theoretical awareness that a certain type of filmmaking was completely *passé* and no longer had a *raison d'être*; and the urgent theorizing of film critics who did not care to take a backseat role and simply mirror the events of filmmaking or to remain fettered to formal models that had lost all meaning.
In Italy, the residual ideology of neo-realism weighed upon film critics who had less of a cultural thrust than in France. After all, this ideology functioned as a model both for the official culture and for the opposition culture, so that even by the late sixties, certain left wing magazines in

Italy were still trapped in that critical approach and were unable to focus properly on the new developments in filmmaking. Nor did the Italian government take any initiative in revitalizing the national cinema; whereas the French government fostered a policy of low-budget production. This was one of several reasons why France developed its New Wave, while all that Italy had was some sketchy beginnings. Indeed, we should not forget that certain Italian directors were making their first films during the early sixties: Pasolini, Bertolucci, De Seta, Bellocchio, Orsini, the Taviani brothers — to name just a few. These directors were creating — or trying to create — a different cinema, with low-budget movies inspired by a living, tangible, present-day reality rather than a mythical past. Nevertheless, they did not constitute a real movement (like the Free Cinema in England); they were merely new directors, new auteurs.

Then, a series of rebellions by young people culminated in the uprising of 1968. And even Italian cinema was forced to give serious thought to its own means of expression and to its relationship between language and reality. The overall Italian film had not yet shaken off the past as had some of the young auteurs (and even not-so-young ones — e.g., Antonioni, Fellini, Ferreri). Admittedly, a very high level was reached: Bertolucci with his poetic vein, Bellocchio with his obsessive focus on a repressive Catholic education, Fellini with his spectacular nostalgia.

One of the merits, or faults, of the "May cinema" was that it endlessly dwelt on cinematic occasions and the same filmmakers: meetings, committees, factories, demonstrations filmed by collectives, dilettante cameramen, weak-willed trade-unionists, and so on. The same thing happened in Italy. There were more and more filmmakers, all with artistic presumptions. In France, this proliferation of the most varied forms of "political" cinema led to more and more thinking about the language of cinema. But in Italy, the proliferation had no effect.

However, there is something far more profound about the failure of political filmmaking in Italy and the abortive renewal of cinematic language. The notion of "political cinema" was presented as a universal concept. It concerned the total liberation from the social fetters of domination in all its forms, especially politics in its specific sense and sexuality.

The goal was to employ cinematic language in order to liberate the traditional images from their ideology, to invent new solutions for producing new ideas on politics (seen as a space for individual and social freedom) and eroticism (seen as the free expression of a desire that had always been pushed back into the unconscious). Such an operation was quite risky, at least in regard to form. Filmmakers had to find a new grammar and a new synthesis to tell what had never been told and to produce what had never existed.

Naturally, not many people, even in France, were willing to take such a risk and go along with the challenge to cinematic language. Aside from a few isolated cases, only Godard can justifiably be called the brilliant innovator of the French (and even non-French) cinema. His "essays" of political cinema, the depth of his images and memories, his formal contrasts, conflicts, contradictions had at least one merit: they indicated a path, directions, they opened up unsuspected roads for the theory of film.

Something analogous took place outside of France: with Rocha in Brazil, Jancsó in Hungary, Kluge

F. Fellini, *Casanova* (D. Sutherland).

and early Straub in Germany, Reisz in England. But what about Italy? As a country that had never taken up challenges historically, Italy found a way of dealing with the problem: either by placing its masters in splendid isolation or by bringing forth an imitation Godardism that, at best, came out in such films as Bertolucci's *Partners*. The Italian cinema saw the new standards of linguistic ideology merely as an opportunity for renewing its themes. The "politically correct images" became images about politics; the eroticism of images became a pornographic image. In other words, the notion of "politics" became a political theme, and eroticism was turned into erotic contents, i.e., pornography.

There was no original renewal of language. Instead, our cinema was enriched with two new genres: politics and pornography.

This was the situation in the early seventies. Political cinema followed its own path for several years; some of these films were of a very high quality but most of them were on a very low commercial level. On the one hand, we had the works of Bertolucci (*The Conformist, The Spider's Strategy*, 1972, with the authentically erotic intermezzo of *Last Tango in Paris*, 1971); Cavani (*The Cannibals*, 1970), Vancini (*Bronte*, 1972), Petri (*The Working Class Goes to Heaven*, 1971), Maselli (*Open Letter to an Evening Newspaper*, 1970, and *The Suspect*, 1975), Giannarelli (*I Have No Time*, 1973), Bellocchio (*In the Name of the Father*, 1972, *Matti da slegare* and *March of Triumph*, 1976), Lorenzini (*Quanto è bello lu murire acciso*, 1976), the Taviani brothers (*Saint Michael had a Rooster*, 1972, and *Allonsanfant*, 1974), Rosi (*Uomini contro*, 1970, *Excellent Corpses*, 1975, *Christ Stopped at Eboli*, 1979). On the other hand, we had an endless number of movies about the police, corruption, power — usually based on formal and ideological vulgarity. Naturally, all the above-listed filmmakers would each deserve a separate discussion; but this is not the place for it.

Anyone who has seen these movies, or at least some of them, must have noticed that the language formally has gone downhill, from an intense and concrete political reflection to a more generic thinking about the world and life, with a symptomatic shift of interest in dealing with the hoped-for revolution. Indeed, the year 1976 seems to have been a watershed in that it was the last year in which "political" films were made (unless we count Bertolucci's *Nineteen Hundred* (1977) as a political work). And 1978 initiated the new era of Italian comedies (Nanni Moretti's *Ecce Bombo*, 1978; Carlo Verdone's *Un sacco bello*, 1980, Maurizio Nichetti's *Ho fatto splash*, 1981, Massimo Troisi's *Ricomincio da tre*, 1981, etc.). These movies were generally short on ideas, and if they had merit, it was in their rejection of the coarse, crude humor typical of Italian film comedies.

P.P. Pasolini, *Salò o le 120 giornate di Sodoma.*

However, we must acknowledge — if any confirmation is even necessary — that the reputation of the Italian cinema rested on the shoulders of the great masters, the "auteurs," who remained above all fads and problems: Fellini (*Orchestra Rehearsal,* 1978, *City of Women,* 1980, *And the Boat Sails...,* 1983); Antonioni (*Zabriskie Point,* 1970, *Profession: Reporter,* 1975, *The Mystery of Oberwald,* 1980, *Identification of a Woman,* 1983), Visconti (*Death in Venice,* 1971, *Ludwig,* 1973, *Family Portrait in an Interior,* 1974, *L'innocente,* 1976), Ferreri (*La cagna* , 1972, *L'udienza,* 1972, *La grande bouffe,* 1973, *The Last Woman,* 1976, *Ciao maschio,* 1978,

Chiedo asilo, 1980), as well as several films by Scola (*The New World*, 1981), Comencini (*Heart*, 1984). There were also several new directors whom we cannot yet define as "talented": Salvatore Piscicelli (*Immaculate and Conceived*, 1980, *The Opportunities of Rosa*, 1982), Marco Tullio Giordana (*Maledetti vi amerò*, 1982, *The Fall of the Rebellious Angels*, 1983); or Franco Piavoli (*Blue Planet*, 1982). No discussion of the Italian cinema can ignore two extremely important filmmakers, atypical as they may be: Pasolini and Carmelo Bene.

Pier Paolo Pasolini was probably the most uncomfortable person that the Italian cinema has ever known; and he was the only filmmaker to have the same courage that we recognize in Godard. He may not have had Godard's inventiveness or stylistic rigor; but he was certainly the only Italian cineast who put himself on the line for his ideas. For Pasolini, the cinema was life, and as such, it is dramatic, contradictory, and both tragic and comic. Indeed, Pasolini seemed to change his stylistic register with every new film; and each film was virtually a stone in the mosaic of the individual and cultural experiences of a mind that was always ready to contradict itself. Perhaps that is why Pasolini was never fully accepted by either the cinema or Italian culture in general: he was always a step above the problems being debated. He introduced cinematic semiotics in Italy when people still didn't know what it meant (Festival of Pesaro, 1966). He anticipated the end of ideologies in *The Hawks and the Sparrows* (1966). And he confronted the question of eroticism profoundly in his Trilogy of Life (*Decameron*, 1971; *The Canterbury Tales*, 1972; *The Thousand and One Nights*, 1974). Then, in *Salò or The Hundred Twenty Days of Sodom* (1975) he desperately experienced the awareness that no redemption is possible for the world. He was the only "curious" moviemaker in Italy, attentive to and thorough about every social and formal problem, for he realized that communication is transmitted by way of a form through a form. He was perhaps the only Italian filmmaker who could have created a "school." And for this very reason, he was the only one who had neither disciples nor imitators, since we have no "Italian cinema," but only Italian cineasts.

Equally extraordinary, although certainly not as rich is the work of Carmelo Bene, perhaps the only (and certainly the most relevant) example of an underground cinema in the Mediterranean area. Deliberately alien to the diatribes about cinematic language and its relationship to politics, Bene tried to film desire in its pure state, absolute individuality against the social and political. His images flow as an enchantment, devoid of any referential ties, creating an interior spectacle in which only the auteur/creator can recognize himself: the mirror of a Narcissus who accepts no interlocutors. *Don Giovanni* (1971), *Salomé* (1973), *One Hamlet Less* (1974) offer the great linguistic alternative to the cinema of traditional logic and narrative. We cannot say that Bene's unsettling questions will remain completely unanswered by our cinema. A cinema that, I repeat, is devoid of almost anything except brilliant inventors who operate in a void.

C. Bene, *Salomé* (Veruschka).

Figures in a Lonely Landscape
The New German Film

Wolfram Schütte

"German films are among the most intelligent and imaginative in Europe today," said Lina Wertmüller in 1976. In 1980 Vincent Canby of the *New York Times* commented: "It seems we're finally entering the decade of the German film." In 1979 Peter Lilienthal's *David* received the Golden Bear of the Berlinale and Volker Schlöndorff won (*ex aequo* with Coppola's *Apocalypse Now*) the Golden Palm at the Cannes Film Festival; in 1980 *The Tin Drum* (*Die Belchtrommel*) became the first German film to win an Oscar, and Werner Schroeter's *Palermo or Wolfsburg* (*Palermo oder Wolfsburg*) was awarded the Golden Bear of the Berlinale; in 1981 Margarethe von Trotta received the Golden Lion at the Venice Film Festival for *The German Sisters* (*Die bleierne Zeit*); in 1982 Fassbinder won the Golden Bear of the Berlinale with *Veronika Voss* and Wim Wenders the Golden Lion of the Venice Film Festival with *The State of Things* (*Der Stand der Dinge*); in 1983 the surprise winner (because not in the competition) of the Cannes Film Festival was Robert van Ackeren's *Femme Flambé* (*Flambierte Frau*), while at the Venice Film Festival it was Alexander Kluge's *The Power of Emotions* (*Die Macht der Gefühle*), which won the International Critics Award (FIPRESCI) (with Godard's *First Name: Carmen (Prénom: Carmen)* winning the Golden Lion); in 1984 Wim Wenders was selected for the Golden Palm of Cannes for *Paris, Texas,* thus winning within two years the two most respected awards of the International Film Festivals.

That's the *crème de la crème* of a bounty of prizes that has showered down on West German films in the past few years wherever they have participated in film festivals. The abundance of other honors as well is proof of the international renown garnered by West German films over the past decade. But even without such outstanding honors, the names and films of Helma Sanders, Helke Sander, Ula Stöckl and Ulrike Ottinger, of Werner Herzog, Hans-Jürgen Syberberg, Werner Nekes, Rosa von Praunheim, Wolfgang Petersen, Niklaus Schilling, Rudolf Thomé and Herbert Achternbusch are no longer unknown to film-lovers outside the Federal Republic of Germany and Europe. Edgar Reitz has just recently been added to the list with his nearly six-hour-long television film *Homeland* (*Heimat*).

The "German Film Boom" that *Newsweek* found worthy of a cover story as early as 1976 is a phenomenon of creative breadth and diversity that seems to unleash an endless stream of new artistic talents with starkly individualistic artistic signatures and themes, comparable to the New Wave in France in the early sixties, the short-lived "film wonders" of Czechoslovakia and Yugoslavia, Switzerland and Italy during the sixties and early seventies.

Why the international applause? What lies behind this phenomenon? What ignited this fireworks display of talents, and what illuminates it? "Among the blind, the one-eyed man is king." The Germans have this saying too. Are the Germans kings now because all about them — in the classical film industries of Italy, Great Britain, Sweden and even France and Japan — blindness reigns? Are we seeing a little stream as a blooming oasis because there's a desert stretching out in all directions around it? Or is this an epidemic of international fashion, soon to be replaced by another?

Many questions, many answers. Fewer than eleven percent of the films shown in the Federal Republic (in c. 3,600 movie houses) are German productions; with over sixty percent, American firms more than just dominate the field. The interest of the German

public in films by its own directors was in fact first awakened by their international success. Even Rainer Werner Fassbinder, the most prolific filmmaker of the postwar German period, had great difficulty making his way on the homefront. What from the outside looks like a field in which, to quote Mao, "a thousand flowers are blooming" is seen from the inside as a tiny scrap of land that more resembles an ornamental garden. For the vitality and creativity of filmmakers, their various approaches, aesthetic credos and imaginative themes are not luxury items to which an intact, commercial film industry treats itself in a moment of self-indulgence. Rather, the "New German Film" exists precisely because there is no film industry infrastructure and hardly a risk-taking producer to be found, and *only for that reason.* A cultural landscape in a commercial desert.
A long battle over cultural politics had to be fought to create the basis for the at first "Young" and then "New German Film" in the Federal Republic of Germany and West Berlin. For the once commercially successful and artistically all but vacuous postwar film industry had dug its own grave with true singleness of purpose. The threat came from television, which radically altered the leisure-time activity of the moviegoing public. The West German film industry did not know how to meet this challenge, at least not strategically. It continued to produce its once successful genres — the provincial-romantic film (*Heimatfilm*), the music-film (*Musikfilm*) and the problem-film, etc. — for a constantly dwindling and ever younger audience that drifted off in ever greater numbers to foreign and especially American and French-Italian films. The coming generation of German filmmakers didn't have a chance: neither through directing apprenticeships nor relevant themes nor new (aesthetic) points of view.
The "hour of birth" of today's West German film is generally considered to be the Oberhausener Manifesto of 1962. At the Short Film Festival in Oberhausen — the only place young filmmakers could express themselves through their first, cheaply made short films — twenty-six directors, cameramen and producers declared "their intention of creating the new German feature film." Under the motto "Grampa's cinema is dead — we believe in the new German film" and encouraged by the first success of the French *nouvelle vague* of Chabrol, Godard, Truffaut, they demanded the means to produce their own ideas. Their spokesman was the disciple of Adorno, attorney and writer Alexander Kluge (b. 1932), who is still today the invaluable strategist, theoretician and practitioner of the New German

R.W. Fassbinder, *Lili Marleen.*

Film. Without Kluge's twenty-year-long activity in the politics of film — in pursuit not only of the influential film industry but also the politicians themselves — there wouldn't be any such thing as the New German Film.
After an initial flickering of a new kind of film in the mid-sixties — especially Kluge's *Yesterday Girl* (*Abschied von Gestern*, 1966) and *Artists in the Circus Tent: Perplexed* (*Die Artisten in der Zirkuskuppel: ratlos*, 1966-68), both of which won high honors at the Venice Film Festival — the flame was smothered again. While the young filmmakers were again reduced to, or continued working within the short film genre and in experimental forms, Kluge kept to his goal of changing the politics of filmmaking from the ground up, despite mounting setbacks. What he was after was a film subsidy program supported by public funds. However since the culture brokers did not (as for instance in France) sit in the national government but in the various state governments, it was necessary to find an instrument that "would support quality films in Germany on a broad basis" without infringing on the sovereignty of the cultural politics of the different states within the Federal Republic.
The Organization for the Advancement of Film, or FFA (Filmförderungsanstalt), composed of representatives from the states, the federal government and the film industry, was established to fill this need. It is financed by channeling to the FFA a percentage of the price of each movie ticket sold. A co-production and option-to-buy contract with the two national public television channels was signed, which contributed further funds to the subsidizing of filmmaking. A complicated mechanism, to be sure, but a highly effective system that fell into the hands of the younger generation of filmmakers as the commercial failures of the old film industry multiplied.
To be sure, the subsidy system thereby relieved filmmakers of the commercial constraints and need-to-succeed of the capitalist marketplace and gave the increasingly powerful television channels that were replacing the old producers a growing say in choice of subject matter and in aesthetic and moral questions — for the public channels are bound by a stricter code of behavior, defined by the parties, than the "Voluntary Self-Monitoring of the Film Industry" or FSK (Freiwillige Selbstkontrolle der Filmwirtschaft) that applies to the cinema. But it was the Film Subsidy Law — frequently updated by the parliament in Bonn over the past two decades — together with various subsidies and awards granted by the Department of the Interior and later the states which created the foundation on which the New German Film could develop in all its diversity.
In certain respects this unique film subsidy program and its successes resembled the varied landscape of German opera and theater which at the very same time was causing a sensation far beyond the boundaries of the Federal Republic with its concept of a new kind of director's theater (*Regie- oder Regisseurstheater*) as defined by directors like Peter Stein, Klaus Peymann, Peter Zadek, Dieter Dorn, Hans-Günther Heyme, etc. A further bond between theater and film directors, many of whom were of the same generation, was the concept of the film *d'auteur*, whose extreme liberty the theater directors adopted for their own work.
What the *Cahiers du Cinéma* critics Godard, Rohmer, Chabrol, Truffaut had earlier articulated as the *politique des auteurs* — namely the continuity of a film director's personal artistic signature (even and precisely in works that grew out of such extreme collaborative production methods as those which characterized the old Hollywood films) — now constituted *one* element in the theory and practice of the German film *d'auteur*. These films were the work of a single individual, on many levels: a single person often both wrote the filmscript, which reflected the author's own world of experience and fantasy, and directed the film, after having first played the role of producer by soliciting funds for the film. Some, like Fassbinder or Schilling, acted as their own cameramen or, like Fassbinder, Helke Sander and Achternbusch, played their own leading roles as well. This radically subjective, extremely intimate form of creative work with and in film is the unique signature of the New German Film. Its great, many-faceted brilliance and its partial failure are both rooted in this, for because the new filmmakers created everything out of themselves alone, they ran the danger of becoming beached on the shoals of their own inexperience and limited capacity to communicate.
Necessity and inclination came together in the making of the film *d'auteur*. Necessity, because the New Film had neither the infrastructure of a mature film industry (studios, technicians,

scriptwriters, stars, etc.) to fall back on, nor a cinematographic tradition. And inclination, because it wanted to make a new start — and in the process, as so often in the cultural and intellectual history of Germany, both genius and its counterpart, the idiosyncratic dilettante, were spawned. The collective mode of production repeatedly encouraged by Kluge, following in Brecht's footsteps, succeeded only twice. "Under dangerous conditions and extreme duress" (to cite one of his film titles: *In Gefahr und grösster Not*), namely when the German intellectuals felt threatened at the height of the terrorist hysteria, the collective process produced *Germany in Autumn* (*Deutschland im Herbst*) and later *The Candidate* (*Der Kandidat*), a film directed against the election campaign of the CSU politician Franz-Josef Strauss. The third project, *War and Peace*, would certainly have been more successful if Fassbinder, who had agreed to the collaboration, had not died before its completion. At any rate, the New German Film (and not least of all Fassbinder with his all-round productivity) has itself now built up a technical infrastructure in the course of its brief fifteen-year history: cameramen, editors, set designers, sound technicians, costume designers, actors and actresses, all of whom have long since outgrown the originally small, tightly knit, loyal teams gathered around a single director, and some of whom have switched now to different directors while others have themselves become directors, such as the film editors Heidi Genée and Dagmar Hirz, or the cameramen Robert van Ackeren, Niklaus Schilling and Xavier Schwarzenberger.

Rainer Werner Fassbinder was incontestably the beating heart of the New German Film just as Alexander Kluge is its theoretician and strategist. Not only was Fassbinder's death in 1982, at the age of thirty-six, a shock for all who admired his work — an œuvre that had taken on the proportions of a Balzacesque *comédie humaine* — but at a single blow it made most of West Germany's filmmakers very conscious of the fact that he was the vital, if unstated, center of the New German Film. His œuvre of over three dozen "big" and "little" films, television series — such as *Eight Hours Don't Make a Day (Acht Stunden sind kein Tag)* — and personal literary adaptations like *Fontane Effie Briest* or *Berlin Alexanderplatz* had reached into the German present and past with a depth and breadth, with melodrama and satire comparable only to Heinrich Böll's contemporary work in the literary field. His films were as indisputably his own as they were works that told all the stories of our times: of the wounds and ruin left behind by a false morality and a society drunk on unrestrained profits; of lovelessness, cynicism, fear and the futility of love; of individuals and groups; of the misery of the guest workers and the loneliness of the old (*Wogs* [*Katzelmacher*]) and *Ali: Fear Eats the Soul* [(*Angst essen Seele auf*]); of the price of emotional and physical self-destruction bequeathed by the restoration of the postwar period (*The Merchant of Four Seasons* [*Der Händler der vier Jahreszeiten*], *The Marriage of Maria Braun* [*Die Ehe der Maria Braun*] and *Lola*); of oppression and exploitation inflicted on one another by possessive lovers (*Martha, Fox and his Friends, The Bitter Tears of Petra von Kant* [*Die bitteren Tränen der Petra von Kant*], *I Only Want You to Love Me* [*Ich will doch nur, dass ihr mich liebt*], *In a Year with 13 Moons* [*In einem Jahr mit 13 Monden*]).

R.W. Fassbinder, *Die Ehe der Maria Braun.*

Fassbinder was capable of doing everything and he did everything, most of it by himself, and he was in every one of his films. Whether he was working for television or for large movie audiences, whether he was pursuing his own personal obsessions or adapting the big-city novel *Berlin Alexanderplatz* (a monumental work of world literature), Fassbinder's genius was one of sensibility and empathy. Above all he was a storyteller in movies who dreamed of making "Hollywood films without their ideological lies." But what made him the heart of the New German Film was his singular artistic ability to reconcile the potential soli*t*ariness of the author with the soli*d*arity of the film public, i.e., to speak so personally about himself, to tell his story intimately and yet do so in a way that everyone could discover themselves in it.

The loss of this *genius of synthesis* who brought together all the various themes, issues, feelings and ideas distributed throughout the New German Film, is inestimable. It is all the more devastating due to the double challenge the New German Film was faced with shortly after Fassbinder's death and that could easily mean its downfall. There is first of all the new film policy of the new CDU/CSU government that set about radically curtailing freedom of artistic experimentation through political censorship and the demand for commercial success. And secondly, the introduction — for which the same government paved the way — of the new privately owned and run media into the Federal Republic, which will rapidly and radically alter the cinema and film landscape, and the public as well. Without its center of gravity, Fassbinder, the planetary system of the New German Film could thus easily fall apart, its rich diversity disappear. And apart from all this, the centrifugal forces of international success have already thrown a number of the best directors of German film into different orbits, i.e., Volker Schlöndorff (*Swann in Love* ["*Eine Liebe von Swann*]), Werner Herzog (*Fitzcarraldo*), Wim Wenders (*Paris, Texas*).

Volker Schlöndorff, who is the only one of the New German Film directors to have "learned" his *métier* (with Melville, Malle), has always been more of a *metteur-en-scène* type who for the most part adapts literary material for his narrative cinema: *Young Törless* (*Der junge Törless*) from Robert Musil, *The Lost Honor of Katharina Blum* (*Die verlorene Ehre der Katharina Blum*) from Heinrich Böll, *The Tin Drum* (*Die Blechtrommel*) from Günter Grass.

Another literary adaptation of his, *Coup de grace*, is of further interest because of his wife's collaboration on the film: Margarethe von Trotta both wrote the filmscript, basing it on a novel by the Belgian writer Marguerite Yourcenar, and played the leading role, a woman of the Baltic aristocracy who takes the side of the Bolsheviks out of political sympathy and her sense of herself as a woman, and forces her lover, a German officer in an ultraconservative volunteer corps fighting the Bolsheviks, to execute her as a prisoner. Directly following this film by Schlöndorff, Margarethe von Trotta began directing her own films certering on self-aware or self-tormenting women looking for a new identity of their own in contemporary, male-dominated German society: *The Second Awakening of Christa Klages* (*Das zweite Erwachen der Christa Klages*), *Sisters* (*Schwestern*), *The German Sisters* (*Die bleierne Zeit*) and *Sheer Madness* (*Heller Wahn*). In *Christa Klages* and *The German Sisters* she addresses the question of why it is young women comprise such a large percentage of the German terrorist scene, while in the other two films she observes the milieu of the leftist liberal cultural chic with an emancipating eye.

She is not the only woman author-director, and not the only one to contribute to the broad and variegated public debate over women's liberation in her work. Women do not constitute a lesser artistic force in the New German Film. The Austrian Elfie Miekesch and Valie Export, who make experimental and innovative films, and Ulrike Ottinger with her grand, Felliniesque phantasmagorias and allegories (*Freak Orlando*, *Dorian Gray in the Mirror of the Daily Press* [*Dorian Gray im Spiegel der Boulevardpresse*]) belong here too, as do Ula Stöckl who, after a long pause, was able to complete her modern version of the Medea story (*The Sleep of Reason* [*Der Schlaf*

U. Ottinger, *Dorian Gray im Spiegel der Boulevardpress.*

der Vernunft]), and Helma Sanders-Brahms and Helke Sander. The latter two have extremely different artistic talents. Sanders-Brahms has moved from documentary film and naturalism (*Shirin's Wedding* [Shirins Hochzeit]) to a melodramatically heated surrealism (*Germany, Pale Mother* [*Deutschland bleiche Mutter*], *The One Who Was Touched* [*Die Berührte*]). Helke Sander, coming from the *Womens Council (Weiberrat: Weib* equivalent to *wench* or *tough broad* in English) of the German Socialist Student Organization (SDS), has preserved an ironic, analytical, humoristic, semidocumentary mode of representation in her films (*All around Reduced Personality-Redupers* [*Die allseitig reduzierte Persönlichkeit-Redupers*] and *The Whole Mess Starts with Love* [*Der Beginn aller Schrecken ist Liebe*]). Her witty montage and often self-critical humor remind one strongly of Alexander Kluge's films. Where Helke Sander in nearly Voltairesque fashion runs through typical, model cases, Helma Sanders-Brahms stages exalted, self-identificatory melodramas of feeling, which she sees anticipated in the neurotic world of Heinrich von Kleist, to whom she dedicated a miscarried biographical film. As much as these works by women differ from one another in temperament, sensitivity, aesthetic form and content, they all share a clear determination to help their own sex to represent itself and declare its own identity.

This feminist attempt to find women's own, independent identity necessarily leads to a dialogue with the other sex. The further the political utopias of this generation have slipped away — almost all of these filmmakers belong to the generation of the events of '68 and student revolts — the more the complex of conflicts surrounding love, marriage and family have moved in on and dominated their mostly openly autobiographical or transparently coded films. A great number of the New German films of the last several years has thus been concerned, with decreasing artistic rigor and urgency, with what can be called the genre of the "relationship film." Among them are seldom the light, comedic variations of an Eric Rohmer, who has turned his intense focus to this subject in his most recent films, or of the late Truffaut, who approached it with ironic charm in so many of his works. Most of the New German films on this topic are tiresome, tortured, Strindbergian dramas full of heavy, melodramatic bombast. The UFA "problem-film" has unfortunately made a comeback here, reduced to the intimacy of a bedroom-film.

P. Handke, *Die linkshändige Frau.*

The question of one's own identity — as a man, a German, an artist — is the dominant theme of Wim Wenders's work. His heroes are homeless, on the road, in search of the fulfillment of their dreams of "return," "homecoming," and harmony. Wim Wenders and Peter Handke are friends who share a love of American rock music, the epic expanses of John Ford's westerns and the semiotic quality and complex simplicity of the works of the Japanese filmmaker Ozu. Both are seeking — almost in parallel, the one in literature, the other in film — a poetry beyond the rigid concepts and everyday language of our normal discourse. And if one of Handke's latest books is entitled *The Slow Journey Home* (*Langsame Heimkehr*), this doesn't necessarily mean for Wenders returning to Germany: it can also mean *Paris, Texas* (or the mythic stringency of cinematographic art). Wenders's first major feature film was an adaptation of Handke's novel *The Goalkeeper's Anxiety at the Penalty Kick* (*Die Angst des Tormanns beim Elfmeter*) and Handke's only feature film, to date, and adapted from his own novel *The Left-Handed Woman* (*Die linkshändige Frau*), was produced by Wenders. In both films, the main character is blasted out of everyday reality by an *acte gratuit*: the goalkeeper Bloch strangles a woman; the "left-handed woman" has a mystical experience that tears her away from love and marriage and family. Bloch starts on a journey that leads him to more and more remote places populated with grownups and children who do not speak. The "left-handed woman" remains in her Parisian suburb, but registers the world around her with a hypersensitive acuity that isolates her from everyone else: objects, streets, houses, sounds all glow with a threatening and at the same time magical beauty and purity.

In another of Wenders's films, the two heroes, who meet by chance after leaving wrecked family and love relationships behind, are sent on a trip along the border with the East German Republic. His "Kings of the Road" travel through a dead region where the movies too are dying — a symbol of the utopian dream of life, which Wenders's heroes also always experience as a separation and alienation from women. Lost in self-preoccupation, these men can act more naturally with children (*Alice in the Cities* [*Alice in den Städten*]). After *False Move* (*Falsche Bewegung*) — also a Handke-adaptation — in which a young writer travels from the North Sea to the Zugspitze — the highest peak in the Federal Republic — in search of his poetic calling without however finding a home for his alter ego, and after the filming of Patricia Highgate's *The American Friend* (*Der amerikanische Freund*), Wim Wenders turned to the object of his own desires, to America and Hollywood.

In the midst of his youthful dreams of the cinema, he awoke, after several years of torturous, humiliating work, as the author of a semi-successful film (*Hammett*) and of a requiem for the dying Nicholas Ray (*Lightning over Water*), who met his ruin in the film industry. Wenders's ideas about the young, open, dynamic European director reviving the Hollywood movie with his fresh spirit are most productively summed up in *The State of Things* (*Der Stand der Dinge*), a synthesis of the improvisational European film and the mythic American film, and at the same time a rejection of the new Hollywood ruled by an unscrupulous Mafia hostile to art and interested only in fast profits.

The chamber-melodramatist Fassbinder dreamt of the Hollywood of Michael Curtiz; Wenders dreams of the Hollywood of Howard Hawks and Fritz Lang as well as that of Nick Ray, Anthony Mann and John Ford. Today the studios are gone and they were never Wim Wenders's idea of a poetic locus for his travel fantasies and the pathways of his yearnings anyway. And in fact he manages — "on the road again" and in "open air" imitation of John Ford — to triumph over the decadence of Los Angeles-Hollywood, which appears only on the distant horizon. Two years after the pessimistic assessment of *The State of Things* he set his obsessions and projections into motion: destination, *Paris, Texas*. And he has come closer here than ever before to realizing all his utopias of homecoming happiness and of the movies, which in turn portray these utopian visions.

But neither did Wenders return home to Germany, as he reported he would to the French press after his triumph in Cannes ("to stand by his colleagues, besieged by the conservative government"), nor was his film shown in German theaters. Because the Authors' Film Company (*Filmverlag der Authoren*), which Wenders co-founded with Fassbinder and others, wanted to start *Paris, Texas* with only a few copies and has handled things unprofessionally, Wenders has become

W. Wenders, *Paris, Texas.*

involved in a tedious legal battle that typifies the recent situation of the New German Film and the cinema. *Paris, Texas* didn't reach German movie theaters until half a year later, and Wenders is currently in the middle of a film project that is taking him all around the world.

All around the world is where three other directors are looking for their "poetic locations," too: Werner Herzog, Werner Schroeter and Peter Lilienthal. They differ in the estreme in their artistic sensitivities. Herzog is the tragedian of the New German Film. Fascinated by Camus's *Myth of Sisyphus*, he has been searching since his first feature film *Signs of Life* (*Lebenszeichen*) for heroes and landscapes that simultaneously challenge the world of matter and of reason and are removed from the everyday normality of "civilized" Central Europe. In his films, he is looking for "images that have never been seen before" (thus the journeys through the Amazon jungles: *Aguirre* and *Fitzcarraldo*). And where he does not play the role of the epic documentarist of human-superhuman madness, as in the just-mentioned films, he becomes the sympathetic partisan of the "de-ranged," (*ver-rückten*), peculiar, ostracized heroes condemned and misunderstood by our technological civilization. Herzog's gallery of outsiders – whose ancestor in Murnau's masterpiece was the model for his own *Nosferatu* – includes *Even Dwarves Started Small* (*Auch Zwerge haben klein angefangen*), the stragglers on the edge of the Sahara (*Fata Morgana*), the soothsayer Kiaserl and the desperate somnambulists in *Heart of Glass* (*Herz aus Glas*), Kaspar Hauser in *Every Man for Himself and God Against All* (*Jeder für sich und Gott gegen alle*), the Büchnerian Woyzeck, Stroszeck, who travels to America with a whore and a cripple, and finally the aborigines of the Australian desert where *The Green Ants Dream* (*Die grünen Ameisen träumen*). Herzog resumes the apocalyptic fantasy world of German Romanticism and Expressionism – often, to be sure, with problematic signs of exertion.

Werner Schroeter's œuvre is characterized by its pathos and irony and derives from the passion and artistic unconditionality of a singer like Maria Callas. She is the guiding star in his artistic cosmos, who, like the grand opera of nineteenth-century Italy and the pop music of today, articulates the truth of feeling, the sensuality of a yearning for a fulfilled life even in her false and

W. Herzog, *Herz aus Glas.*

exaggerated notes. Most of his works have a semidocumentary character that is transcended in the art world of opera and melodrama by the music and the theatrical body language of his actors. So too in his most recent film *The Laughing Star* (*Der lachende Stern*), a grand scale, complex montage of historical and contemporary materials on the history and present of the Philippines: a highly poetic and at the same time political *Canto General* (Pablo Neruda) on the exploitive relationship of the "First World" to the Third World. This is a theme that has preoccupied the director in two of his three feature films to date: in *The Kingdom of Naples* (*Regno di Napoli*), a chronicle of postwar Italy which is indebted to both Brecht and to Italian folk drama, as well as in his polemical film *Palermo or Wolfsburg* in which he emphasizes the irreconcilability of and

estrangement between Sicilian honor and poverty, on the one hand, and German rigidity and consumerist wealth, on the other.
The sympathy for the Mediterranean and non-European cultures that pervades Werner Schroeter's œuvre as a counterpoint to the German *misère* recurs in Peter Lilienthal's work as political sympathy for the oppressed peoples of Latin America. Shortly before the outbreak of World War II, Lilienthal's family was able to flee to Uruguay, where he grew up. After the war, he returned to Germany and filmed extremely sensitive and artificial literary adaptations for television. Disoriented by the politicization of the student revolts and stirred by Salvador Allende's promising experiment with a leftist People's Front government, Lilienthal turned his attention to Latin America.
In Chile, during Allende's time still, he filmed *La Victoria*, a semidocumentary eyewitness report on the changed conditions of life among the poor. After the Chilean military putsch, Lilienthal made another Latin-American film in Sandinist Nicaragua, *The Uprising* (*Der Aufstand*). Here and in the movies he filmed in Portugal that portray fictional Latin-American dictatorships, Lilienthal the humanist focuses his sensitive narrative attention on the hidden signs, the gestures, the epiphanies of resistance that the people under these brutal, flagrant dictatorships exchange with each other in order to preserve and announce their dignity and determination to change the political conditions of their lives. Through its largely unsentimentalized testimony, Lilienthal's work serves as a reminder of the social and political misery of the Third World and of the "power of the weak" (*Die Kraft der Schwachen* — to quote the title of a cycle of stories by Anna Seghers written during her exile in Mexico).
But the most radical expression of the German film *d'auteur* is certainly to be found in the œuvres of two diametrically opposed and yet often equally perplexingly hermetic filmmakers: Alexander Kluge and Herbert Achternbusch. Kluge, the author of large volumes of avant-garde stories and philosophic and sociological studies, for instance, *History and Stubbornness (Geschichte und Eigensinn*), has combined experimental montage techniques (Wertov, Pudowkin) with narrative film in all of his works — comparable only to the complex poetics of Godard's œuvre. His films are many-layered on both the vertical and horizontal axes. They tell the story of the "stubbornness" of mostly female heroes who subversively tinge the everyday reality of life with their fantasies and wishes, their dreams and practical deeds. At the same time, he situates his laconic, elliptical narratives in a dense network of associations that work with numerous visual and sound image quotations. The aim of his latest films, *The Patriot* (*Die Patriotin*) and *The Power of Emotions* (*Die Macht der Gefühle*) is a philosophical and sensual reflection on the contradictions and conflicts in both the individual psyche and the corpus of German society.
Where Hans-Jürgen Syberberg attempts with pathetic nostalgia to stage a Purgatorio, a revue of German cultural and intellectual history (*Karl May*, *Hitler*, *Parzival*) in which the German people are confronted with the irrational night apparitions of their historical divagations, Kluge searches the "construction site" of German history for materials that might be used to illuminate and fight the fatal affinity of the Germans for drama, tragedy, destruction. How is one to offer resistance to the seductive, self-gratifying *Power of Emotions* — those passions that always lead the impetuous heroes of the opera, i.e., melodrama par excellence, to their deaths — so that life can succeed? With action, solidarity and the highest possible degree of "mental alertness" (*Geistesgegenwart*, as the currently widely read young philosopher Peter Sloterdijk put it in his *Critique of Cynical Reason* [Kritik der zynischen Vernunft]). What one might call Kluge's program is summed up in the parable at the end of *The Power of Emotions*: a man close to death is rescued by two people who dedicate themselves to him with intelligence and common sense — and so, in shared work, learn to love one another (while the practitioners of emotional bathos always crumble up and die). In this way, Kluge's films, which always require the audience to pay very close attention, also always speak about our immediate reality.
The literary and cinematic work of Herbert Achternbusch is more difficult of access. He is a radical poet who builds all of his works solely on his own powers of imagination and memory. One would be hard put to find more revealingly autobiographical books and films in Germany today than those of the born-out-of-wedlock Achternbusch, who grew up in one of the remotest of all Bavarian provinces. A "backwoodsman," but

H. Achternbusch, *Der Neger Erwin.*

an artist, too. Achternbusch, a radical anarchist who initially wanted to be a painter, does not tell realistic, straightforward stories about his life. Fantasy and vision, dream and experience are thoroughly permeated by his eruptive, sign-like, "wild" poetry. Because he has played the leading role himself in nearly all of his films to date – a sad, downtrodden clown and failure, a "crazy" and a "dolt" – his works all become "fragments of a great confession" ("Bruchstücke einer grossen Konfession," Goethe), the testimony if not manifesto of a man who is searching to find himself as a human being. The more autobiographical films like *The Olympic Winner* (*Die Olympiasiegerin*) or *So Long Bavaria* (*Servus Bayern*) are equally tensed between the poles of love and death, yearning and refusal as are the "freer" fantasies such as the bleak reflection on the Germans in *The Last Hole* (*Das letzte Loch*) or the complaint over the destruction of the Bavarian world by the stupidity and vanity of the politicians in *The Wandering Crab* (*Der Wanderkrebs*).
Allegory and Punch-and-Judy theater, visionary panoramas of the world and puns and language games are melded together in Achternbusch's "unformed", "reason-defying" phantasmagorias. In the process, Achternbusch not infrequently breaks the "grammatical rules" of cinematic language, but he simultaneously shows that this is intentional, that he is deliberately attacking and destroying art, for he also knows how to wring moments of great beauty from his art, a beauty that lies hidden in the alienating, enigmatic poetry of this wilful surrealist of the ego.
All the works of New German Film speak of the personal experiences of their authors in an idiom of their own – at least in so far as they do more than just illustrate a literary text (especially those of Thomas Mann). They are mirrors of Germany's past and present that have been broken by their creators. These works participated in the social utopias of an entire generation. The richness and diversity of the New German Film, its vitality and creativity were a parallel phenomenon to the worldwide but especially European rebellions of youth around 1968.
Perhaps it would be possible to see this artistic uprising as "the work of mourning" (*Trauerarbeit*) carried out on a broad collective and individual plane. Freud's term for this self-enlightening occupation with one's own past and the dark paths of its projection into the present was cited already at the outset of the New German Film in Kluge's *Yesterday Girl* (*Abschied von Gestern*; literal translation: "Goodbye to Yesterday"). This process of examining oneself and one's own society took place in the light of possible reforms and utopian yearnings for a different, truer, juster life.
This light is waning, if perhaps not yet entirely extinguished. The atomic and ecological threat to human life has become overwhelming and hopes for utopian thought have grown dim. Does this mean that a whole generation of German filmmakers has consumed all its artistic energy? Many signs point in this direction. What has been articulated of late lacks the urgency and autonomy, the artistic force that New German Film once possessed. "And when the times turn dark, will people still sing?" ("Und in den dunklen Zeiten / Wird da auch gesungen werden?") asks Brecht in a poem written during the days of fascist dictatorship. "Yes, people will sing then too" ("Ja, da wird auch gesungen werden.") he answers himself, "about the darkness of the times" (von den dunklen Zeiten). But the New (or newest) German Film has yet to find the language of these dark times – much as has the most recent German theater and literature.

The Situation of Industrial Design

Gillo Dorfles

Many students of industrial design felt that the disappearance of the artisan class would destroy many of the best national and regional characteristics of individual products, and that the design product would lose all originality with the advent of mass production.

Such fears have not come true, however. In the sector of utilitarian objects, furnishings, decorations, fashions, as well as in industrial design per se, Italian production has maintained its identity, even in the advanced phase of industrialization that it has reached today. This fact confirms that a designer's personality can come out fully even in the area of design. He can retain a good part of the authentic artistic prerogative that distinguished the craftsman of the past. I find it useful to establish this brief premise because I consider it essential in pinpointing the presence of a specific quality in Italian design. It is difficult to translate this quality into words, but it unquestionably exists everywhere, and anyone can recognize it in the majority of Italian products.

Other nations, other production systems may have gone further than Italian industry. But I believe I can state that one of the most typical features of Italian design is its ability to combine state-of-the-art perfection with a remarkable level of formal invention and good taste. To repeat a slogan of more advanced countries, we fuse "whigh tech with high touch." During the past few years, this blend has led to the outstanding quality of our design.

At this point, a broad outline of the history of Italian design would be useful. However, it would take us too far afield, forcing us to review centuries and perhaps even millennia of an artistic tradition that undoubtedly played its part in the development of the utilitarian object both in the past and in the present. Indeed, as we may assume, the inventive genius that produced the masterpieces of our Renaissance painting and architecture has now concentrated on the new sectors of industrial production. I will therefore limit my focus to a few of the basic stages in the history of Italian design after World War II. If we want to go back to earlier times, we must realize that we cannot speak of true industrial design. Unlike such countries as England or Germany, Italy lacked an industrial tradition rooted in the nineteenth century. It is only with the end of the interwar period that we can note a few examples of autonomous design rather than imitations of filtered models from Germany or England. I am thinking of certain electric household appliances and certain automobiles.

We must, however, wait for the postwar era in order to witness the first real examples of a design that has attracted the attention of both Italians and foreigners. Among the earliest products to elicit an immediate response both in Italy and abroad were the two famous motorscooters: Piaggio (the Vespa) and Innocenti (the Lambretta). These soon made our industrial design famous, and it became known in other countries as well. During that same period, Italy produced some of its best-known car bodies (Pininfarina, Bertone) typewriters (Olivetti's Lexikon), kitchen appliances (Necchi, Borletti; designed by Nizzoli and Zanuso), and many other domestic items. There were the lamps of the Castiglioni brothers, Mangiarotti, and Asti, the furnishings of Zanuso, Albini, Magistretti, Cini Boeri, and Sambonet's steel silverware. There were the plastic objects of the Kartell (Colombini, Anna Castelli); the Sambonet watches. This was an area in which Italy was the first to invent new forms with the plastic materials perfected by the chemical industry. There were the electric appliances of Bellini, Bonetto, Rosselli, the Brionvega television sets (Zanuso), the electronic calculators of Sottsass jr. and Bellini (Olivetti), and, more recently, Giugiaro's car bodies.

Rather than dwelling on a roster of names and products that can only sound sterile, I would prefer to describe the immediate repercussions of Italian design and its stylistic direction during the past few years. This is the only way that we can understand the appeal of certain designs and the struggles behind them.

We cannot hope to understand the present-day situation in Italy if we do not grasp two essential phenomena:

1) the evolution of industrialization taking place all over the world, especially in the West, and causing a reduction and even disappearance of craftsmanship;

2) the particular situation of the applied arts in Italy.

Mechanization and mass production may have just about replaced manual labor. Nevertheless, the ancient traditions survived in such Italian sectors as ceramics, glass, wood, and textiles, so that industrial production has retained some of the intrinsic features of craftsmanship: imagination and good form. For this reason, industrial products, although coming off an assembly line, have maintained the formal originality that has become one of the hallmarks of our industrial design. Furthermore, even the fashion industry has hooked up with industrial design, for example when Missoni textiles were used in automobiles or when Gucci leathers were used for purses and luggage.

Basically, Italy has always tried to bring out those formal aspects that were not obvious and yet assisted the function of an object without submitting to it entirely. Thus, during the era in which aesthetic theory, plainly deriving from the Bauhaus, preached the absolute identification of form and function, Italian design interpreted the function more broadly than utilitarian functionalism did. Italians leaned toward a functionalism that was both psychological and semantic. In other words, the form of an object had to correspond not only to technical and functional data, to the economy and adherence of form, and to the peculiarity of the material, but also to the precise "semantics." Form had to make the meaning and function of the object immediately obvious; and the meaning, I might add, had to be symbolic as well as practical.

This conception, often entirely instinctive, may be the reason why Italian design managed, at least partly, to avoid the excess of styling that infected design both in the United States and in Europe.

While the above description applies to the initial phase of Italian design — the heroic period of the affirmation of the first models — the situation changed somewhat during the relative boom of the sixties. With mounting prosperity and a rise in exports, Italy went through a time of relative styling and hedonism of the product. Then, especially because of the first oil crisis, Italians began to have second thoughts; they realized the futility of dwelling on redesign and stylization.

Next, during a period dominated by economic and ideological issues, Italy briefly verified utopian or radical design. Various avant-garde groups (such as Archizoom, Superstudio, Ufo, Global Tools) tried to materialize several of their ideological hypotheses about a "counter-design" — ideas taken from the sociological aesthetics of the moment.

However, even this phase of the crisis was soon dealt with. In fact, during the past five or six years, Italian production in the areas of product design, especially fashions and furniture, is again at the vanguard. Our products are being exported to all the most industrialized countries, and Italy is partly taking paths that have been carefully explored. At the same time Italy is developing new tendencies that have made for a decisive shift in the panorama of our design.

On the initiative of several teams, especially Alchimia (Mendini) and Memphis (Sottsass jr. and colleagues) a new approach has been taken to the problems of furniture, textiles, and utilitarian objects. This is due chiefly to an intense return to ornamental motifs, which terminates the long ostracism of all decoration. During this phase, i.e. the past five or six years, the designers that I have listed have continued to produce and to be appreciated: e.g. Zanuso, Aulenti, Castiglioni, Bonetto, Bellini, Stoppino, Scarpa. They have been joined by a younger generation: e.g. Branzi, Deganello, De Paz, Domazzi, D'Urbino, MID, Cortesi, De Cursi, De Lucchi, La Pietra, Giugiaro, Carla Venosta, Mari, Sapper, Piretti. To some extent, the younger designers have followed in the footsteps of their predecessors by insisting on the functionality and imagination that have always

inspired the older designers. On the other hand, the new generation preferred to emulate Mendini and, above all, Sottsass jr., taking over decorative models and neglecting the principles of the most rigorous rationality.
If we wish to review briefly the works of the designers in this exhibition, we can easily see that they effectively represent the basic trends in Italian design today. Castiglioni, for instance, has certainly managed, for the longest and most continuous period, to experiment not only in furnishings, interior decorating, and above all, lighting (he has created some famous prototypes), but also in the mounting of large-scale expositions. His highly personal style, which is both functional and fanciful, is the finest example of respect for the dictates of functionality as well as the investigation of always new and different forms. Ettore Sottsass, who is unquestionably one of the most interesting figures in the Italian panorama, has displayed his great professionality in his Olivetti projects (typewriters and electronic calculators). Within the design evolution of the past few years, his task has been highly unusual: he has been at the hub of the new movement, and he has managed to break away from the excessively severe patterns of International Style. Together with his followers in the Memphis group, he has reintroduced decoration within environments and interior design, inventing totally new, if paradoxical forms, which undoubtedly constitute a fixed point within the movement of Italian design.
A similar situation is that of De Lucchi, who has focused on the "banal object" (in terms of a poetics partly sustained by Alessandro Mendini). De Lucchi has transformed the panorama of the domestic object by introducing a wide range of colors and sometimes excessive frivolity.
Deganello, on the other hand, although following some of the most traditional currents, is nevertheless anchored in an excellent practice of product design, which has been confirmed by the well-known AEO armchair (for Cassina). His focus on asymmetry and odd profiles in furniture design has made him one of the subverters of Italian design practice.
In conclusion, we can state that Italian design, in industry as well as fashion (here, the personalities of Armani, Ferré, Krizia, Versace form an enviable quartet) constitutes a basis of the Italian economy. Products such as Olivetti's personal computer, the Brionvega television, the furniture of Cassina, Arflex, Busnelli, Kartell's plastic objects, Giugiaro's automobiles, etc. are appreciated everywhere and frequently envied. And many of our designers, such as Bonetto, Bellini, Zanuso, and Aulenti, are often invited to other countries to provide an Italian look for foreign products. We can only hope that Italian designers will maintain their high standards and not endanger our situation by seeking new forms for their own sake, forms devoid of any authentic technical, aesthetic or functional need — without which good design can never survive.

A Formal Balance

Vittorio Gregotti

What has happened to the "design" of Italian furniture in the last twenty years? Although the separation of a particular type, such as furniture, from the global context of the process of transformation of industrial design in its broadest sense is an entirely abstract application, we think it possible to attempt a formal balance.
1964, one can say, is a particularly significant year for the culture of design in Italy.
In 1964 the first agitation begins in the faculty of architecture, the influence of the supertechnological neo-avant-garde of the English group Archigram has already been affirmed; in 1964 at the Biennale of Venice there is the large exhibition of American Pop artists: the groups of the artistic, literary, and visual neo-avant-garde begin to consolidate.
Finally in 1964 the crisis of the political prospects of the program of governmental planning of the center-left coalition become manifest. Above all a new conception reached maturity in 1964, after long and difficult debate conducted primarily by the Gruppo 63; a new conception of the relationship between ideology and language and a different evaluation of the possible contributions of the creative culture in the formation of alternative social images.
Thus, in 1964 a long anti-institutional exploration of one part of the culture of Italian design also begins. There are, naturally, international influences to which credit must be given: from Pop Art to Archigram, as we have already seen, to Hans Hollein (his antifunctionalist manifesto is from 1962), the French group Utopie, the rediscovery of Kiesler, in addition to a certain influence of unconventional technologists such as Frei Otto and Buckminster Fuller.
Then during the sixties, primarily from the American avant-garde culture, the influences of Oriental religious and communitarian thought begin to grow. In this context develop the anti-industrial ideological positions, with the idea of a return to the land and to agriculture and a general anti-consumption polemic which was manifested, to tell the truth, in rather contradictory ways, primarily by the younger generations.
But in order to explain the condition of furniture design at that date in 1964 it is necessary to take a step backward to understand what connection links the activity of the generation of Albini, Gardella, Rogers, Molino — for whom furniture represented a demonstrative example of the method of the modern movement in architecture, and of that of the following generation.
This connection is represented on one side by the historicist movement of the then younger generations and by two great personalities: Carlo Scarpa and Ettore Sottsass.
The influence of the first on design is entirely indirect. He was, in the thirties, the designer for the Venini glassworks but did not, up until the end of the sixties, design a single piece of production furniture. His is a lesson in broadmindedness and also of highly refined craft filtered through (in spite of the explicit inspiration of Frank Lloyd Wright) capable of traveling across and of recovering all the sensibility of the experience of the plastic and pictorial avant-garde. He is the author of some museum interiors, which together with those of Franco Albini, are certainly among the best in the world. The extraordinary sense of spatial stratification obtained through the care for and invention of detail, the sense of the value of materials and the continuity of environmental image are the determining ingredients in the best Italian design that originates with the lesson of Carlo Scarpa.
With Sottsass, on the contrary, the culture of

design (even if understood in a most original way) is the most profound and continuous commitment. Sottsass came to design as a result of a veritable disappointment with regard to the situation in architecture, of its state of presumptuous approximation. He has been a painter from the beginning of his career, he participates in an intense way in the world of contemporary literature, particularly American literature. After his first trip to America in 1955, his vocation is confirmed and his way of doing interior design reveals itself up until 1960 (when it culminates in the anti-rhetorical atrium of the XII Triennale) in a patient recomposition of a series of fragments of images where painting, fabrics, objects, furniture are as many materials for a great spatial collage.
In the meantime his realizations in the area of business machines for Olivetti: electronic devices, typewriters, adding machines, are numerous. All are based on a vocation toward a severe and highly controlled image, full of inventions but which does not ever evade the sense of pleasure of a multicolor game, of the plastic presence in the environment played precisely on its extraneousness and together with the attempt to construct a normal relationship of the technical device as object in the context of household objects.
This sense of the "multicolor pleasure" shows up even in his activity in the field of furniture: but can one still talk about furniture? Absolute presences, centers and elements of magical reference, new altars where everything depends not only on the symbolic relationship with the formal object, but rather on a ritualistic approach (Indian and Far Eastern culture had a very heavy influence on him); places intent on provoking pre-ideological awareness in terms of the idea of dwelling, the attention to and the love of manipulation and of use.
The attempt was made, however, even if it was unfortunately abandoned by the same Sottsass, of contrasting the advancing sense of precariousness in the use of the object as a consumer object.
The influence of Sottsass has been, I believe, very strong; the attractive quality of his personality has been very strong; deriving from this research into the continuity between work and a lived life, of the lack of distinction between the world of activity and the moment of play.
In an analogous way, although through very different paths, the successive XIII Triennale of 1964 (the theme of "leisure time" was often a mere pretext for the demonstration that was desired) represented in the culture o Italian design a notable turning point and long term indirect influence. In the first place the net break with respect to the direct confrontation of the theme of art-production which had characterized the last three or four editions of the exhibition; in the second place with the change of generation, of which the younger was the protagonist (the same in large part as the exhibition "New Designs for Italian Furniture"); in the third place because it placed in view many elements which characterized Italian design in the successive period.
In the first place the notion of the physical environment in its totality is clearly identified and thus the task becomes available for the designer of industrial objects to attempt to regulate the relation system that every product involves. In the second place the XIII Triennale put into discussion the idea that environmental control, the opposition to its degradation, can be proposed in terms of the rational construction of the single object.
Nothing guarantees that the sum of a series of well designed objects produces a positive environment: overcrowding, poorly established relations, superimpositions or poverty of relations can negate that which the object affirms. In the third place this Triennale carries to the front row the theme of consumption as the fundamental component of the process of the formalization of the object, criticizing at the same time its limits and its prospects.
These themes are reconsidered the following year and rendered theoretically explicit in issue no. 85 of *Edilizia Moderna*: they codify and render evident a process which had already been taking place for a long time but which had its definitive cultur codification only after 1963. In these years the number of theoretical contributions to the theme of design had increased notably as did the pressure for the constitution of an institute for design research and instruction on a university level.
Venice, in 1960, was the first to try to create an experimental institute but it rapidly dissolved: then Florence (still in existence) tried and finally Rome. All with the ambiguous prospect of the transformation of the old Art Institutes into Schools of Design.
In Milan many programs were presented, many meetings were held but without any success: from

as far back as 1959 ADI (Italian Association for Industrial Design) and the Pagano Foundation proposed a university level school and in the architecture schools the space given to the various instruction of industrial design was and remains entirely marginal. That which the XIII Triennale represented under the form of negative criticism, is in some measure fixed as positive by the accomplishment of Tomás Maldonado, who in those years became, after the experience of the direction of the Hochschule für Gestaltung of Ulm, integral element and protagonist of the design culture in Italy.
The practical activity of Maldonado as the person in charge of the image of the department store of the Rinascente group lasted just three years: these were enough to show how it was possible to apply in a total way the methodology of design to an entire sector: that of mass distribution. From graphics to architecture, from equipment to space planning and internal distribution, he succeeded in impressing a dynamic unity to the entire arc of the image of Rinascente. What was important was that one was dealing with a systematic proposal completely new for Italy, in which the only precedent was found, even if in very different ways, in the experience of Olivetti.
An analogous attempt at systematic design is that of the work of Gae Aulenti for FIAT showrooms of the beginning of the seventies.
In those years the work of Franco Albini moved along the same systematic and environmental lines.
Starting in 1960 he received responsibility (along with his collaborator Franca Helg and with Bob Noorda for graphics) to design the typical station of Line 1 of the Metropolitana (subway) of Milan. The project was conceived as a single system, the Italian example of the environmental definition of a public means of transport through design. One must remember that in the second half of the sixties urban congestion and social tension provoked by internal immigration reached their culmination in Turin, while the role of exportation became decisive considering the capacities of the internal market. In those years the split between the North and South grew instead of diminishing. The Cassa del Mezzogiorno (Fund for the South) and the program of poles of development did very little nor did the law which established that 40% of the investments of state-owned companies had to be made in the South.
The role of state participation grew throughout the sixties. In 1962, IRI (the Italian government agency which controls state owned businesses) was one of the most important organizations in Europe. After 1963, even with the advent of the center-left the conditions of social-economic disequilibrium seemed for a moment to change radically: the contraction of profit margins had as a reaction on the part of capitalist interests a push toward growing inflation, and that created a climate of general nervousness which had to then explode with renewed vigor in labor clashes. This tension was also the result of a broadened maturity and strengthening of the unions themselves.
The small and medium industries, on the contrary, particularly those operating in the area of consumer goods and domestic items for medium term use, the not to be underemphasized locomotive of the "economic miracle," solidifies in these years its already established links with the culture of design. It is true that they are in large part placed in the advertising budget rather than in that of design and it is also true that the question is above all determined by problems of marketing instead of by those of production, but in spite of it all the designer became a normal collaborator of many businesses. The designer ceases to have a function of cultural elite and enters in an area more solidly professional.
A condition which must also be carefully considered and which explains in both a positive and negative way many things about Italian design is the type of work relationship with the structures of production. Almost all Italian designers are professionals who work outside the productive structure even when their respective relationships with the firm extend over a long period of time. Even more unusual was the type of mixed general consultancy on a part-time basis with a firm, and the uncommon arrangement during those years was an actual design department. Beyond this, businesses, on their own initiative, moved into the area of design either, in a broadly imitative way with respect to situations which have been established including those based on profit, or on the other hand reached sometimes novel and ingenious solutions through internal paths as in previously indicated examples.
At times these internal programs were set up so that the designer either was given excessive responsibility (marketing, typological invention,

distributive proposals), or he was limited to a promotional level placed in the advertising budget. Only in rare cases did he end up being organically positioned in the company's organization chart.
From 1960 on, Zanuso is certainly the designer in Italy that precisely through his relationships with business has demonstrated the greatest capacity of professional continuity.
Even in quantitative terms the number of interesting objects designed by him is notably high, yet the products are always of very high quality.
Each of his projects seems to benefit with sagacity from the preceding experience, capable of avoiding the temptations of fashion by entrusting to professional seriousness the function of objective mediation between creativity and the exigencies of the products.
The beautiful chair for children in polyethylene of 1964, fantastic and ironic game of construction, the folding school desk designed in occasion of the XII Triennale; then the series of television sets, the entire repertory of household objects, pure instruments at times plastically cancelled as with Black in 1970 or with the small portable receiver reducible to a compact volume based on joinery as in a Chinese puzzle; or for example the logical invention of the Grillo telephone in 1967. In the sixties even the best of his architecture seems to adhere with continuity to the methodology developed in his design experience. In this area the valuable support of Richard Sapper cannot be forgotten: a support which reached the level of morphological exchanges between different activities.
The work of Alberto Rosselli, interrupted by his premature death, can be placed, along with the work of Rodolfo Bonetto, in a perspective analogous to that of Zanuso. Bonetto was not trained as an architect but his profile resembles in this sense the "cultured" worker image of Marcello Nizzoli. The work of Bonetto was also applied in a solidly professional manner in the sixties and seventies to more structurally industrial themes with a seriousness and rigor not very frequently found in the traditions of Italian designers. His work is based on a direct and profound awareness of techniques of fastening and of the technological processes of materials.
The other determining group for the formation of the Italian approach to furniture design is without doubt that of the Castiglioni brothers: their sense of assemblage, of technological reduction, their sense of irony.
These characteristics are accentuated and become more precise in their activity of the last few years to the point of becoming caricature (screwdriver table 1966) and impersonation (Poretti beer dispenser 1964), and to the point approaching the "ready-made" dadaist!
Beyond having the formal and technological knowledge of the designer, as applied for example in a most beautiful series of radio receivers, phonographs, cameras, or through the employment of minute details (switches, bulbs, and sockets), there is a strong sense of the transportation of the object, of its out-of-context placement typical of the dadaist experience: a transformer + a fishing pole + an automobile headlamp, or a leaf spring + a wooden pin + a tractor seat. Their interiors also reflect this type of discourse in which highly refined objects are intermingled with the most humble and quotidian things. Design recovers this collage at the last minute through the process of design, but it continues to show ambiguity which allows a different angle of penetration. All of the lighting devices are based on the principles of reflection, transparency, and mobility. Then there is the taste for citation.
There has not been an Italian design object which has succeeded in restating with so much sagacity the Futurist experience, and that of Boccioni in particular, as that of the San Luca chair (1960). This was accomplished through methods that were totally unusual.
No one has been able to connect the specificity of his own cultural roots with the absolute modernity of approach in such a clear manner. Magistretti, Aulenti, Joe Colombo, Tobia Scarpa, and then Stoppino, Boeri, Frattini, Asti, Vignelli and others furnish, with brilliant quality of invention, with the elegance of plastic solutions, a truly new culture of design of the home which, even with different solutions and values, will remain in the future the most complete and significant fact of Italian design in the seventies.
A separate discourse would be necessary for each of them since each possesses a unique expressive poetic. There is the naïvely mechanistic futurism of Joe Colombo, the refined nostalgia of "craftsmanship," the mastery of he who, like Magistretti, succeeds in fulfilling with invention an authentic necessity of moment, or the case of Gae Aulenti who demonstrates the capacity to

construct on the basis of concrete environmental occasions an image for the aspirations of cultural status for the ruling class of an ideally modern and non-sectarian society. It is necessary to say that Gae Aulenti, in spite of her large and sophisticated production of objects remains principally, by virtue of approach, an architect: it is not happenstance that her work as a designer rarely proceeds in a pure context of production but results instead from the placing into production of objects born as components of an architectural strategy that forms a specific whole, hence they are like structural parts of a narrative which pass from the common language to the composition of other texts.

The inventive precision of Mario Bellini must be considered separately. The important role he has had with Olivetti electronics and in the automotive sector are not the only aspects to be considered: Bellini places at the basis of his own creative process the faith in being able to construct a design procedure which is authentically integral for the construction of the industrial object.

In certain ways Bellini represents that which Zanuso was for the preceding generation. The industrial world certainly is not a marvelous discovery in the eyes of a designer, but rather a natural component even when he seems to be playing close by in a way which is diversely experimental with the world of significative plasticity. The marvelous Bellini seems to look for it elsewhere: in an experimental curiosity, in the mimesis of processes of organic formation apparently far from his creative obstinacy.

The group which works with Danese represents, in spite of the modest diffusion, a position which is anything but secondary in Italian design. The exercise in the use of the small object of high quality (which is thus fatally the luxury object) of the knick-knack rigorously placed inside the sphere of visual and communicative research according to figurative principles of programmed art and the paradigmatic processes of construction (and the mimetic processes of industrial production) sheds light in an extraordinarily exemplary way upon the optics of contradiction in which design moves.

Yet while for some exponents of the group, such as Munari, often the sense of the game, and an extremely fine irony are able to reestablish a possible contact, an understanding, for Enzo Mari, contradiction becomes actual creative material. The production of Mari is notably well documented in its quality and in its continuity in a monograph which he himself edited. What is interesting in this sphere is to explain his position as exemplary of an entire attitude diffuse particularly among the younger generation at the end of the sixties.

Someone like Enzo Mari is more committed to reducing in the use of an object the possibility of error rather than increasing the combinatory morphology of the object. The polemic against improvisation, the commitment to establishing a hierarchy of values in which the project and the time necessary for its proper development are given considerably more importance than the resulting product are at the center of his self-interrogation on the meaning of design and on the reduction of every "visual" operation to design.

The return to poverty of means, the active participation of the executor in the project of projection-execution, the critique of the creation of ideological need become in the creative tension of Enzo Mari, principally poetic materials rather than instruments of revolutionary politics. And yet the position of Mari is solely explainable through a lively sense of ideological contradiction that the world of design represents in his eyes. And his eyes are those of a person who has lived intensely, as have many others, the most important questioning of the fundamental ideals of the collective life of the years between 1967 and 1970.

The interrogatives set up by this "questioning" have created different answers in the world of design of the industrial product, yet these answers are essential for a judgment on the products of the seventies. A widely practiced response has been the questioning of the industrial object through a return to direct manual intervention and to the transformative power of the imagination on the common object, or one dealt with a tension towards the total dissolution of the object in the environment and no longer that of rational control, but rather symbolically suggested or projected control on a utopian level. One dealt with an authentic polemic against formalist reduction, the spiral of consumption, which continually constructs objects with ever more eccentric meanings in the search for diversification (which is also social diversification) to such a degree as to have it lose all credibility.

But one also dealt with, beyond the self-involvement in this same process of the creation of merchandise, identifying openings for the useful transformation of space, of relationships, of behavior, developing that non-constructivist tendency of the avant-garde tradition which has followed a destiny separate from that of design. Through techniques acquired from the experiences of the plastic arts, from the object of the popular industrial culture, of the enlargement, of the out of scale, of the "happening," of the recourse to stylistic incoherence, of the collage obtained through the evocation of the magical gesture and regression to childish fable of the UFO group, of the ironic and at the same time radical experiences of Archizoom, or the utopian terrorism of Superstudio, culminating in the cultural organization of these groups in the *Casabella* directed by Mendini and the interesting didactic attempt of the "Global Tools". Then the multiplication of the groups was tied to the imitation of pop discoveries, from the anthropomorphisms inspired by the feminine furniture of Allen Jones, to the soft object such as the "sack" chair of the Paolini group.

In another sense, there were strong counter-influences from Arte Povera and Conceptual Art or the entire reaction against the decorative neo-Oriental superabundance resulting in the total absence of the object.

Design had become the symbol of integrated youth, of the order and of the institution that had to be put in question. But the tumultuous and strongly imaginative linguistic and ideal system which derived from it, remained without an authentic correspondence of political and social transformation, was rapidly transformed into merchandise, hence into a caricature of itself, or better, the institutional world re-absorbed in terms of fashion and merchandise, the authentically transformative tendencies which were mainly founded in the great hopes of 1968. After the great questioning of 1968 and the relative disappointment (no imagination went to power nor did any power fall as a result of that extraordinary impetus), the problem of the neo-avant-garde is concentrated on the aesthetic operation, the temporary, the banal.

From 1972-1976 *Casabella* becomes the official organ of this area and in 1973 also founds the design school: the "Global Tools." Broadly open to influences of neo-avant-garde sisters (Arte Povera, Conceptual Art) this part of the culture of design fragments its own experimentalism with very interesting results, in a series of operations in which the center of the ideal questions seems deliberately abandoned in favor of a strategy of action based above all on the vigor of decorative discoveries, of the contiguousness with the idea of fashion, and thus of temporariness, as a value. The actors in this area, of uncertain and uneasy boundaries, are many, with many exits and entrances.

The tension towards the signification which overcomes the pure manipulation of the object, becomes thus decorative redundance, representation of a liberty which is totally without basis. The infraction of this neo-avant-garde, which displays no ideal tension, returns to the super-aesthetic tradition of D'Annunzio, to arrive at the saddest renunciations: that of trying to construct with one's own design work an international horizon but trying to coincide, by means of the notion of banality, with simple existing as a value, with the opinion of the silent majority, with an anti-institutional indifferentism barely disguised as fashion by some innocuous operation of caricature.

The portrait of ideal disillusionment could not be more complete. But that same ideal disillusionment is not completely absent from that "culture of the factory" that we have seen running parallel and which surveys with mixed sentiments of contempt and admiration the rapid convulsion of high culture.

Between 1965 and 1971 there was an explosion of worker conflict in almost every sector, a conflict which used new and articulated methods of protest: and that was the tangible sign of a series of problems of ideals and identity which go beyond the structural level in which Italy progressively found itself in the seventies. The fall in productivity, the international situation, the growing debts of public industry, the lack of planning, the price increases of primary materials and energy, the growing costs of applied research and the impressive tardiness in that research represent different aspect of this crisis.

On a practical level certain factors such as the increase of the specific importance of the small industry (representing at the end of the seventies almost 25% of national industrial production and benefiting from the transfer of certain types of processing from the large factories), the broadening of the activity of the so-called "underground economy," and finally a new distribution of industrial density in the national territory (from the Venetias to the Marches) with

a loss in the absolute preeminence of the traditional industrial triangle, have all contributed to counterbalance, in a rather weak way, the general industrial crisis.
The handicraft manufacturing sector has assumed, in the economic and industrial context of Italy, a position of importance.
This is manifested by the passage from the limiting role of simply perpetuating traditional crafts to the more contemporary role of serving industry for the specialized supply of parts and components yet at the time retaining autonomous productive and structural configurations.
This explains how in the actual reality of handicrafts one finds the most disparate figures: from the traditional craftsman with his workshop like the carpenter or the goldsmith to that type of worker — autonomous through antonomasia (plumber, electrician, etc.) - who is specialized in "custom" intervention, offers a direct quality of service with potent artisan implications, and finally the veritable craftsman-entrepreneur placed in the contemporary phenomenon of being a secondary supplier to small, medium, and large industry.
Such a particular type of productive decentralization — defined as secondary supplying — interests the numerous independent firms which conduct production-runs sporadically or continuously or entire processing cycles for business clients.
It is, for example, evident in this context the very special position which Italian fashion has assumed in the last twenty years. Between the traditional fields of fashion and design particularly intense processes of relations have developed in Italy in recent years. This is also in merit of the great Italian fashion designers such as Versace, Armani, Ferré, Krizia, and Missoni who have had an extraordinary success and have displayed extraordinary creative capacities in the last twenty years, also as a result of precisely that very special relationship between craftsmanship and industry.
If this extended phenomenon of the complementarity of handicraft and industry underwent its greatest expansion in the years 1972-1973 appearing as a strategy to counteract the economic crisis, today decentralization in general, and secondary supplying in particular, have assumed all of the characteristics of a truly structural strategy which constitutes the most interesting prospect in the handicraft sector.
There are many technical and economic reasons that have induced large-scale businesses to entrust a part of their production processes to outside firms. The most typical case in the secondary supplying of a speciality which occurs when the artisan firm offers particular technical requirements which the large business does not possess and which has an interest in integrating that speciality in its productive cycle. In Italy, this relationship between handicrafts and production is present in almost all the productive sectors and not only in those which are more typically artisan. One can distinguish in this relationship of secondary supplying the "textile-garment" sector, the "lumber-furniture" sector, the "leather and hides" sector, and the mechanical sector.
Beyond this, the fact that in our country production specialities in given fields have been maintained and strengthened, hence developing craft values and skills, explains the productive vitality and reconversion capacity of the sector, which has come about through the introduction of technologies which reflect the specific and original qualities of different artisan groups.
In terms of the industrial project one must remember how much importance craftsmen have who participate with the production of prototypes, models and tools to the important phase of technological research which has as its goal the design and expressive definition of the product.
The principal characteristics of design in the seventies were above all the constitution of a double line (in some cases of a double consciousness deriving from the same personality) of design activity: on one side we find design linked to the world of industrial production (and as a novelty, linked also with large industry) which performs according to a decided leap toward the specialization and the sophistication of methods and controls.
Upon this link weigh, even in the most professional examples, both the doubt of the authentic social necessity of the designer's work as well as the fall of an authentic ideal tension beyond that of his own personal creativity. On the other side, we find the world of poetic license, of the lucid activity which monitors the relation with the visual arts, fashion, and rapid changes of social taste.
Often the same group of designers work in the two fields which to some degree compensate each other. Sometimes the phenomenon of an inversion

of tasks is verified where the production of consumer goods tends, for reasons of tooling costs, towards a requirement of product durability which inhibits the same designers' impetus towards innovation and renewal.
It is important to reveal that the culture of the industrial product separates almost totally after 1970 from that of architecture in technical discussions. The architectural culture seems more interested in comparing its own factory culture with that of the designer.
One must note that there have been occasional reasons (in the seventies clothing and furniture realize a new season of intense expansion) but on the whole the phenomenon involves many other areas of production in a longlasting way.

Italian design thus finds itself partially in a situation which must be considered as a crisis, precisely because of its specific characteristics. It is not a crisis of creativity nor is it a crisis of the capacities of the production units, but rather a crisis which derives from a subjectivization of ideals so strong as to dispense any common sense of social progress. And in a design field as in Italy which is capable of a notable idealistic as well as aesthetic sensibility it counts very much.
That from such a fragmentation someone tries to find evidence of overall progress does not alter the difficulties against which one tries to restore to the modern material culture that design represents, a civil statute and significance.

1

1. *Frisbi*, 1978.

2. Drawings for objects designed between
1945 and 1984.

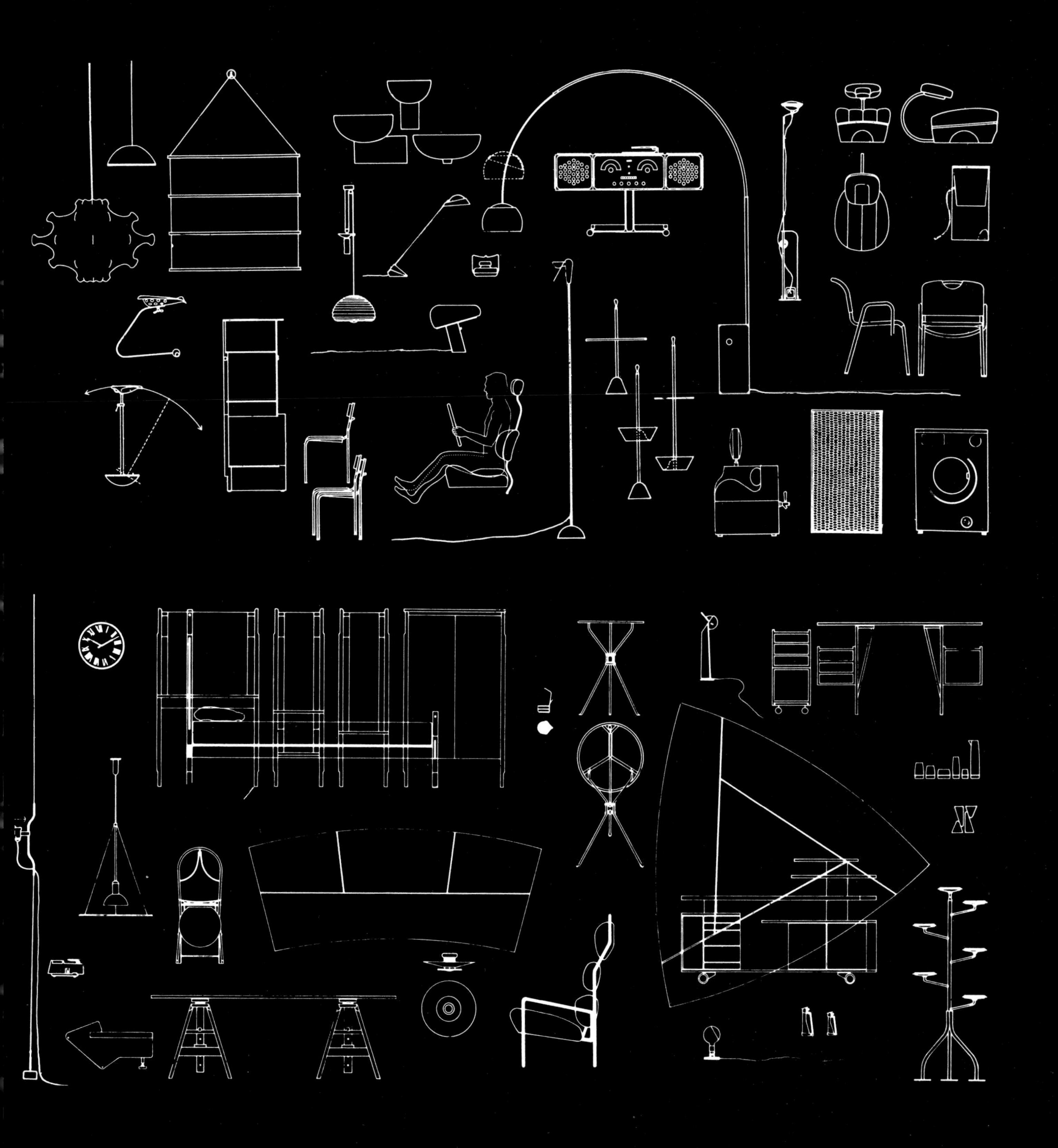

Paolo Deganello

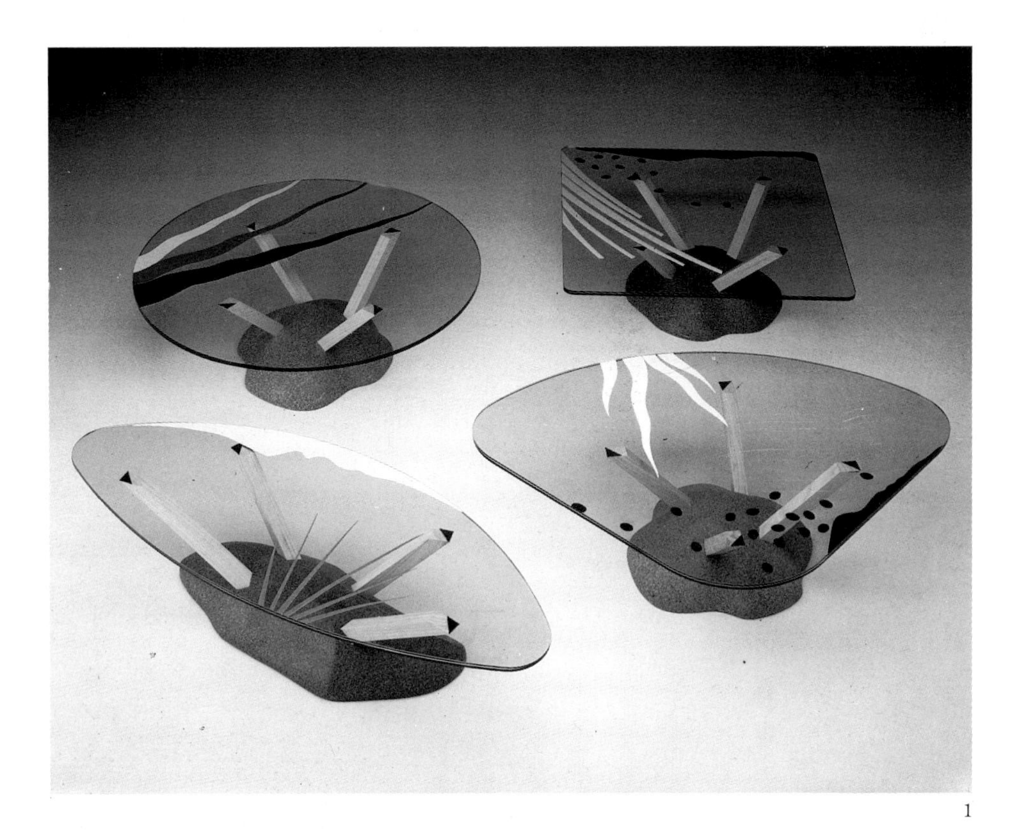

1

2

1. *Artifici*, 1985.

2. *Palomar*, 1984.

3. *Common House*, 1983.

3

Michele De Lucchi

1. *Cadetto*, 1984.

2. *Cyclos*, 1983.

1

2

1. *Clark Scheid PV 60.*

PV 60
PV60

Herbert Lindinger

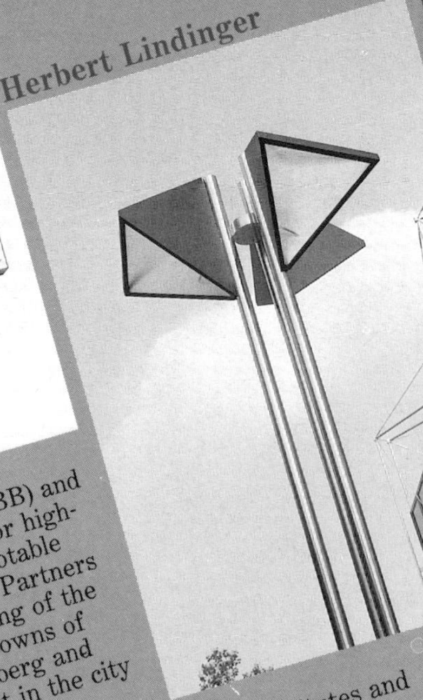

Lindinger & Partners Hannover
Town planning is becoming more and more a question of functional and aesthetic qualities of urban traffic systems, as well as its effect on streets and squares.
The group of designers, Lindinger & Partners Hannover, specialize in this type of urban design. They took part in the design of Hamburg's underground network, as well those of Stuttgart and Hanover and are currently involved in the design of the new Berlin underground system.
The conception of the design for the Standard City Bus used by all important transport manufacturers until 1984 was proposed by Lindinger & Partners.
You often find Lindinger & Partners projects in major German cities, such as underground stations, busstops, waiting rooms in glass and steel, information points, pictographs and corporate designs of complete town traffic networks including everything from transport to uniforms. As well as these activities Lindinger & Partners also design helicopters (MBB) and cars (VW) and concepts for high-speed trains. The most notable projects by Lindinger & Partners have been the redesigning of the largest squares in the towns of Darmstadt and Heidelberg and the pedestrian precinct in the city of Hanover.
Professor Herbert Lindinger, founder and senior member of the group, born in Austria in 1933 studied at Ulm's graphic high school, where he taught from 1962. Following this he became guest professor in USA and India. He is now teaching industrial design at Hanover University, a post he has held since 1970.
Professor Lindinger belongs to the board of directors of the German Design Council. From 1971 to 1976 he was the president of the German Designers' association and in that capacity was invited to be a member of the panel of jurors for numerous design institutes and competitions.
The works of Lindinger & Partners have been awarded the Berliner Kunstpreis, the Gold Medal of Biennial International Design, the Silver Medal, the Triennial of Milan, as well as many national awards for urban planning graphics and design.

121 St.Pauli Spielbudenplatz

Street Furniture
Lampposts and fittings for waiting rooms designed by Lindinger & Partners during the work on Darmstadt's Luisenplatz (Lindinger, Boss, Mitscherlich, 1978).

Standard City Bus
Prototype for the German standard city bus commissioned by the German minister for Science and Technology, design Lindinger & Partners (Lindinger, Medugorac, Kusserow, 1975-77).

Stuttgart Underground
Design Lindinger & Partners (Lindinger, Kusserow, Staubach, Weinert, 1979-1984).
Contractor: MAN/DUWAG
Stuttgart city traffic network.

Hi-Fi System
H. Lindinger and Hans Gugelot Ulm 1958, for Braun AG Frankfurt.
Since 1962 Braun has been manufacturing and varying the system.

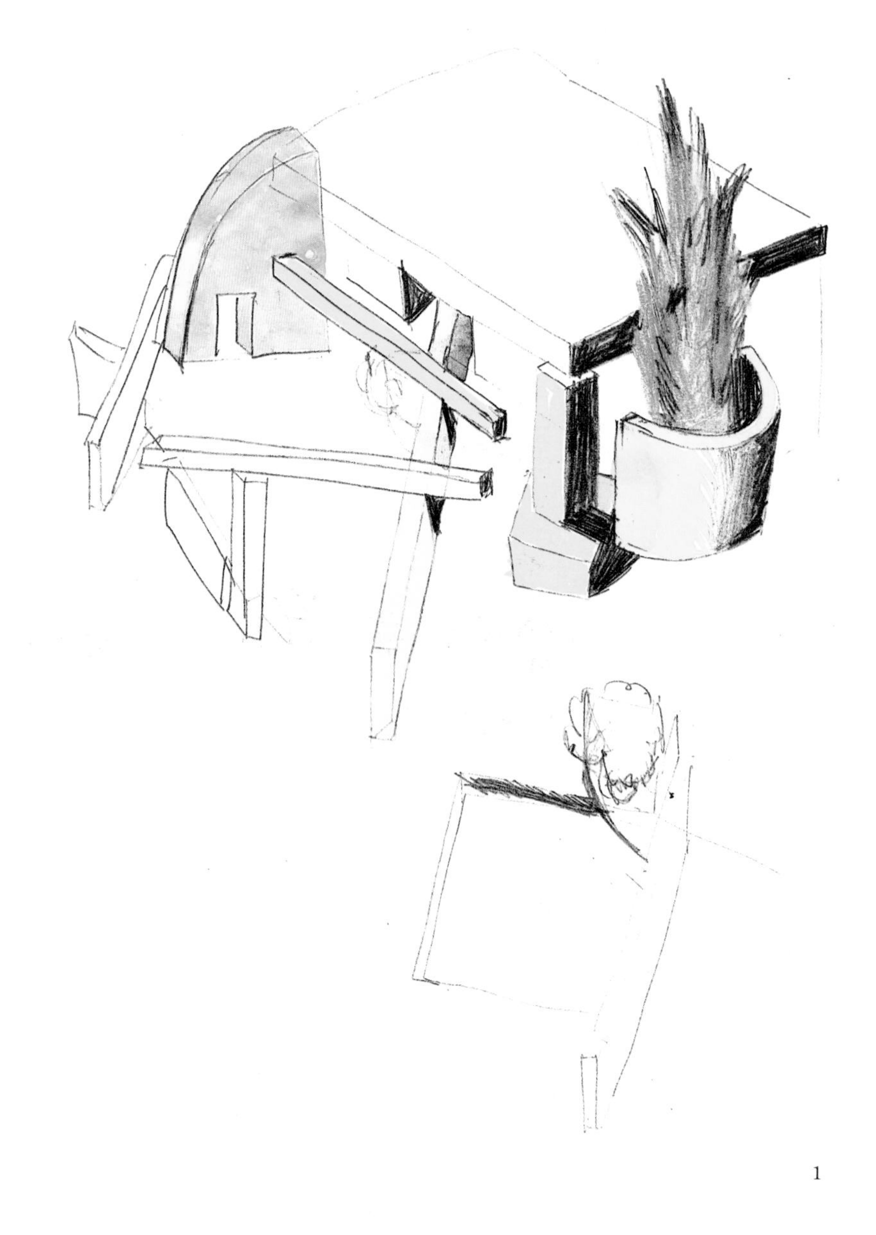

1

1. Progetto (Project), 1980.

2. Progetto (Project), 1984

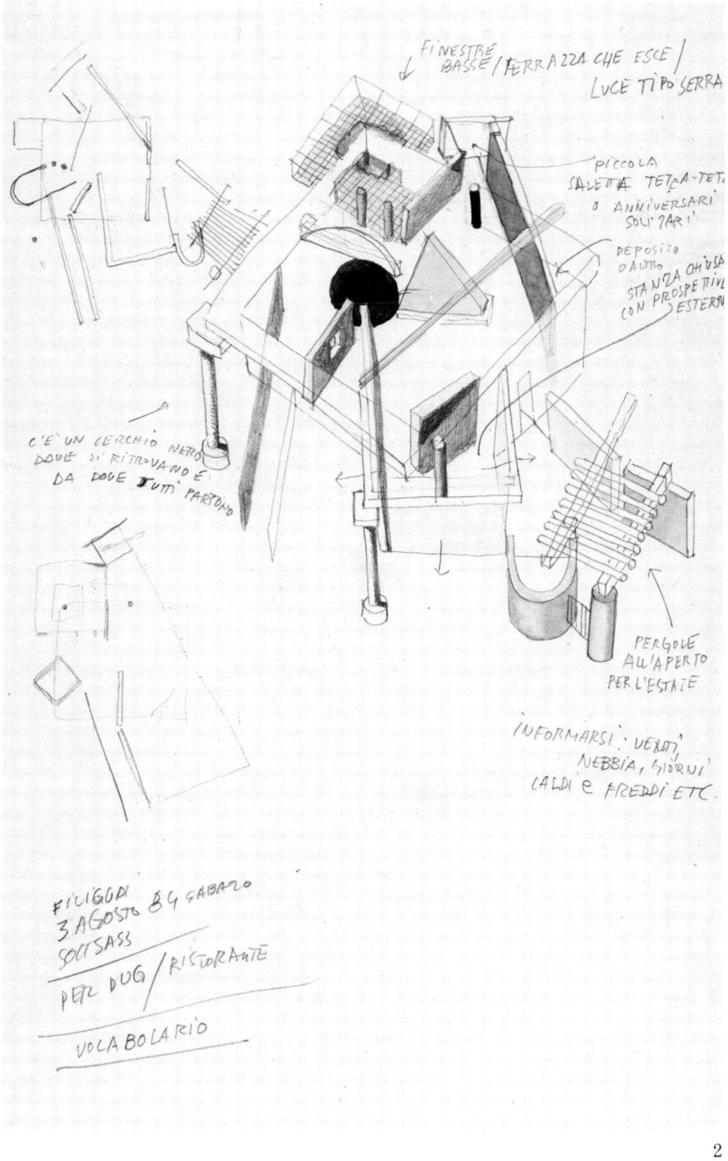

FINESTRE BASSE / TERRAZZA CHE ESCE / LUCE TIPO SERRA

PICCOLA SALETTA TETE-A-TETE O ANNIVERSARI SOLITARI

DEPOSITO O ALTRO

STANZA CHIUSA CON PROSPETTIVE ESTERNE

C'È UN CERCHIO NERO DOVE SI RITROVANO E DA DOVE TUTTI PARTONO

PERGOLE ALL'APERTO PER L'ESTATE

INFORMARSI: VENTI, NEBBIA, GIORNI CALDI E FREDDI ETC.

FILICUDI
3 AGOSTO 84 SABATO
SOTTSASS

PER DUG / RISTORANTE

VOCABOLARIO

2

Dieter Rams

1

1. *Coffee-machine*, 1984.

2. *Atelier*, 1980.

2

Fashion & Mode

Fashion World

Nicoletta and Andrea Branzi

When we speak of fashion in Italy, we are defining a highly creative macroscopic phenomenon, Italian style, in the economic sector. But actually, it is not so easy to pinpoint the details, causes, background of such an overwhelming success story. On the one hand, we might look to entrepreneurial inventions and desk decisions: Milan became one of the fashion capitals of the world, and the label saying Made in Italy became a powerful standard.
Milan, however, proved to be a fertile ground for the growth of other activities as well: photography, printing, graphics, advertising. We may therefore ask whether the fashion story was a natural phenomenon rather than a deliberate choice — an array of coincidences that have made this city a magic center of the fashion industry.
Milan has also become a capital of design, spectacle, and fashion journalism. During the past few years, it has been the setting for a whirlwind of meetings, discussions, articles, publications and shows that have brought out the relations between fashion and the areas around it, next to it, parallel or overlapping. Other disciplines, more noble ones, seemed to have given fashion an official position among the visual arts and the mass media.
There was some danger that the fashion world, which had surged up so unexpectedly, might be tempted to develop the technologies and communication methods characteristic of other areas.
However, fashion was and remains a productive phenomenon based on its own intrinsic culture and completely independent of all other areas. The fashion designer, as he is understood today, is his own producer. He combines roles that, in other industrial activities, are performed by several different people. This fact alone sharply distinguishes the fashion industry from other sectors, but it does not suffice to define the complexity of this difference or to explain what Italian fashion represents with respect to fashion industries in other countries.
Interestingly enough, from the first official appearance of Italian ready-to-wears at the Sala Bianca of the Palazzo Pitti, Florence, in 1951, to the Milanese fashion parades of today, Italian designers have gone through convulsions, transitions, and periods of calm and settlement. Ultimately, they have succeeded in producing their complex image of a "national" style.
At the outset, they still revealed the influences of their great French "fathers." But as the years went by, what looked like real or psychological subjugation was transformed into a gradual autonomy that nevertheless maintains close ties and contacts with fashion developments outside of Italy.
It would be a mistake for the designer to lock himself up in his own image and ignore outside experiences, if only because exchanges and communications among various cultures have broadened so greatly as practically to wipe out geographic borders.
The standard-bearer of this attitude of cultural exchange by means of the fashion world has been Elio Fiorucci, who slaughtered a lot of sacred cows during the seventies. He unceasingly brought home the meaning of "communicating by means of clothing." During the sixties, Italy looked to London, the concentrated source of the new youth culture. From there, we imported skirts, boots, jackets, graphics, that could help our people find a more coherent identification in their behavior and in their tastes in music, spectacle, and entertainment. Fiorucci didn't care whether his style was Italian or foreign, because the changes determining the new modes of behavior were not to be viewed purely as characteristics of a specific

Genius Group, *Diesel*, 1984.

Genius Group, *Goldie Italia*, 1984.

geographic area. The important thing was to give people the means, i. e. clothing, allowing them to feel that they were in the thick of a new lifestyle. Outside the Fiorucci front, there were other designers who achieved success during that same period. Today, they are considered the leaders of the Made-in-Italy fashions: Armani, Versace, Krizia, Lagerfeld, Ferré, Fendi, Missoni. They came from different backgrounds, with different experiences and training, but they assumed leading roles in the fashion sector because of their sound professionalism and their solid faith in their own ideas. This professionalism was evident in their choices of textiles and the perfect balance between newness and the security of tradition in their collections. It was also evident in their policy of an image accompanied by efficient marketing strategies — an image that has become the best-known and most powerful external symbol of our fashion industry.

And yet, even these factors do not fully explain the phenomenon known as Italian Style.

Not everyone can buy Armani's exclusives, just as not every Frenchman or Frenchwoman can buy those of Yves Saint-Laurent. Yet one of the most obvious facts of current Italian fashions is that when we walk the streets of Italian cities, towns, or villages, we can see that the people are dressed better than in other countries — including those with long traditions of fashion. This Italian situation is easily explained. Aside from the big names, there are many small and medium-sized clothing firms with a level of quality far above that of similar enterprises in other countries. Even the smallest, family-run business can quickly react to the latest fashion trends. It always grasps the changing taste of its customers, and it can even put its own stamp on its production.

This phenomenon goes beyond the canonic area of Milan. Just think of the hosiery factories in Carpi, the Venetian clothing-makers concentrated in Treviso, where two of the most important and interesting fashion firms have developed: Benetton and the Genius Group, with their numerous brands.

Another very exciting phenomenon at this moment is the activity of the yarn producers. Here, Prato and a huge number of daring and enthusiastic companies are outdoing one another in their efforts to present new and revolutionary yarns. The development within the hosiery sector has led to an ever more pressing demand for yarns with

characteristic techniques and particular aesthetics. During the past few years, the renaissance has taken place exclusively in style (cutting and tailoring), aside from the use of colors, naturally. But today, designers tend to re-evalutate the feel, the consistency, the quality of the textile from which they might make clothes in the simplest of styles.
Thus, on the whole, the Italian garment industry is in good health, and we can only hope that it will remain so for another thousand years. However, this state of fitness does not leave much elbowroom for a younger generation of designers. The situation is like that of an upside-down iceberg: the tip is submerged under an enormous mass of ice, which, understandably, cannot submit to the natural laws.
During the past few seasons, we have witnessed the unexpected success of such young Japanese designers as Rei Kawacubo, such British ones as Vivienne Westwood, and such French ones as Jean-Paul Gaultier. These former *enfants terribles* have become major figures, paving the way for new conceptions of clothing.
In Tokyo, Yoshiki Hishinuma, a young designer, is sponsored by a private company, which allows him to dedicate himself to "pure research," with no concerns about or involvements in marketing and merchandising.
In Milan, a similar case would be hard to find. Any attempts at non-commercial activities are not regarded as being part of the fashion world per se. Rather, they are seen as personal and self-indulgent extravagances. For years now, this has been the attitude toward the work done by Cinzia Ruggeri. Her garments are made of a textile smeared with liquid crystals that changes color when it touches the skin. She has also produced ziggurat sculpture clothing, as well as embroideries and inlays in post-modern style.
We may regard as exceptional the success achieved by Franco Moschino, who attended the Academy of Brera and also studied with major foreign and Italian designers. His performance at the Galleria Vinciana, Milan, for the presentation of his Mister Luna Collection was more than just a break with the traditional structures of classical fashion shows. It gave Moschino a chance to show the possibilities of expressing oneself beyond the traditional canons and taking control of the realization of the image, the music, and the environment in which a designer's products are presented.

Shop Zeus in Milan.

Altogether, this is a new approach to be found among other young designers as well. They place the garment design at the center of a more complex activity, which is no longer that of the famous designer who also sponsors perfumes, furnishings, notebooks and pencils. Instead, we find a certain attitude towards a particular type of eclecticism. The stronghold of the "new stylism" is the Ticinese Quarter, and one of the chief centers is Zeus, a store that sells fashions, art, and design, and sports such names as Gianfranco Spada, Mizio Turchet, Antonio Donato, Cinzia Tomachiello, Lorenzo Dossol, and Titti Urt. These and others , such as Stefano Baccari, are serene, eclectic, and very self-assured; they have a whole new concept

C. Ruggeri, *Ziggurat*, Winter 1984-85.

C. Ruggeri, *Ragnatela*, Summer 1985.

of what the designer's profession can be. They are not so taken with the idea of becoming a famous designer who puts out masses of collections. Rather, they are determined to plan and realize, from time to time, certain objects, some music, or a video that contain the best and most immediate possibilities for their self-expression. This does not mean giving free rein to creativity for its own sake, *l'art pour l'art*; for these younger people have also been seeking new technologies and materials, as well as new approaches to the practical demands of the garment industry.
This type of problem is one of the focal points in the fashion course given at the Domus Academy, Milan, coordinated by Gianfranco Ferré and Vern Lambert. We note a further sign of a trend toward deepening and developing fashion with the appropriate instruments.
We could say that while the Italian fashion world confirmed its successes during the first half of the eighties, the current assumptions will lead to the realization of new possibilities during the second half of the decade. Even though, for several seasons now, there has been talk of a coexistence of so many diverse styles, the next few years will bring new approaches to clothing design. The tip of the upside-down iceberg can resurface without forcing the whole mass to submerge.

Cultural and Artistic Development in West Germany from the Sixties to the Eighties

Bazon Brock

Were we really alive? Yesterday — a thousand years ago. Op, Pop, and Hopp in the habitat of the sixties.

The Throwaway Plan on Credit

Hopp typifies our partly roguish, partly martial participation in the market wars of the sixties. "Ex und hopp" was the German slogan for throwing away empty bottles. Hopp had lived in the twenties as "hoppla," Jenny's (Lotte Lenja) expression in Brecht's *Threepenny Opera*, for offing the heads of the decadent smart set, drunk on its own decline. The children of the ruling classes used to chant "hoppe, hoppe Reiter" riding pony on Daddy's knee — thus learning at a tender age to savor the cries of the falling.

Then Hopp, the later hero of the throwaway culture, was trained for a new role. Matter of factly and mostly with bored indifference, he learned to accept "Ex" as the rule of the day, following in the footsteps of generations of university students who eagerly complied with the order to slug it down: "Ex!" Only now it was blood, not beer. Now it was the earth and the sea chugging down the guzzlers' vital liquor. "Ex!" And then came the new command, on smiling lips, "Ex und hopp," urging consumers to do their duty: suck, munch and throw away. Full speed ahead, out of ship's bellies and factory waste lines and into the rivers. But pissing in the bath water or, heaven forbid, in a public swimming pool was a social abomination.

Certain words... were not to be touched even with a ten-foot pole: they were filthy. Others only became polluted by human touch, like "Vaterland" and "Heimat" (fatherland and homeland). Ex and hopp.

I used to hand out refugee identity cards to West Germans so they might note in time that their "Heimat" was being taken away from them (though with different methods) just as it had been taken from us, the refugees from the East. The poker game with property was up. No one could stay in the bidding, not even the rich, who bought on credit and paid no taxes (there were enough low wage tax payers to fill the till). Ex and hopp: evictions, foreclosures, unhonored insurance claims — powerlessness. Ex and hopp. But, milk to the rescue: a hearty little chug of the stuff will fix up your black lung, your lead poisoning and, with a flick of the wrist, the one-way bottle lands in the gutter on top of some torn paperbacks.

Throwaway books! Ten years earlier they'd been marketed as an educational resource for the lower classes. But now at long last the poor had also finally attained the appointments of true culture: books for display, not for reading. After all, who would show off with "Ex"-books, all scrawny and yellowed, and tattered?

Everything half-eaten, not quite pleasing, slightly scratched or dented went straight into the garbage can. Throw it away! This was the greatest change in the cultural behavior of the German people in the sixties. While the hits of the fifties had, understandably, still been shirts made of new synthetic materials, indestructible even by tanks (as demonstrated in the news-reels), the up-to-date shirt for the sixties was the one guaranteed to be wearable only once. Paper, by the way, is not only a tolerant material, as they say, but also has the advantage of being more easily disposable than any other substance. Imagine newspapers of a material that's difficult to destroy: a nightmare.

The sixties were the memorable years when industrial progress justified the citizen's duty to consume. The goods were not supposed to last long; if they did, their owners or users would for years to come have to do without the new and improved products introduced in the meantime.

But there were other, more convincing arguments Hopp could campaign for. Imagine the projected (exponentially expanding) continuation of mass

production for several decades. The world would soon be so filled with goods that the question of where to put all the stuff couldn't even be raised anymore, because any place one wanted to put it would already be filled up.
Such projections didn't use to be frightening. On the one hand, people used to live in a society of shortage. And on the other, despite a hundred years of disarmament conferences and "down with weapons" slogans, one could firmly rely on the fact that at regular intervals and according to need, wars would be staged which would destroy everything one wanted to get rid of that could have prevented people from continuing as before. Of course, violent and destructive wars were fought in other parts of the world in the sixties. Wouldn't it have been profitable, as I suggested at the time, for us to drop our surplus food and consumer goods from airplanes onto the Vietcong, say?
No, it's against the rules: strictly prohibited. "Don't throw anything out the train window," let alone from airplanes! Besides, that would not have been an act of war, but just "throwing away" things. War means using objects to destroy other objects. That is sacrifice! Peace means using objects by throwing them away. That is freedom! Woe to those who, for example, want to preserve old buildings. That is harmful to society, hostile to liberty, and unsanitary. Thus consumption becomes war, with the sacrificial duty to clear and destroy, make room. *Volk ohne Raum (A People without Lebensraum* — a novel by Hans Grimm; its title became a Nazi slogan) were now consumers with no more room to put anything. No one knew what to do. Not even Hitler's boys from the General Staff, who had made a seamless transition to the Corporate Staff and were now busy planning market strategy. They had their orgasms of success in the sixties, but planned obsolescence was all they could come up with now. I had more ideas. For instance, I suggested training in throwaway exercises in back of the Hotel Kempinsky in West Berlin — but as practice in not wanting to own things. My strategy was affirmative: you can only beat the enemy with his own weapons. The only way to fight the law against abortion is by mass self-denunciation; a sweet tooth can only be remedied by stuffing yourself with chocolates till you puke; bad working conditions can only be improved by sticking strictly to the rules and regulations.

Eulenspiegel, Nietzsche, and Schweijk have always been misunderstood. Pop artists, Happening instigators, and agit-prop advocates understood this all too well, but remained the "court jesters of capitalism, clowns, compliant tools in the hands of the class enemy." Meanwhile, the gentlemen from the Left raked in one cultural prize after the other from these very same capitalists. They practiced throwaway gestures of indifference after bagging the bread, these arrogant *mafiosi* of underground progress through history.
But there was another slogan-justification of the high cultural value which throwaway behavior attained in the sixties. The throwaway habit was immunization not only against raking in but also against keeping. In the fifties, Germans still held onto things in an old-fashioned sort of way, particularly things that had been held in high and holy esteem during the Thousand Year Reich of National Socialism. "You musn't throw anything away," said old auntie, formerly a member of the BDM (*Bund deutscher Mädchen* - Nazi organization for girls), who was now busy applying her "Untermensch" knowledge to the protection of the

Body Builder.

State against communists. Not only would it have been inhumane to do without the collaboration of Globke's generation (Hans Globke was Secretary of State under Adenauer; from 1933 to 1945, in the Nazi Ministry of the Interior, elaborated the National-Socialist racial laws) especially as they had all only been doing their duty; no, above all, it would have been a waste of resources.
Well, in the sixties one could little by little afford both more doing without and waste. Occasionally someone even dared to throw away old notions of German unity, the German Reich, of Bismarck as the Anointed of the Lord and Hitler, as the Elect. There was nothing left to be repaired, and a new unity would in any case be cheaper and better than the old one. This too, was a liberating tactic of the market economy: buying a new object must be cheaper than repairing an old one, or people won't buy. After all, even surgeons were no longer snipping and mending a bit here and there: no, total hysterectomy, total lobotomy. Yes, even ideologies, theories, doctrines of salvation and proofs of truth had to go. There could be no winner in the dispute between positivism and the dialectics of enlightenment. As Max Planck had already observed, true scientists can't be convinced by better arguments to give up their own theories. The old nonsense only ceases and makes way for the new because scientists die and take their truths with them to their graves. In the sixties established scientists declared their readiness for the first time to give up their convictions for duty's sake. Obedience to progress required increased efforts to come up with something new, not just new weapons all the time but new ways of making more money, too. Actually only military research guaranteed true freedom of science: spare money was being handed out unbureaucratically and, unconventionally, with no strings attached. During market wars, consumer research might also increase profits, even double them if the criticism of this concept were sold at the same time, packaged as the "aesthetics of consumer goods." Then the customer knows that the scientists and scholars really think of everything, and its opposite. Thus the formula — people really have forgotten Professor Ludwig Erhard was a scientist — for a completely new conception of credit was created. After all, the consumer's overriding duty to throw away had to be financed somehow. People who have to earn money don't have to be told not to throw it out the window. But those who have credit love to buy all the stuff that deserves to be thrown out fast anyway. "Fear of poverty eats the heart" (allusion to R.W. Fassbinder's film *Angst fressen Seele auf, Fear eats the heart*), credit only eats the future and there was enough of that. You could make the future any way you wanted. The future could be created in any size, shape or fashion. Future was overtly advertised in department stores, a hot sales item for the masses' new purchasing power, a revolutionary invention of the sixties: "Come and visit our credit office. Reasonable installment terms for everyone. No security required. Statement of earnings sufficient." The financing costs were borne by the raw material producers in the Third World, see! And indeed, we were not ungrateful: on every conceivable occasion we were asked to remember the poor of the Third World. "Three cheers for the poor!" And after that, the twist. And the rustling of golden tassels, a suggestion by Beatle Paul to his frenzied female fans.

Marlene Dietrich.

Op and Pop — On the Body and in the Pad
Sex and Hopp — which came first, the contraceptive pill or the miniskirt? "She's throwing herself away," they said in imperial-republican times of loose lower-middle-class girls; in Hitler's day this was reserved for Jewish girls. "Ich bin am Ort das grösste Schwein und lass mich nur mit Juden ein" (I am the biggest swine in town and only mix with Jews) was jeered by the snubbed customers. They had nothing against an

amorous adventure — but this racial pollution!
All this changed with the pill. If you didn't live through the transition from the terror of "what-if" to the pleasant irresponsibility of "as you like it," you can't begin to imagine what the introduction of the pill meant. Today's enemies of the pill can't imagine it either, because at the time there was absolutely no possibility for abortion, except the illegal one which made you a criminal. Not to mention the fact that the pill brought about a fundamental change in sexual practices and pleasures. The only limitation on these pleasures was the pointedly expressed opinion that sexual liberality would quickly blunt the senses. Only heightened stimulation could remedy this: i.e., the total exposure of the legs in the miniskirt. The ups and downs of hemlines have always been regarded and evaluated in relation to the changes of morals and income, of aggressive potentials and of ideas about physical and mental hygiene. But it had always been the ruling classes that set the trends in these matters. Mary Quant was the first to prevail with lower class ideas of fashion against the much more powerful middle class, and even against the upper classes of the Western world, who in all other regards were still aristocratically decked out and stand-offish.
The English sales girl from the industrial suburbs as the Queen of fashion! The only thing that made this possible was that the miniskirt finally sanctioned everybody's ideas about fashion, the gentlemen's as well as the prole's, i.e., more attractiveness, that is to say, female seductiveness. Ever since grandfather's day, that little naked, fleshy zone of a handsbreadth between stockings and panties — neatly bridged by the legendary garter strap following the introduction of the girdle — has exercised the greatest seductive power. This strap apparatus, though introduced some seventy years earlier as health-reform underwear, restrained just that freedom of movement which the miniskirt was designed to liberate. Moreover, the unobstructed view of front and back yard to which the miniskirt gave permanent access was irritating. Without at least a hint of veiling, no unveiling effect! Hence, the invention of the panty hose, a typically drawing-board concoction of the hosiers' guild actually, but which sold like hot cakes. This seemed to be the end of the girdle — but also, sadly, of that little seductive zone at the top of the thighs, as well. But this loss could perhaps be offset by interestingly designed peekaboo panties to be worn on top of the panty hose (a new source of profits, too). This turned out to be a bit problematic, however — otherwise we wouldn't have had those endless discussions about whether one should throw all hygienic and medical advice to the winds, and considerations of comfort, too, and wear the panty hose under the panty or rather, etc...
These highly momentous questions were not only discussed in women's magazines. I myself was asked for a contribution to the underwear discussion for the feature section of the weekly *Die Zeit*. The first clubs against the abolition of the garter strap were also founded at this time, and today even young men, who for reasons of age cannot possibly have a merely nostalgic attachment to the straps of yore, are joining this opposition movement. A Euro-anthropological constant, perhaps, on which the Order of the Garter as well as the garter as pledge of love were long ago founded? The question of whether the mini created the pill or the pill the mini must thus be suspended. In any event, the new panty hose were much less titillating, even disillusioning — a

Space-age clothes.

loss that could not be ameliorated by transferring the eye-catching panty from the tennis court to the office.
Constantly discussed issues surrounding this problem in the sixties included "the pill and cancer, the pill for men, the pill and partner-swapping, the pill and professional prostitution, the pill and the legalization of pornography." But before it could come to that, before the socially hygienic function of pornography was generally accepted and legalized à la Scandinavian model, *Playboy*'s playmate of the month was succeeding in checking energies that otherwise might perhaps have led to criminal acts. Slowly, very slowly the owners of newsstands dared to display the magazines in question ever more prominently in hopes of increasing their turnover.
Even *Playboy* largely accepted the notion that naked women are only really attractive when transformed by the artist's hand. Vargas, who had an exclusive contract with *Playboy*, was of course an excellent draftsman and had a corresponding influence on a number of pop artists.
The first nude photographers practiced their artistic freedom altogether in the tradition of nude painting. But with the advent of cheap color films and cameras, artists lost their monopoly on representing the naked body. Millions of amateur photographers began showing each other and their lovers what the lens had sharply taken in. Artists were no longer needed. First of all, it was no longer necessary to constantly justify erotic images by reference to their artistic content. And secondly, the lens allowed panoramic and intimate views of the body that are inaccessible even to the most brilliant artist's eye. But this is a different subject. The artists were able to salvage some of their privileges only by turning their skill to comic strips, more or less soft pornocomics, of course. In the mid-sixties, this genre celebrated its first climax with Guy Paellert's and Pierre Bartier's *The Adventures of Jodelle*. Stark naked and with everything showing, this timeless specimen of the French big-city girl's fights against would-be usurpers of women's power and the overbearing weapons of virility. Like the Asterix comics that were taking Europe by storm at the same time, Jodelle's adventures also played on an overly explicit analogy between the Roman and the American craving for world power.
Jodelle appeared in the movies as Barbarella, successfully played by Jane Fonda, who later became one of America's most famous opponents of the Vietnam War. Barbarella's costumes looked like they were donated by the synthetics industry for advertising purposes: naked bosom and behind, but all neatly framed in a transparent foil under which Miss Fonda didn't seem to perspire even under the duress of the most vehement exertions. Synthetic outfits, plastic sculptures on living stands! Expressions of germ-free sterility, like sex in the operating room? Or a contemporary form of the veil Lukas Cranach breathed onto his nudes? The transparent umbrella, at least, was acceptable because it made sense: fewer collisions on sidewalks. However, a really philosophical penetration of the new synthetics was first achieved by Rudi Gernreich, the Parisian from Vienna. He created the NOBRA, the non-brassiere.
He made sense of the dialectics of concealment and provocation — the game of transparency and veiling — with his brassiere, that indeed is one according to its function but does not look like one. Gernreich's bra is extremely thin and nearly invisible because of its transparency. It still molds, but only as a support for the natural forms of the breast. From grandmother's solid bra to its negation, the topless — propagated by many representatives of women's lib who regarded the bra as a straight-jacket concocted by men — Gernreich developed the negation of the negation with his NOBRA: bra, but still nude. Thesis: the bra is necessary for aesthetic and medical reasons. Antithesis: the bra is to be rejected because it contributes significantly to the sexual objectification of women. Synthesis: the NOBRA supports the natural forms and offers almost no resistance to an eye-catching view and the movements of the breast. Naturally this did not remain the only recourse to the young Marx in the sixties.
It is still uncertain today whether Gernreich is also to be credited with the invention of the so-called "body-stocking," a bra, so to speak, for the whole body, or a stocking from head to toe. What is certain, though, is that it was no success.
Paco Rabanne and Courrèges attempted an altogether different kind of mediation between nudity and clothes; that is to say, they tried to find new answers to the question of how to dress in order to be undressed. The tectonic solution of constructing dresses from thin metal plates, like houses whose doors and windows can be easily

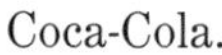
Coca-Cola.

opened and closed, was not exactly convincing. Nor did the many slits and openings produce particularly seductive results except when the lady stood bending forward or walked in a bowed position, which, after all, is not possible for any length of time. At any rate, Courrèges' and Rabanne's designs transformed the thus attired ladies into figures of the future, straight out of science fiction: the plain geometric forms and the machine-like austerity of their designs lent the women an air of distantness that could be read as indifference to attacks of male desire. The sight of Courrèges-women tended to remind many men of turning machines on and off. In any case: even these avant-garde garments would have to be comparatively inexpensive and — unfortunately — all too quickly thrown away. Dior's successors made an heroic attempt to prevent the world's fashion center, Paris, from being divided into multiple centers: Tokyo, London, New York, Florence, Milan, Rome, Berlin. After heated struggle, the Parisian masters brought themselves to sell their haute-couture designs to the ready-to-wear manufacturers for mass consumption. According to the laws of probability, the million-fold copies of the exclusive model dresses that were distributed all over the world would hardly ever cross paths. The fear of such encounters is really the only reason for buying haute-couture dresses since it has become practicable to copy almost any cut and style for mass production. The boutiques chose a middle path between department store and haute-couture, and quickly became the fastest-expanding branch of the ready-to-wear business.

Because of its extravagance the fashion of the sixties was predestined to become a very controversial topic for critics of consumption and culture. Fashion remains scandal-prone as it is absolutely unpredictable; it makes no difference whether one relies on intuitive predictions by consumer experts or on the most sophisticated scientific methods. The actual development of the mostly short-lived trends remains a complete mystery, and thus a thorn in the capitalist's eye — even millions spent for advertising can't promote a desired fashion — and a thorn in the eyes of critics of capitalism as well (obviously money and market power are not unlimited; the system's vitality derives from particularities of social behavior which can't simply be put aside as stupidity or brainwashing). The emancipatory potential of fashion and mass consumption is much greater than the not entirely unjustified fear that the fetishism of goods might reduce the individual and also the masses to the level of domesticated pets of capitalism. In any case, this was one of the most important themes of the cultural and socio-political discussions of the time.

If the defenders of the emancipatory effect of mass consumption were right, it was hard to see how the capitalists would be able to succeed in defending their hegemony with wars like the one in Vietnam. Were the capitalists afraid of the consequences of their own system? Mass consumption without freedom of choice is inconceivable — and freedom of choice is at least a freedom that encourages a claim to higher freedoms. Did freedom, which seemed to have become the property of the capitalists, perhaps defeat its own masters? Was the Vietnam War perhaps a war of liberation on both sides?

But there were very few who didn't believe the United States could win the war if it just slugged the hell out of Vietnam and disregarded humanitarian self-restraint. I, for instance, believed the US could win because it refrained from granting the Vietcong the same fighting conditions it had set up for itself. My suggestion of giving the Vietcong the same weapons the Americans used could only be considered nonsensical interference in the tough business of power by silly artists — a typical pop-maneuver, a happening hullabaloo. Of the scientists, politicians and journalists who seriously tried to illuminate the trends of the time, hardly a one understood that there was method in this hullabaloo. Nor could they get through their heads why Pop, Happening, and Fluxus artists seemed so determined to imitate in museum settings what was happening anyway and everywhere, in the cities and living rooms of the Western world, on television and in magazines, visible to everybody and for no particular reason — unless perhaps for reasons of entertainment and advertisement, which just seemed to be another form of entertainment. At best, they understood that the artists were strangely fascinated with trivial myths — that is to say, the discovery of new myths in the daily life of mass consumption and in the world of the media. The children of the hamburger-and-Coca-Cola generation obviously felt the need to see their lives elevated in a few fragments of lyricism and half-ironical stereotypes, at least. At first they just went to the movies together to get some encouragement from Wild West heroes and Red Injuns. Then they tried living together and behaving and dressing alike, or similarly unalike. The children of flower power and communes, the hippies and freaks, the city-roamers and joggers, they all became trendsetting stars of the gossip columns, thanks to the mythification of their lives. They acted like characters in an age-old myth whose narrator couldn't begin the tale because he wasn't supposed to exist yet, or any more. A lovely mishmash, a polychrome picture of continuous folkloristic performances.

The music of the Beatles also had more emancipatory power than the organizers of teen festivals could wish. Long hair as a symbol of resistance was a legend in Biblical times already. But above all, long hair levels the differences between the sexes, as far as they can be observed from the outside, that is. In particular, unisex styles were a problem for the police who, after all, couldn't completely repress their chivalrous instincts towards women. Some male demonstrators, for instance, masked their sex to take advantage of the policemen's inhibitions, which they weren't entitled to as males of the species. But all this changed in 1968. I.e., everything remained pretty much as it had always been. Before the development of the Pop program, that is. Now this program was very effective, but little understood. The Pop program recommends an artistic attitude that no longer comes from open confrontation with the pervasive nonsense of the consumer world and mass society, of Hollywood and television trivialities, and that no longer goes along with just protesting everything that can claim to be genuinely democratically criticized and thus legitimized precisely because it's protested. The Pop program no longer recommends quoting the holy claptrap of high, sublime, eternal cultural values against the cynicism of bread and circus. It recommends affirmation as the sharpest form of criticism. It recommends first of all accepting all the unavoidable rationalizations of power positions, then taking them at face value and exaggerating them to the hilt, thus unmasking their unacceptable consequences and robbing them of any claim of absolute validity. For example: instead of long-winded, ineffective polemics against the rabbit-cage or KZ architecture of Germany's postwar cities, a demonstration of the very attitude that created this kind of architecture, namely the demolition mentality that welcomed the horrific bombing raids of World War II with open arms as a way of finally modernizing the old German cities. Consequently I plead for "blessed bombs for Germany's residential pissoir architecture" when the first monsters sprouted in the concrete suburbs of Frankfurt. Andy Warhol formulated the gist of the Pop program like a true master: "The most beautiful thing in Tokyo is McDonald's. The most beautiful thing in Stockholm is McDonald's. The most beautiful thing in Florence is McDonald's. Peking and Moscow don't have anything beautiful."

It would have been simply too absurd for a brush-packing artist to try to oppose the mechanisms of consumption that moved millions of dollars. Since Campbell's soup cans had already conquered the whole rest of the world anyway, they had to stake their claim to the sublime world of culture as well. Under no circumstances could one act as if culture were any different from a department store sale item. The only remote possibility of bringing about any change at all lay perhaps in demonstrating to people in the most total, radical way the consequences of their behavior — by stuffing them so full of the chocolate they craved that they puked.

In short: the Pop program was affirmative. Unfortunately, old Marcuse didn't get the picture and kept on trying to convince young people to pursue the same kind of cultural criticism he had

learned as a young man in the twenties. And he published an old essay of his scourging the affirmative character of culture. "Affirmative" here meant: defending and agreeing with. That certainly wasn't what Pop Art had in mind, though there were naturally plenty of artists who gleefully embraced the chance to join the Heavenly Host of art history with their poster painting talents and advertising expertise, ascending to the new Pantheon with the blessing of Man and God. At any rate, Marcuse's trivializing pseudoconcept of the "affirmative" created so much confusion that the philosophically unobjectionable use of the term got mangled. Affirmation is negation of negation as a new starting point. Perhaps we should have said "negative affirmation" when describing the attitude of Pop. Ah well – in the meantime, everybody knows that following the rules to a tee is the best way to sabotage them. Even some trade unionists have figured out what affirmative strategy means, and what it meant to Pop artists. Whatever is still noteworthy today about Pop Art is a product of this attitude. The rest, which may well mean most of it, is just bad ad art.
Just as Mary Quant with her miniskirt triumph was the first to succeed in establishing the fashion leadership of lower class tastes, Pop Art first succeeded in turning the entertainment business, kitsch, camp (as Susan Sontag called kitsch in the service of affirmation strategy) into the leading weapons of effective social criticism. For who would dare to oppose the entertainment industry with its 150 percent backing for that insanity dressed as everyday logic, which a mere 99 percent of the public clamored after? Pop Art transformed the entertainment industry's scenery magic into an unmasking trick, much like what Brecht or Krakauer or Benjamin might have come up with for the early phase of mass-consumer society at the end of the twenties. These transforming and unveiling tricks required the above-mentioned readiness to give up the materialistic habit. Away with everything that wanted to make us believe it was precious and valuable in itself. Better still, don't even want to own anything that isn't just an instrument, or means. The time-honored forms of Pop actions were happenings and the Fluxus concert, events that left no baggage, no cultural rubbish that had to be sent to museum dumping grounds.
The museum itself was to become a department store, transit depot for groceries and articles of everyday use.
It is strangely touching (particularly for the stars of the Pop scene) that absolutely nothing has remained of all this, neither in the field of design nor in architecture. Disposable cardboard furniture – it really existed, and we're hung onto it, not being strong enough to throw it away. We were completely filled with the subversive spirit of affirmation, which was considered the only true standard at the time. We looked with suspicion on anyone who still played with the wishful idea that his ad art in the garb of Pop cultural revolution might become a Rembrandt ersatz. There is no Pop furniture or architecture any more except what was designed for Las Vegas, fairs, television shows and theater sets. Nothing has remained except the bad painting of mediocre artists, who never really were Pop artists at all but really only

Young Chineses.

wanted to be academic painters. Nothing has remained. Everything dissolved into actions, particularly the actions of the student revolutions in the United States, France, Italy and West Germany. Nothing has remained, and that's a triumph, because it proves the efficacy of the Pop program.

The Sanctification of Felt Slippers against the Heoism of Permanent Self-Transcendence
The Goods of the Change on the Way to the Beyond
To define long-term historical trends in terms of vogues is very questionable. It is reasonable, though, to define short-term changes in the surface behavior of a society as vogues. But the question remains, what do we gain by the acknowledgement of such styles or vogues, and should we follow them or not?
No vogue is like another. And still they all are only vogues; that is to say, they can neither be predicted nor imposed. Even though innumerable trends of history have been analyzed, the resultant knowledge does not help us to recognize the drift of the immediate future. But when we compare vogues with respect to their common characteristics, we are no longer making statements about vogues themselves but about the forms of long-term historical developments. And the alternation of vogues or styles is clearly a characteristic of historical developments.
How can the transitions between short-term vogues and long-term trends of historical developments (traditions) be defined? The West German social-liberal coalition — in government for twelve years — can certainly not, as a historical fact, be regarded as a vogue. However, the enthusiasm of many young people who actually supported this coalition between 1969 and 1973 can perhaps be considered one.
Meanwhile young people have adopted different political and socio-psychological styles in the movements of idlers, punks, the "I don't feel like doing anything" people, and finally the Greens. Do these young people follow a style only as long as it's a movement and then abandon it as soon as the movement turns into a political party?
In the field of the arts, the appropriate question would be: do artists abandon fashionable trends as they abandon a lover or leave an employer? Do artists switch avant-gardes when they don't seem to offer surprising, provoking and new ideas any longer, or do only those artists skip around who haven't got the discipline for continuous work or the visionary imagination for ambitious life-work? Was the RAF [Red Army Faction — West German terrorist group in the early seventies] a vogue paralleling the heroic gestures which painters like Kiefer, Baselitz, Lüpertz, and Penck developed at the same time? Or did the RAF and the German artistic geniuses of the seventies only demonstrate a constant of human potential, i.e., did all of them, even at the risk of their lives, aim at the highest assertion of their own claim to power?
In the early seventies, this style was expressed as a program emphasizing radical subjectivity, which in turn, however, was considered an objective phenomenon.
The fact that many RAF members were killed and the movement destroyed — without regard to who these individuals were, what they thought and felt — is an objective fact of the historical process. Moreover, posterity has transformed the ideas and feelings of its martyrs or public enemies, absorbing the individual and psychological motivations of the RAF members into its collective consciousness.
How are the individual and psychological motivations of artists transformed into the collective consciousness? An artist only achieves recognition when his/her personality and work transcend the individual. Does the same criterion transform an avant-gardist into a classic? Are classic works of art thus those that are at all times considered interesting, regardless of current vogues? This is certainly not the case, for many Picassos of yore were not recognized as such by their respective contemporaries.
Furthermore, what is considered classic and thus worthy of attention changes according to current vogues. The best-known example of this in the seventies is Francis Picabia, who came to be viewed as one of the most interesting artists of the twentieth century only in light of the modes of perception and representation developed by Sigmar Polke and his followers.
The seventies changed our attitude towards the fashionable avant-gardes quite radically. I speculated on a theory to explain this recently (see *Kunstforum*, no. 40, 1980). This theory of the avant-gardes suggests that the function of vogues is to establish new traditions. I define as avant-garde only those striking innovative artistic trends that force us to rewrite the history of art and culture from new and different perspectives. In

Punk.

this century the Bauhaus was truly avant-garde, because it obliged us to completely rewrite the history of architecture between Brunelleschi and Palladio. The German Expressionists were true avant-gardists because they forced us to rewrite the history of baroque painting; as eminent a painter as El Greco had to be essentially re-discovered as a historical personality. (Space does not allow going into further examples here.) This concept of the function of the new provides quite an efficient criterion for evaluating vogues in relation to traditions, i.e., to long-term historical tendencies of development.
It allows us, for instance, to fairly accurately judge the actual meaning of many post-modernist programs and buildings. One could even say that post-modernism is a program of mediation between the vogues and traditions of architecture. And Joseph Beuys, who did much to shape the seventies, proves to be a great and true avant-gardist, for he was able to force almost the entire art world to regard objects in museums of prehistory and ethnology in a completely new and visionary way. Through Beuys, the avant-gardist, we have rediscovered our culture's oldest stories in the present.
The whole history of the seventies cannot of course be reconstructed here. The following is only an attempt to describe a trend that has proved to be the most effective of contemporary avant-garde movements where it has become visible in the fine arts, literature, the humanities, and in politics as well.
In politics this trend is called "the new spirituality," the trademark of the new conservative coalition in Bonn. It would be superfluous to deal with it here, as it is dealt with almost daily in newspapers and political journals.
In the humanities, the same trend is defined as the "rebellion of the elites." This means: the ruling classes no longer want to allow anyone and everyone into the universities, as in the seventies. The university is henceforth, and once again, to be reserved for the education and character formation of the intellectual elite. Since this trend toward abolishing the educational policy of the social-liberal coalition is also widely discussed in the media, I will refrain from giving a more detailed account here.
The same holds for the fine arts, for Baselitz, Kiefer, Penck, Immendorff, and the groups of young painters in Hamburg, Cologne, and Berlin, who only started working around 1980. As this trend is undoubtedly important not only for Germany but for a great part of the Western and Eastern world as well, I will describe it in more detail with reference to some literary examples. The developments of the seventies culminate in this trend, though its effects have not yet reached their climax. What it all means is that the literary, the artistic, the political, and the scientific public is allowing itself — timidly, for the time being — to glorify those aspects of the German past that shocked the entire world in Hitler's day. Those Germans who are following this trend as avant-gardists want to be regarded as gods again. This is much more dangerous than President Reagan's ambitions: for him it is sufficient to be the Supreme Judge of good and evil in East and West. In short: the little country of Germany is in a state of ruin as no other nation of the First World because of the advanced development of her

industries and military installations. In Germany, the future of all other countries has already begun. The United States and Japan lag far behind in this respect: the Americans do not know the problem of countrysides completely destroyed by the indiscriminate spread of settlements, and the Japanese are not obliged to maintain such enormous military force as the Germans.
What else remains but to re-style the road to hell and the end of the world as the ascent to the eternal abode of the gods and the spirit? Dirt, noise, a poisoned environment and corrupt politics have to be justified by all available means, because they nourish our irresistible longing for greatness and the sacred. From Luther to Karl Marx, Adolf Hitler, the RAF and the new intellectual and artistic saints, this longing has been maintained throughout our history as a particularly German characteristic.
We have to be prepared for the worst. That is to say, a great part of the world will soon adopt German characteristics, in this particular sense: the East has already done so, and the United States is practising very diligently.

"Why does the supreme good so often express itself as a wrong tendency? Because nobody can understand himself if he cannot understand his fellow men. Therefore, first of all you must believe that you are not alone, you must always guess infinitely much and not tire of trying to understand the meaning of things until finally you find the origin and the essence. Then the genius of time will appear to you and cautiously suggest what is appropriate and what not." (Friedrich Schlegel, *Fragments*)

We should indeed like to imagine that we are not alone. This was the reason the traveling companions met so often under the patronage of Petrarch. What I had in mind here I have tried to convey in the first volume about the Petrarch Prize. On the basis of those ideas, I should now like to cautiously suggest what is appropriate and what not, and what in this sense may be original and essential.
The supreme good that presently often expresses itself as a wrong tendency is the willful act of self-transcendence, by which, as it seems, a whole generation of German artists is trying to liberate itself to normality and from historically imposed self-restrictions. We thought that along with the politics of ecstasy, which seemed to have disappeared in the apocalypse of National Socialism, the art of ecstasy, the heroism and

Bob Marley.

monumentalism of "life transcending itself" (Arno Breker) had also been overcome and rejected as a historically obsolete artistic attitude. This was not and is not the case, and capable artists can hardly be expected to renounce expressing the supreme good which according to Schlegel actually means to renounce expressing the highest goal of human action.
In a general sense this highest goal may be supposed to be a transcendence of the individual as well as the general human limitations of life on earth, i.e., a transcendence of life itself.
Western, Mediterranean culture has during the course of its history very rarely awarded prizes to concepts and strategies of the transcendency of the "mortal little man" (Petrarch). Self-sacrifice for others, martyrdom for confessions of faith and knowledge, virtuosity in developing extreme and rare talents, ruthless crimes causing unforgettable horror, titanic strength in founding states and the

creative power of towering works, those have been the dominating concepts and strategies of human self-transcendence in the west.
Only now do we begin to understand an attitude that has primarily been developed in other countries: the heroism of idleness, of renouncing the great deed, the pathos of unpretentiousness; and thus we start learning to rediscover our own German history. Wasn't this West Germany's most remarkable achievement — if there was any at all — to be satisfied with the basics of life, and since the end of the fifties, to renounce all possible attempts at restoring Great Power illusions? Wasn't it a sign of maturity to demand that the new parliamentary democracy should be created by the average man, not the pretended elites? Weren't all of us important contemporaries by virtue of deliberately choosing to live as Philistines who renounced the yearning to be geniuses and heroic creators of new worlds?
If anything was sacred to us, it was the ordinary, the unostentatious matters of everyday life. People who had experienced the fact that the self-evident is not self-evident at all, voluntarily sacrificed heroic greatness for the miracle of normality and the calm and harmony of an extremely uneventful life. Blessed be the man who does not want to achieve anything great to justify his bloodthirstiness. Blessed be provincialism, the self-sufficient self-limitation to immediate needs. Blessed be the felt slippers that prevent us from being swifter than cripples. Blessed be the moment of repose and the hands in lap. Blessed be the leaf that is not threatened by any gardener's maintenance. Blessed be what remains the same as it has always been. "Small is beautiful" (Schumann); only the smallest possible modification is justified (L. Burckhardt); the dismissal of heroic principles (Marquardt) is necessary if the whole is not to decline.
Kant developed these positions systematically long ago and he came to the striking conclusion — which to this day has hardly ever been accepted — that the only form of justifiable desire for self-transcendence is the acknowledgement of the extreme limitation of human capacities.
Only the admission that we are dependent on ineradicable prejudices, on uncontrollable emotions, on conventions of thought that are always being replaced by new conventions, enables us to see that we are lacking in everything that would allow us to be more than we actually are.
We concede greatness to anyone who acknowledges this as being valid for him — or herself.

The Basic Law of Germany's Postwar Intellectuals
Of course it may be doubted whether all German Philistines trembled at this idea and consecrated their felt slippers. However, we should remember that the majority of ruthless criminals, titans, virtuosos, and above all those who sacrificed themselves all went the route to immortality in frightful ignorance. Nietzsche ascribed narrow-mindedness to heroes of this ilk; and his skepticism towards the heroism of the great deed is accompanied by a general warning against too much thinking, because it supposedly makes people incapable of action. Skepticism must certainly not be exaggerated into a universal principle of interpretation, casting mankind and its history of heroic nihilism as an entertaining interlude in the history of nature.
In 1948 Günter Eich included a matchless poem in his *Abgelegene Gehöfte* (Remote Farmsteads) concerning the Philistines' sole possibility for expressing the supreme good:

Aurora, Morgenröte.
Du lebst, oh, Göttin noch!
Der Schall der Weidenflöte
tönt aus dem Haldenloch.

Wenn sich das Herz entzündet,
belebt sich Klang und Schein,
Ruhr oder Wupper mündet
in die Ägäis ein.

Dir braust ins Ohr die Welle
vom ewgen Mittelmeer.
Du selber bist die Stelle
von aller Wiederkehr.

In Kürbis und in Rüben
wächst Rom und Attika.
Gruss Dir, du Gruss von drüben,
wo einst die Welt geschah.

Aurora, dawning red.
O goddess, still alive!
The sound of meadow flutes
sighs from deep in the earth.

When the heart is aflame,
sounds and sights come alive,
Ruhr and Wupper flow
into the Aegean.

You hear the pounding wave
of the eternal Mediterranean.
You yourself are the site
of all return.

In pumpkins and in turnips,
grows Rome, grows Attica.
Salutations to you, o salutations from afar,
where once the world took shape.
(Günter Eich, 1948)

When and what enflames the heart? When do we become the site of all return ourselves? Exactly when we do not scale walls in Speer-like heroism or let walls collapse on our way to oak-leaf cluster with swords and diamonds but, instead, when we remember Rome and Attica, i.e., historical greatness, among pumpkins and turnips, or on coal stocks, or on the river Wupper, a dirty trickle. Such memories of what we are not and can never be, of what mankind has lost forever and can only keep present as something lost, enflame our hearts, allowing us to hear the roaring waves of the eternal Mediterranean Sea. Pumpkins, turnips,Wupper, coal stocks, i.e., the most ordinary, banal, obvious and unostentatious things must be taken seriously, must even be venerated. This was Günter Eich's basic law for Germany's postwar intellectuals. Here, the supreme good was comprehensible as an objective tendency.

Longing for the Heroic Life

Today we are confronting the Philistines with the same pathos with which Don Quixote confronted his fantasies. Today we polemicize in the name of supreme goals against the levelling of everything. Today we hail iron chancellors and iron ladies whose horizon is limited enough to let them all out for the realization of high heroic principles. Our longing for the heroic life is understandable because we are too unimaginative to be satisfied with the ordinary and obvious. Our desire to rise from anonymity and to be recognized and praised as creators and leaders is understandable because it is all too human. But in truth, we do not even approach the level of the ordinary. These indisputable facts are revealed by their consequences: presently there are more writers than experts, more artists than purchasers of paintings, more professionals than gifted students, more biographies than great personalities.
We boast: "Out of our interest in the element of destruction, we reject a view of literature that understands it as guidance for living, that misconstrues the writer as a producer of meaning, and that constructs solemn identifications between artist and reader, the former, heroic, the latter in search of a guide. But where could the falseness of this view... be better and more literally contradicted than where literature serves as a preparation for suicide?... Hence, let us leave aside harmonizing, intellectual and existential defenses of suicide and refer to Achim von Arnim's immediate and brutally formulated horror over Kleist's death. He wrote: 'It is a death like that that befell Wolfdietrich [a medieval knight,] where the skeletons of all those he had once slain slew him in return'. This is the first reference to the phenomenon we are interested in, namely the anticipation of Kleist's suicide in his own writings, in prose that is murderous because horror is presented in a composed, cold and detached way that suggests the author's secret complicity" (Karl-Heinz Bohrer, *Merkur*).
If we should try to find some possible meaning behind the strange logic of this argument (for ridiculing literature as guidance for the living and considering it interesting instead as preparation for death can indeed be disregarded as Junkerism) then the program would seem to be that the author must identify with the fictionality of his own work. In contrast to the reader in search of a guide, the writer is a secret accomplice to his own work, like the priest of his god, like the victim of the evildoer. Whether or not this is heroizing the writer, his work still remains a guide for living — or dying, as the case may be — for himself at least.
For the sake of his own self-elevation, the writer disregards the fact that the average reader most willingly identifies with authors of murderous prose, precisely because they represent horror in a composed, cold and detached way suggesting the reader's secret complicity. Today every newspaper presents the most terrifying facts in a composed, cold and detached way, and the journalists admit their complicity quite openly.
Official government releases, court opinions, contracts, and political programs have long been noted for the cold detachment of their prose style, still admired by many today for its particularly interesting artistic qualities. The authors of such documents are above all accomplices in making allowances for themselves for their complete lack of philosophical, poetic or artistic substance. To

smugly polemicize against readers who try to identify with authors by superelevating them to heroes is a prerogative of those writers who are accomplices, and who are so because they have not been submitted to the murderous juridical and journalistic prose of arrogant officials and narrow-minded functionaries.

The indisputable naivety of many readers who demand guidance for living from literature does not at all surpass the unworldliness of the aforementioned writer who wishes to reserve murderously cold prose for himself and his colleagues.

The heroic radicalism which artists and writers are opposing to Philistine attitudes today is even less worthy of attention than the mass media rubbish currently so popular. Andy Warhol has already drawn our attention to the fact that even the most brillant of achievements are rarely remembered longer than a quarter of an hour — but hardly anybody believed him. Here too, the entertainment industry proves to be more enlightened than the school of philosophy: nobody would be interested in a top-ten hit list if the same names appeared on it for three weeks in a row.

Design by Courrèges.

Self-Elevation in Full Array

The supreme good as a wrong tendency, i.e., the wrong conclusions about the human longing for permanence, greatness, and fame, has recently been demonstrated by Ulrich Horstmann, another heroic nihilist, in the final paragraph of his book *Das Untier* (*The Beast*): "Let's pluck up our courage and transfer the transcendental ideal of the moon to sub-lunar reality! Let us transform our metabolically diseased planet into a moon! Because until the sickle of the moon is reflected in thousands of crater lakes, until moon and earth have become indistinguishable and quartz crystals wink at one another above the abyss in the light of the stars, until the last oasis is desolate, the last sigh unheard, the last germ withered, there will be no Eden on earth."

Has anybody ever spoken about such an Eden before? How would the above-quoted condition transform Earth into an Eden? German-style convulsive thinking has always considered a dog's barking at the moon an expression of the most sublime poetry, because our heroic minds and souls have always been moonlike. The shameless presentation of one's personal intellectual and emotional state as an expression of the supreme good is undoubtedly meant to serve as a proof of one's super-elevation, one's barbaric pride in one's own ignorance: to be man no longer but to have become an interesting, pitiless, and unpredictable beast.

But who actually knows whether he prefers the wolf in a sheepskin or the sheep in a wolfskin? The artistic circles of the chancellery would certainly prefer the latter. Unfortunately the author rejects both roles for himself. He says straight out, because it is his opinion, that "the arsenals of ABC weapons for the first time in history offer the chance of relentlessly extinguishing mankind now, a chance that must not be missed." Horstmann calls his conception "relentless" towards himself, which only a true titan is supposed to be without any self-censure or maudlin sentimentality. He does not play roguish tricks like Eulenspiegel. No negative affirmation that causes the collapse of an absurd idea through its total realization. He rather appears in the petty glory of a "partisan of the anthropophagous resistance knowing defeats of the truth represented by him but no capitulation."

"Ever since the sixties, in spite of fierce humanistic maneuvres of disturbance, a phase of new stabilization and consolidation can be stated permitting us to hope that the beast — as is due to its intelligence — will strike that apocalyptic blow against itself and the suffering creature with a seeing and understanding eye, the blow it has been preparing feverishly ever since the second war of preparation " (Horstmann). This misanthropic thinking "does not at all compete with humanism which it regards as a functional sedative of the last phase of armament and which it accepts as inevitable. It does at no time define itself as a majority doctrine, a secular religion or as an ideological-social cement, but always as a minority perspective, a philosophy of a small, exiled fraction of meditative minds " (Horstmann).

Well then, the coronation array of the self-transcendent man has been designed: in solitary greatness, he relentlessly contemplates the end. His dedication to the end, which all other creatures are trying to escape by all possible means, is unparalleled. He does not smile, he suffers. He cannot smile, because he does not know how ridiculous he is when — as a university professor — he stalks the jungle of our recreation areas in carnival costume in order to terrify harmless passers-by by revealing his diabolic clubfoot.

In our country, the heroes of courage to the bitter end have always been like that. But whenever someone threatened to put their designs for the salvation of all mankind into action they turned out to be like children full of self-pity: "It'll serve my mother right if my hands freeze! Why doesn't she buy me some gloves!"

Fifty years ago Carl Schmitt, another university professor, glorified the program and the personification of the beast. When the SS-newspaper *Schwarzes Corps* criticized him publicly, a criticism far less radical than what he himself, this blossom of science, had on dozens of occasions shamelessly levelled against the victims of Nazism, calling even for the extinction of their names, this titan of radical philosophy, this giant of ruthless schemes for final solutions, this hero of pure logic immediately felt persecuted by the National Socialist regime.

A Call Like a Thunderbolt

A third author bears witness to the wrong tendency that West Germany's intellectuals, writers, and artists have been following for five years now in order to elevate themselves from their normal irrelevant lives to the highest goal, i.e., their self-elevation as gods. "When rereading *Minima Moralia* a feeling of home — which, however, is no abode — fills me. How conscientiously and ostentatiously one used to think, even in my time. It seems as if several generations have passed since then. (Without dialectics we immediately become less intelligent. Still, this is how it has to be; we have to do without dialectics.) Instead, we are now instructed by some satirical young philosophers as well as ethonological and anarchic essayists who incessantly provide us with brazen-faced ideas and giggling offenses against rigid Marxist dogmatics, as against orthodoxy at the university generally. But they are much too deeply involved in their antiphilosophy to let their imaginations be even modestly stimulated. To waste so much effort in combating ignorance that will take care of itself anyway does not demonstrate a strong desire for knowledge. One does not make elegant parries before scarecrows. Such people are only witty as critics, but they do not provide any imaginative solutions, either liberating or disturbing, and this naughty confusion will entertain us only as long as no one more powerful intervenes" (Botho Strauss, *Paare, Passanten — Couples, Passers-by).*

Of course the writer regards himself as this great man, who is referred to in several sections of the text as being deeply longed for. As yet, though, he has not got the command, and therefore the writer can — as quite a few of his colleagues applaud with conviction — consider himself Baptist and pioneer of something yet to come.

Away with naughty confusion, witty criticism, dialectical thinking! The longed-for great man will doubtless be left behind, as the writer states with the self-confidence of all political functionaries of the century, because they can only get others to accept their claim of being greater than everyone else if they are more ignorant than rule by representative democracy will tolerate. The Philistine is perplexed when faced with this poet of the supreme good who sees his goal in becoming more ignorant than he already is; he is perplexed over the dictum of the anthropophagous philosopher who says that we immediately think more radically when we relinquish our humanity. Indeed, we do not have to waste energy on nonsense that takes care of itself. But the hatred that comes of self-pity, the killing out of love, the fear of virtue certainly do not take care of themselves. They have to be studied seriously until everyone understands that he or she is at least potentially such a criminal of lost honor. Such self-critical suspicion is both bewildering and liberating. It liberates us from the fantasies of omnipotence our cultural heroes ramble about in as if they were revelations of extraordinary intellectual significance. Of course our intellectual geniuses must forbid the satirists' and anarchists' offenses against orthodox teachings at the university since their elevated heroic status can only be adequately praised by themselves in orthodox university teaching. And of course Botho Strauss recommends the formulae of praise he uses himself: "Hymnic beauty — if only deep enough and from the most confused origins — is always the highest goal of poetry, beauty clarifying the muddle; this is what we should like to be convinced of again and again when trying to escape the nightmares of everyday life; we do not find any support in the shredded forms of contemporary poetry, but rather in Rilke's *Elegies.* Even to slip into pompousness is imperative as a fertilizer for the creation of an incomparable line, for the precision of triumph, for the magnificent effect."

Magnificent, magnificent, magnificent! Triumph, triumph, triumph! Hymnic, incomparable, deep!
The intellectual level of this pathos of adoration effortlessly reaches the level of the nation's everyday reading matter, and every day the shapers of public opinion decide again not to think dialectically, i.e., to think more ignorantly.
What actually does the writer want to say when boasting about such goals? Why is he not content to be your average pompous great man, as he actually proves to be, judging by the ideas and ambitions expressed in the excerpts. What is it that turns these very gifted contemporaries into figures of derision, who do they pen thoughtless imitations of certitudes of faith that were once valid?
"The doctrine that is important to me is not derived from the rules... but from enthusiasm — never from ecstasy, i.e., the poem — for those things that are still valid: sun, earth, rivers, winds, trees and bushes, cattle, fruit (in baskets and jars), tools and utensils" (Peter Handke, *Der Chinese des Schmerzes).* Why does he say this? Is he just fascinated with stubbornly praising things not even kitchen maids — if they were still available — would sing about any more and even illustrated magazines only rarely dare offer their readers as a nightcap? Why does one of our most eminent writers recommend the worship of nature, earth, rivers, winds, trees etc. even though meanwhile no one can go for a walk without uttering at least one mournful sigh about the transitoriness of nature? Naturally our poet knows all this, too, but he considers himself great, precisely because he does not have to see and understand what everyone sees and understands. This is only another form of the much-deplored mediocrity expressed in the appeal to the masses, which has developed into a standard measure of psychological health.
What are these people who are mentioned in encyclopedias proud of, hovering over the illiterate Philistine masses? Friedrich Schlegel wrote in his *Fragments:* "What am I proud of as an artist? I am proud of the decision that separates and isolates for all eternity me from everything common; proud of the work that divinely surpasses every invention and the intention of which nobody will ever completely understand; proud of the capacity of worshipping everything that opposes me; proud of the awareness that I can stimulate companions to more efficiency and that everything they create is to my benefit."

Imitatio Imitationis
The fact that this declaration — with one slight emendation — can still serve today as a credo for the above-mentioned members of the Club of Idolatry in Bonn, for the acrobats who identify with heroes, saints, geniuses and political criminals, provides us with insights into what moves and motivates such mediocre men. Every conversation with motorcycle fans, lovers of Westerns, or would-be Richthofens reveals that they too are proud of precisely the same things as

our exceptional intellectual heroes. The way they drive at the brutal speed of 180 km per hour — an arbitrary limit — sets them apart from all other road users; the way they push their wantonness to the point of inhumane acts, the intent of which no criminologist or social psychologist can ever understand; the way they worship what has subjugated and still enslaves them; the way they can stimulate their companions' efficiency as members of criminal gangs, and the way they claim their companions' gains as their own profits: all this also appears on the balance sheet of the heroic poets and artists whose intention it is to actually rise above these masses.

And what is the slight emendation we ought to keep in mind? Well, the adoration of these new gods isn't all that widespread as yet because Germany's geniuses only oppose themselves and, hence, can only worship themselves.

One or another of the aforementioned writers also dares to worship power, though secretly and indirectly. Unscrupulous everyday criminals, hardened by ignorance, are superior even in this respect to the writers: they are proud of being gangsters and worship power openly.

However, Friedrich Schlegel's declaration is not the only noteworthy statement about defeat and victories, gains and losses, reality and appearance. Renate Liebenwein-Krämer reveals in her unexpectedly up-to-date essay on *Secularization and Sacralization* some of those background influences to which Schlegel and his companions referred. The "sacralization" of rulers and heroes, the heroes of work and art, is presented and analyzed in a way that makes even the most arrogant and boastful attempt to bear our miserable life seem touching and pathetic. When, for instance, Friedrich Schlegel and Novalis try to convince each other of the other's greater suitability for becoming the baptist or rock of a new religion, then this servile gallantry of the late rococo period becomes a farce of sheer foolishness on the one hand. But on the other, these "fools" transpose into poetry and reflection what dominated the era as objective tendencies, which seem to be becoming dominant tendencies of our era as well.

Friedrich Schlegel declared the French revolution, Fichte's *Theory of Science* and Goethe's *Wilhelm Meister* as examples of genius in his sense. For the sake of his author's vanity, he could not simply declare the things that interested him as expressions of an already present general tendency: he wanted to see himself as the successor of Moses and Mohammed, the personally identifiable founder of a new religion; he wanted to transpose the Bible into poetry and philosophy, as it were. Art actually was only a continuation of religion by different means. The artist wished to be indebted to himself alone, to his historical mediation of anonymous texts, songs and rituals. Art became a secularized religion, and the critics, theater directors, the editors and pedagogues considered themselves their priests. The prophets of this secularized religion were the philosophers and scholars of art. Their apostles were Dürer, Raphael, Dante and Shakespeare, the martyrs. But most important of all were new artists themselves who sought to inscribe their names into the book of history — the Newest Testament — by relentlessly and unscrupulously sacrificing their health, their happiness and peace, and finally their lives.

Dürer could still represent himself as Christ, and Renate Liebenwein explains why: "In order to humbly and publicly trace his individual capacities back to the grace of God and to visibly follow the Imitation of Christ, while his suffering makes him more and more similar to Christ." Following Friedrich Schlegel's program, dozens of artists appeared now as imitators of Dürer or Raphael but, of course, even great suffering by no means made the imitators' works any more similar to those of Dürer or Raphael.

The pompous enthronement of art as religion, which led to strictly rejecting any true art in the service of the church, of emperors, robber barons, and merchants, necessarily resulted in an almost total isolation of the artist in the autonomy of coffee-houses and attic life. Artists who did not believe they could survive this self-imposed asceticism of radical artisthood and who yielded to the temptation of accepting commissions were stigmatized as second-rate artist-craftsmen. But these outcasts who supposedly fared badly and who were denied recognition by their priestly colleagues and experts, united to form a faction that took bitter revenge: they quite openly offered themselves as partners to everybody outside the field of art, i.e., to institutionalized power, and they provided their customers with promises of salvation of the old kind, reaching their peak during National Socialism, in socialist realism, and in the capitalist advertising agencies of our time.

In order not to be completely eclipsed by these annoyingly honest artist-craftsmen who acted brilliantly in the forecourt of power, the representatives of art as a secularized religion felt obliged to even more extravagant self-elevations so they would no longer be ignored and they grew to be real monsters of self-mutilation and became negative attractions.
Artists, poets, writers, and musicians, whose embarrassing pathos has been quoted in a few examples, plead for acknowledgment as geniuses, though the attractions currently on display in our capital village of Bonn are more disturbing than anything provided by art literature. These intellectuals no longer imitate Dürer and Raphael, but Nietzsche and Klages, Goethe and Spengler, Baudelaire and Wagner. And if they want to rise really high they even imitate Hitler who actually was an artist in the first place. He had the strength for consistency to the bitter end. He was the great man of power for whom the *homo homini lupus* has always been valid and who offered his murderous prose to his readers as guidance in dying, as euthanasia.
Hitler: an irresistible politician and brilliant military leader? Others may judge that! But Hitler the greatest filmmaker of all times, a master sculptor of social behavior, a cultural hero? With this Hitler we compete.
"Art is a sublime mission," he proclaimed, "obliged to fanaticism." Great! When, in contrast to that, I state: "art is the human longing for permanence sanctifying banalities," I probably can't count on the approval of our contemporary geniuses who would certainly consider this notion crude and grotesque. Peter Sloterdijk at least says so: "To pick one's nose while Botho Strauss is conjuring his daimonion, discussing the divinity of the soul? Have we got better words than 'vulgar' for the farts Rühmorf directs at Handke's theory of ideas or should these too be considered one of the ideas God released from his cosmogonic meditation? And what does it mean when this philosophizing city tramp answers Bohrer's subtle theory of eros with public masturbation?...To present a theory means to make oneself its medium. This is the opposite of what is demanded by moralistic pleaders for strictly idealistic concepts. While listening to what can be presented and lived, we remain protected from moralistic demagogy and from the terror of radical, liveable abstractions."

Texas Instrument.

This analysis leads us to depressing conclusions. Precisely because such geniuses cannot embody their theories, they terrorize us with their radical, unliveable abstractions. Precisely for the reason that they cannot critically examine their lives and because they are not destined to live what they say, they are never obliged to reassess their postulates. Instead, they follow the role models for philosophers and poets which were derived, some 180 years ago, from the formal analogy between art and the church as the power that institutionalizes universal entities. Hardly anybody would doubt that there is widespread interest in beauty, eternity, splendor, paradise, triumph, grace, and the like. However, these universals will not be transformed into realities by poetry or by politics. People who are still trying to work this magic cannot denounce those as narrow-minded Philistines who reject such attempts on historical grounds. That is not appropriate, Mr. Schlegel!
If it were only a case of exposing ourselves to yet another kind of exhilarating satanism, we would be able to cope with it up to a certain point. However, unfortunately, we are confronted with ignorance and not with evil. We have got used to accepting this idea ever since Hannah Arendt referred to the "banality of evil." But the objection to this idea is that we do not want to endure the banality of the sacred any longer. Is evil banal? Everybody would certainly like to believe so. However, the fact that the sacred is banal as well has been demonstrated so far only by

enlightened artists by their utilization of waste materials and employment of working methods that are accessible to everyone. But, still, the artists created unique works of art with these methods.

The sanctification of the sacred is again being demanded and, as in the past, artists are being required to be mystagogues and priests. Of course they welcome this sanctification — which is forgivable, for it increases their self-assurance. After the years of National Socialism we could only expose ourselves to the sacred in the ordinary. And the experience that though nothing corresponded to its inner logic and laws society still did not collapse was quite wonderful indeed. It was marvellous to have to deal with people who would say: "Why should I care about what I said yesterday?" or "Programs are written on paper, that's why we don't have to take them seriously." Everything worked, because nothing really worked.

Now, though, things are expected to function according to plans and programs, and *that* will certainly not function without major disasters.

The sanctification of the sacred derives from a congenital defect of the Enlightenment. The enlightenment suffers from this defect because it understands itself as clearing up a crime never actually committed. There were investigators even in the arts: they directed their spotlights of enlightenment on a work of art, long and hard, until it finally confessed to a crime it had not committed at all. The banality of the artists' inspiration and motivations was denied. But the culprits were not diabolical. To admit crimes one has not committed is a result of the kind of apologia artists have been required to endorse ever since the age of Romanticism.

Our understanding of enlightenment is not without consequences: if we understand enlightenment generally the same way we understand sexual enlightenment, specifically, then facts only become a problem because of enlightenment. For instance, before a mother asked their children whether they knew where little babies come from or what interest rates are all about, neither sexuality nor capitalism were at all problematic.

Enlightenment should rather be called "problem consciousness," then it could be extremely effective, inasmuch as it would not stress the banality of the miracle but the wonderful banality of the interest rate policies, as well as of the proliferation of mankind.

"Even the strongest man sometimes looks under his bed, even the most beautiful woman has to go to the toilet every now and then." There is no secret that should be illuminated in order to destroy it.

It is not higher insight that enables a person to rise above others, but it is the courage and readiness to acknowledge the banalities of power; that is to say, acceptance of the evident, not better insight but comprehension.

The actually frightening fact about art as a religion is its insistence on confronting the world open-heartedly, its readiness for self-sacrifice, its fervent desire to concern itself only with the supreme good, with life, nature, cosmic law!

In politics this program was pronounced in the denunciation of parliamentary process — *the* form of mediation — and of politics in general as a form of dispute relying on mediation alone. After all, it was not the National Socialists who invented parliament as the meeting ground of blather heads. Once, the recommendation to blow up parliaments was considered in a serious way by many artists, but today many of them again think that this would be very funny indeed. They would like to watch their own decline, being sure of their ability to enforce their personal ascension. But salvation can't be enforced, either in the arts or in any other religion.

(Translation provided by the author)

Graphic Design

Pierluigi Cerri
A.G. Fronzoni
Michael Klar
Karl Heinz Krug
Italo Lupi
Massimo Vignelli

Graphic Axes

Giovanni Anceschi

1. Several current directions in the study of cultural phenomena tend to ignore notions based on the accumulation of modern and contemporary scientific knowledge; instead, they draw on "sapiential" knowledge, i.e., lore and wisdom, what Mircea Eliade calls "traditional" knowledge. City planners who are tired of functional trees and quantitative diagrams are now trying to base their activities on conceptions pertaining to the *axis mundi* and the ties between macrocosm and microcosm, between faculties, colors, and cardinal points.
Other areas, for instance, anthropology, are trying to bring out elementary archetypes of communication. These elements are seen not in terms of the technoid metaphor of the constructional combination, but as genetically primary and original components: *Urelemente*, common to every kind of cosmic grammar, biological structure chemical table, human preference. The intuition underlying the desire to bring out a guiding rule of cultural propagation and exchange (in our case, graphic culture) seems to be part of that system of thought — analogical and synthetic thought about correspondences and connections. And, as we shall see, the fact that this hypothesis is confirmed by a multitude of historical and factual data — even if we cannot find logical foundations for the *truth* of the method — emphasizes its heuristic brilliance. And that is what really counts for any method.

2. By stressing the European north-south orientation, i.e., Germany and Italy, we find a robust marriage of opposites —opposites that have attracted one another since time immemorial. And with an anachronistic reference that, I hope, is as fertile as the "sapiential" method, I would like to recall the first German visual designer active in Italy: Bohemund of Taranto, to whom we owe nothing less than the corporate image of the First Crusade. According to medieval chronicles, the Swabian baron Bohemund did something consistent with the best handbooks on visual design.
Before trying to unify the identification systems of the entire army, he informed himself about those identifications that (to use a technical term) we may call the "communicative preexistences." He gathered information on the various types of armaments of the troops converging on Brindisi from the most disparate parts of the Christian West. He also found out about the various war cries and the various kinds of *ostensio Christi* displayed on shields and banners (i.e., a cross of St. George, St. Andrew, etc., the color, etc.). All this in order to hit upon the clinching solution of a unifying *white background*, a *Dieu le veult*, and the well-known red cross as a trademark.
And for anyone who finds my terminological usage far-fetched, i.e., too anachronistic, I would suggest a later *graphic* event that cannot be called irrelevant by any stretch of the imagination. I am obviously referring to the invention or discovery (or fusion of invention and discovery) credited to Johannes Gänsefleisch von Gutemberg. And to the lightning spread of typography with movable characters and typographic printing from the place of origin toward the south. And I think of the completely mature situation of a publishing industry that was putting out deluxe elitist editions *(Hypnerotomachia Polyphili)* and mass editions (of classics during the sixteenth century). This occurred during the second generation of printers, when Aldo Manuzio in Venice used a visual designer for all seasons: Alberto Griffo, a Bolognese engraver. Griffo created a typeface that met the technical and aesthetic demands of the

new market and overall context: *antiqua cursiva cancelleresca*.

3. The north-south route followed by the Dürers and then later by the Goethes was — to use the German word — a *Wandern* toward a vital cultural center or toward the vestige of a cultural area whose center of gravity could still aspire to the title of *caputmundi*. The direction of the main cultural flow coincided with the return of the travelers: perspective knowhow and the worship of ruins headed from south to north.
The great transformation came at the turn of the nineteenth century, when industrialization publicly celebrated its triumphs. This massive and magistral change was fundamental for communication, for turning the masses into a *passive protagonist*; and this spelled the turning of the tide of influences. Italy's cultural primacy was replaced by technological backwardness. The new myth became the (Germanic) model of mechanical precision or even the futuristic myth of electromechanics.
We can effectively cite the great Peter Behrens as the unequivocal anticipator or rather inventor of the corporate image and design coordination for the AEG. In Italy, he was seen as projecting the stand of the industry of electromechanical pumps for the navy; and his extremely rigorous displays of public illuminations dazzled the visitors at the Turin World's Fair in 1911.
Then, for (technical, scientific, and philosophical) publishing, the productional and also formal model became Leipzig. A more artistic publishing involved the so-called *Adornatori del libro* (book decorators) headed by Cesare Ratta of Bologna and involving De Carolis, the illustrator of D'Annunzio. Even this refined publishing referred to, and adopted the aesthetic banner of the Nordic technology of the woodcut. On the other hand, while poster art (*peinture d'affiche*) referred more to Chéretiana lithography, advertising graphics in periodicals followed the black-and-white creativity of the Central European newspaper network controlled by Rudolf Mosse, a pioneer of advertising management.

4. Right after the war, Antonio Boggeri, the true father of the creative explosion of Italian graphics, applied the word *studio* (in the French sense) to his graphic projects laboratory; however, the great majority of artists and colleagues had, as Pierluigi Cerri termed it, a huge number of non-Mediterranean consonants in their names. This was a time of pioneering for Germany and indeed all of Central Europe, which exported ideas to Italy — and also such leading figures as Imre Reiner, Herbert Bayer, Xanti Schavinsky, and so many others. Boggeri tells us, "We needed *finished graphics*," that is, completely formed and *impratichito* (expert), as Italian tailors say. Here, Boggeri implicitly puts his finger on the fact that the creation of and training for graphics came from outside Italy. We may therefore say that the Italian school of graphics, which is so highly appreciated for its creativity and its flexible improvisational character, actually resulted from the encounter between an anything but improvised graphics and a new vital context that craved innovation.
The Italian-German axis (which passes through Switzerland (especially Max Huber) is an *anti-historistic* axis, as Nikolaus Pevsner would term it. It is entirely of the twentieth century and in its break with the nineteenth century, it is full of pioneering originality and opposed to the idea of cultural production based on stylistic categories. This attitude removes styles or rather places them in parentheses; it tackles the problem of communication with all the immediacy and openmindedness that Tomás Maldonado calls "technological intelligence." It is only *a posteriori* that the result can be recognized as a style. Examples of a similar anti-stylistic approach (which has its Italian origins in Futurism, according to Carlo Belloli, in a now legendary special Italian issue of the magazine *Neue Graphik*, 1959) are the procedures employed by such figures as Luigi Veronesi, one of the direct interlocutors of the Bauhaus, and Dradi. Their magazine *Campo Grafico*, edited by Attilio Rossi, reveals a deep interest in normal graphics, the kind that we may call *graphic material culture*, and that others, with a more collective attitude, call *ephemera*, from the architecture of a book page to a streetcar ticket.
Thus, it is at least curious that this north-south axis of reference is to be read altogether contrary to the idea of the Rome-Berlin axis. Indeed, we can even perceive underground veins of resistance. Albe Steiner, the grand master of Italian political graphics, certainly looked at Hartfield, while the Nazi regime rejected the cosmopolitan Akzidenz Grotesk in favor of the Gothic Fraktur; and the

typography of Italy's fascist regime, despite some philo-industrialist uncertainty, wallowed in lapidary monumentalism.
A further vein of the thread linking the north with the graphic south can be seen in the development of how the situation was comprehended. That is, the development of conceptual tools that could deal adequately with the existence of communications production. More generally, this refers to the relationship between new architecture, design, graphic and new philosophies and epistemological approaches. A major factor was the exchange between Husserl's phenomenology and the Milanese school of philosophy headed by Antonio Banfi. And in particular, for visual design as well as the entire sector of design and costume, a large number of connections passed through the cosmopolitan and Central European figure of Gillo Dorfles, who was certainly not a marginal member of that circle. This applies to both graphics and visual communication, if we recall a text like the one that Dorfles (who, so to speak, rubbed elbows with the principal visual creators of the time) produced for the yearbook *Pubblicità in Italia*, 1958. In this text, Dorfles toppled so-called pure art off its pedestal when he described stimuli that painting receives from posters and design objects. These reflections were in tune with the emergence of Pop Art.

5. This long history of connections and influences forms a variegated background. And we then have something unique, something undeniably peculiar: Italy was linked to the School of Ulm, a German

Tomás Maldonado with Ettore Sottsass jr. at Ulm.

The building complex of the A&G in the project by Max Bill. Axonometric.

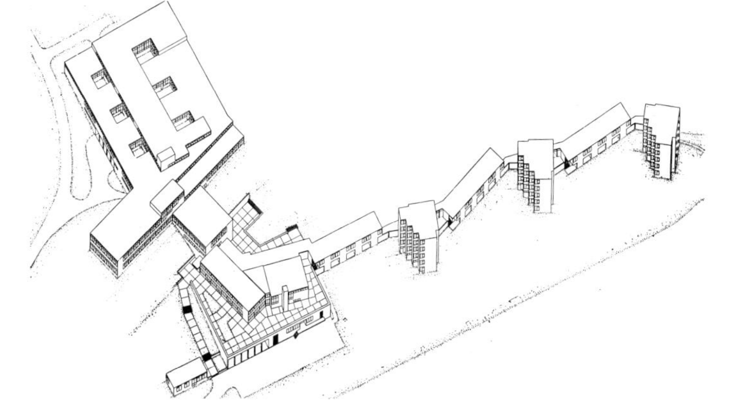

institution for teaching design and visual communication after World War II.
The representative of Italian architecture could be Enzo Frateili, a scholar of design methodology and history. We can also identify product design with Rodolfo Bonetto, now the outgoing president of the ICSID and, back then, the only Italian to give a regular course at Ulm. Within Italian architecture and product design, links were forged with a third component, indeed an extremely important one: Italy gave birth to kinetic and programmed art, and Germany parallelled this and reacted. The first blossoming of the relationship between culture and cybernetics was primarily theoretical. In 1960, Max Bense, a teacher at the School of Ulm and a writer on information theory and aesthetics, published a book with an emblematic and, indeed, provocative title: *Programmierung des Schönen* (*Programming the Beautiful*). But focus on the relationship between *research art*, which is kinetic and programmed, and *basic design*, the ensemble of exercises originating at the *Grundkurs*, basic course, of the

Bauhaus. The results were the propedeutic basis, the very foundation of construction at the School of Ulm. Furthermore, *programmed art* in Italy overlapped in a fertile way with functional visual communications. First of all, it directly affected the work of many graphic artists such as Grignani and Garboni. Secondly, we should recall the participation of the chief exponents of *programmed art* (Munari, Gruppo T, Mari) in the so-called *Operazione Natale* in Milan in 1962: a collaboration with professional designers on the Christmas decoration of the city.
One of the most brillant participants here was Massimo Vignelli, who worked out a modular system of lights — and it caused a sensation. Vignelli, together with another "Nordic," this time the Dutchman Bob Noorda, founded Unimark, the great international studio, which took on many graduates of Ulm, for instance an industrial designer like Frank Hess.

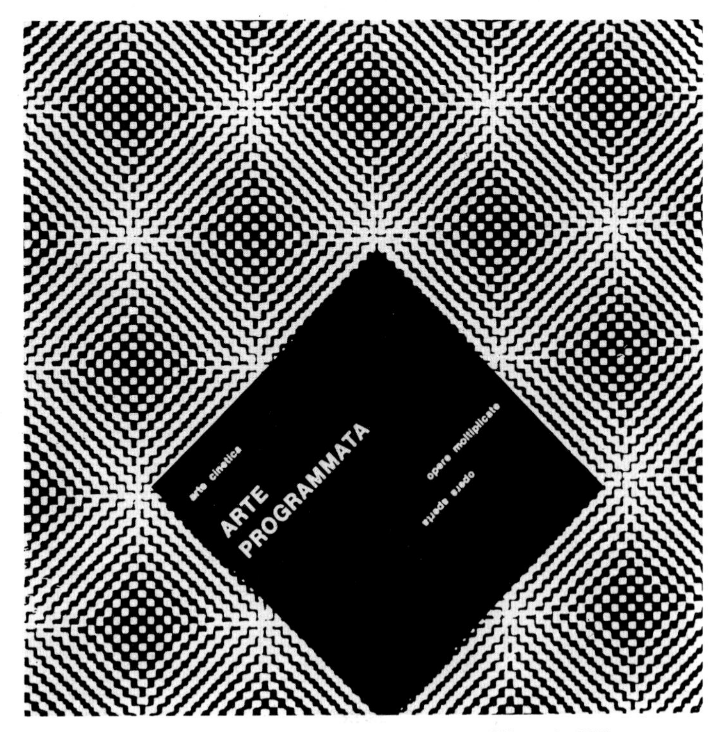

Cover of the catalogue *Arte programmata,* Olivetti, Milan, May 1962.

6. Since World War II, Fronzoni's graphic output has been accompanying these developments, intensifying graphics language to its extreme consequences, with emblematic and (may Fronzoni forgive me) baroque solutions. All this together with a cultural curiosity that moves toward areas of linguistic, verbal-visual research, including such topical efforts as visual poetry.
In contrast, Lupi and Cerri, take off from architectural culture to design elitist or mass-communication instruments and products, which however are also theoretical reflections as well as pragmatic projects. And for Lupi, we can speak of an extremely mature rational and constructional approach. For instance, his free and easy relationship with the chief tool of printing graphics: the layout grid system, as it is called by Joseph Müller Brookmann. Pierluigi Cerri, a book designer and exhibition designer, who also has his antecedents in avant-garde art with Manzoni and Castellani, has a direct if deferred kinship with Ulm. This was evident in his collaboration with one of the school's most prestigious members of the visual communications department. The two designers cooperated in producing the graphic layout of the review *Casabella* when it was published by Tomás Maldonado. By then, the School of Ulm had closed, and its teachers and students were scattered throughout the world, with a certain predilection for Italy.

Cover of catalogue *Nouvelle Tendance,* Musée des Art Décoratifs, Paris, April- May 1964.

7. At this point, we have to digress in order to make a, so to speak, methodological observation. Until now, we have been speaking from a particular viewpoint, we have seen things from the Italian perspective. But we must also point out that any Italian elements in German graphics can be readily noticed and brought out only by a German viewer.
Just as Fronzoni, Vignelli, Lupi, and Cerri constitute a profile of Italian graphics that stands out strongly against the graphics of other countries, so too Krug, Klar, and Edelmann emerge sharply from the German panorama. Krug is not only a graphic artist in the strict sense of the term, he is also a "graphic editor", something like an art director, for the review *Form*, to which he has dedicated all his professional and cultural energies. Michael Klar, in contrast, is a graphic artist's graphic artist, as well as, and perhaps mainly, a graphics teacher at the Hochschule für Gestaltung in Schwäbisch Gmünd. However, his most salient characteristic is something he is particularly aware of (see his text entitled *Gestalter als Autoren* — designers as authors): he aims at and practices a professionalism that diverges from the traditional model of the communication process.
The graphic artist no longer plays the ancillary role of translating between a "transmitter" (the customer) and a target (the mass audience). Now, the designer is an *author*, that is, he shares responsibility for the contents. And here, we are close to the ethical and political position of an Italian like Albe Steiner, who is graphics editor of Elio Vittorini's *Politecnico*. The sense of complete involvement, of a *powerful* reflection on the part of the graphic artist, of a strong presence in the design and communication process is obvious in the "gestural" work of Edelmann; he is certainly far removed from the stylemes of Ulm, but he is also very close to several of the most topical efforts in international graphics.
Edelmann — and this is yet another confirmation of the powerful nexus between north and south — is certainly a design figure who is looked at (and *copied*, according to Gianfranco Torri's malicious self-accusation) in the latest development in Italian graphics. We need only leaf through the catalogue of the most recent *Biennale della grafica italiana*, which took place in Cattolica during the summer of 1984.

Pierluigi Cerri

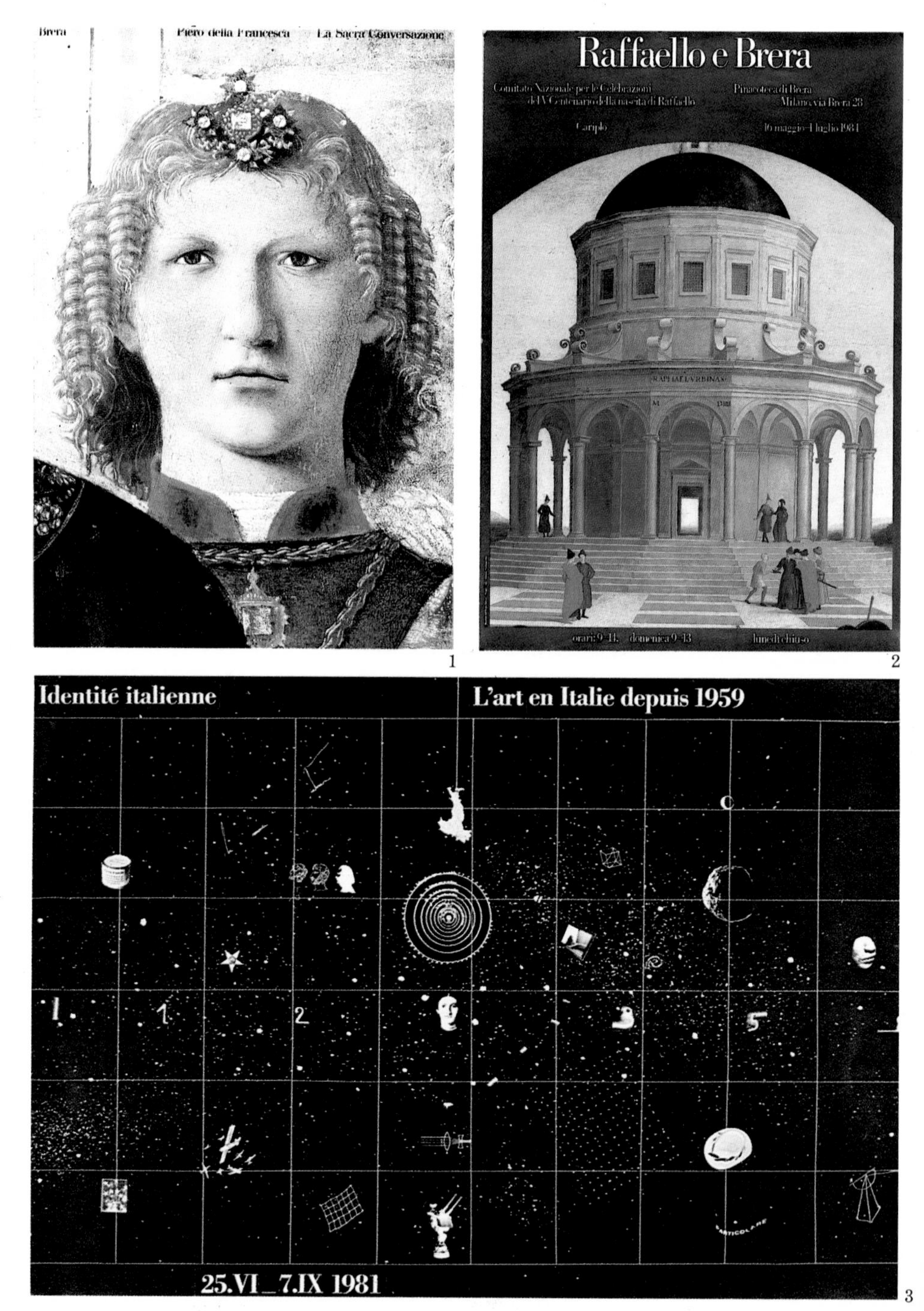

1. *Piero della Francesca*, Brera's altar-piece restoration, 1982.

2. *Raffaello e Brera*, 1982-1984.

3. *Identité Italienne - L'art en Italie dépuis 1959*, Paris 1981.

4. *Alexander Calder*, Turin, 1983.

5. *20 projects for the "Lingotto"*, Turin, 1984.

6.7.8. XXXVII Biennale, Venice, 1976.

CALDER
Mostra retrospettiva
Torino Palazzo a Vela
Luglio Settembre 1983
Città di Torino Toro Assicurazioni
LINGOTTO
ex Cantieri Navali alla Giudecca
5 GRAPHIC DESIGNERS
Roman Cieslewicz / Paul Davis
Milton Glaser / Richard Hess
Tadanori Yokoo
(– 28 agosto / 10 ottobre –)
B76
Cantieri navali / la Giudecca
Attualità internazionali 72/76
Un panorama sull'attività degli ultimi cinque anni.
85 artisti di ventuno paesi
(– 14 luglio / 10 ottobre –)
La Biennale di Venezia
B76

4 5 6 7 8

A.G. Fronzoni

1

1. *Fontana*, 1966.

2. *Un raggio di sole (Sun Beam)*, 1980.

2

Italo Lupi

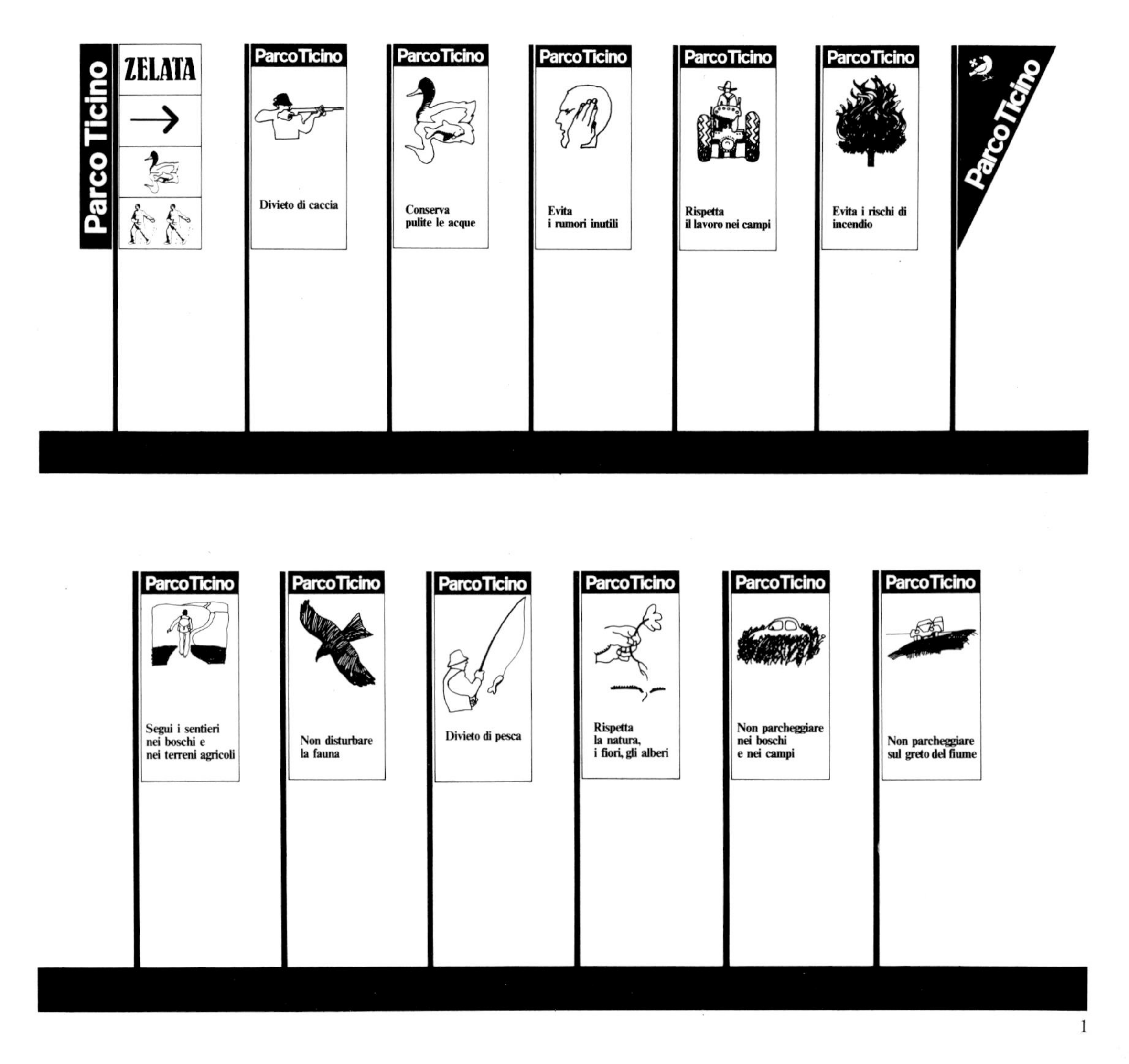

1. *Parco del Ticino (Ticino Park)*, 1980.

2. *La contesa in architettura (Architectural Contest)*, Milan, 1983.

3. *Belice*, 1980.

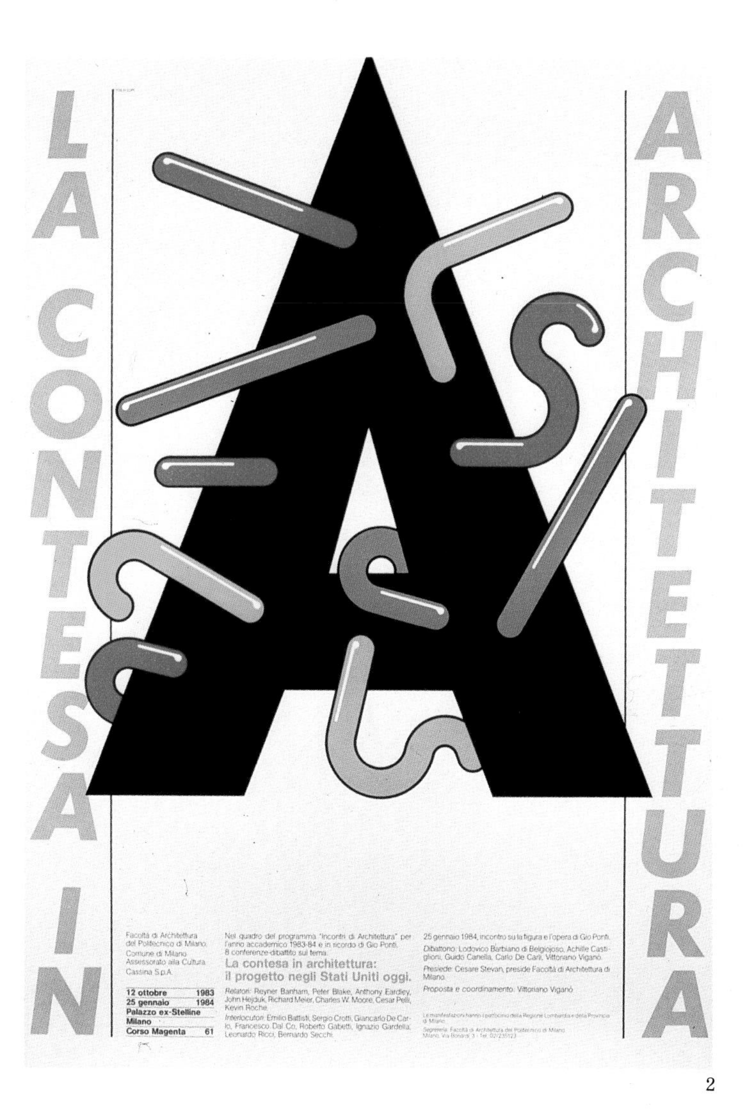
LA CONTESA IN
ARCHITETTURA
Facoltà di Architettura del Politecnico di Milano.
Comune di Milano
Assessorato alla Cultura
Cassina S.p.A.
12 ottobre 1983
25 gennaio 1984
Palazzo ex-Stelline
Milano
Corso Magenta 61
Nel quadro del programma "Incontri di Architettura" per l'anno accademico 1983-84 e in ricordo di Gio Ponti.
8 conferenze-dibattito sul tema:
La contesa in architettura:
il progetto negli Stati Uniti oggi.
Relatori: Reyner Banham, Peter Blake, Anthony Eardley, John Hejduk, Richard Meier, Charles W. Moore, Cesar Pelli, Kevin Roche.
Interlocutori: Emilio Battisti, Sergio Crotti, Giancarlo De Carlo, Francesco Dal Co, Roberto Gabetti, Ignazio Gardella, Leonardo Ricci, Bernardo Secchi.
25 gennaio 1984, incontro su la figura e l'opera di Gio Ponti.
Dibattono: Lodovico Barbiano di Belgiojoso, Achille Castiglioni, Guido Canella, Carlo De Carli, Vittoriano Viganò.
Presiede: Cesare Stevan, preside Facoltà di Architettura di Milano.
Proposta e coordinamento: Vittoriano Viganò
2

16ª Triennale di Milano
17
BELICE 1980
PROGETTI ALTERNATIVI
15 DICEMBRE
31 GENNAIO
1982
PALAZZO
DELL'ARTE
AL PARCO
FERIALI:
SABATO
E FESTIVI
3

Michael Klar

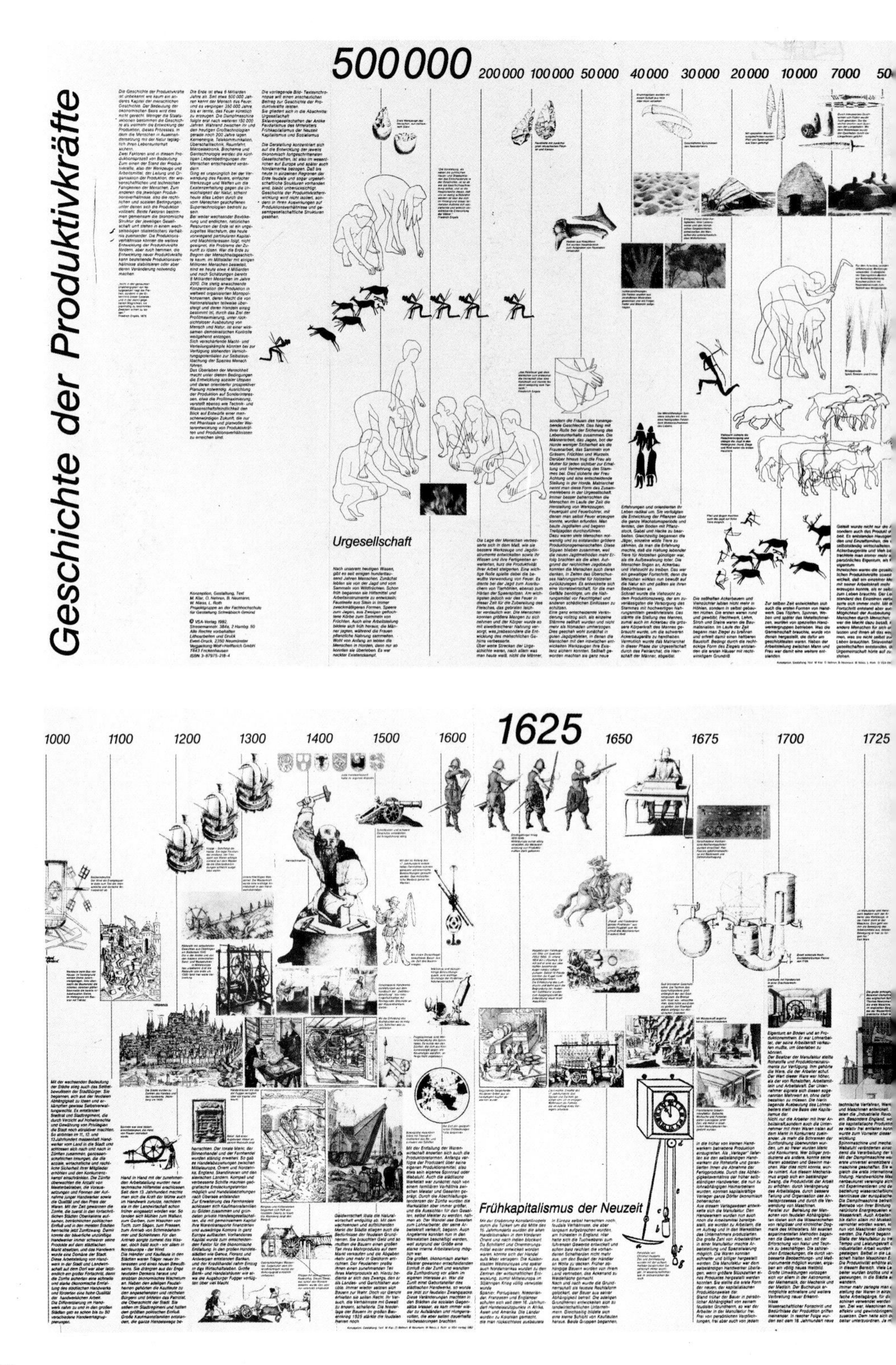

1. *Geschichte der Produktivkräfte (History of Productive Power)*, 1982.

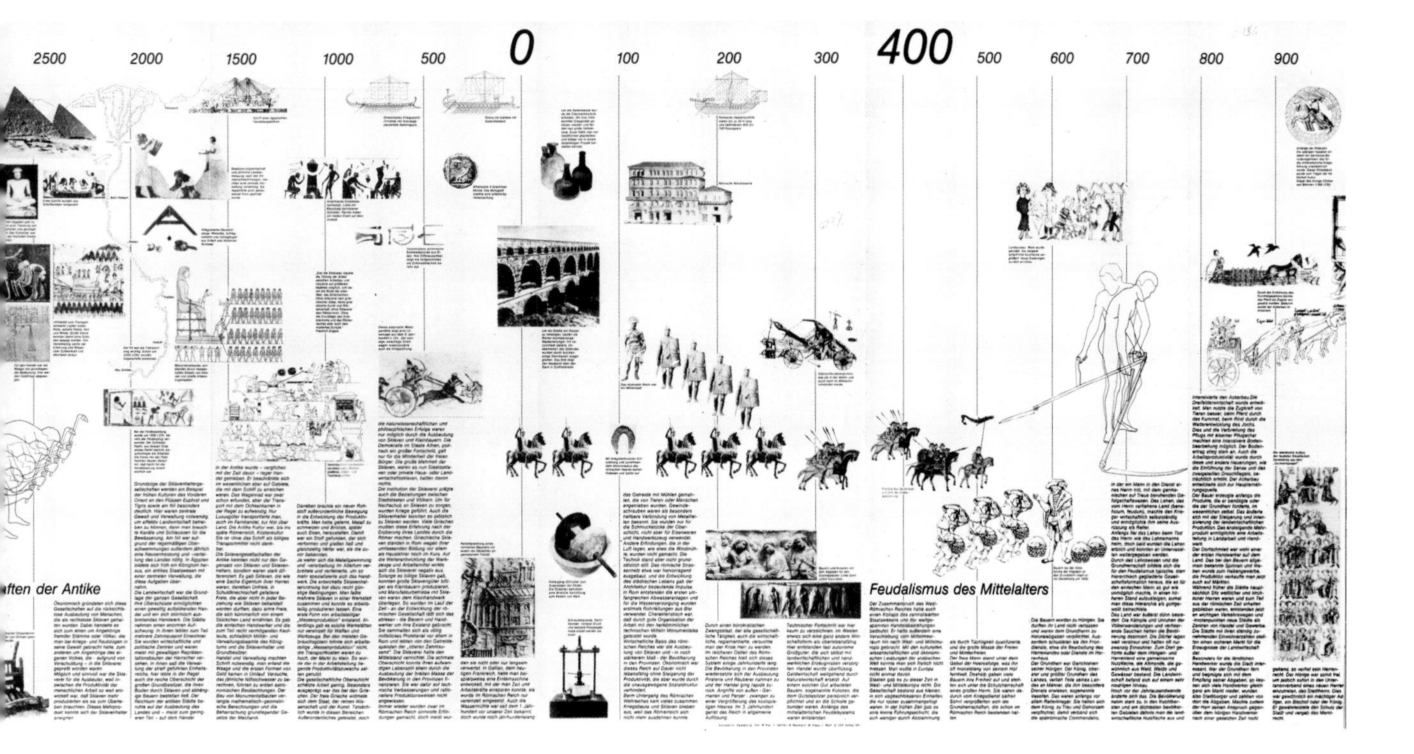
2500
2000
1500
1000
500
0
100
200
300
400
500
600
700
800
900
aften der Antike
Feudalismus des Mittelalters

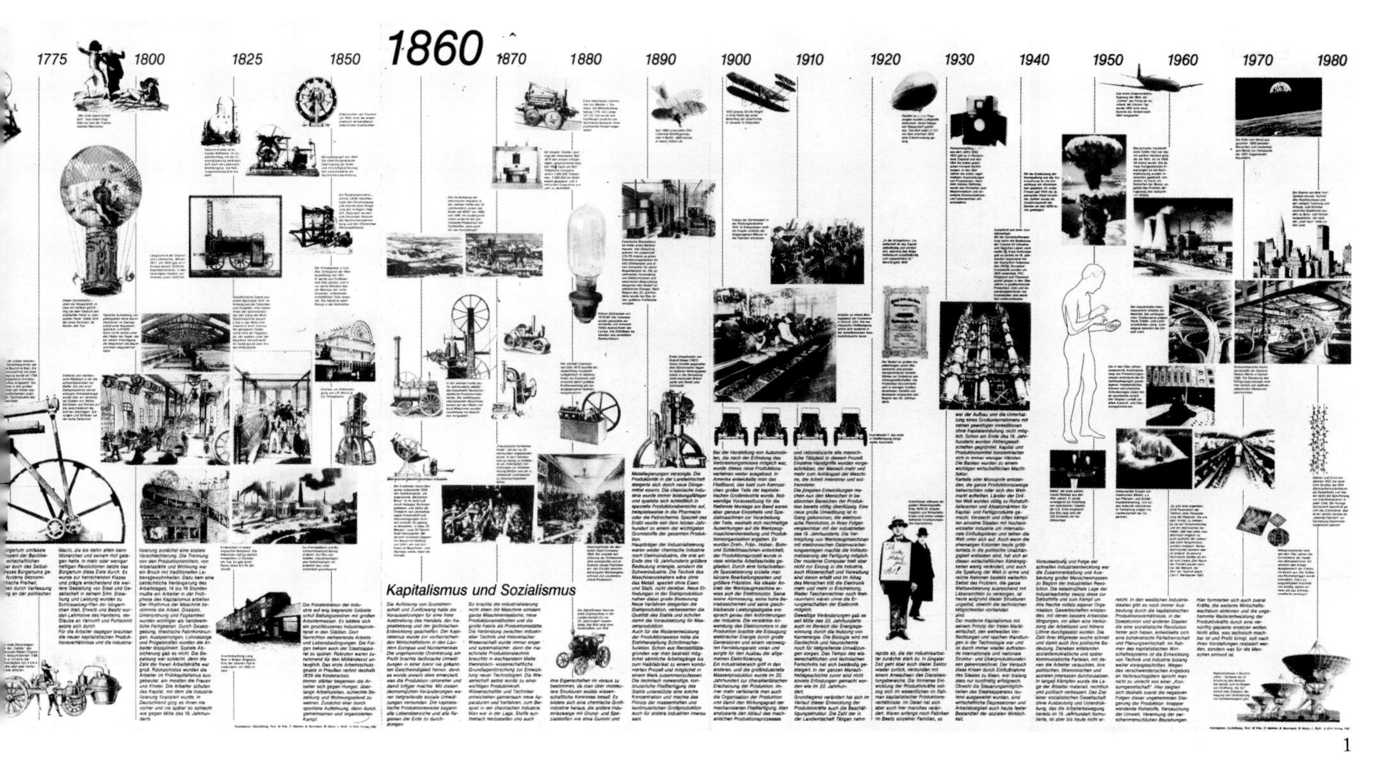
1775
1800
1825
1850
1860
1870
1880
1890
1900
1910
1920
1930
1940
1950
1960
1970
1980
Kapitalismus und Sozialismus

1

Karl Heinz Krug

1

1. - 13. *Form*. Covers and inside pages, 1957-1984.

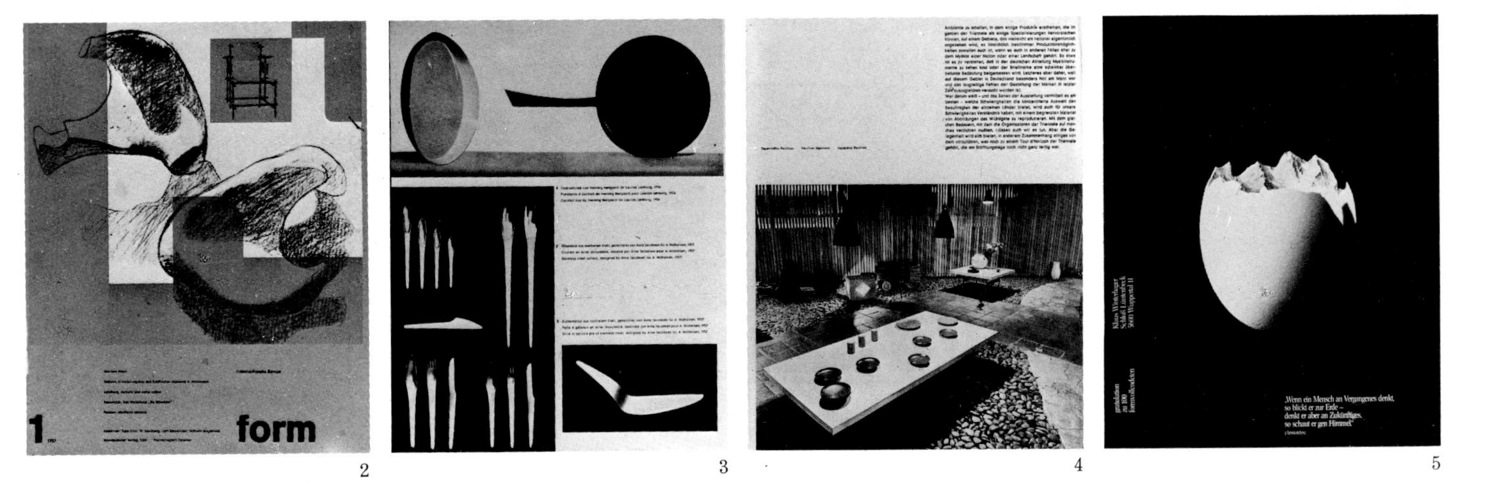

2 3 4 5

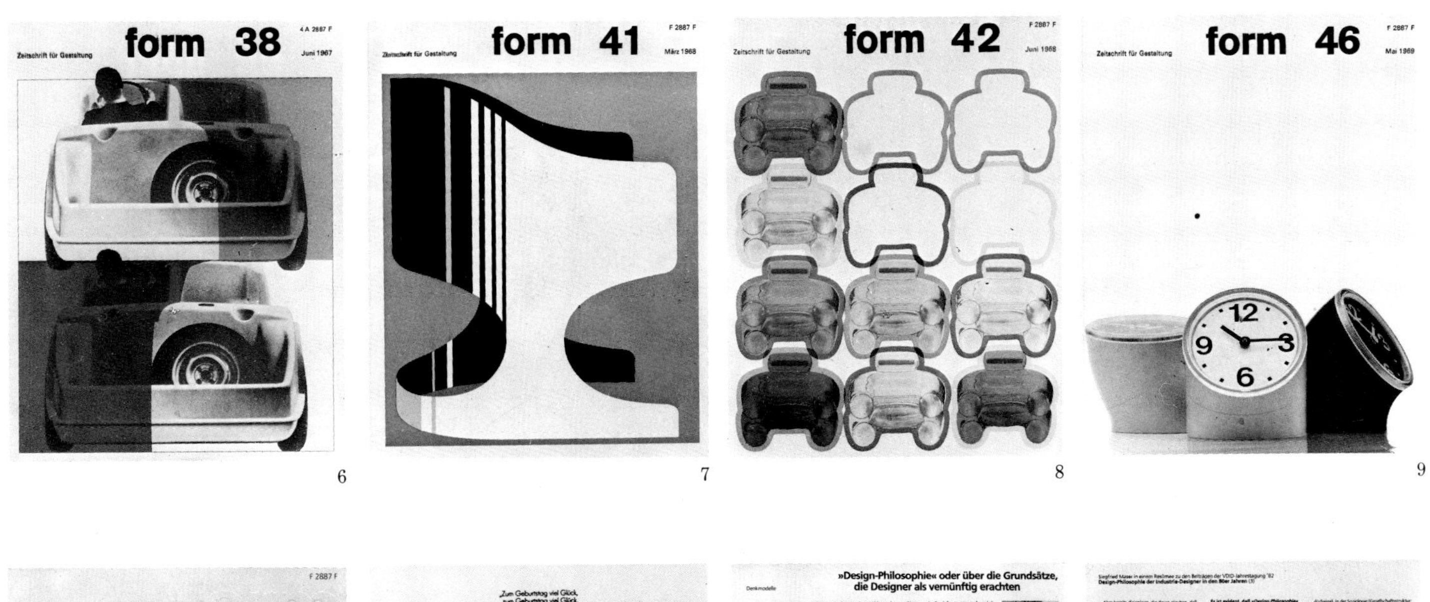

6 7 8 9

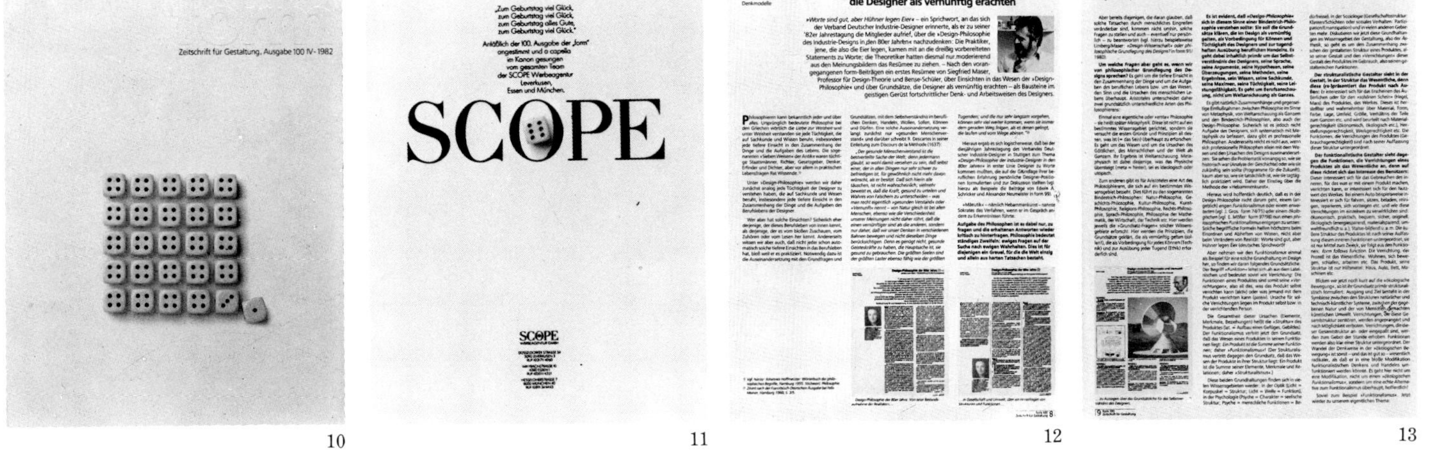

10 11 12 13

Some publications designed between 1963 and 1980.

SKYLINE
The Architecture and Design Review
One Dollar
AMERICAN HERITAGE
Knoll au Louvre
Eric Larrabee Massimo Vignelli
Knoll
Design
Peter Eisenman
HOUSE X
RIZZOLI
Graphic Design
for Non-Profit
Organizations
Butterflies

Photography

Vincenzo Castella
Verena von Gagern
Luigi Ghirri
Mimmo Jodice
Klaus Kinold
Nino Migliori
Philipp Scholz Rittermann
Wilhelm Schurmann

Photo/graphy

Arturo Carlo Quintavalle

During the past few years, the debate on photography has become livelier and livelier. Now, the historians of the official culture of the image are about to join the fray alongside the art historians. I believe, however, that a certain contradiction and even misunderstanding have developed in regard to photography. The contradiction concerns the entire history of photography, which is generally viewed as the history of realism, the history of the depiction of reality. This attitude obviously regurgitates old ideas, old academic models; however, it also involves an evasion of the history of photography in its various aspects and functions. The misunderstanding concerns the relationship between a technological assumption and an artistic one — or rather, between a code, several codes and their users. I would like to deal with this problem within the brief space allotted here.

If we review the history of photography, we discover things that challenge the view of the photo as a revolutionary device. At first, there was the dagherrotype (leaving aside Niepce and Fox Talbot, whose fundamental work, as we realize, was never widely known). The daguerrotype was a single work for a specific customer. Replacing the miniature portrait, it was certainly an elite product — nor could it be anything else. It never had the revolutionary function of a multiplied image, precisely because the daguerrotype icon existed in that single, unique copy.

It was deliberately preserved as a model, an archetype, as proof of a real image, as an icon replacing the depicted person, a family album of the dead, a province of the Lares, an area of regressive culture, and always to be viewed analytically in terms of the clients. A customer wished to elude his own death by opting for the icons of those who are "alive" through the "realistic" hypothesis of the photo. Preserving the true image was a way of living forever, escaping the reality of the end by means of the convention of the image, which was a reality in its own right.

Realistic culture in photography did not come until later, triumphing with the Paris-centricity of Nadar's *Ville lumière* and its relationship first with Balzac, then with Hugo and ultimately with the entire history of the serialized novel. The installments were illustrated with Doré's academic drawings, which were imbued with the anything but random surreal presence of things. Meanwhile, the existence and function of the daguerrotype may have helped to maintain the notion that photography is indeed an icon of reality.

There were two lines of tradition: the group portrait and the individual portrait. However, they were preceded by a culture of composition and imagery that was certainly not realistic but unmistakably painterly. I am speaking of the group portrait of the seventeenth century as well as the ostentatious "display" portraits and family portraits that made up the galleries of the "regal" culture of nobles and hence the bourgeoisie. In their development, these models became the legacy of the lower classes — needless to say, without changing the key to their interpretation.

If we shift from this tradition to the use of the photograph by academicians, specifically painters, we find ourselves dealing with a genre that has to be tracked down and excavated. Nevertheless, this genre was highly important, given what we know about the way the Impressionists used the photograph and the way the academicians used it in the school of photography. Here, however, we have different photographies and certainly diverse functions.

The important thing for the academicians was the length of time involved in photography, the conviction that by condensing a certain amount of shooting time in the image, photography profitably substituted the shooting of the model for its sketching and drawing. For the Impressionists, however, the main interest of photography was its renovating function, which the new emulsions gradually attributed to it; the mythology of the snapshot, of the duration of the momentary, apparently coincided with the mythology of the Impressionists (though these were snapshots of poses lasting minutes), with that of the *soleil levant*, which was naturally that of many artists, from Monet to Sisley, from Renoir to Degas. The idea that photography is a snapshot, capturing the instant, is an assumption that comes to us from history; above all, however, this assumption is actually part of the cultural model that we are used to and take for granted. Yet, I repeat, this is a poetic, an ideological datum — i.e., closely tied to the culture of idealism: first Hegelian and post-Hegelian; then, in our century, Bergsonian and Croceian.

But there are only those poetics in the history of photography, even if an ideological analysis could point out their substantial and internal contradiction. These investigations are actually only an (admittedly well known) portion of a far more complex experience. For instance, take a thread that is only being rediscovered now, in a revival of "realism." I mean the Nadar area. Not the Nadar linked to Balzac, but the one linked to Hugo's "populism." Nadar not only as a portraitist, but also as the man who mythically documented reality. An almost canonical example could be his so-called reportage of the *caves*, the Parisian catacombs, filled with Hugo-like dramatic effects (granted, with artificial lights, and mannequins replacing men who would have moved). This, and the post-Courbet culture of realism, led to the documentary photography of the world that, from Michetti to Verga, has filled and will continue to fill our research.

It would be useful to understand the cultures behind the so-called realistic transcriptions. Once and for all, we should stop applying terms like verismo, realism, document, etc., to an operation like photography, which is characterized by a precise encoding. We are, in sum, dealing with a major problem: how have these experiences contributed to changing our conception of photography as an invention, a choice — an idea that our critical tradition about specifics has never dreamed of suggesting that a photograph is a *compte rendu*, a report, a recording of reality. Even worse: let us recall postwar neo-realism, a mainly cinematic culture, rooted in Marxism and also linked to Lukacs by its chief practioners, e.g. Luchino Visconti. Its photographers were all connected to the magazine *Il Mondo*, and it operated substantially in terms of idealism in that it constructed "beautiful," obviously emblematic, and even non-contextual images, which, in this periodical, were seen in a sense, dependent on the texts. The complete antithesis to this was what Vittorini did in *Il Politecnico*, with sequential photography that was dependent on the culture of the ESA. His work was ignored by subsequent research, since, as we know, this important experiment was soon terminated. Thus, even realism ultimately told us that photography is an "art," and that a photograph depicts reality.

What about the discussions on photography outside Italy? Bresson is always being quoted, and he should be as an eponymous cultural figure, with his reportages. If we read his writings, we find that these reportages function as documents of reality — a reality, however, that (as Bresson himself says) is given only by the photographer's eye, which sees what the ordinary eye fails to see. Hence: the intellectual who sees beyond, the intellectual who virtually creates on the skin of the figure and the audience, the intellectual who knows when others do not know. Knows that? Is the problem of the reportage, implicit in our reference to Bresson, the problem of the analysis of reality or the problem of the acculturation of the masses and therefore of the creation of the consensus? No one would dare to say that any painter in the world documents reality with his image. Yet this statement is made about photographers, all photographers, even if we know perfectly well that only the shooting, the printing and hence the mass reproduction, the editing of the images and their sequential construction determine the sense of them, not to mention the titles, captions, etc., which, in a situation of the prevalence of the written language, constitute the interpretation factor, the phase in which the entirety has meaning. The history of photography agencies in general is the history of reporters, the history of the invention of a reality and its use. Yet when we reach this point, when we come to *Life* in 1936, for example, we see that photography had taken directions that were different from those that the great experiences of cultural revolution during the early twentieth century had wanted to give it. What I mean is that if we survey the history of the ideologies of photography (a history still to be written), we discover the following. This type of consumer product, or rather, this model of the consumption of a product conceived of as totally different, yet read and understood as a uniform function of the ideology of the buyer — this product has a very different and far richer history. I am attempting only a very swift reconstruction by means of examples in order to clarify what I will be saying more specifically about various figures in this horizontal cross-section of the Italian situation.

Let me indicate a few items in a survey that ought to be done in a more profound way. I am thinking of the work of Marey or Muybridge, who were so important for Duchamp (*Nu*) and the futurists — especially Bragaglia, but also the other painters. That work represents simply one aspect of a complex cultural context, the cinema, which tends to depict time — a problem that is seen (specifically) only as part of a problem of many other "intellectuals," in terms of European idealism. Naturally, the scope of this problem is much vaster, since it involves the theme of the machine and its relationship to man. However, the poetics of futurist photography — not one poetics, but several — and its use would not exhaust the question of the avant-garde.

When Man Ray completed the greatest revival in the history of photography, by discussing the work of Fox Talbot and off-camera contact printing, his approach sounded like a direct critique of the academic function, i.e., of the academic functionalization intrinsic to photography. Man Ray's approach, extrapolated from any context, seems to have no meaning other than the neo-romantic meaning of genius; but actually, he was performing a historical operation, he was rejecting the photographic culture of realism. And all his photographic acts (tinted, as I have indicated elsewhere, by alchemical colors, hence by the white of calcination) existed outside the culture of the camera, because they consciously recovered a system of codes that is different from the system proposed by the contemporary civilization of the image.

I am alluding not to official photography, but to picture postcards and to the documentation of Historic Monuments, the eponymous architecture of the city, symmetrical with the documentation of the eponymous faces of the eponymous figures of the city. On the one hand, the portraits of Queen Victoria, the official albums of the British nobility, Hanfestaengl's commissioned photos; on the other hand, the landscape photos, which are a similarly official aspect of how to chapture, and wherefore conceive urban structure.

Every country has its Alinaris and its Brogis; and they are always tethered to the pictorial culture — as a continuation or integration of that pictorial culture. We are dealing here with a substantial contradiction inside the medium itself: photography is apparently revolutionary, potentially revolutionary (according to Benjamin) because of its possibility of multiplication; and yet, in substance, it is reactionary, an official supporter of the conditioning culture of the academy.

There are many exceptions, many possibilities of pinpointing "styles" of the various practitioners; there are and will be many salvages. The so-called realist code is still a weighty and enduring code within our culture, and it has many variants; yet it has never operated officially in any part of Europe. This was the reference point for every photography that we would now call an "alternative" photography, that of the "avant-gardes." However, photography *without* cameras constituted a history that spread its roots beyond the foreseen limits. Painting with the objective was within official history and the class history of painting. But operating without a camera, i.e., without perspective, was tantamount to rejecting these assumptions and landing in the ambiguous zones in which codes blur into one another. Printing, engraving, photo-engraving, which were crucial factors in the nineteenth century culture of the image, newspaper illustrations, book illustrations and the problem of multiplication immediately became issues for photography as well. If photography means placing scissors and a spool of thread on a surface and letting light pass through it, what would it mean if someone did the same thing with a series of techniques considered peculiar to painting? This was a problem that had to be coped with and must still be dealt with today.

But now we come to the problem of editing, which has been so neglected by critics. It is wrong and unacceptable to negate the editing of the image in terms of *camera* photography. After all, we know perfectly well that if a photographer chooses a lens, an objective, a certain type of film, the format, and the size, or else trims the format in terms of the printing, then that photographer is actually editing an image and constructing its significance. Far from being the univocal representation of an icon, the photographic "writing" is actually a conventional search for an image, a construction of various pieces in terms of a meaning which the photographer assigns to the image itself, and which the users take upon themselves to assign. These users do so on the basis of the captions and the various lines of sequential editing (if they are there); or else, they go by the system of the context or contexts in which the icon is presented. As we can see, the meaning is merchandise; and there is no stable meaning of the image except in the idealistic imagination of the person talking of writing about it.

Hence, we are dealing not with histories of realistic shooting as opposed to histories of non-realistic shooting, but with verbal conventions that are obviously analyzed case by case. As Jakobson pointed out, there are multiple realisms rather than one single realism, and realism is always a problem of relationship, not an absolute system. Thus, an image may be realistic for us today; yet people who lived a century ago would not have qualified it as realistic. But let's get back to the avant-gardes and to the moment in which editing, invented some time back, is demonstrated *in vitro*, that is, "on paper." Naturally, I am referring to Dada in general and to the Berlin activities of the Dada photomonteurs, from Hartfield to Hoch and Hausmann. We will not analyze them in depth, if only because that would lead us outside of photography, as the expert of specifics might say; it would be a history of "manifestos" or illustrations or collages. With all these specifics we might very easily misunderstand the historical reality, we might fail to realize that using a canvas for a cityscape is like cutting up a figure (collage) and forcing it into an alien system. Hence, photography means constructing, editing, and the photomonteurs are the photographers who have made this problem so obvious to our culture.

We should now examine several other experiences, especially the impact of surrealism on photography. This discussion would take too long, however. For one thing, psychoanalytical interpretation is part of any critic's instrumentarium and therefore applicable to any situation; furthermore, the leaders of the surrealist movement clearly employed photography in their works, constructing a kind of mirror game. Thus, this history must be read as a whole and not in separate sections, as has usually been done.

How, then, can we proceed correctly after dealing with the first problem, i.e., the failed analysis, hence contradiction, in reading the history of photography? How can we proceed in order to understand the misunderstanding that I spoke of at the beginning of this article? I mean: writing histories of technologies (a vice typical of critics who live totally within the mythologies of the consumer society) and pitting them against one another.

Once, there was something interesting about a serious mistake in the historical perspective — i.e., constructing the opposition of painting and photography, which are actually functions of one another, forming a single history.

This mistake was fruitful, however (at least for us), because it showed the cultural level of the critics and made us realize that we have to write not histories of technologies, but the history of the technologies linked to the ideologies. Thus, this mistake shed light on the methodological poverty, the disarming naïvité of the "experts." However, not even this mistake

developed as we might have expected. We dread a history of engraving as opposed to a history of photo-engraving, of handwriting (ah, the romantic antithesis between the hand and the machine, a distinction that design — to cite just one example — reduced to outer trappings and hence to urban design — eliminated in the day of the Bauhaus) as opposed to a history of brush-writing (called pure painting, as we know), etc., etc...
This is why I have felt it would be useful to offer, within this survey of Italy and Germany, a group of individuals who have contributed to the medium. These are not all the people who have worked in this direction, only a few. I would venture to hope, however, that despite their small number, they are the most important ones, or else those who have shown a larger, richer and more complex awareness of the problems within the context of the overall phenomenon, which has to be delineated in the proper time and place.

Vincenzo Castella

1

1. *Monte S. Giacomo, Salerno*, from *Geografia privata*, 1982.

2. *Pescara*, 1983.

2

Verena von Gagern

1

1. *Bild vom Fluss (Picture of the River),* 1983.

2. *Bild vom Fluss (Picture of the River),* 1983.

2

Luigi Ghirri

1

1. *Scandiano*, from *Viaggio di ritorno (Return Journey)*, 1984.

2. *Sassuolo*, from *Viaggio di ritorno (Return Journey)*, 1984.

2

Mimmo Jodice

1

1. *Castellammare del Golfo*, 1981.

2. *Chateau de Sully, Loire*, 1984.

2

Klaus Kinold

1. *Sylt*, (Germany) 1982.

2. *Chicago*, 1983.

1

2

Nino Migliori

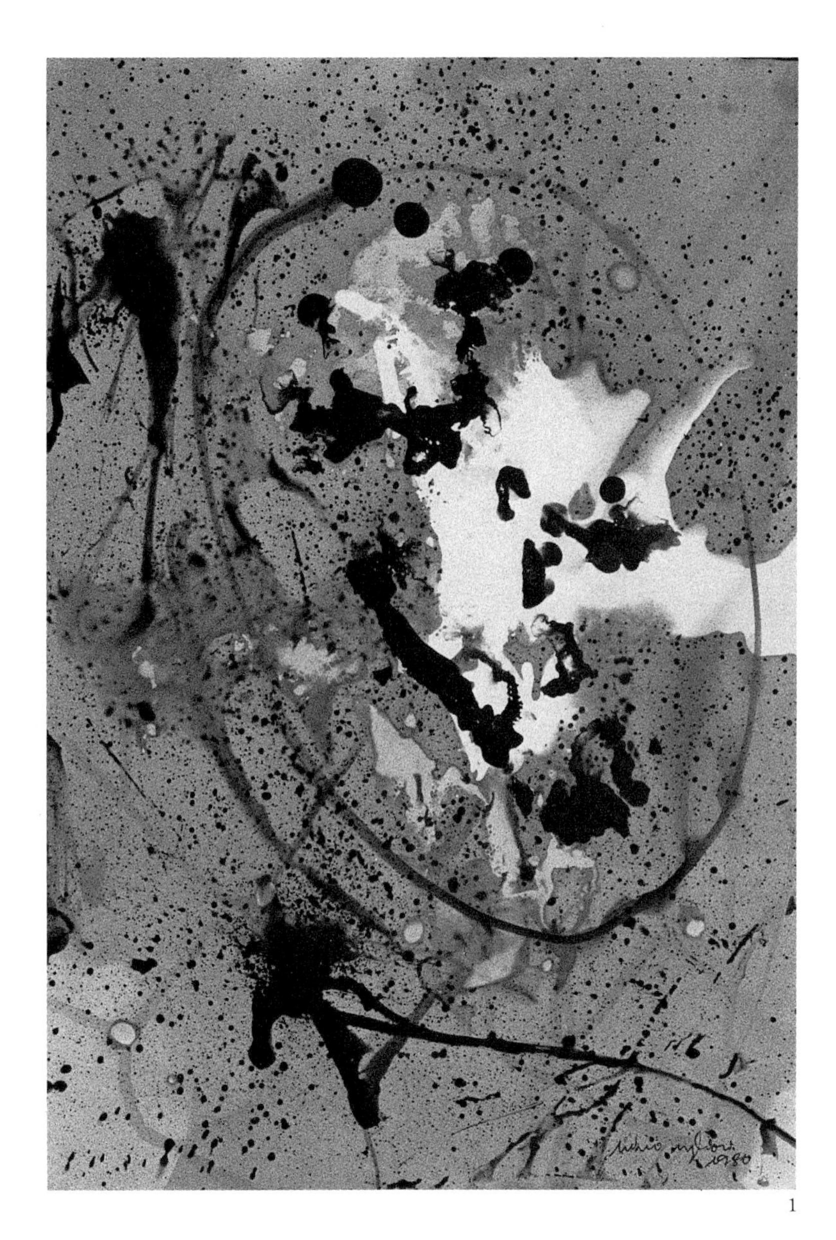

1

1. *Ossidazione (Oxidization)*, monotype, 1980.
2. *Ossidazione (Oxidization)*, monotype, 1984.

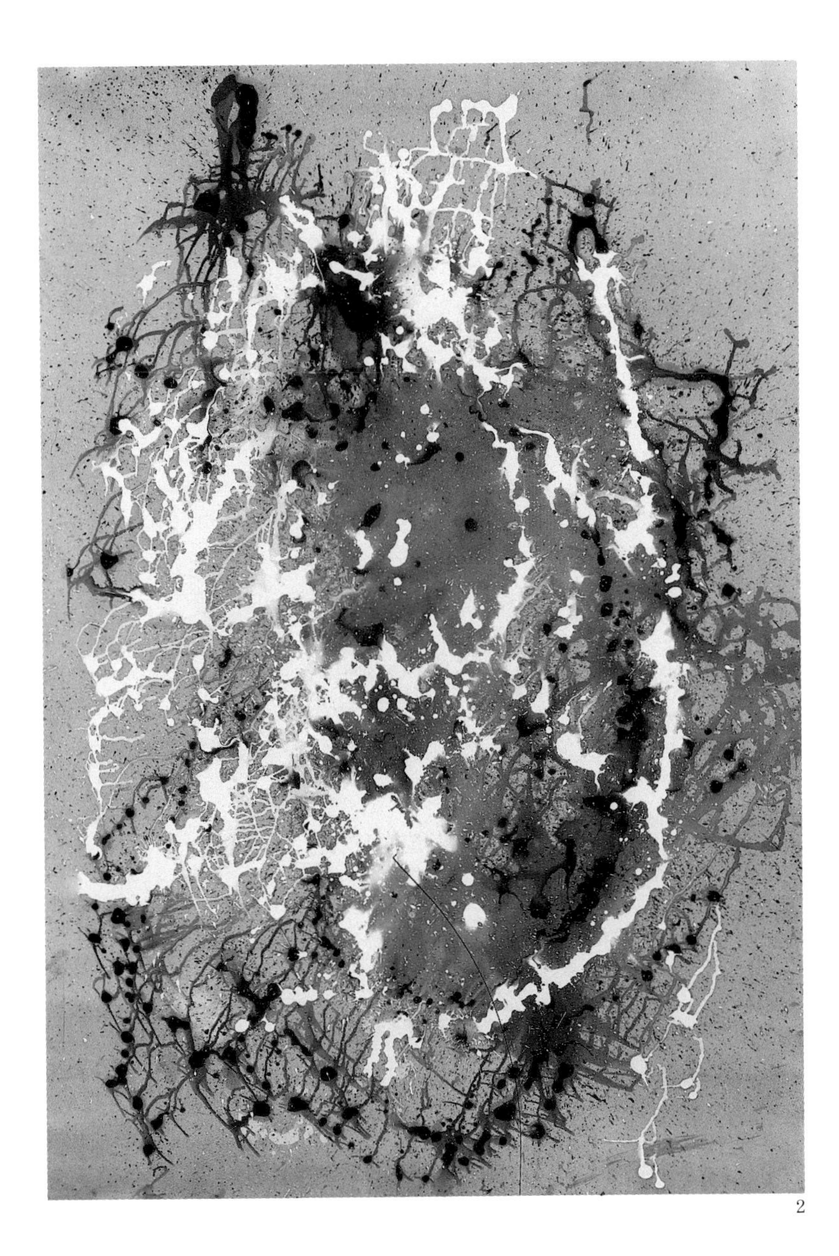

2

Philipp Scholz Rittermann

1

1. *Cementwarehouse with Bulging Door, Port of San Diego, California*, 1984.

2. *Railway Workers, Del Mar, California*, 1983.

2

Wilhelm Schurmann

1. *German Infantry*, 1984.

MARPOL
Marmor
und Stein
pflege
Mit Sicherheitskappe
WORLD WAR 11
GERMAN
INFANTRY
3.95
HO/OO
Scale
AIRFIX
48
PIECES
Model Figures
Making 43 Assemblies
FIGURES SUPPLIED UNPAINTED
NOT ACTUAL SIZE

Theater

From Traditional to Modern and Contemporary The New Italian Theater of the Eighties

Giuseppe Bartolucci

Foreword

These notes on the Italian theater focus on several features from the traditional theater to the modern and the contemporary theater, down to the most recent experiments of the postwar Italian stage, which has had its own origin, its own development, and its own crystallization in our day.

Naturally, these elements are only brief samples; but taken together, they constitute a good method of information.

In regard to the post-avant-garde , we can go into the movement itself and its dissolution, its cultural reference points and its specific qualities. As for earlier times, the examples of authors and plays are articulated and concentrated enough to clarify the development of the artistic work and its social background.At this point, the information becomes formation and belongs not only to the foreign reader, but re-enters the dynamics of Italian conflicts.

The Tradition

We cannot speak of tradition in Italy without citing Giorgio Strehler and his work as the assimilator and interpreter of a Central European theater world. Thus, his encounter with the Goldoni of *The Servant of Two Masters* can be seen as proof of a tradition in the sense that Strehler devoted all his poetic sense and his sense of craft. His poetry was shown in his quest for a gesture that began far away and reached us, not as nostalgia or as culture, but by demonstration and expression. And his craftsmanship was revealed in his total demand for precision and for references in synchronizing words and situations in an era if not in a style.

Modern

It is impossible to avoid mentioning modernity and Ronconi in the same breath. Ronconi was one of the first directors to feel the weight of an interpretative, dramaturgic, and theatrical tradition. From the very first, he went back to the actors as irreplaceable elements for a renewal of playwriting. At the same time, he moved to the space, as an inadequate vessel, which had to be upset from time to time, by excess and by omission of resemblance and fancy, by the destruction of habits and by the free play of invention. Ronconi even respected — in his own way, of course — the dramaturgy that he took over from time to time, almost always faithfully, and often with a particular approach.

Nevertheless, he always maintained a distinction and a link to certain — tendentially — classic playwrights. Thus, his work is modern precisely because of all these components, which we find in *Orlando furioso* as well as in his interpretation of romantic and ancient dramas, from the *Oresteia* to Kleist and Ibsen.

Dario Fo gave the best of himself in *Mistero buffo*; he resisted the temptation (not always an artistically useful one) to preach ideology, assault reality at any price, attack the occasions of the day, exchange them for inevitable dramaturgic material.

Instead, he wisely returned to the narrative of a tradition in revolt and admirably fished out moments and situations in a state of conflict. Even more important, he rediscovered or invented a low, comic, popular gesture full of energy and clashes, demanding participation and extremely provocative, yet natural and cultivated, acute and very simple, transparent and straightforward.

Here, comedy radiates and becomes tragedy, turns into madness and then reattains great wisdom. It makes itself available to all: a comical Italian *being*, vulgar and crazy, the face and the madly desirous body, the bitter smile and the agitated hands, saving itself from the torrent of anti-literary prevarications and landscapes miracoulously suspended between falsehood and reality, recomposing an overall gesture of an actor-author on the threshold between today and yesterday.

G. Strehler, *Arlecchino servitore di due padroni.*

L. Ronconi, *Orlando furioso* (Edmonda Aldini).

When the late Eduardo De Filippo was on stage, he knew how to drain his own physiognomy and throttle his words and gestures, either because his work was primarily a quest for essence and simplicity, or because what he said and how he said it established a series of naked and complex communication signs that are transparent and multiple. This explains his extraordinary primordial and yet contemporary vein, his tragic and quotidian stage presence as a witness to and accomplice of artistic situations or states of grace. For example, with Pirandello's *Il berretto a sonagli*, more than for other interpretations of his work, Eduardo proceeded by draining, by excavating the Pirandello dramaturgy. This is an elevated isolation of the interpretation of the protagonist and his environment. The resulting spectacle was exemplary as a communicative tension, with no expressive rhetoric and no oratory influence. We saw an interpretational construction/destruction; Pirandello's meaning was extracted from literature and staged *en bloc*, even in the details, with no betrayal of its nature and motion. A Pirandello in search of a multiplication of reality as well as a white-hot fission of dreams was cultivated by Eduardo in terms of steep, rocky precipices and wounds inflicted by glances and gestures. The glances were from a physiognomy that is both mobile and empty; the gestures were within an absence of approximate recognitions and a presence of irregular and insidious demands.

Carmelo Bene, our contemporary, is offensive to many and he is not a secret for a few. He is contemporary as someone who, in passing through the fragments and warpings of the avant-garde, was not taken in by the false and immobile battle between tradition and vanguard; as someone who, naturally choosing the modern as his banner, hence the renewal and contemporary relevance of dramaturgy for interpretation and production, never yielded to the temptation of anti-classical rigidity or environmental destruction. Thus, he has worked and perjured himself on specifics, stupendously alternating between stage, cinema, video, and music, always getting to the gist, the essence, by way of dramaturgical and interpretational fragmentation and depopulation. He refused to save himself by means of a

D. Fo, *Mistero buffo.*

romantically sterile vindication of artistic primacy. Instead, he affirmed himself in a productive artistic modality that is able to act upon the poetic reality and its practice.
In *Un Amleto in meno*, Carmelo Bene created the landscape and the faces, the images and the lights, for an illuminated cultural encounter and for a subjective invasion of data. Faithful to his Baroque interlacing of nature and theater, of interpretation and disloyalty of literary writing and the way it takes possession, his *Hamlet*, painted on the face, the eyes, the hands, is read in a visionary fashion, in slices of light and physical impressions: since any other legitimate encounter and any other pertinent observation would deprive it of substance and uniqueness. The contemporary quality of Carmelo Bene also resides in this grip on his own self on which he unleashes all those stimuli and all those other signs.

Part Two

It is as hard, indeed as impossible to present the new theater in Italy as it is anywhere else. The avant-garde has exhausted its alternative energy; tradition is more of a nostalgic repetition than a verification or resumption. The modern is continually reabsorbed by tradition and eludes the imperative of the avant-garde. In Italy, we see a simultaneous wealth of possibilities.
We have the poetic exhaustion of tradition (staging by interpretation and dramaturgy: Strehler); the constant display of the modern (dispossession of subversion and interpretational reinvention: Ronconi); the simultaneous state of agitation in artistic and theatrical language (Carmelo Bene: by way of extreme subjectivity and high sonority); the display of the actor and the author by Fo and Eduardo as examples of going through the theater in terms of a total interpretation and a dramaturgical re-elaboration.
In addition, the past few years have brought several other groups into new situations and with various kinds of creativity. They have been collectively labeled a post-avant-garde, to distinguish them from the alternative theater of the sixties, that of Ricci and Quartucci, and the so-called image theater of the Perlinis and Vasilicos of the seventies. Initially, these groups of the post-avant-garde aimed at a staging without actors, without texts, by means of lights and sounds, with an urban route and a basement specificity (Simone Carella and the Group '72). Or else, they expressed themselves in terms of existential pathologies and minimal analyses, offering an extremely rigorous and penetrating subjectivity (Magazzini Criminali). Or else, they arranged movements and gestures, behaviors and measures by means of grace and balance in steady variations (Gaia Scienza). With their methods of working and staging, these groups introduced a vast number of experiments, a singularity of ideas, often involving other art forms (music, cinema, video, architecture, etc. — Falso Movimento), and utilizing quotations with complexities of signs, even close or distant influences (Raffaello Sanzio). Thus, for the Italian stage of the eighties, the post-avant-garde constitutes a valid reference point, not only at home but also abroad.
The events at the Festival of Poets in Castelporziano probably represent the best of the new theater, that is, the environmental display of a method of operating externally without falling short of a basement practice. In other words: the ability to arrange the vanguard elements and materials in a spectacle with the purpose of creating communication beyond messages and contents. This hinges on the lucid and pitiless, yet open and passionate guidance of Simone Carella, as well as the poetic sensitivity and underground tension of Franco Cordelli. And thus the seascape setting — the moon and the water line, the desert and the horizon — was distributed among tens of thousands of spectators and dozens of Italian and

international poets. The result was an explosion that blasted several contradictions between artists and poets embracing the crowd and the crowd's demand that it not take part in the consoling and aesthetic game of making art and poetry. And yet, even with the development of a true dramatic action, with so much diffusion, with an irregular use of the time/space continuum and with no network of communication and information.
Imagine the situation: poetry and poets physically *in situ*, gradually winning over a fierce and inattentive audience of "accomplices," the flights due to the inability to both exist and resist at the same time. And then, victory by means of violence, ambiguously uniting, say, the political intensity of Leroi Jones and the sensitivity of Ginsberg, and yet manifesting itself in chorales and sacredness. Now, at a distance, all these factors allow us to nimbly overcome the famous actions of the claque against the poets, the insidious fears of the very young in the throes of terrorist narcissism, the exercises of mass communications, the display of similar residues or relicts in the constrained representation of poetry.
Environmental music and desert crossing, science-fiction decorations and natural descriptions, repetitive electric gestures and modern surface situations, fashionable quotations (Eno, Mendini, Hassel) betrayed at the outset and running as various reprises of interpretation (music, future space), battles to the death amid the loss of meaning and its possible recovery, amid surface descriptions in other styles and perforations of beauty by means of profound discardings: as usual, the Magazzini distinguish between what counts at the moment and what needs to be discarded, between what is inevitably to be offered and what must be cruelly abandoned (*Ebdomero*, *Crollo nervoso*). They are accustomed to analysis and pathology, to showmanship and mass media; and now they are on the threshold of the invasion of myth; yet the results of *On the Road* are like a challenge to adventure and also a proof of emotion, a fictitious game, a theatrical seduction (here too Hassel and Liberatore have taken direct hold by means of an interweaving of heat and light, percussions and accelerations, visionary energies and movement, etc.). The latest work, *Genet in Tangiers*, gets to the heart of a poetic sensibility that, by inflating expectations and playing a bit outside the house, finds within itself an interpretational standard based on a visionary perception and on reflexes of collective behavior. This spectacle does not enfeeble a center that is not regarded as such; nor does it play at its own marginality by means of reassurance. Instead, it manipulates a mechanism of communication, in which the eye and the idea, the ear and the imaginary gaze at one another and infiltrate one another on a basis of passion, on an unimpeded rapture. All this is given an absolute depiction, a rendering of aesthetic accounts with a fine tactical reversal and with a splendid poetic provocation under the insignia of a Genet crisscrossed by Fassbinder, Ginsberg, and Burroughs.
Gaia Scienza knows how to administrate itself quite well in the sense that for years now the members have added superfluous things to their own work, elegantly safeguarding it, that is, measuring themselves continually with their own sensibility and with their own work. However, this superfluousness is their energy, or rather their mode of existence and self-expression; here, a

Magazzini Criminali, *Crollo nervoso*.

Falso Movimento, *Tango glaciale.*

Gaia Scienza, *Cuori strappati.*

Raffaello Sanzio, *Kaputt Necropolis.*

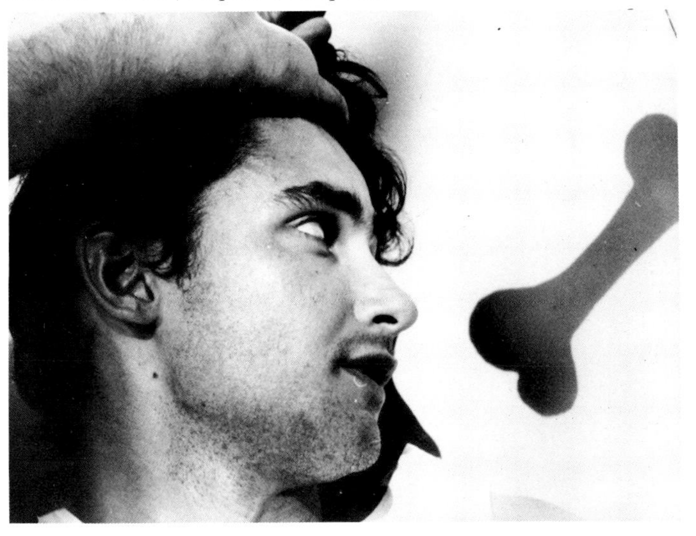

certain lightness fuses with a particular snobbery, and a certain attractiveness blends with a specific fleeing. The members of this group gave their gesture a diffraction and suspension beyond the original lesson of post-modern dance. They "befouled" themselves with internal and external drama navigating over roofs or sliding over squares, beyond any more or less occasional showmanship. And, finally, they culled the new sensibility of inside/outside, from fashion shows to natural landscapes, from back-court exhibitions to tableaux vivants by which the contemporary dramaturgical line is judged, beyond the notion of speech loss as a label and formula for a doomed experimental theater. Using losses of meaning and multiplications of seduction, the members of Gaia Scienza have set up a structure that is mobile in interpretation and scenery, both unprotected and constructed; they can expand and pretend to be masters, they can believe themselves to be traitors and reassure themselves with their own existential rages and their interpretational frenzies. All this in the name of a fashion/counter-fashion, which exists in the play of the whirlwind of transitions of the contemporary and, at the same time, finds a shelter, feigning a defense, betraying its own behavior, even its own work. There is no better way of surviving the exposure of "broken hearts" — to quote the title of their famous presentation. Mario Martone (with his people) has commanded attention with his use of technological materials and his combinations of interpretational elements. He has surprised not only those who watched him experiment with analyses and spectacle, minimal and communicative; but also in a certain sense he has remained himself, and his approaches, from the installation of *Tango glaciale* to *Othello*, and from the perfection and practicability on a public level of these productions. In these two shows, Martone employed a spatial environment that is simply a decoration in terms of a contemporary decorativeness; he also used an expository narrative that involves decorative bodies and objective emotions in an ambiguity of interpretation. From this point of view, the work of Mario Martone and Falso Movimento virtually draws a final balance of the new theater and overcomes the very notion of a metropolitan image, while retaining his very personal compositional design and his very particular showmanship. The eye — and the ear — clear a path for themselves, taking command by means of

receptions and diffractions that are neither marginal nor warped, but tendentially global and compact.
We cannot conclude this survey of the contemporary Italian theater without a look at the work of Leo-Perla. The tragic nature of Leo-Perla is so manifest that it responds to a habit and a judgment; a naturally comic tragedy that elevates and lowers the dramatic materials, turning expectations upside down. Leo-Perla know how to live concealed and to suffer the agonies of hell, mixing the afflictions of life and artistic elevations, continually proving and obliterating those everyday poetic exercise which they are accomplices to and executors of. Thus, their productions are always noisy and elicit passionate and curious detractors and fans, they are generally masses of irregularity, arousing both intimate and spectacular reactions. In particular, the lapses, with which they wreak havoc to dramatize the situation, are almost always to the up-and-down, alto-bass pedal and the physical and mental diffusion that are the foundation, the motor of their work. For many years now, Leo-Perla have been concentrating and decentralizing themselves, miraculously unscathed by negligence and habit, naturally paying for that rather expensive irregular behavior, either in terms of a legitimate productiveness (which always runs through their fingers, marginalizing them beyond vindication) or in terms of a slow and insidious wear and tear in the comforts of life and, at the same time, in art and poetry.

Action - Learning - Suffering
Success and Crisis at the Berlin Schaubühne at Lehniner Platz

Peter Iden

Among the attempts to redefine the work of the theater in the early eighties, a number of productions by the Berlin Schaubühne stand out in high relief. Redefinition today means the development of aesthetic positions within a diffuse situation that is marked by disappointments in society as well as in the arts and that demands at the very least a re-examination of the vocabulary of the theater of the sixties and seventies in the search for a new orientation.
From the time Peter Stein and his group began productions at the Schaubühne in 1970, it rapidly became one of Europe's leading stages, exemplary in both its organization and results. For a decade, the latest productions of the Schaubühne dominated every discussion of the theater. It is a singular event in the history of the German theater that such enormous energy, which has again turned Berlin into a capital of world theater reminiscent of the twenties, has not slackened for so many years: no other stage has been able to maintain its pre-eminence for a comparable period of time. The continued influence of this theater is testimony to the great individual artistic power of the directors Stein, Grüber and Bondy, the dramaturges Dieter Sturm and Botho Strauss, the set designer Karl-Ernst Hermann and the actors and actresses who have made the Schaubühne a reference point for the international theater public from *The Mother* (*Die Mutter*) and *Peer Gynt* (1970-71), *Kalldewey*, *Hamlet*, and *The Negroes* (*Les Nègres)* (1982-83), to *Three Sisters* (1984).
According to some, the Schaubühne passed its peak once Peter Stein and his Ensemble left the crumbling theater on Hallesches Ufer on the edge of Kreuzberg to move to the center of Berlin on the upper Kurfürstendamm. The city had engaged the architect Jürgen Sawade to transform a famous, old movie house of the thirties, Mendelsohn's Universum, into a theater for the Schaubühne. Many questions preceded this change of location: didn't the move to Kurfürstendamm mean a step into the Establishment? Wouldn't the new house be too luxurious, too fine, too chic for the critical purposes of Stein and his people? Wasn't there a danger that the Ensemble might lose its love of improvisation, so often inspired by the very inadequacies of the old theater on Hallesches Ufer? And finally, wouldn't the presence of several theaters in the rebuilt Mendelsohn building put the Schaubühne under production pressures that Stein had long sought to avoid for the sake of quality?
But when the new playhouse, jointly designed by the architect and the theater people, was presented to the public in August 1981, the architectural critics gave rave reviews — here was a house that had been expressly created for Germany's premier theater and provided with unparalled facilities. The critic Heinrich Klotz described his first impressions in the following words: "You find yourself standing in a theater whose unusual appearance at first glance resembles a work hall but soon reveals itself as an enormous basilica with side aisles and apse. The steel ceiling is an open lattice from which the sets, lights and acoustic equipment can be lowered as desired. The entire hall can become a stage, or an auditorium. There aren't any fixed places or hard and fast partitions for this or that function anymore. The conventional categories of picture-frame stage and the newer arena-stage are no longer relevant, for the space can be divided, cut up, lowered or raised; can become whatever you want, even a picture-frame stage or arena, or then again an open unpartitioned hall, or even a kind of Roman stadium. The floor can slope toward the apse in regularly stepped intervals, or form a

depression in the middle; it can be perfectly flat or descend into a pit, making a sacred hall of what had just been a plain secular room. The character of the space is as variable as the stage-forms it can assume. Almost every aspect of the architecture is transformable; hardly anything is fixed. To speak here in terms of the currently popular notion of 'flexibility' would be wrong, for the degree of plasticity here is far greater than what this hackneyed and misused word can express. The key to this transformability is in the 3 × 7 meter floor plates which can move up and down individually and lift or lower great weights like power jacks. The entire floor, thus, is subdivided into movable rectangles that can be raised and lowered by hydraulic pistons. There are, further, two huge retractable walls which can partition the hall into three separate transverse spaces. The apse area can accomodate three hundred guests, the two longitudinal aisles six hundred each, or a total of fifteen hundred. Each of the transverse spaces can become a chamber theater or rehearsal theater. And while sets in one of the spaces are being changed, the performance can continue in another. The audience then finds itself directly behind one of the raised walls facing the new stage set, and can enter the acting space and climb up or down the stepped floor. Like the floor and walls, the segmented ceiling is also completely movable. The grids and screens can be entirely removed, as well, allowing huge sets to be lowered at any given spot. A workshop." (*Frankfurter Rundschau*, 20 August 1981.)

As Klotz further observed, the model for this new theater behind the renovated façade of the old Mendelsohn building was not traditional theater architecture but rather the improvised sets of the Schaubühne itself; both in the old house of Hallesches Ufer and in the studios and workshops it was from time to time necessary to move to for various projects already in the seventies. In this regard, then, continuity existed between the old and new locations.

Nonetheless, Peter Stein treated the move with great caution. There was no special premiere of a new production and thus none of the pressure of public scrutiny invited by an opening. The *Oresteia* was first performed in the old theater on Hallesches Ufer in October 1980 and was taken to the new house almost a year later. Stein wanted a smooth transition and he used smaller works at first to approach quietly and test out the new instrument.

Within the Ensemble of the Schaubühne itself, however, lay further reasons for such caution. From 1970 to Botho Strauss's opening of *Big and Little* (*Gross und klein*) in December 1980, almost every single one of the theater's productions had been an undisputed success. A deep skepticism and — its prerequisite — a heightened perception of subjectivity in all its uneven, irregular structures and projections had led the Schaubühne to a theme that preoccupied it throughout this period: brave new departures that come to naught. The performances all told of these foundering efforts, crushed under the most varied social and personal circumstances. In fact, they portrayed failure as an inevitable component of every new beginning. The plays often bore the message that only beyond the experience of failure and in the consciousness of defeat might hope re-emerge. (For a detailed study of this recurrent theme of the productions and its aesthetic consequences, please refer to the author's *Die Schaubühne am Halleschen Ufer 1970-1979* [Hanser-Verlag, Munich, and Fischer-Verlag, Frankfurt, 1979 and 1982].)

For many years the Schaubühne confronted the theme of failure without foundering itself. After 1979 that was no longer the case. The premier theater of West Germany experienced a number of defeats. This was due in part to changes in the Ensemble, but the productions in question are not worth mentioning any more, for the Schaubühne has been able to sustain its skill at daring and accomplishing the extraordinary despite these miscarriages. The productions to be discussed, Stein's *Oresteia*, and his *Three Sisters*, Bondy's *Kalldewey*, Grüber's *Hamlet* and, at the end of our list, Stein's staging of Genet's *The Negroes* in the early summer of 1983, are proof of this continued excellence. At the very latest, Grüber's production of *Hamlet* in 1982 in the Mendelsohn building, using its dimensions to the full, proved despite earlier skepticism that the new house could augment rather than diminish the quality of theater at the Schaubühne.

Despite differences in temperament between the directors and in the times and subjects they treated, Stein's *Oresteia* and Grüber's *Hamlet* have a number of things in common. Most importantly, the attitude of both towards the old texts differed strongly from that found in contemporary theater generally and in the public at large in its emphasis on the priority of the dramatic action over a particular interpretation. For this reason, both productions — like that of Chekhov's *Three Sisters* — were criticized as being "conservative." This so-called "conservatism," which for some time now has no longer been definable in opposition to — and especially not in pejorative opposition to — what is "progressive," this "conservatism" is precisely what gives these productions their particular importance in the discussion of the renewal of the theater today.

Hermann Lauser and Ilse Ritter in *Macbeth,* Schauspiel, Cologne.

Peter Stein: Oresteia

The Schaubühne's preparations not only for the production of the *Oresteia* but also of the public were extensive. The actors and actresses, in particular, were intent on making the production — their second Greek piece, after *Project-Antiquity* (*Antikenproject*) of 1974–more accessible with the help of a number of explanatory workshops. Similar preparatory workshops had been used at other theaters and they attracted a good deal of interest at the Schaubühne now, where they were of such high quality that they became an event in themselves, alongside the main event.

These pre-noon presentations were led by Peter Stein to acquaint the public more closely with the director — what moved him, his thinking and his work. From the very beginning, Stein's work in the theater has sought to establish connections with social reality. The stage action always has for him an element of "someone's life is at stake here."Although these public seminars on the *Oresteia* sometimes began on a rather pedantic note, they quickly evolved into sharp, witty, enjoyably thought-provoking excursions into the world of the Greeks. One never came away feeling one had been force-fed a dogmatic program; one had the sense, rather, that Stein was arranging the course of the afternoon's events with the public. It was a pleasure to watch him respond to questions or comments from the audience or be willingly diverted from his line of thought for a while and then decisively steer both himself and the others back on track. A brilliantly staged example of spontaneity and intellectual agility.

Take for example a Sunday morning in May 1980. Stein is sitting with several of the younger members of the Ensemble in front of the closed curtain in the theater of Hallesches Ufer. These are the performers who will appear in the play later that day. Stein introduces them to the audience and draws them into the already almost familiar circle of guests. Distance is overcome; one and all embark on a common journey — destination: the Greeks. The purpose of such conversations with the public for those involved in the performance, Stein explains, is to find out what associations people have with names like Apollo or Athena, for instance. He says, "It makes me think right off of 'Pizzeria Apollo' and I see Athena in the Citroen logo." He asks, "What do you think of theaters 'messing around with all this old stuff?" The beginnings are modest, but the off-hand tone does not obscure the seriousness of the effort to understand the ancient themes nor the respect, even awe, elicited by the energy and beauty of the old poetry.

With a leap we move from the eponymous pizzeria, the trivial residue of Grėek culture, to Hesiod: a precipitous change of mood following a leisurely preamble. The actors and actresses read passages from Hesiod's 2,600-year-old narration of the creation of the world. Stein points out a formal connection to the *Oresteia*: Hesiod's cosmogony is not a linear one; existing alongside Chaos from the very beginning is Gaia or Earth, who brings forth Uranos, the Heavens. So too in Aeschylus's trilogy, complexes of motifs stand side by side, independent. Then a change of pace again. As though it has just occurred to them that very moment, Stein and the actors open the stage curtain on the space where the *Oresteia* will be performed, and then move on to problems of the structure of the text, the translation, the means of representation. (Stein, not without rather heavy-handed coquettishness, suggests that when Apollo purifies the temple of the Furies, "it would be nice to have a full-blooded American director to do the job.")

There are a number of fractures during the morning session, but also many new ideas, connections and pathways into this remote material. Even an argument in favor of the Humanistic Gymnasium gets thrown in. And in fact, the lesson here is that when antiquity is presented not as cultural dead weight but, as by Stein and his Ensemble, as a reservoir of cultural knowledge that trains the mind and the imagination, then looking at "all this old stuff" not only makes sense but is imperative.

And all the hard work the Schaubühne has taken on makes sense too: an effort to counteract the sloppy practice of so many contemporary theaters. Stein: "I think we will be subsidized for the continuity of our efforts, even if the preparations take months. That's our special task."

The production followed barely half a year later. It must be seen against the background of a theater-praxis throughout Germany that was devoid of orientation, lacked self-confidence and often took refuge in cynicism. The climate of the times was one of breakdown and crisis: Where to go from here? What can we do? How valid are the means at our disposal? Such questions and such a frame of mind favour a return to the classics in the cultural sphere. What can that reasonably mean? Stein's production remained in repertory almost two years and was enthusiastically received on numerous tours. During one guest performance in the spring of 1980 in Caracas, over a thousand spectators in an open-air theater put up with pouring rain till late into the night to see the performance out. Stein's response — "We'll keep playing till the electricity gets knocked out" — has become legendary. This more than nine-hour-long production of the *Oresteia* is an attempt to go back to the beginnings of theater and political thought in order to find the basis and justification, the form and measure of artistic work and a political philosophy for today. Unique is Stein's abstention from commentary, his refusal to impose a self-assured interpretation on the action of the tragedy and the questions it raises. Interpretation appears here primarily in the form of disclosure: reconstruction on the basis of what we know about the Greeks and their theater. The extraordinary thing here is the absence of the kind of speculative interpretation that characterizes so many West German productions of the classics. Questions of success or failure here therefore must be framed in a different context. Reservations, for instance, about the competence of individual performances must be given less weight in consideration of the significance of the approach itself, which encounters the historical text with new humility and uncovers structures and contents that illuminate the old text.

The production does not however get stuck in theatrical archaeology, an obvious risk of staying close to the text. On the contrary, patient, insistent attention to the historical text here produces insights of undeniable contemporary relevance. The *Oresteia* tells the three-part story of Orestes: his avenging of the murder of his father, Agamemnon, at the hand of his mother, Clytemnestra, by murdering her; his pursuit by the Furies, goddesses of revenge, and atonement before Apollo; and finally his exoneration by Athena, whose purpose it is to establish a new rule of law on the Areopagus. In the unfolding of this story of events and of a society very distant from us with roots reaching back into prehistory, three central concepts emerge — action, suffering, learning — that form a single web in the end. The message we hear is that no one, at any time, can escape this web. Stein bases his political philosophy on an acceptance of the inevitable interdependence of these three elements of human experience and thus rejects all the doctrines of salvation that paint seductive pictures of painless life in a society without problems.

That is the one message: to act is to suffer. The other, hardly less relevant for today, is that suffering can be diminished by insight into the necessity of order — specifically, the necessity of

an order of law that is universally binding on all members of a society and that guarantees freedom by imposing just limitations on it.
The third segment of the production, *The Eumenides*, profiles these ideas forcefully, with barely a hint of irony. In Orestes's trial, a luminous Athena (Jutta Lampe) institutes the new order of law. She glows with reason and hope, having finally transformed the Furies into the Eumenides and integrated them into the new order (the hideous figures are literally transformed on stage by wrapping them up in colored sheets). At the conclusion of the almost nine-hour-long performance, this celebration of the founding of a social system comes nearly as a confession of faith. Order alone — i.e., a mutually acknowledged order of law, the triumph over anarchy — can make life in society viable. Stein is obviously taking direct aim at the problems we have with the concept of order today. It's as if the sum of many discussions (and not just at this theater) were being tallied up. And in fact it has been a long way for the Schaubühne from its production of Brecht's *The Mother*, with which the theater opened in 1970, and even from its first anarchy-tinged *Project-Antiquity* (1974) to this *Oresteia*. It has now arrived at a conservative position which is not to be confused with the misuse of the concept of conservatism in everyday politics. In his review of one evening's performance — of which he wrote, "at times it rises to the height of making theater history" — Joachim Kaiser accurately described the Schaubühne as "a democratic-moral institution with a preserving-conservative ethos" (*Süddeutsche Zeitung*, 20 October 1980).
What does the audience see? Since Greek theater did not rely on complicated decorations and sets, Karl-Ernst Hermann's stage design also avoids them. The audience sits on a gently rising, stepped floor in a half-circle facing an enormous portal on the stage. Until the third part of the trilogy, the portal remains sealed by a black wall with just a single opening in the middle, the palace gate. The Watchman sits in semidarkness high up on the upper ledge of the wall at the beginning of the play, waiting for news of the Trojan war. Far below, directly underneath him, women are conducting a sacrifice, a slow ritual with songs, candles, incense. The floor is wetted with water from their bowls; from time to time their outstretched arms make signs in the twilight. Intimations of a religious ceremony.

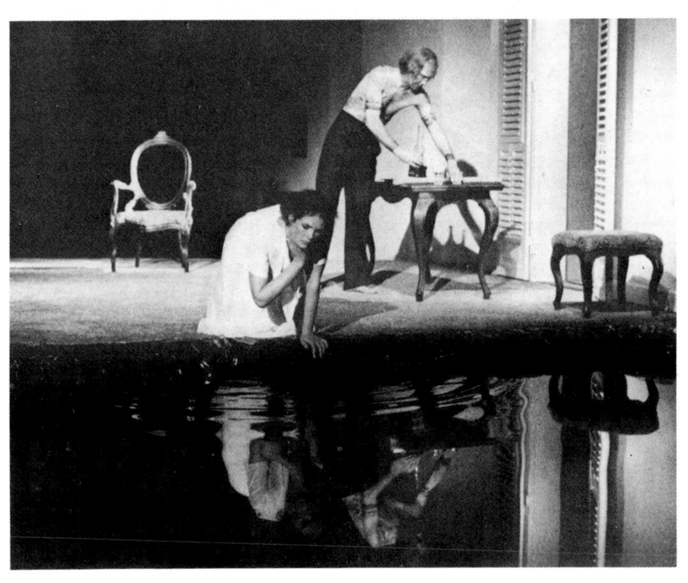

Elisabeth Trissenaar and Edgard M. Boehlke in *Iphigenie auf Tauris*, Schauspiel, Frankfurt.

Then the Chorus becomes audible and visible, old men dressed in gray street clothes. At times they stand in a group, or sit around a table; at others, they are driven apart, feel their way through the rows of spectators, make contact with each other above the heads of the public or start talking to themselves.
The men are both a group and separate individuals. They speak as with a single voice, but their voices are also distinct. Complex textures of sentences develop, webs of words full of superimpositions and jagged edges, moments of intensification and moments of slipping into the babble of old men. Through the medium of this bold orchestration of language, the play presents an image of a society, its shared experiences, its contradictory perceptions and expectations, its questions.
We learn what it is that moves this Chorus. We see the same fears that move us, the ever-repeated sameness of history that each generation, each individual experiences as something unique: namely, that there is no home, that defeats are already contained in victories, that life is a rising and falling in which the hardest thing to find is the proper balance. Agamemnon (Gunter Berger) — victor in the war that has just ended, strutting tall, armed to the teeth, a butcher — is pulled diagonally across the stage on a cart on tracks. His wife, Clytemnestra (Edith Clever) advances towards him, moving at first with precious,

mannered gestures and exhibiting herself in the circle of light. Then, growing harder, her strength feeding on her rage, she lures the hero into the palace, without warmth, the memory of their previous life together completely eradicated. But another memory remains fresh in her mind, the memory of Agamemnon sacrificing their daughter Iphigenia to procure favorable winds for the Greek fleet on its journey to Troy. And fresh rage inflames her hatred: the victor has brought home with him Cassandra as war booty and lover. Thus the wife justifies the double murder: Cassandra (Elke Petri) must be done away with too. The prophetess sees all, knows that death awaits her in the palace and, in a long, pain-filled scene, takes leave of this life before entering the palace gate. Part I closes with a horrifying tableau. The bloody bodies of the slain lie before the wall and above them, smeared with blood, stands the murderess, sword in hand, butcher of the butcher. Stein and Clever moved boldly here, pushing the representation of the gory deed to the very limits of dangerously excessive pathos.

In Part II, Aegisthus, now ruling in the house of Agamemnon as the new husband of the murderess, appears small against the monumentality of this image. In the middle of the stage, Electra (Tina Engel) and the other women circle about a steel plate as they raise their cries against the mother's adulterous murder of her husband. Here too Stein composed for the Chorus a sensitive vocal texture that mixes and separates the individual voices: a wreath of wails. Orestes, who has come as liberator, is drawn forward by the lament. Udo Samel plays him as a man crushed by the weight and burden of history, but also unswerving in his determination. Samel sustains a strained, pinched tone to the end; the words are always more powerful than the man and one understands that the deed is greater than the doer. Before he can murder his mother, there is a carefully articulated period of hesitation, an exchange of final arguments, as it were, and Orestes's horror at the deed. And Clever as Electra defends herself in words that show she doesn't truly believe in her salvation. It's as if she were standing next to herself, observing the fate that will destroy her.

In Part III, the hideous, monstrous, clammy Furies race through the rows of spectators, embodiments of the madness that has befallen the liberator turned mother-murderer. Apollo stands by him. Athena, descending on a rope, alights on the now-opened stage, an angel of reason. She calls the jury of citizens together to decide the case. They throw their stone ballots into the urn: five for, five against Orestes. Athena casts the deciding vote, acquitting Orestes of the crime of matricide. But more important by far is the cessation of the cycle of vengeance, of furious personal revenge followed by equally brutal counter-revenge. The innocence or guilt of the individual is to be judged henceforth by the law of democracy, to which all submit, and no longer by the rule of personal revenge. The Furies rage long against the acquittal before finally submitting to the new order of law. And the shocked jurors fall from their seats — a caricaturizing of the action on the part of Stein that is also meant to be critical of the practices of democracy, as is the idea of sending the actor who plays Orestes among the spectators to shake their hands in gratitude for his acquittal: an exonerated man taking his leave of us democrats (being now, as we know, in a not unproblematic state of interdependency).

Aside from this scene, the production did not resort to other such shortcuts. Stein's *Oresteia*, which undoubtedly had the longest rehearsal time of any play in the history of German theater — a kind of cathedral of the theater world — developed a clear canon of means, an instrumentarium of language, gesture, ideas and movement. This was carried out with the kind of consistency that always exacts its price. There were long dry stretches: for instance Part III seemed dissociated from the whole until Athena's assertion of herself. It was difficult to keep in mind the deed narrated earlier during the trial. There were doubts about the translation, too. Stein himself translated the ancient text into German prose. He had tried, he wrote, "to stay as close to the original meaning as possible and to reproduce the order of the meaning-bearing words as far as feasible." The spoken text was never careless or casual, but a number of irritating formulations did crop up that were obviously descended from certain overused colloquialisms that bury rather than disclose reality.

The limits of reconstructability set by the material itself are revealed in these linguistic problems. But, like the length of certain passages, they were offset by the repetition and variation of the expressive values in which Stein had trained the Ensemble, especially in the Chorus passages, and which incrementally familiarized the audience with the sign-language and linguistic idiosyncrasies of the production. (And in regard to length, it should be further noted that following the premiere performances, the three parts of the triology could be seen on consecutive evenings.) The performance truly offered the audience a chance to become part of the action, to observe in itself how thoughts and associations gradually began to move with greater confidence on the archaic foundations of classical form. Anyone open to this invitation could have remained in this world of the *Oresteia* for much longer than the nine hours of the performance, without having to leave his own times.

By emphasizing the intertwining of action, suffering and learning in his production of this ancient tragedy, Stein stirred up a great number of contemporary issues. Stein's interest in his own times — which is not hampered by, but grounded in and supported by his passion for the past, for history — came to the fore again the following year, in June 1981, in his production of a new English play. While the youth of Berlin protested the housing shortage by throwing stones through boutique windows on Kurfürstendamm, Stein was staging Nigel William's *Class Enemy*, almost too brilliantly for the unwieldiness of the subject matter. William's play is a slice-of-life that portrays a group of youths driven by their social milieu and their own predispositions into a self-destructive rage and hatred of the world that is barely expressible in language. There is no way out for them and no possibility of their being integrated into a livable community.

That evil begets evil was one of the lessons of the *Oresteia* and so too of the English play, though in the latter there was plainly no realistic way of assimilating these socially ostracized and self-ostracizing youths, not even via the institution of the theater, even if they provide the subject of the drama. The production thus dealt with the limits of the theater's capacity to integrate certain extremes. One could observe here and at other performances of the play elsewhere in the Federal Republic that the middle class audiences experienced the misery of these youths as something exotic, while people from the youth "scene" who happened upon these performances found it amusing to see their own wretched lives portrayed on stage. Nevertheless, it is important for the theater to push forward to the limits of its capacity for assimilation.

It must want the present, with all its risks.

Peter Stein: Three Sisters

Did Peter Stein violate this imperative of the present in his production of Chekhov's *Three Sisters* (February 1984)? Some critics clearly thought so. Henning Rischbieter (*Theater heute*, 3, 1984) for instance called it "dead theater." Such critics saw the production simply as a rigor mortis of the Schaubühne. In the textual accuracy of the staging, in Stein's abstinence from willful contemporizing and in the exacting detail of Karl-Ernst Hermann's set designs they found nothing but paralysis. "Chekhov's play is buried under the bell jar of its own historical era" (Rischbieter, *ibid.*).

Drei Schwestern, Schaubühne, Berlin.

For others, the production drew its beauty precisely from the intensity of its connection with the past. The center of attention was a debut. For the role of Irina, the youngest of the three sisters, Stein had found a young woman in her early twenties who was to make her first appearance in the large theater that day. It was an extraordinary event. One must go a long way back to the opening appearances of Edith Clever, Jutta Lampe, Barbara Sukowa, Bruno Ganz, Heidemarie Theobald (in Kortner's *As You Like It* in 1963) to find anything comparable. Corinna Kirchhoff has an earnestness which is, even in lesser degree, rare in performers her age. She is a slender, tall, gracious young woman with all of youth's hopes and desires, excitement and love of the new, but with a prescience of age, a presentiment of futility, of early sorrow. To see her between Edith Clever and Jutta Lampe is to recognize how much she draws from and has learned from them, and yet see something altogether different: the signs of having grown up in a different time, an element of tension that breaks through the sometimes curiously conservative, even old fashioned quality of her appearance.

Das Wintermärchen, Schauspielhaus, Bochum.

Peter Stein fixes and liberates this element of tension in Corinna Kirchhoff's interpretation of Irina. He repeatedly focuses attention on her by the way he structures the scenes, separates her from the others, gives her space for herself. The young actress can then show us her ability to create a mood, an impression of a life and fate, even when she is alone on stage and even without speaking. Irina is the one who most fervently wishes to leave the province for Moscow and experience real life, for which reason she is willing to marry Baron Tusenbach (Ernst Stötzner, who finds brittle yet soft tones for the young man's foreboding of death in the last act) although she does not love him. The whole tragedy of this play that Chekhov called a comedy is encompassed in Corinna Kirchhoff's portrayal of this young woman. Here is a woman who is ready to pay almost any price to change the conditions of her life, but whose hopes are wrecked when the baron is killed in a duel. There is shyness and directness, a gift for silence and eruptions of temperament, and above all sensitivity to the words and movements of the others in her performance. Through this sensitivity, Stein can allow everything that happens with the other characters be reflected in this one figure. It is in Irina's reactions, above all, that this production tells what all the characters suffer because of the meaninglessness of their lives and their fear, written in all the feelings and situations of the play, of being forgotten — an old and very contemporary pain. The first act plays in a very broad, moderately shallow room. Windows open onto a garden. To the right, separated off by columns, the dining room. It is spring and Irina's name day. The production leaves time to get acquainted with the individual characters. As so often at the Schaubühne, a patient introduction to a slice-of-life, to life stories. Almost all the performers have been acting together in the Ensemble for a number of years and one senses that in the precision of their playing to one another. These people know each other, like a family. The oldest of the sisters is Olga. Edith Clever presents her as composed, tight, seamless. Mascha is the next in age and is played by Jutta Lampe. She wears the color of mourning. At times she springs from the shadows and assumes a beguiling vivaciousness. Only in the last scene, when everything is ending, does Lampe fuse the elements of this character to a single fate. Werner Rehm plays Mascha's husband — always intent on illusory reconciliation, on concealment of contradictions. His cheerful moods are exaggerated, but one senses behind this excess an awareness of his own weakness.

Tina Engel plays the robust, vulgar householder to the sensitive sisters while Peter Simonischek portrays her husband as a walking self-reproach.

Then there are the officers, stationed in the garrison town and on the lookout for girls. Otto Sander's performance as Werschinin, the Battery Commander, is somewhat too sketchy and lacking in depth. Schäfer's Captain is driven, "more interesting," stretching the boundaries of the role. Jochen Tavote and Nikolaus Dutch are the Lieutenants. Stein places the characters in the large room in changing constellations, a choreography of hastened and tempered paces that is not entirely lacking in artificiality. At table, someone toasts with, "Things are bound to go wrong." But despite all the disorder of the events, the composition of the scenes remains precise, orderly. Stein's problem: even the detours often keep the characters on charted tracks — a fear of losing the overview. At the end of the first act, everyone stands in a row listening to the magical sounds of a humming yellow top.

The second act is played in semidarkness, but our view of the individual characters that come and go grows sharper, their suffering and hopes flickeringly illuminated. The third act: a restless night, a fire in town; the catastrophe is outside, a mirror of the questions, doubts, desperations for which people find no solution. From the first setting to this third one we follow a steadily narrowing path. But then for the collapse of all hopes in the fourth act, the set opens up wide and grand. To the left is the house, now from the outside, with peeling paint. An avenue of magnificent trees, autumn leaves on the ground. In the distance, light on a gentle landscape. It smells of woods and streams. Pathos of nature. This detailed set by Karl-Ernst Hermann does not become an autonomous element here (as does the forest in the Schaubühne's production of Shakespeare's *As You Like It)* because the constancy of nature versus the restlessness of the heart is a theme in the Chekhov play. To look at the trees is to participate in life: one of the characters says, "How beautiful it must be to live under the trees." But departure is in the air. The officers are leaving town, the girls remain behind, embracing one another. Olga: "Why are we living, why are we suffering... If only we knew." She repeats the questions three times. This last set, the alley of autumn trees, the land in the distance, the people and the way they turn from each other, to each other, the separations and the hopes that transcend them — there is hardly anyone who can resist the sorrowful melancholy of this tableau. And for a moment the question of where and when real life takes place seems to be answered after all: in the theater.

What do we expect of the theater? That was the question that sparked the critics' debate over the production of *Three Sisters*. Peter Stein fanned the flames of the discussion himself when shortly after the premiere he unexpectedly announced his "definitive decision" to step down from the directorship of the Schaubühne in a radio discussion with Berlin high school students. He said he "had had it." His allusion to "objective pressures" was not very convincing. Some more light is shed on his reasons for stepping down in an interview, shortly before the radio panel, that appeared in the Parisian journal *Théâtre en Europe*, edited by Giorgio Strehler. What he says there reveals his self-doubts as a stage director, which necessarily affect his role as director of the Schaubühne as a whole as well. "I notice that I'm tending more and more to the purely conventional. I would like as far as possible to leave the structures of the plays and theater texts as they are and avoid every intervention, every arbitrary addition... When I see my own and others' productions today, I get the impression of an irresponsible, almost pubertary display of knowledge that does injury to the theater, to the text — which can't defend itself — and to the reality that surrounds us. Because in most cases these interventions are justified as references to reality today. For a man of the theater like myself, it is particularly dangerous when he starts perceiving today's reality in such a dogmatic way and attempts to draw absolutely air-tight conclusions about how we should live." Earlier productions by Stein such as *Tasso* (1969) and *Peer Gynt* (1971) also fell into the wake of this self-criticism: "I will never let another production like *Peer Gynt* see the light of day... The same goes for *Tasso* too."

These remarks must also be understood as an expression of exhaustion. For one and a half decades, Peter Stein has defined the shape of the Schaubühne (and of European theater). No era of German theater has lasted as long. Exhaustion shouldn't come as a surprise. The new house on the Kurfürstendamm requires a different kind of approach than the theater on Hallesches Ufer: it is more difficult for a single director to control. And Stein senses that his grasp on the operations as a whole is slipping. He plans to continue to direct

individual productions at the Schaubühne however: "I built up a theater that is perfectly suited to my needs. I'll never find another instrument to compare with this, whether in regard to facilities or location or genre."
Who will take over the directorship of the Schaubühne? As long as Stein himself is still working there, another director is inconceivable. A predicament for the house itself and the public as well. If even Stein himself doesn't want the directorship of his theater anymore, who could possibly fill his shoes? Has the time come when management pure and simple will take over what for Stein was — as he often proved — an instrument of knowledge and of magic? The problems facing German theater today, problems of redefining itself structurally and substantively, are nowhere as visible as in the crisis over the directorship of the Schaubühne, which for so long has been a model of organization and results.

Klaus Michael Grüber
and Dieter Sturm: Hamlet
The relationship of the theater to the present was the topic of many discussions following the Schaubühne's premiere of Klaus Michael Grüber's and Dieter Sturm's *Hamlet* in December of 1982. In this production the present was to be arrived at *ex negativo*, via a completely self-contained counterimage, an image built up by the most extreme concentration on the language and figurations of the old poetry and without the slightest concession to contemporary attitudes. Grüber was suspected of having betrayed the boldness of his earlier work at a single devastating blow (a suspicion that was also expressed concerning Heyme's *Demetrius*). The Berlin *Hamlet* seeks a grand form for Shakespeare's tragedy. The melodies of Schlegel's and Eschenburg's translations and the pathos of the heavy, meaning-laden motions of the performers are set off against a vast space in which they seem like lost wanderers. The *Hamlet* is not a reconstruction of the original Shakespearean production — Peter Zadek's staging of the play came much closer, one presumes, to the Globe Theater spectacles than Grüber's — but much more a performance in the spirit of Romanticism. Its effectiveness is the result not so much of a high level of energy (as with Zadek) as of the sustained mood of sorrow: sorrow in the knowledge of the insufficiency of all actions and the impotence that isolates the figures in a world filled with death.

Die Neger, Schaubühne, Berlin.

This atmosphere sucks up the dramatic movements and contradictions of the tragic action and neutralizes them. One recognizes in this a response to the tenor of our own times, but also experiences the resultant near-paralysis of dramatic energies here as a loss. But this loss is compensated for by a quality of dramatic presentation which has long seemed unattainable on the German stage. The frequent emphasis on the language of individual passages carries us beyond the reality of the specific scene: the play's meaning, relevance, validity are contained in a transcendent world of ideas. The tragedy, Grüber and his collaborator Sturm argue, does not lie in the actions but in the minds of the characters, that is to say, in the language their thoughts assume. That is what is new about this production. On the other hand, this *Hamlet* is inconceivable without Grüber's earlier work. What concerns Grüber in *Hamlet* is the same thing that intrigued him in his productions of Shakespeare's *The Tempest* (1969,

Bremen), Kleist's *Penthesilea* (Stuttgart, 1970), *The Bacchae* of Euripides and Hölderlin's *Empedokles* (Schaubühne, 1974 and 1975) and also in *Faust* (Paris, 1975): the problem of pathos, the dramatic representation of an emotionality in which human experience seeks magnified expression.

The production does not fall outside the perimeter of Grüber's previous work, as some have claimed, but it is intimately related to his earlier formulations. It is true that the path has led to picture-frame theater and historical forms of presentation. But this is not moving backwards, (let alone an "about-face"); rather it has been a process of compressing tension: an extraordinarily risky endeavor to refound the theater — with acknowledgement of his earlier work, however, to which the Berlin *Hamlet* refers.

Was *Hamlet* a good choice for this project of reconstituting the theater? Was it a good choice for examining the theater's means and potentials for new departures in a time of hazy concepts, broken enthusiasm, weakened motivation — a time that nevertheless insists on passionate deeds, the capacity to act in the first place, clear goals? Although it may seem to be an appropriate selection at first glance, the question should not be answered prematurely in the affirmative.

Hesitation — be it that of the Danish Prince who cannot raise his hand against his father's murderer — is perhaps better described by those who can overcome it, who possess an inner counterforce, than by those like ourselves who are completely immersed and overwhelmed by it. At any rate, it is true (and relevant to the choice of *Hamlet* in connection with the present times) that no production of *Hamlet* can avoid confronting basic questions concerning the first principles, the significance and means of theater. For this tragedy — in which the Prince expects enlightenment, insight and motivation to action from a theater troupe — is very direct about the theme of the theater itself, for Hamlet's experience of the world as groundless illusion surely mirrors the imagined reality of all inventions of the stage.

Where to begin with illusion and invention? How close, how far away should the old story be? And what kind of space should be used? Which also means: in what format are the human players to be seen and with what sense of themselves? These are always the first questions in a theatrical production. In a production of *Hamlet* they never cease.

At the Schaubühne the answers to these questions appear to have come easily (at least as spectator, one must think so) and to be convincing. The astonishing thing about the production is its absolute self-assurance. Is it perhaps too sure for this restless drama that, though it tells of hesitation, presses nervously forward, setting so much in motion? Everything about the production is firmly structured and decisively articulated: the characters, their gestures and movements, even the folds of their garments, as designed by Moidele Bickels.

There is an almost unfailing fixedness about things, hardly any inconstancy (surely an important component of *Hamlet*), rarely a sudden blurring of contours. Even in Ophelia's madness scene there is, in Jutta Lampe's performance, the cold orderliness of intelligent, thoughtful construction: a high degree of technical skill in the composition of the scene, but so regulated that we are more likely to admire the control and technique than be moved by the scene. Ophelia leaves a lute behind on the otherwise empty stage, and in the next scene a sailor picks it up, lost in thought. One notices immediately: someone has to get that instrument offstage, that's his function. Often just as calculated and obvious as this handling of a prop is the generation of certain effects, where the stakes are higher. The performers always know exactly the impression they want to create in this production — and go about doing so. Never before has a Grüber production had this degree of control.

The first thing that sets the tone is the architectural set, designed by the French artist Gilles Aillaud: an imposing semicircular structure of concrete ashlars, with four openings on the lowest level and the two rows of three openings above that, all equally spaced. Associations with Samuel Beckett's house of the damned in his story *Le Dépeupler* come to mind: "A place where bodies are constantly searching, each for the one who orphaned him. Large enough for a futile search. Crowded enough to thwart any effort to flee." Perhaps one thinks too of the mathematically conceived, almost pure architecture of the last Staufer-Burgen Friedrich II films in Apulia, at Castel del Monte. Unfortunately, Albert Speer comes readily to mind as well: monumental, alienating backdrops without

any relation to the people in front of them. In various scenes large platforms are hydraulically raised before the wall, for instance, when Hamlet visits his mother. This is the signature of our times: machinery, heavy equipment, fearful in its inexorable forward momentum. After Hamlet's death scene, the corpse is laid out on just such a slowly rising platform and motors set the iron curtain in motion. The sound of the motor is imitated by the ponderous music that pompously accompanies the very, very slow lowering of the curtain.
At any rate, this would not be the proper setting for Ulrich Wildgruber's fidgety, flighty Hamlet in Bochum, 1979, nor for Lambert Hamel's cumbrous dreamer in Munich, 1980, nor again for the little dropout (Ignaz Kirchner) in Jürgen Gosch's middle class drama in Bremen, 1981. The stage in Berlin demands a different kind of character, people who despite all their fears can measure up to this monumental environment and who do so with an expressive vocabulary that has had to be reinvented after lying buried under interpretation-mad productions for years.
A director has to start from the ground up if the figures set before this concrete monolith (the apse of the Mendelsohn building described by Klotz) are to find their proper form and come into their own. He must begin with one of the most fundamental issues for the theater: what constitutes a scene? This production answers: an actor and a text, first of all; then the stage space, the lighting, the costumes; and further, the movements of the actors with the text on stage. This reduction to fundamentals, which subordinates the scenic translation, the visual metaphor, is what gives the production its particular tone. A strip of light across the semidarkened stage alone constitutes the connecting path on which Hamlet and Ophelia meet. A simple circle of light draws the Queen (Edith Clever) out of the darkness, magnifying the figure and lending it the pathos of one entangled in an evil deed. A row of torches up front on the ramps represents the flickering threat to the King of his crime being revealed, not just a metaphorical but a real threat, for the unsteady light multiplies his fears and distrust.
All the long crossings of the stage and the heavy gestures (Hamlet's raised, glaringly spotlit hand is for a moment the only thing visible on the gigantic stage) are carefully considered. Not breathlessness, as in Zadek's *Hamlet* in Bochum, but patience characterizes this performance. Patience is called for not just as a response to a specific situation but as a universal attitude towards the transitory nature of man, whom death awaits at every corner. The high solemnity of this theater is the solemnity of *memento mori* — remember that you must die. The forms of pathos this production boldly presents are a stand against the end, a desperate, rebellious assertion that the individual human being can after all be someone in the face of all this finity, a king perhaps, a queen, a prince — or an actor. (Bernhard Minetti's performance as the first player embodies this kind of dignity.)
It was Ernst Bloch's perception (in *Das Prinzip Hoffnung*) that Hamlet's inability to act was a consequence of the emancipation of Renaissance man from the medieval worldview. Emancipation through reason does not inspire optimistic, active initiative but on the contrary: "The extinguished transcendence sends nothing but coldness to the rudely disenchanted; it magnifies their distance from the real world, and what can be reasonably accomplished therein, on a cosmic level too" (a judgment that is bitterly affirmed by contemporary feelings that our — at least allegedly — emphatically rational interventions into reality only heighten our sense of the irreality of the real). It is as if Bloch were describing what we are seeing here in Berlin. High above the sets, pale blue stars shine faintly from very far away and in the enormous space beneath this heaven the people feel a great coldness. It is in them; it mantles their movements and their relationships to one another. And it makes them very alone. All this is in fact apparent in Grüber's and Sturm's perception of the tragedy. In their *Hamlet*, there is no society, no connection between individual human beings. A court of loneliness surrounds each. When several are present at once, one immediately senses the forced artificiality of the situation. Society, says this production, is always just an arrangement, provisional and inadequate, that only scantily veils our true condition. An illusion that easily dissolves.
Even such a love as Ophelia has for Hamlet — accented in the production for the length of one scene — this most radical expression of the idea of communion, is nothing but a passing closeness. Everything becomes a plant. And perhaps the most beautiful moment of the Berlin production is a lament: Edith Clever, moving all the way to the

front of the stage and fully facing the audience this one time, tells of Ophelia's death:"Es neigt ein Weidenbaum sich über'n Bach..."("There is a willow grows aslant a brook..."). There is a wonderful luminosity in Schlegel's translation: from ages past, the eternal lament and sorrow.
For the moorless, stranded theater of the present day and against the background of a society that no longer understands itself, the important challenge of this production of *Hamlet* is contained in the fact that it often concretizes the language of the text, as in the just-mentioned passage; that it patiently develops forms utterly unlike those that are fashionable in our imbecile times; and that it examines a vision of humanity from the past and dares to see the characters as isolated individuals (like the three philosophers in Giorgione's famous painting in the Kunsthistorisches Museum in Vienna, the figures are particularly separate when they are not alone).
At the Schaubühne the past is presented to us as a challenge. But there were perils in Berlin that can't be overlooked. The recollection of the past to which the production subscribes also leads it to the verge of paralysis. At times this theater not only uses death as a theme but threatens to succumb to the Grim Reaper himself. When, for instance, Peter Fitz visibly forces himself into convulsed postures and rolls off the King's texts in gloomy tones, or when Werner Rehm shuffles Polonius along, or, at the other extreme, Rosencrantz and Guildenstern (Gerd Wameling and Udo Semel) rush all too trippingly over the stage, then the dust of stale conventions lies over this production, too.
And Hamlet? Bruno Ganz, returning to the Schaubühne after a long absence to take this role, has grown more skillful but not deeper through his work in film. He plays the shadow of Hamlet. Wrapped in the black veil of mourning he kneels at the King's throne. The veil remains about him even when he has cast it aside. Hamlet has but one hue, the shadow-color of his consciousness of impermanence. Ganz distances himself from Shakespeare's — as Bloch remarked — concave, diversion-seeking character as well as from the madness which Shakespeare's Hamlet suffers or perhaps only feigns. In many of his earlier productions, for instance in his Paris *Faust*, Grüber was fascinated by the motif of travel. But his *Hamlet* has none of that urge, however problematic, to pick up and leave, none of the "blocked embarcation" that Bloch identifies as the source of the play's tension. From the very start Ganz is — at the end. A broken character, doubtless with a high degree of inner tension, but without a break in the visible surface.
As in Ganz's performance, so too in Edith Clever's, Jutta Lampe's and Peter Fitz's, the resigned autonomy of the figures diminishes the tragedy. The characters do not swerve, nothing breaks forth in them, they do not appear to be free agents. Thus the important duel scene at the end is staged without any uncertainty of outcome as a ritual battle to the death, the fatal end is speedy and sure. The tragedy is prefigured everywhere. What we are shown here is not the possible fateful turn of one man's life but a preordained judgment against all of life.

Edith Clever and Bruno Ganz in *Hamlet,* Schaubühne, Berlin.

List of Illustrations
Catalogue of the Exhibition
Bio-Bibliographies
Statements

Catalogue of the Exhibition and List of Illustrations

Works marked with an asterisk are in the exhibition. Text refers to the work or the project. Many of these works were built in situ or especially for the Toronto show. This means that the catalogue is incomplete. The definitive list of works displayed will be added to the present publication when the exhibition opens. Titles are as indicated by the creators of the works.
In dimension, height precedes width.

Architecture

Gae Aulenti

Musée d'Orsay, Paris, 1980-1986.
Transformation of the Gare d'Orsay into a Museum of French Art, 1849-1914.
Project: Gae Aulenti with Italo Rota and Pietro Castiglioni.
Client: Etablissement Publique du Musée d'Orsay, Paris.

...Theoretically, when tackling our work, we have never referred to any ideology aimed at the different practices of reuse. On the contrary, we have confined our task to an analytical and articulate observation of the three existing "bodies" on which we must work: the Laloux Building, its form and its typology; Michel Laclotte's museographic program, the collections and their order in terms of a period of French art history running from romanticism to the various avant-gardes; and the ACT Architecture project, winner of the competition for transforming the station into a museum...

...The geometry of the grand nave contains a powerful illusion of symmetry. The longitudinal axis, along which the first part of the museographic passage is articulated from the rear entrance of the grand nave was flanked by two parallel axes and countless axes at right angles. The side rooms have axes that intersect the longitudinal axes of the two parallel galleries across the openings corresponding to the doors; the central transept runs through the entire structure, from one side to the other. All these crossings coincide with the structural law in the typology of the Laloux Building, its main entrance being composed of porticoes and oval salons on the long side toward the Seine and with a back aperture on the short side toward Place Bellechasse across the Marquise.
The museographic program, the concrete analysis of the works, their arrangements, their logical rhythms, their sequences, have determined an articulation of rules according to which the restructuring of the totality of the museographic course is a sum of specific typologies of museum traditions: rooms, galleries, passages, balconies — but transfigured by the different formulations set by the act of their foundation in the Laloux Building. This structure, in turn, has imposed its laws upon the program; one of these laws, for instance, has led us to bring out, in the Pavilion Amont, a sequence of rooms for a vertical movement through the Museum of Architecture: a veritable museum within the museum.
The multiplicity of the different typological units has thus permitted the invention of other types of original spaces as in the towers, autonomous structures, buildings within the building...

...The Laloux Building, with its iron structure (pilasters, girders, structural work, projecting bands, joints), stone walls that reveal or conceal the iron, stucco work and decorations — that is, the laws of its existence — has imposed the "territory of the new construction." We viewed the building as a contemporary object, without a past : the architect Laloux helped us design the metamorphosis of the station into a museum.
The compositional principles operate by means of a clash, a systematic opposition and not in a naturalistic or stylistic continuity, so that the buildings constructed within the building analytically demonstrate the process of this decomposition and fragmentation, giving form to the constituent elements of their own language...

...In regard to its own constructional goal and purpose, the project employed the same analytical method used by its relationship with the museographic program and with the existing building. No shape, no construction element came into being as a definite and finite form; they emerged as combinations, as fusions of different parts that were decomposed and then recomposed. From here, the observation of different details, seen as parts of the whole and as their effective and concrete possibility of being produced in a place of quantitative industrial production. The diversity of materials, varied but controllable, thus excludes the possibilities of traditional craft, but it does not turn industrial production into a repetitive law...

...The study of the museum's lighting went through the following process: research into the different typologies that the museographic route would create, isolating the different space and articulating the different technological possibilities — defined, however, under the common denominator of "indirect light." Articulation of the countless specific signs that the Laloux Building offered in relation to the natural illumination, and the decision to combine and overlap the natural and the artificial light (zenith light in the roof galleries, light in the large nave, light in the windows overlooking Rue de Lille, light in the ovules of the oval rooms). Finally, order and sequence of all the different elements and their articulation.
This procedure caused every different space to be illuminated in a different fashion and yet with the same technological qualities...

Gottfried Böhm

Administrative Building of the Züblin Company, 1982-1984.

Project: Gottfried Böhm.
Collaborators: D. Gatermann, J. Minkus, F. Valda.

Stuttgart — Administrative Building of the Züblin Company - 1982-84
The new administrative building is located at the edge of the city and consists of a series of large structures without any potential for integration into urban planning.
The new building is conceived, thus, as an independent structure which in profile has the form of a house with a hipped roof.
The space between the two office wings is glassed in on both sides to provide a view of the relatively unspoiled landscape here looking out in both directions. The location was used to best advantage and the landscape was optically unified with and through the building by placing rows of trees in the glass hall.
The hall is roofed in glass and the interior walls are constructed so as to give the impression of a city square.
Collaborators were: D. Gatermann, J. Minkus and F. Valda.
The construction plans for the administrative building of the Ed. Züblin Co., Inc, were by Stuttgart-Möhringen (Vaihinger Strasse 167).
Specifications for the Licensing Board, September 1982 (Drawings No 185/100 to 108 and 114 to 123). Reference is made to the preparatory discussions in March, 1982.

Construction Site
A description of the lot includes the land register: number 5573/8,
real property: number 2326/1,
and the area: size of 16,149 m^2.
The construction plan is as follows: Mö 135-810.2, "Commercial zone, Vaihinger Strasse Süd" as notarized in Document no. 35, Aug. 26, 1976. It is a corner lot: Vaihinger Strasse/east. Albstadtweg, with a southern boundary consisting in elevated trolley tracks.
The size of the lot is: width (Vaihinger Strasse): c. 95 m, length (Albstadtweg): c. 170 m. Access is afforded, entrance and exit, via Albstadtweg. Utility mains run from Albstadtweg.
Topography is as follows: Vaihinger Strasse — averages 430.50 m above mean sea level; entrance via Albstadtweg c. 428.27 m above mean sea level; southern boundary: trolley ca. 425.50 m above mean sea level; north-south falling gradient ca. 5.00 m. Transportation from the north is by Vaihinger Strasse - L 1205, from the south by trolley station, from the west by Albstadtweg - Stichstrasse (with parking lots on both sides — parallel parking). Parking space: see enclosure.

Architectural Plans
The building consists of two wings on a north-south axis (13.2 m wide - 94.0 m long). Distance between wings is 24.0 m. Height is ground floor and six upper stories (4.0 + 6 ×3.0 = 22.0 m) while ground level is 429.4 m above mean sea level.
The distance from top of foundation to top of seventh floor is 451.4 m above mean sea level.
The attic is 0.6 m high.
The gutter line is 452.0 m above mean sea level (=permissible height of structure). Grid unit is 1.2 m. Unit spacing is 7.2 m. Subdivisions are created by exterior semicylindrical stairway towers at 28.8 m intervals, measured from the mid-axis of the towers.
The profile is symmetrically stepped at the sixth and fourth stories at the north and south sides.
The space between the wings of the building is roofed over in glass, with enclosing glass walls between the wings: the whole forms a glass hall that functions as a climatic envelope for passive solar energy.
Within the hall, the two wings are connected by open footbridges with stairs leading to all floors. In addition, there are two elevators in the middle of the hall.
The lower level of the hall (first basement level) has various structures, ramps and stairways as well as troughs and planters for trees and shrubs that make a visual connection with the terrain surrounding the building and visible from the hall.

Foundation. The building is constructed on a basement consisting of two levels which will serve primarily as an underground garage. The entrance to the garage is situated under the main entrance. It is roofed over by a 22-m-wide platform. Access and egress are from the southern turning circle on Albstadtweg via an insignificant cut of c. 1.5 m in depth across the grounds.

Building Plans and Maintenance System. The upper stories contain exclusively office spaces of differing sizes, arranged in parallel rows. The hallway between is formed by walls of closets (F30).
The ground floor of the west wing is the reception area with foyer, reception desk, waiting room and computer facilities. On the ground floor of the east wing are located the conference and meeting rooms, and the photocopying service and stockrooms. The built-in galleries of the library and the cafeteria occupy the southern side of the office wings on the floor.
The library and cafeteria and kitchen are located on the same level as the lower hall, i.e., first basement level.
The southern part of the west wing also houses two small apartments for chauffeurs and a family-sized apartment for a superintendent.
The midsection of the basement contains a two-story garage, surrounded by the building maintenance rooms for the technical systems, as well as storage and archival rooms, which in part occupy two stories.
All floors are accessible to the handicapped by specially fitted elevators. The size of the elevators is sufficient to accomodate freight.
The building maintenance systems and technical apparatus for drainage, water pipes, heating and air conditioning systems, electrical systems and lightning-protection system, elevators and conveying plant, sprinkler system and fireproofing, kitchen equipment, photocopying facilities, print shop, computer facilities, are as described in a separate technical prospectus.

Construction and Materials. The building is to be constructed in prefabricated reinforced concrete units.
The containing walls of the basement floors and ground water containment basin are made of on-site poured concrete; roof supports for the glass hall are constructed of reinforced concrete headers and steel beams.
Roofing and walls are of galvanized steel frames.

Interior. In the reception area, in the outer zones and in the glass hall and built-in units in the hall there are stairways, ramps, parapets constructed of brick pavements and masonry. On the office floors in general there is carpeting with sound-proofing over concrete floors without plaster finishing, the same in halls and passageways.
Stairways, outer galleries, footbridges in the glass hall, utility rooms all have molded rubber flooring.
The entrance hall has brick tiles and natural stone, in an ornamental pattern.
The walls are coated with textured wallpaper, painted over and in the entrance hall, glass construction blocks are set in concrete (F 90). The ceilings are in general, sprayed plaster (acoustic).
The hallways have suspended metal or panelled ceilings, and the same is true in

the utility rooms. Lecture and conference rooms have suspended sound-proofed ceilings. Windows are made of wood or aluminium. Exterior glass walls on the ground floor have steel frame construction; tinted, thermopane glass. The glass walls of the climatic hall are single pane. Doors are in general, wood doors in steel frames, varnished or laminated, while the hallway and exterior doors are of glass and steel construction. Exterior walls have insulation and moisture barrier; walls of utility rooms have ceramic tile from floor to ceiling. Roof construction includes plans for a walkspace in which the air conditioning system will be housed. Fireproofing consists of a sprinkler system with hose attachments as well as chemical fire extinguishers in all stairwells on each floor. Smoke ventilation vents in the sides of the cone-shaped glass roofs of the stairway towers. In the glass hall at both eaves lines and at the apex are air vents that also function as smoke vents, which take up one percent each, i.e., three percent of the total glass roof surface.

Vittorio Gregotti

Università degli Studi di Palermo, Nuovi Dipartimenti di Scienze a Parco d'Orléans (University of Palermo, New Science Departments in the d'Orléans Park), 1969-1984.
Project: Vittorio Gregotti and Gino Pollini.
Collaborators: S. Azzola, H. Matsui, C. Fronzoni, R. Brandolini.
Client: Università di Palermo.

Photographs by Mimmo Jodice, Naples.

Hans Hollein

Haus 8, Rauchstrasse, Berlin, 1984-1985.
House of 5 floors containing 25 apartments.
Project: Hans Hollein.
Client: IBA, Tiergarten, Berlin.

Josef Paul Kleihues

Maasprospekt, Rotterdam, 1982.
Project: Josef Paul Kleihues.
Collaborators: Mirko Baum, Jean Fammang with L. Brands, R. Hoelscher, F. Moeller and G. Sunderhaus.

Few cities can boast such a marked functional and visual dialectic as Rotterdam. One sees it especially clearly in the relationship between the Old City and the *Koop van Zuid* with its warehouses and crane-lined piers. In between lies the broad, sluggish Maas which bustles with shipping traffic.
The visual contradiction between the two banks is a sign of Rotterdam's tradition-mindedness and engagement in the modern world alike.
Bourgeois conventions and a healthy mercantile spirit have coupled the crafts with technological curiosity in a most favorable union. Expressions of Anglo-Saxon empiricism can be seen in the historic segments of the city. The artificial reshaping of the flat topography, the man-made landfill and waterways have created a new reality with a specific homogeneity.
The brutal destruction of Rotterdam in World War II deeply scarred the cityscape. Reconstruction has healed most of the wounds but it also established new proportions that were strongly influenced by CIAM. For a good ten years, the architectural focus has been concentrated on the conservation and restoration of historic sections of the city and their careful expansion through new construction. The principle of citizen participation is firmly established in this work. There have been very notable successes in the area of urban renewal here, but alongside these, one notes the unambitious quality of much of the new planning and especially of future-oriented urban development projects which could take the prospective structural changes in the inner city port into consideration.
In this situation and within the context of AIR, the "Rotterdamse Kunstlichting" together with the City Council, has invited four architects to work up proposals for future urban development of the *Koop van Zuid.*
The panorama presented here for the banks of the Maas represents one segment of an overall plan for seven residential sections, two large inner city parks and a number of individual projects. The term "panorama" is used in reference to the exposed site of this segment of the project, facing the Old City of Rotterdam. Directly above the waterline and optically underlined by the blackened walls of the quay, this new "crown of the city" (Peter Rumpf's characterization of this project) emphasizes the silhouette of the *Koop van Zuid* on a frontage of six hundred meters. Flow of the river and flow of time, the movement of the ships, the up and down of the cranes and the integration of these motifs into the building, whose length it experienced in temporal and visual subdivisions created by the supports and serial steel constructions.
And the technological conception of the whole refers directly to the craft traditions of Holland as well as to the modern technology of the port. Up to the fifth floor, the building is laid in the traditional red brick that has been used in Holland for hundreds of years. This very traditional structure is crowned by trim steel constructions whose dark profiles stand out against brilliant white wall panels. It's easy to imagine these units being prefabricated in the neighboring Ruhr, in Duisberg or Essen, loaded onto ships and transported by waterway directly to the Koonings pier. There, on-site cranes need only unload and position them to complete the construction of the building. One of these cranes, or a row of cranes, would remain in place, ready for future use. This proposal by no means follows the usual practises of modern urban renewal. It is intended as a visual and functional plan, simultaneously.
Especially in the last twenty years, empirical social research and analytical methods have led much too often to a new routinization in architecture and urban development. Belief in processes and methods has too often taken priority over ideas. On the other hand, the constitutive elements of the historic city cannot simply be repeated, imitatively and nostalgically. But they are and remain the point of departure for the underlying conception of many new projects whose function and appearance are often only fragments but which neverthless can be of fundamental significance.
If we succeed in creating new urban environments that achieve their effectiveness and legitimization from their artistic quality and social commitment, they will be accepted by the public. If we succeed, that is, in creating a number of unique sites — here a garden and park, there a street and a square, a composition of constructed elements in new living spaces weaving together new strands of social life — we will have laid the foundation of and fulfilled the desire for what a city should represent: an identity. The city as process is only then bearable when unique identities stand firmly against the dangers of being ground down by the city and depleted of one's sense of self.

Renzo Piano

IBM Itinerant Exhibition, 1982-1984.
Project: Renzo Piano, S. Ishida, A. Traldi.
Client: IBM Europe.

Temporary exhibition hall built in pyramidic shapes using polycarbonate, laminated wood and aluminium, to be set up in the city's green zone.
Client: IBM Europe.
General Co-ordination: G. L. Trischitta.
Image Co-ordination: R. Lanterio.
Architects: Building Workshop srl, Renzo Piano, S. Ishida, A. Traldi, assisted by F. Doria, G. Fascioli, O. Di Blasi.
Co-ordination for the installation: Atelier Piano, Nori Okabe, assisted by P. Vincent, G.B. Lacoudre.
Engineers: Ove Arup & Partners, P. Rice, T. Barker, assisted by D. Atling, A. Guthrie, R. Kinch, A. Sedgewick, J. Lewis, G. Calow.
Main Contractors: Calabrese Engineering spa, M. Valeriani, N. Del Re, N. Panzarsis, G. Brandi, N. De Tullio, D. Di Candia, M. Palumbo, assisted by V. Calabrese and A. Gnoato.
Subcontractors: Calabrese Veicoli Industriali spa, F.lli Loda snc, Leonelli & C. snc, Loctite Italia spa, Officine Termotecniche Breda spa, Officine Termotecniche Breda spa, Radaelli spa, Tecno spa, Woodplastic-Alberani spa.

Photograph: G. Berengo Gardin, Milan.

Aldo Rossi

Teatro del mondo (World's Theater), Venice, 1979.
Project: Aldo Rossi.
Client: La Biennale, Venice.

The Project of the World's Theater (Teatro del mondo)
I recently designed a small scientific theater as a site of pure performance: a platform, sets, scenery. The auditorium made no difference, I was not creating a theatrical space. It was more like the puppet shows of childhood, stages set up in any room, usually only a section of a building. Thus, the houses, mansions, churches, cut in half by bombings and surviving in the cities of postwar Europe, displayed public and private life as a spectacle.
The project of the World's Theater is an entirely different matter. This Venetian theater is characterized by three facts: it has to have a precise usable space even if this space is not precisely pinpointed; it has to be set up as a volume according to the form of Venetian monuments; and it has to be on the water.
Its location on the water is obviously its chief hallmark — a raft, a boat: the limit or confine of the construction of Venice. And all cities, not only Venice, have different tasks to assign to water.
The barges coming from Ticino in the Lombard mist turned into carnival boats; the waterside constructions mark the incisions of Northern Gothic cities. The Limmat, the river which flows through Zurich, was lined with houses or towers (actually mills), but also mysterious, evil places, situated between water and land. The Oriental cities were and still are surrounded by this world of boats. The image of Venice, a synthesis of foggy, Gothic landscapes and Eastern insertions or transpositions, establishes it as the capital of waterside cities. And hence the capital of possible passages — not only physical or topographical ones — between the two worlds. In this way, the Rialto Bridge is a passage, a market, a theater. These analogies of place in a building design are of decisive importance for me, if they are properly read then they are the project. If the building is planned for a foreseeably brief time, this is not just a Venetian caprice. In earlier times, great architects were summoned for urban decorations.
Today, the vast divisions by lots leave a moderate freedom for architectural culture — *sine pecunia* projects, irrelevant compared with the large-scale operations of the system. This insensitive system has destroyed and corrupted our cities, but the competition projects, small-scale works, are beginning to constitute an effective alternative.
I do not know if or how this Venetian theater will be constructed; but it will grow in my designs and others', because it has a character of necessity: its limited capacity will allow the staging of direct spectacles of various types — above all, in a central part of the city. Its structure has to be made of wood, which is an extremely solid and lasting material. The use of wood, however, in the architecture of this theater goes beyond its purely functional meaning: just think of the wooden boats, the black wood of the gondolas, the maritime constructions. In the American state of Maine, we can still find marvelous and eminent wooden constructions: the lighthouses — houses of light that observe and are observed.
Finally, the theater, whether stable or temporary, was a huge work of carpentry that was barely masked by the gold and stucco.
These brief notes on my project are independent of the possibility of its construction and its use. But they are certainly not independent of a Venetian construction, a mode of design that seeks fantasy purely in reality.

Gino Valle

Banca Commerciale Italiana, One William Street, New York, 1981-1983.
Project: Gino Valle.
Collaborators: Alfredo Carnelutti and Marco Carnelutti.
Partner: Jeremy P. Lang & Associates.
Client: Banca Commerciale Italiana.

"One William" — Architectural Concepts of the BCI Building
The design decision, according to the conception of architect Gino Valle, has been to preserve and restore the Kimball building and to build a new building on that portion of the lot made available by the demolition of the annex. In this manner, the construction on the block was completed, starting from the existing building, its structure, morphology and typology.
The old building has a ground floor consisting of a circular atrium on the corner of William and South William Street, and a main hall, rectangular in shape and covered with travertine, with a ceiling of golden caissons with painted panels.
The group of four elevators at the South William Street entrance has been preserved and restored. Two new fire stairs have been built in the annex. The two-building complex has therefore been integrated into a single building which covers the entire block. This blending of the parts has led to the arrangement of all the offices on the outside perimeter around a central core that includes the staircases, the oval-shaped conference room form on the seventh floor, the elevator lobby and the service functions.
The oval form, which is located on the bisector of the main corner, gives rise to the axis of the tower of the new building on the corner of Stone Street and Mill Lane, opposite the tower on William and South William Street.
The grouping of the new windows mirrors the central motif of the three-bayed and five-bayed windows found on the ninth and tenth floor, and the horizontal axis

follows the rhythm set by the Kimball building.
Combined with this integration is the close dialogue and comparison between new and old in the materials of the facade, in the detailing of the stone and grouping of the windows and in the alignement of the setbacks and horizontal cornices with the new black granite bands, in either a polished or matte finish.
The top parapet repeats the motif of the oculi of the Kimball building, and will be complemented by a stainless steel tower. This new corner tower will be surmounted by an open circular stainless steel structure that will rise to a height equal to that of the old tower.

Art

Giovanni Anselmo

1. *Il paesaggio con mano che lo indica mentre verso oltremare i grigi si alleggeriscono (The Landscape with Hand Pointin toward It while in the Direction of Oltremare the Grays Gradually Fade Away)*, 1982.
Pencil on linen paper, stones, steel cable, and Oltremare, size variable.
Collection the artist.
Photograph by Paolo Mussat Sartor, Turin.

2. *Il paesaggio con mano che lo indica mentre verso oltremare i grigi si alleggeriscono (The Landscape with Hand Pointing toward It while in the Direction of Oltremare the Grays Gradually Fade Away)*, detail, 1982.*

3. *Grigi che si alleggeriscono verso oltremare (Grays Gradually Fade Away in the Direction of Oltremare)*, 1982-84.
Stones, steel cable, and Oltremare, size variable.
Collection the artist.
Photograph by Paolo Mussat Sartor, Turin.

Marco Bagnoli

1. *Metrica e Mantrica (Metrics and Mantrics)*, 1982-1984.
64 + 1 prototypes in wood, cm. 160 × 18 × 18.
Installation, Cappella de' Pazzi, Santa Croce, Florence, June 1984.
Photograph by Paolo Mussat Sartor, Turin.

2. *Albe of Zonsopgagen*, 1984.
Earth, air and fire. Laren (20 km from Amsterdam), September 1984.

3. *Anti-Hertz*, 1979.
Installation, Salvatore Ala Gallery, New York.

Georg Baselitz

1. *Ohne Titel (Untitled)*, 1982.
Beech wood, cm. 50 × 45 × 45.
Courtesy of Mary Boone-Michael Werner Gallery, New York.

2. *Deutsche Schule (German School)*, 1979-80.*
Eggtempera on canvas, diptych, cm. 324 × 200 each.
Courtesy of Mary Boone-Michael Werner Gallery, New York.

3. *Das Atelier (The Atelier)*, 1980.*
Eggtempera on canvas, diptychon, cm. 324 × 200 each.
Courtesy of Mary Boone-Michael Werner Gallery, New York.

4. *Die Familie (The Family)*, 1980.*
Eggtempera on canvas, diptychon, cm. 324 × 200 each.
Courtesy of Mary Boone-Michael Werner Gallery, New York.

Lothar Baumgarten

1. *Monument für die indianischen Nationen Südamerikas (Monument to the Indian Nations of South America)*, 1978-82.
Installation, Documenta 7, Museum Fridericianum, Kassel, June 1982.

2. *America*, 1983-84.
XLI Biennale, Pavilion of the Federal Republic of Germany, Venice, 1984.
Marbles: negra marquina (Spain), estremotz (Portugal), Sicilia royal (Italy), 480 square meters.

Joseph Beuys

1. *Einschmelzaktion (Smelting Action)*, 1982.
Documenta 7, Kassel, June 1982.
Photograph by Ute Klophaus, Wuppertal.

2. *Das Ende des 20. Jahrhunderts (The End of the Twentieth Century)*, 1983.
Felt, clay, 48 stones cm. 190 × 60 × 60 each.
Courtesy of Schmela Gallery, Düsseldorf.
Photograph by Ute Klophaus, Wuppertal.

3. *Hinter den Knochen wird gezählt-Schmerzraum (Behind the Bones Will Be Counted - Space of Pain)*, 1983.
Lead, silver rings, incandescent electrode, telephone.
Courtesy of Konrad Fischer Gallery, Düsseldorf. Photograph by Dorothee Fischer, Düsseldorf.

Alberto Burri

1. *Cellotex C 1*, 1981.*
Cellotex and acrylic, cm. 228 × 366.
Collection Minsa Craig, Los Angeles.

2. *Cellotex C 3*, 1981.*
Cellotex and acrylic, cm. 228 × 366.
Collection Minsa Craig, Los Angeles.

3. *Cellotex C 2*, 1981.*
Cellotex and acrylic, cm. 228 × 366.
Collection Minsa Craig, Los Angeles.

4. *Cellotex*, 1976.
Cellotex and acrylic, cm. 250 × 376.
Collection the artist.

Pier Paolo Calzolari

1. *Senza titolo (Untitled)*, 1984.
Pencil and pastel on paper.

2. *Senza titolo (Untitled)*, 1984.
Pencil and pastel on paper.

3. *Rideau V (Curtain V)*, 1984.*
Oil on canvas, cm. 200 × 560.
Courtesy of Peter Pakesch Gallery, Vienna.
Photograph by Evelyne Tietze, Vienna.

Enzo Cucchi

1.2. *European man.*
Painting, and along with it, the land,
comes into being only in Europe.
In recent years this land
is the mirror
of this extraordinary development.
Almost as the same time?...
Perhaps even earlier in some cases?...
Man, before turning to painting...
learns to domesticate animals,

and then to raise them. 1984.
Ink on paper.

3. *Un millenario trasporto comincia a muoversi attraverso la preistoria (A Thousand Year Transport Begins Moving across Prehistory)*, 1984.*
Oil and fire on canvas, cm. 130×750.
Courtesy of Bruno Bischofberger Gallery, Zurich, and Mary Boone Gallery, New York.
Photograph by Salvatore Licitra, Milan.

4. *Succede ai pianoforti di fiamme nere (It Happens to Pianos with Black Flames)*, 1983.*
Oil on canvas, cm. 207×291.
Private collection, Zurich.
Photograph by Capone and Gianvenuti, Rome.

Hanne Darboven

1. From left to right:
12 Months with Postcards from Today of Flowers, 1982; *12 Months with Postcards from Today of Dogs*, 1982; *12 Months with Postcards from Today of Kittens*, 1982; *12 Months with Postcards from Today of Horses*, 1982.*
Postcards and mixed media on paper; each piece consists of 12 sheets representing the months of the year; each sheet cm. 37×51.

2. *12 Months with Postcards from Today of Horses*, 1982.
Postcards and mixed media on paper, 12 sheets, each cm. 37×51.

3. *12. Months with Postcards from Today of Horses*, detail, 1982.

Nicola De Maria

1. *L'angelo del 1983 (The Angel of 1983)*, 1983.
Fresco and oil on canvas; dimensions of canvas, cm. 40×30.
Installation, Kunsthalle, Basel, 1983.

2. *Sorridi faccia! 2 fiori 2 occhi (Smile Face! 2 Flowers 2 Eyes)*, 1980-82.
Mixed media on canvas, cm. 150×110.
Courtesy of Karsten Greve, Cologne.

3. *Tu (You)*, 1983.
Mixed media on canvas, cm. 40×30.
Courtesy of Karsten Greve, Cologne.

Luciano Fabro

1. *La Germania (Germany)*, 1984.*
Lamppost (height 900 cm.), iron form (cm. 900×300), sand bags (50, kg. 50 each).
Courtesy of Paul Maenz, Cologne.

2. *Habitat di Aachen (Habitat of Aachen)*, 1983.
Variant for Venice, 1984. Paper and steel, cm. 600×600×400.
Collection the artist.
Photograph by Francesca Del Col Tana, Milan.

3. *Esprit de finesse, esprit de géométrie (Spirit of Finesse, Spirit of Geometry)*, 1984.
Marble, cm. 400×58.
Collection the artist.
Photograph by Francesca Del Col Tana, Milan.

Ludger Gerdes

1. *Zwei Vorhangwände. Allegorie der Freundschaft - Künstler und Architekt und drei Freundinnen (Two Curtainwalls. Allegory of Friendship - Artist and Architect and Three Girls)*, 1982.*
Oil on canvas, cm. 500×250 each.
Collection Lutz Schirmer, Munich.
Photograph by T. Struth, Düsseldorf.

2. *Ohne Titel (Untitled)*, 1983.
Pencil and water-colour on paper.

3. *Ohne Titel (Untitled)*, 1984.
Installation at Produzentengalerie, Hamburg.

Rebecca Horn

1. *Kopfextension (Headextension)*, 1972.*
Performance, Documenta 5, Kassel, 1972.
Black fabric and wood, cm. 540 h.

2. *Der Pendel (Pendulum)*, 1984.*
Steel and goose's egg.
Collection the artist.

3. *Das Quecksilber Bad (Quicksilver Bath)*, 1984.
Steel, glass and quicksilver.
Collection the artist.

Body-Space-Reflexes
Touching Hammers. The tapered ends of the two hammer heads meet in the middle. At 180-second intervals they bang sharply on the wall behind and then slowly move towards each other again, waiting in this stationary position for the next bang-impulse.
Quicksilver Bath. Triggered by the same impulse, a small hammer bangs against the rim of the quicksilver bath, sending ripples through the large pool of mercury.
The Pendulum. At the same moment, a 3.30-meter-long pendulum suspended from the ceiling begins to swing. Directly below the tip of the pendulum lies a goose egg, which the swinging pendulum nearly grazes.

Jörg Immendorff

1. *C.D. beben/heben (Quaking/Lifting)*, 1984.
Oil on canvas, cm. 285×330.
Courtesy Mary Boone-Michael Werner Gallery, New York.

2. *Hü*, 1984.*
Synthetic resin on canvas, cm. 285×400.
Courtesy of Mary Boone-Michael Werner Gallery, New York.

3. *Akademie Ost - Aufgabe Hans Albers (Academy East - Task Hans Albers)*, 1984.*
Synthetic resin on canvas, cm. 285×400.
Courtesy of Mary Boone-Michael Werner Gallery, New York.

4. *Akademie Mitte Aufgabe Städte der Bewegung (Academy Middle Task Towns in Movement)*, 1984.*
Synthetic resin on canvas, cm. 285×400.
Courtesy of Mary Boone-Michael Werner Gallery, New York.

Anselm Kiefer

1. *Der Ölberg (Mount Olivet)*, 1980.*
Oil on canvas, cm. 219×300.
Courtesy of Sonnabend Gallery, New York.

2. *Landschaft mit Flügel (Landscape with Wing)*, 1981.
Oil, straw, lead on canvas, cm. 330×500.
Collection Sidney and Frances Lewis Foundation, Richmond.

3. *Des Malers Atelier (The Painter's Studio)*, 1983.*
Woodcut, straw, oil on canvas, cm. 280×280.
Collection Edwin L. Stringer, Q.C.

4. *Untitled*, 1984.*
Oil and mixed media on canvas, cm. 280×280.
Courtesy of Marian Goodman Gallery, New York.

Jannis Kounellis

1. *Metamorfosi (Metamorphosis)*, 1958-84.
46 iron shelves, smoke, oil on wood (shelves each cm. 40×13).
Collection Crex, Schaffhausen.
Photograph by Paolo Mussat Sartor, Turin.

2. *Metamorfosi (Metamorphosis)*, 1975-84.
Iron structure, wood, fragments of plaster casts, table, mixed media.
Collection Crex, Schaffhausen.
Photograph by Paolo Mussat Sartor, Turin.

Markus Lüpertz

1. *Il principe (The Prince)*, 1983.*
From the series "Die Bürger von Florenz" (The Citizens of Florence), painted bronze, cm. 49×19,5×24.
Courtesy of Mary Boone-Michael Werner Gallery, New York.

2. *B.C.*, 1983.*
From the series "Die Bürger von Florenz" (The Citizens of Florence), painted bronze, cm. 60×35×23.
Courtesy of Mary Boone-Michael Werner Gallery, New York.

3. *Der Mohr (The Moor)*, 1983.*
From the series "Die Bürger von Florenz" (The Citizens of Florence), painted bronze, cm. 45×19,5×32.
Courtesy of Mary Boone-Michael Werner Gallery, New York.

4. *Tourist (Tourist)*, 1983.*
From the series "Die Bürger von Florenz" (The Citizens of Florence), painted bronze, cm. 32×32×40,5.
Courtesy of Mary Boone-Michael Werner Gallery, New York.

Gerhard Merz

1. *Nude Woman*, 1984.
Silkscreen on canvas, copper frame, cm. 170×140.
Collection Bazon Brock, Bonn.

2. *Juan Gris*, 1982.
Silkscreen on canvas, cm. 220×160.
Collection Ludwig Rinn, Giesen.

3. *All'Italia (To Italy)*, 1984.*
Oil and silkscreen on canvas, 4 panels, cm. 140×35 each.
Courtesy of Elizabeth Kaufmann, Zurich.
Photograph by Bruno Hubschmid, Zurich.

4. *All'Italia (To Italy)*, 1984.*
Oil and silkscreen on canvas, wood frames, triptych, cm. 230×130 each.
Courtesy of Elizabeth Kaufmann, Zurich.
Photograph by Bruno Hubschmid, Zurich.

Mario Merz

1. *Senza titolo (Untitled)*, 1979.
Installation, Castello Colonna, Genazzano-Rome.
Metal tubular structure, stones, neon, mixed media on canvas; measures variable.

2. *Crescite senza fine (Endless Growths)*, 1984.
Oil, enamel, spray and neon on canvas mounted on wood, cm. 278×486.
Courtesy of Christian Stein, Turin.
Photograph by Mario Sarotto, Turin.

Reinhard Mucha

1. *Lampe (Lamp)*, Kunsthalle, Baden-Baden, 1981.

2. *Astron-Taurus* (two details), Kunsthalle, Bielefeld, 1981.

3. *o.T. (Untitled)*, Kunstmuseum, Düsseldorf, 1982.

4. *Hagen-Vorhalle*, Kunsthalle, Bern, 1983.

Mimmo Paladino

1. *Cordoba*, 1984.*
Oil on canvas, cm. 300×400.
Courtesy of Waddington Gallery,London.
Photograph by Salvatore Licitra, Milan.

2. *Viandante (Wayfarer)*, 1983.*
Oil, wood, plaster with papier maché on canvas, mounted on wood, cm. 320 diameter.
Collection Art Gallery of Ontario, Toronto. Gift from the Volunteer Committee Fund, 1984.

3. *Camera in tempesta (Room in Storm)*, 1984.
Pencil and pastel on cardboard.

Giulio Paolini

1. *Delfo*, 1965.
Photograph on canvas, cm. 180×95.
Private Collection, Brescia.

Delphi. The elusive character of the painting is questioned in relation to the identity of the painter. This photograph shows a concept accomplished by the painter in front of an unaccomplished painting. The photograph is equal to the moment in which the painting exists in the mind of the painter although the painting is not yet physically there.

2. *Giovane che guarda Lorenzo Lotto (Young Man Looking at Lorenzo Lotto)*, 1967.
Photograph on canvas, cm. 30×24.
Collection Rentchler, Laupain.

Young Man Looking at Lorenzo Lotto. A reconstruction of the time and place occupied by the author (1505) and spectator (now) of this painting.

3. *Caleidoscopio (Kaleidoscope)*, 1976.
Plaster stainless steel, cm. 100 h.
Collection the artist.
Photograph by Paolo Mussat Sartor, Turin.

Kaleidoscope. Nothing remains permanent, nothing remains transient. He who would imagine superimposing one column on the other, would reproduce an image, that would already have been reproduced (in the mirror) by itself.

4. *Casa di Lucrezio (Lucretius' House)*, 1981-82.
Plaster and fabric.
Collection Christian Stein, Turin.
Photograph by Paolo Mussat Sartor, Turin.

Lucretius' House. In the maze, once you have not managed to find your way out, you are free to imagine other innumerable mazes which take, everyone, back to the starting point.

A. R. Penck

1. *Was ist Gravitation? II (What is Gravitation? II)*, 1984.*
Acrylic on canvas, cm. 250×350.

Courtesy of Mary Boone-Michael Werner Gallery, New York.

2. *Wechseln, verwechseln (To Change, to Exchange)*, 1983.*
Synthetic resin on canvas, cm. 260×350.
Courtesy of Mary Boone-Michael Werner Gallery, New York.

3. *Wichtige Begegnung 2 (Important Meeting 2)*, 1982.*
Synthetic resin on canvas, cm. 250×330.
Courtesy of Mary Boone-Michael Werner Gallery, New York.

4. *Standard 6*, 1983.
Synthetic resin on canvas, cm. 350×260.
Courtesy of Mary Boone-Michael Werner Gallery, New York.

Giuseppe Penone

1. *Vegetal gesture, trace, distance, virtual adherence, gesture fossil, static action, expectation, vegetal structure. Finger traces as channels, bundles of fibers traversed by bronze. The leaf on the hero's back, point of death, point of life.*
The hero as a tree trunk, dragon's blood as a wound, the leaf as a suture. Dragon's blood as non-corruption, the leaf as the life cycle, corruption and death. The leaf has the strength to strike down the hero, it possesses the secret of his life, it protects the natural cycle of things, it gives order to exception, it inhabits the attempt to subvert the true duty of things to death. The vegetal gesture fills up with leaves, a natural vessel of the transience of a form.
Ink on paper.

2. *Quattro paesaggi (Four Landscapes)*, 1984.*
Cast bronze, cm. 180×70×40; cm. 150×80×100; cm. 200×70×40; cm. 80×70×150.
Collection the artist.

The patina of bronze; with great facility, bronze translates, fossilizes the vegetable, the gesture of its growth, and its vital color.
We admire the landscape of the patina of bronze which is neither rust nor color, but seeps out from the metal with the same natural freshness as the greens, grays, and reds of mosses and leaves.
The metal is subject to the elements of air, rain, wind, the sun's heat; and, as with vegetable growth, color is formed by these elements.
The dense and compact air in perpetual tension, biting and subtle, penetrates the bronze and corrodes it, it joins with it, making the brilliant splendor of a landscape appear (flower) on the surface.

3. From left to right:
Paesaggio verticale (Vertical Landscape), 1984.
Cast bronze, laurel and baked clay vase, cm. 210×110×110.
Verde del bosco (Wood Green), 1984.
Leaves rubbed on canvas, cm. 283×262.
Courtesy of Christian Stein Gallery, Turin.
Photograph by Paolo Mussat Sartor, Turin.
The green, the jewel-like Greek of the leaves and the inert moss, the greenery, fresh repose, woodland refuge.
To capture the green of the woods.
To encompass with a gesture the green of the woods.
To rub in the green of the woods.
To imagine the depth of the green of the woods.
To work with the splendor, with the consistency of the green of the woods.
To consume the green of the woods against the green of the woods.
To repeat the woods with the green of the woods.

Michelangelo Pistoletto

1. *Leoncini (Little Lions)*, 1984.
Travertine Samanta, cm. 240×120×350.
Installation, Forte di Belvedere, Florence.
Photograph by Paolo Mussat Sartor, Turin.

2. *Figura che si guarda (Figure Looking at Itself)*, 1983.
Carved styrofoam and red acrylic, cm. 250×100×120.
Collection Giorgio Persano, Turin.
Photograph by Paolo Pellion di Persano, Turin.

3. *Figure che guardano nel pozzo (Figures Looking down a Well)*, 1983.*
From left to right:
Figura che guarda nel pozzo (Figure Looking down a Well), 1983.
Carved styrofoam, cm. 340×120×40.
Seconda figura rossa (Second Red Figure), 1983.
Carved styrofoam, cm. 340×120×120.
Prima figura rossa (First Red Figure), 1983.
Carved styrofoam, cm. 340×240×120.
Courtesy of Giorgio Persano, Turin.
Photograph by Paolo Mussat Sartor, Turin.

Sigmar Polke

1. *Schnee und Hagel (Snow and Hail)*, 1983.*
Lacquer on canvas, cm. 300×200.
Courtesy of Schmela Gallery, Düsseldorf.

2. *Filmschleife (Film Ribbon)*, 1984.*
Mixed media on fabric, cm. 300×200.
Courtesy of Schmela Gallery, Düsseldorf.

3. *Regenbogen (Rainbow)*, 1983.*
Lacquer on canvas, cm. 300×200.
Courtesy of Schmela Gallery, Düsseldorf.

4. *Tafel: Vermessung der Steine im Bauch des Wolfes und das anschliessende Zermahlen der Steine zu Kulturschutt (Sign: Measurement of the Stones in the Wolf's Belly and the Subsequent Grinding of the Stones into Cultural Rubble)*, 1980.*
Oil and mixed media on fabric, cm. 300,5×185.
Collection Art Gallery of Ontario, Toronto.

Gerhard Richter

1. *Lilak (Lilac)*, 1982.*
Oil on canvas, cm. 260×400.
Courtesy of Durand-Dessert, Paris.

2. *Abstraktes Bild (Abstract Painting)*, 1984.
Oil on canvas, cm. 225×200.

3. *Tor (Gate)*, 1982.*
Oil on canvas, cm. 250×250.
Courtesy of Sperone-Westwater Gallery, New York.

4. *Tisch (Table)*, 1982.*
Oil on canvas, cm. 224×294.
Courtesy of Sperone-Westwater Gallery, New York.

Salomé

1. *Ultramarin (Ultramarine)*, 1982.*
Mixed media on canvas, cm. 400×300.
Collection the artist.

2. *Im Morgenlicht (Light of Dawn)*, 1982.*
Mixed media on canvas, cm. 400×300.
Collection the artist.
Photograph by J. Littkemann, Berlin.

3. *Zeitgeist VII (Spirit of Time VII)*, 1982.*
Mixed media on canvas, cm. 400×300.
Collection the artist.

4. *Im Abendlicht (Twilight)*, 1982.*
Mixed media on canvas, cm. 400×300.
Collection the artist.

Remo Salvadori

1. *Aim*, 1984.
Vegetal colours on paper, cm. 21×29,9.
Collection the artist.
Photograph by Carlo Cantini, Florence.

2. *Modello (Model)*, 1979-83.*
Baked clay, cm. 170 h, cm. 45 diameter.
Collection the artist.
Photograph by Carlo Cantini, Florence.

3. *L'attenzione divisa (Divided Attention)*, 1982-83.*
Vegetable colours on canvars, cm. 210×470.
Collection the artist.
Photograph by Carlo Cantini, Florence.

Thomas Schütte

1. *Studio I*, 1982-83.
(For sculptor), model 1:100, in cardboard, Private collection, Germany.

2. *Studio II*, 1982-83.*
(For painter), model 1:100 in cardboard.
Collection Hartford Museum, Hartford.

3. *Beckmann Building*, 1982.
Pigment and paint, cm. 110×130.
Collection the artist.

4. *Haus für zwei Freunde (House for Two Friends)*, 1983.*
Model 1:100 in cardboard.
Collection Dr. Lawrence, Hamburg.

Ettore Spalletti

1. *When the atmosphere is pierced by the intensity of light on days of calm, the blue and violet radiations produce the azure coloring of the sky*, 1982.

2. *Anfora, bacile, vasi (Amphora, Bowl, Vases)*, 1982.*
Installation, Museum Folkwang, Essen.
Photograph by W. Hannappel, Hessen.

Emilio Vedova

1. *Rosso '83-IV - (Red '83-IV-)*, 1983.*
Painting on canvas, cm. 300×190.
Collection the artist.
Photograph by G. Mazzetto, Venice.

2. *Omaggio a Dada Berlin (Homage to Dada Berlin)*, 1964-65.*
Mixed media on wood, collage, and iron hinges, cm. 305×180×300.
Collection the artist.
Photograph by Paolo Mussat Sartor, Turin.

3. *Rosso '83-VI - (Red '83-VI-)*, 1983.*
Mixed media on canvas, cm. 300×190.
Collection the artist.
Photograph by G. Mazzetto, Venice.

4. *Rosso '83-VII - (Red '83-VII-)*, 1983.*
Mixed media on canvas, cm. 300×190.
Collection the artist.
Photograph by G. Mazzetto, Venice.

Design

Achille Castiglioni

1. *Frisbi* hanging lamp, manufactured by Flos, 1978.

2. Drawings for objects designed between 1945 and 1984.

Paolo Deganello

1. *Artifici*, manufactured by Cassina, Meda, 1985.
Tables with base made of an amalgam of quartz grit, marble and polyester resin in two color variants: gray-green and pale bordeaux.
The tops are held up by four cherry-wood supports. Tops in glass with possibilities for inserting decorative elements in non-slip plastified fabric. Height cm. 37.5. Square top measures cm. 100×100. Circular one measures ∅ cm. 120. Triangular one is cm. 114×114. Elliptical one is cm. 160x63.5.
Some of the decorative elements only go with certain tables; others can be used with all of them. Other decorative elements can also be fitted in between the glass tops, according to personal tastes (rose petals, photos, drawings etc.).

2. *Palomar*, manufactured by Ycami Collection, Novedrate, 1984.
Coat stand in extruded aluminium. Cast iron base, umbrella stand in marble, clothes hanger in ceramic. Natural aluminium structure with decorations below in pale yellow and red.

3. *Common House*, 1983.
The claiming/reappropriation of *time* and its measuring according to people's self-determined existences urgently magnifies the need for widespread construction of community *space*.
Heterogeneity and pluralism of life forms: there is a movement away from universal measure, producing polymorphism, and a movement toward individualization and a pluralism of societal aggregates, languages, cultures.
Toward individuality — "a room of one's own" — : knowledge of one's body, one's sexuality; the development of creativity; the construction of biography; a search for solutions to anxiety.
Toward community — "a concrete and self-determined space/time" — flight from metropolitan machines; creation of a pace different from that of the system; migrations toward a different relationship with space, with nature, with society; the conglomeration and gathering of local knowledge; the self-construction of landscape and environment; the refocusing of activities and technical, scientific knowledge upon self-determined ends.
But, *in the telematic universe:* there is an explosion of relationships, messages, symbols, control over concrete actions, within the aspatial and instantaneous domain of the "global village."
The contradiction: time itself moves toward individuality, and the community reclaims concrete space/territory, architecture, nature, space for interaction: "the local village."
This homologizing implosion of the telematic universe is juxtaposed to the explosion of diversities that seek out actual concrete places of existence: the identities of women, men, experts, and local communities, young people, old people, nomads, areas for non-work activities, and so on. All these exist now, within the typology of the industrial city and the family dwelling. And all seek out typologies that identify and recognize their existence. Typological research is an investigation into a new system of relationships wich can be substituted for the abstract order of work, the

marketplace, mass production. Within the realm of the informational marketplace, the community is both rooted and nomadic. It reclaims concrete spaces and at the same time travels at the speed of light.
Is the local village being reappropriated by the "global village?"
There, perhaps, lies some hope for design — to translate the dominant mode into an exchange among diversities.
Living places (built by the people and the community and not the product of the labor force!) are clearly a point of intersection for the exchange between individual and societal research. The places given over to this exchange — once they were the marketplace, the stock exchange, the bank — are now places for representing an exchange of information about the forms of existence among diverse communities. For to live within the wealth and redundance of the informational metropolis implies to produce.
Thus one accomplishes typological research, one arrives at a project, via a process of naming and identifying; designing workable forms for the self-recognition of individuality and community; designing tools, stimuli, symbols, territories for the self-determination of the concrete space/time of the community.
We have chosen four subjects who seem to us to be representative of the redefinition of and the breaking away from the consolidated typology of the family dwelling (living room + kitchen + hallway + bedroom), defined according to elementary functions and roughly representative of the reproductive function. We have asked these four subjects to describe both their requirements for a living space in today's urban world and how these needs relate to their histories. From these four subjects we have been able to piece together certain — not all — aspects of an emerging identity of habitable space.

From the story by Augusto (militant worker in Marghera, then an ecologist, he now creates and sells, along with Daniela and Emanuele, papier-mâché masks, costumes, paintings made of dried plants, watercolors, etc.): "...I need for my living place to recognize, to identify, my presence. I need a mobile equilibrium, fluctuating according to my mood, but also a stratification, a solidification of my experience which accepts the 'site' — the four primal elements impressed by the directionless passage of time — as the physical manifestation of my origins."

From the story by Grazia (teacher, traveler, feminist activist, she prefers living alone): "...When I was eight years old I was given a room of my own; it was clearly a question of *decoration*, without any personal touch. I hid behind the bed, and they looked for me all night long, such was the extent of my alienation from this environment...One must compare space as the representation of women's work to the symbolic space of consciousness and states of being...
I would like a bedroom with a bed resembling a ship. I would like only that — a house where there is only a place of repose and of love — there are no other functions. It is important not to have to make your bed every day...The collective space would contain a level for relaxation — a room looking out into a veranda, a room which has nearly everything on the floor, pillows, coffee tables, etc. An aesthetic space, extremely pleasant and comfortable; a space capable of looking outward, filled with light and plants..."

From the story by Sandra (university instructor, an active participant in the social and personal revolutions of the seventies, she and her three sons live in a large city): "...A house in the belly of a courtyard — an Arabic house, the courtyard intimate, lived-in. I no longer want to live within a community, even if in my dreams the community intersects my life... This is a children's house, the pace is that of the mother and her children. It is a protective shell having no relationships with the external world except through the children's holidays. This is a house of dreams: used by an aspatial community, it has nothing to do with the neighborhood or with collectivity. Its spatial arrangements can vary, and life within can be seen as a performance. Life with children. Living according to this tempo, without the intrusion of a man, seems a great pleasure to me. I feel irritated if a man's glance intrudes upon this erotic picture."

From the story by Silvio (post-movement city-dweller, photographer, artist): "...Within my pyramid, my tomb, I would have my teddy bear, which I would place on my night stand, a telescope, a Chinese tapestry given to me by my grandfather, and some of my photographic work... This house of mine is a large empty space with few objects, only those which I would place in my tomb. It is a totally private space, but sometimes it can accomodate others; I could never live with other people, except for my woman, and my house is also my photography studio... and sometimes it is a space for public events — selective art shows, performances, celebrations..."

Each of the above four people was asked to design along with us their idea of a living space, one which would show traces of the person's biography and experiences, as well as specific desires for a house.
Each representation is organized on three levels:
— places of individual identity, of solitude (areas on the ground level; each area presented in facade view, seen through a "terrace" or "window" opening, individualized for each specific subject);
— places for collective activity, adjusted to each individual's experiences (spaces beneath ground level, completely open to the undefined space of informational exchange and experience typical of the urban enviroment);
— the undefined urban space of informational and experiental exchange (effectively continuous surfaces, not designable, site of informational totems).
The totality of sites is protected by a transparent dome which creates an enclave condition with respect to the metropolitan "machine" and which acts as a separation between the protected and the polluted enviroment.
Paolo Deganello and Alberto Magnaghi

Michele De Lucchi

1. *Cadetto*, Morphos collection, manufactured by Acerbis, Seriate, 1984. Table in lacquered wood and metal, disc diameter cm. 56, height cm. 80.

2. *Cyclos*, manufactured by Artemide, Pregnana, 1983.
Wall light in painted metal and glass, diameter cm. 40.

Frank Hess

1. *Clark Scheid PV 60.*
Design and development of construction equipment, corporate graphics and product color and graphic identification. Client: Clark Equipment Company, Benton Harbor, 1972-76.

Herbert Lindinger

1. *Hi-Fi System*

H. Lindinger and Hans Gugelot, Ulm, 1958, for Braun AG Frankfurt.
Since 1962 Braun has been manufacturing and varying the system.

2. *Street Furniture*
Lampposts and fittings for waiting rooms designed by Lindinger & Partners during the work on Darmstadt's Luisenplatz (Lindinger, Boss, Mitscherlich, 1978).

3. *Standard City Bus*
Prototype for the German standard city bus commissioned by the German minister for Science and Technology, design Lindinger & Partners (Lindinger, Medugorac, Kusserow, 1975-77).

4. *Stuttgart Underground*
Design Lindinger & Partners (Lindinger, Kusserow, Staubach, Weinert, 1979-1984).
Contractor: MAN/DUWAG, Stuttgart city traffic network.

Dieter Rams

1. 10 cups *Coffee-machine*, 1984, Braun Aromaster Kf 45.

2. *Atelier*, 1980, Braun Production.

Ettore Sottsass jr.

1. Progetto (Project), 1980.
Pencil and pastel on paper, cm. 22×19.

2. Progetto (Project), 1984.
Pencil and pastel on paper, cm. 22×19.

Graphic Design

Pierluigi Cerri

1.2. *Raffaello e Brera*, 1982-1984.
Posters.

3. *Identité Italienne - L'art en Italie depuis 1959*, Paris, 1981. Project for the poster.

4. *Alexander Calder*, Turin, 1983. Poster.

5. *20 Projects for the "Lingotto"*, Turin, 1984.
Project for the logo.
Photograph by Mario Carrieri.

6.7.8. XXXVII Biennale, Venice, 1976.
Posters.

A.G. Fronzoni

1. Poster for the "Fontana" show, 1966, offset, cm. 100×70, Galleria La Polena, Genoa.

2. *Un raggio di sole (Sun Beam)*, from the volume *Immagini per la pace (Images for Peace)*, 1980, offset, cm. 70×50, Associazione Nazionale Amici dell'Unità, Roma.

Michael Klar

1. *Geschichte der Produktivkräfte (History of Productive Power)*, 1982.
Synopsis on five posters which can be folded, size Din A2.
Conception, shaping and text by M. Klar, O. Nehren, B. Neumann, W. Niess, L. Roth. Published in 1982 by VSA Hamburg.
The Designer as Author
History of Productive Power is a foldable poster that chronicles electronic data security systems, psychiatry, animal experimentation, the Weimar Republic, worldwide hunger, *Bildzeitung*, the labor movement, the constitution, counter culture, destruction-by-renovation, and many of the other projects I have worked up with students as video-photo-film, posters with text, wall-sized posters, exhibitions, or synopses.
In my program, dealing with content is of equal importance with solving problems of visual presentation. The designer chooses the theme and works with the contents as an author. The design solutions derive from working with contents, not the other way around.
The goal is not to simulate so-called on-the-job experience but to communicate and practice planning and design as part of a broader kind of activity.
Practical work on projects, even at the learning stage, does not occur within a static situation but is a way of engaging in and changing the processes of social life.
My goal is not to train designers to work out prescribed themes and contents on demand or be "creative" in inventing and racing through forms and fashions in ever faster turnover in the service of questionable propaganda for consumer goods.
Now as before, exciting, necessary tasks for the visual designer lie in the largely ignored sphere of didactic, scientific, technical, administrative, social and public communication. Here are to be found perspectives and points of departure for a program of emancipated, enlightened design practice.

Explanation of the Project
Less is known about the history of the forces of production (*Produktivkräfte*) than about almost any other chapter of human history. This is out of line with the importance of the economic basis. Acts of government shape history much less than does the development of productivity, that process by which the human race secures its survival in daily battle with nature.
There are two important factors in the processes of production. First, the level of sophistication of the forces of production, i.e., the tools and methods of work, the management and organization of production, the scientific and technological competence of a society. Second, the relations of production (*Produktionsverhältnisse*), i.e., the legal and social conditions under which production procedes. These two factors taken together define the economic structure of a given society and stand in mutual (dialectical) relation to each other. The relations of production can further the development of the forces of production, or hinder it; the development of new forces of production can stabilize existing relations of production, or it can necessitate their change.
"Freedom does not lie in the dreamt-of autonomy of natural laws but in the recognition of those laws and in the possibility inherent therein of systematically harnessing them to specific ends." (Friedrich Engels, 1878)
The earth is approximately six billion years old. For about the last 500,000 years, the human race has known the use of fire and 350,000 of those years passed before it learned to produce fire artificially. The steam engine didn't appear for another 150,000 years, whereas a mere 200 years lie between the steam engine and today's supertechnologies. Nuclear energy, telecommunications, ultrasonic technology, outerspace exploration, microelectronics, biochemistry and gene technology will decisively alter the conditions of human life.
Where the use of fire, simple tools and weapons originally served to help the

human race survive nature's overwhelming forces, the supertechnologies created by man today seem to threaten all of life.
Given the population explosion and the finiteness of natural resources, unlimited growth, today primarily in the service of certain capital and power monopolies, is not suited to solving the problems of the future. At the beginning of our history, the human population of the earth was very sparse. In the Middle Ages, there were several million human beings. Today the population is approximately four billion, and by the year 2010 it is expected to reach eight billion. There is virtually no effective democratic control over the continually growing concentration of production in internationally organized corporate monopolies, whose power in some cases exceeds that of nations and whose activities are determined solely by the goal of profit maximization, involving reckless exploitation of human beings and nature.
Given the available tools of destruction, ever sharper power struggles and battles over distribution could lead to the self-elimination of the human species.
If the human race is to survive under these conditions, the development of social utopias and future planning related to these visions are imperative. The organization of production around special interests — such as profit maximization — as well as generalized hostility towards science and technology blind one to possibilities for a more humane future, which can be achieved only with imagination and systematic further development of the forces and relations of production.
The following picture-text synchronopsis is intended as a visual contribution to presenting the history of the forces of production.
It si divided into the following sections:
- Primitive Society
- Slave-based Societies of Antiquity
- Feudalism in the Middle Ages
- Early Capitalism in Modern Times
- Capitalism and Socialism.

The presentation concentrates on the development of the economically most advanced societies in each case and is therefore primarily concerned with Europe and, later, North America. No reference is made to the continued existence today of feudal and even primitive societies in various regions of the world. The history of the forces of production is not considered in isolation but in the context of its effects on the relations of production and overall structures of society.

Karl Heinz Krug

1. *Form*, 106, Leverkusen, February 1984. Cover. Size cm. 30×24.
2. *Form*, 1, 1957. Cover (illustration: Le Corbusier).
3. *Form*, 1, 1957, pages 20 and 21.
4. *Form*, 100, May 1982. Special project to celebrate the hundredth issue.
5. *Form*, 38, June 1967. Cover.
6. *Form*, 41, March 1968. Cover.
7. *Form*, 42, June 1968. Cover.
8. *Form*, 46, May 1969. Cover.
9. *Form*, 100, May 1982. Cover and pages 8, 9.

In 1960 as a student of the HfG in Ulm, I criticized the only German language design magazine (*Form*) because in my opinion it was superficial. The publisher invited me to discuss the possibility of finding more interesting contents for the magazine. The following year I began working for the magazine and in 1963 I became editor.
At that time it was not easy to work on a new cultural project such as a design magazine. Expectations were high. We wanted to be "organs for the publication of all industrial design products" ..."and be open to all objects produced..."
Form 1 published the declaration: "...we are not a technological magazine, we are not dealing with the preoccupations of those who create, nor with the problems connected to industry...; and precisely because we do not want to philosophize about the spiritual and sociological backgrounds of a "Gestaltung of form" which has become a discipline, we have the best excuse for not filling our pages with coffee cups, vacuum cleaners, electric razors..., on the contrary we want to give these objects only the importance they really have in life. We believe that this is sufficient." The areas of interest were: "Industrial design of form, architecture, figurative arts, theater, cinema, dance — forms within the area of the perceptible."
After a few years, the "Artistic design of industrial products" became a technological discipline known as "Industrial Design." Ulm's HfG summed up the conceptions of a new culture of the product. After his frequent criticism of the magazine *Ulm*, it was precisely a graduate of the HfG (Yours truly) who was named editor of *Form*.
In 1966 *Form* became "the magazine for design," a technological magazine open to the fascinating and vast area of design. The year after it became the official organ of the German Federation of Graphic Designers, of the Federation of the Free Association of Photographers and Designers and of the German Association of Industrial Designers.
Independently, a specific editorial conception took hold which did not express itself only with produced samples, the result of product design, with graphics and photography but which was forced to deal with political themes.
Because of its technological contributions the magazine gained international status and only once did it risk becoming "politically dependent" when its small scholarly publisher was bought by a large concern. It was perhaps the most decisive turning in *Form's* history when, that year, the readers of the magazine stepped forward to ensure its editorial independence. In 1974, a graphic artist, a printer, a merchant and the editor of the magazine himself, bought *Form* so they could handle it personally. Form GmbH publishing house was born. Last year the magazine published its 100th issue.
Despite other responsibilites and the 22 years I have dedicated to *Form*, it still remains a fascinating thing, just as on the day when, as a designer fresh out of Ulm, I entered the field of advertising graphics.

Italo Lupi

1. Examples of signs designed to unify communications in public parks in Lombardy. Drawings by Ferenc Pinter. Consorzio Parco Lombardo della Valle del Ticino e Regione Lombardia, 1980.

2. Poster for a conference cycle at the Architecture Faculty.
Facoltà di Architettura del Politecnico, Milan.

3. Poster for exhibition of alternative projects for rebuilding the Valle del Belice. In collaboration with A. Marangoni.
Milan Triennale 1980.

Massimo Vignelli

Some publications designed between 1963 and 1980.

Publication design has constituted a considerable part of our activity. We are particularly interested in designing books from the initial concept stage through the collection of the material to the final selection and sequence.
Here also the grid has been a most valuable tool. It helps to structure and give character to the book, and throughout all the production phases it serves as a quality-control device.
The design of books has taught us to consider problems in a whole, complete way, in a cover-to-cover sense, so to speak.

Photography

Vincenzo Castella

1. *Monte S. Giacomo, Salerno*, from *Geografia privata*, 1982.
Photograph, color, cm. 30×40.

2. *Pescara*, 1983.
Photograph, color, cm. 40×30.

Verena von Gagern

1. *Bild vom Fluss (Picture of the River)*, 1983.
Photograph, b/w, cm. 20×30.

2. *Bild vom Fluss (Picture of the River)*, 1983.
Photograph, b/w, cm. 20×30.

Luigi Ghirri

1. *Scandiano*, from *Viaggio di ritorno (Return Journey)*, 1984.
Photograph, color, cm. 30×40.

2. *Sassuolo*, from *Viaggio di ritorno (Return Journey)*, 1984.
Photograph, color, cm. 30×40.

Mimmo Jodice

1. *Castellammare del Golfo*, 1981.
Photograph, b/w, cm. 18×24.

2. *Chateau de Sully, Loire*, 1984.
Photograph, b/w, cm. 18×24.

Klaus Kinold

1. *Sylt (Germany)*, 1982.
Photograph, b/w, cm. 12×40.

2. *Chicago*, 1983.
Photograph, b/w, cm. 12×40.

Nino Migliori

1. *Ossidazione (Oxidization)*, monotype, 1980.
Photograph, b/w.

2. *Ossidazione (Oxidization)*, monotype, 1984.
Photograph, b/w.

Philipp Scholz Rittermann

1. *Cementwarehouse with Bulging Door, Port of San Diego, California*, 1984.
Photograph, b/w, cm. 28×35.

2. *Railway Workers, Del Mar, California*, 1983.
Photograph, b/w, cm. 28×35.

Wilhelm Schurmann

1. *German Infantry*, 1984.
Photograph, color, cm. 30×40.

Giovanni Anceschi

Born 1939 in Milan.
From 1957 to 1959 he studied philosophy at the University of Milan and began his art activities by writing for *Il Gesto* magazine and exhibiting at the Azimuth Gallery and the Pater gallery along with Boriani, Colombo and De Vecchi. The association with these artists led to the foundation of the Gruppo T. In 1960-1961 his research was in the area of image production as "programmed variation." The result was the electromechanical operation of works such as *Percorsi fluidi* (1961) or more explicitly *Grafica programmata* (1961) published in the *Almanacco Bompiani.*
In 1962 Anceschi enrolled in the HfG (Hochschule für Gestaltung) in Ulm and graduated with a thesis on "schematic illustration."
His professional activity as a visual designer began when the Algerian government asked him to create an image for the Sonatrach (National Hydrocarbons Company).
Back in Italy he worked in graphics for publishing, interior design, information and communication systems, both public and private. He won first prize in the competition for a logo for the Rome Chamber of Commerce in 1980.
He taught at the University of Rome from 1969 to 1971 and the Faculty of Architecture in Venice from 1971 to 1974. He is presently professor of Graphic Systems at the Communications Institute of the University of Bologna, directed by Umberto Eco (the only place in Italy where this subject is taught).
Among his scientific and critical contributions: translation, introduction and overall supervision of Max Bense's *Estetica* (1974) and B. E. Burdeck's *Teoria del design* (1977).
He writes for *Casabella, Domus, Ikon* and has a column "Grafica e circostanze" in *Il Verri.* He recently published *Monogrammi e figure, teorie e storie della progettazione di artefatti comunicativi* (1981), *Progettazione visiva: convenzioni e procedimenti di rappresentazione* (1981) and the essay "Il campo della grafica italiana: storia e problemi" which appeared in *Rassegna.* Moreover he wrote the introduction for *Lo studio Boggeri* (1981) and for *Max Huber: Progetti grafici* (1982).

Giovanni Anselmo

Born 1934 in Borgofranco d'Ivrea. Lives in Turin.
One-man exhibitions: 1968 - Turin, Galleria Sperone. □ 1969 - Turin, Galleria Sperone; Paris, Galerie Sonnabend. □ 1970 - Turin, Galleria Sperone; Milan, Galleria Toselli. □ 1971 - Turin, Galleria Sperone; Turin, Galleria Multipli. □ 1972 - Turin, Galleria Sperone; New York, John Weber Gallery. □ 1973 - Brussels, Galerie MTL; Lucerne, Kunstmuseum. □ 1974 - Bari, Galleria Bonomo; Rome, Galleria Sperone/Fischer; Naples, Studio d'Arte Rumma; New York, Galleria Sperone; Warsaw, Galerie Foksal. □ 1975 - Florence, Galleria Area; Genoa, Samangallery; Bremerhaven, Kabinett für Aktuelle Kunst; Turin, Galleria Sperone; Rome, Galleria Sperone. □ 1976 - Genoa, Samangallery; Milan, Galleria Ghiringhelli/Sperone; Brescia, Nuovi Strumenti. □ 1977 - Biella, Galleria Il Tritone; Bremerhaven, Kabinett für Aktuelle Kunst; Rome, Galleria Sperone; Rome, Galleria De Crescenzo. □ 1978 -Milan, Galleria Ala; Turin, Studio Russo; Cologne, Galerie Maenz; Paris, Galerie Durand-Dessert; New York, Sperone-Westwater-Fischer Gallery. □ 1979 -Basel, Kunsthalle; Munich, Galerie Schöttle; Modena, Galleria Mazzoli. □ 1980 - Eindhoven, Stedelijk van Abbemuseum; Amsterdam, Galerie van der Meij; Cologne, Galerie Maenz; Rottweil, Forum Kunst; Grenoble, Musée de Grenoble; Ghent, Vereniging voor het Museum van Hedendaagse Kunst; Turin, Galleria Sperone. □ 1981 - New York, Ala Gallery. □ 1982 - Turin, Galleria Stein; Paris, Galerie Durand-Dessert; Milan, Galleria Ala; Amsterdam, Galerie van der Meij. □ 1984 - New York, Goodman Gallery; Antwerp, Galerie M. Szwajcer.
Selected bibliography: 1968 - *G.A.*, GianEnzo Sperone, Turin (texts by G. Celant, M. Fagiolo). □ 1972 - G. Anselmo, *Leggere*, GianEnzo Sperone, Turin; T. Trini, "Anselmo, Penone, Zorio e le nuove fonti di energia per il deserto dell'arte," *Data*, no. 2, Milan, January. □ 1973 -*G.A.*, Kunstmuseum, Lucerne (text by J.C. Ammann). □ 1974 - *G.A.*, Galerie Foksal, Warsaw. □ 1975 - G. Anselmo, *116 particolari visibili e misurabili di INFINITO*, GianEnzo Sperone, Turin; U. Castagnotto, "G.A.," *Data*, no. 18, Milan, October. □ 1978 - "G. A.," *Data*, no. 32, Milan, Summer. □ 1979 - *G.A.*, Kunsthalle, Basel/Stedelijk van Abbemuseum, Eindhoven (texts by J.C. Ammann, R. Fuchs)*. □ 1980 - *G.A.*, Musée de Grenoble, Grenoble (texts by J.C. Ammann, R. Fuchs).

Gae Aulenti

Gae Aulenti graduated from the Faculty of Architecture at Milan Polytechnic in 1954.
Her careers as an architect, interior designer, teacher and editor have been concurrent since that time. She worked with E.N. Rogers on *Casabella - Continuità* until 1965, and has been a member of the Board of Directors of *Lotus International* since 1974. Her memberships in design societies include honorary positions in the National Society of Interior Designers and the Association of Industrial Design, of which she became vice-president in 1966. She has participated in numerous architecture and design exhibitions in Italy and abroad: among them, several Triennali in Milan, receiving the Grand International Prize for the Italian Pavilion in 1964; "Italy: The New Domestic Landscape" at the Museum of Modern Art in New York in 1974; and a one-person show at the Padiglione d'Arte Contemporanea in Milan in 1979. Often invited to conferences, she was a panelist at the

International Conference of Design of Aspen, Colorado, and the Women's International Congress in Iran. A strong interest in theater design has led to collaborations with Luciano Berio and Karlheinz Stockhausen and work on a production of *Wozzeck* for Teatro alla Scala with Claudio Abbado and Luca Ronconi. She produced the design for *La donna del lago* at the Rossini Festival in Pesaro with Maurizio Pollini. From 1976 to 1979 she collaborated on figurative research at the "Laboratorio di Progettazione Teatrale di Prato" directed by Luca Ronconi and in 1980, a book was issued which sums up the conclusions for the editions Ubulibri. All aspects of her work have been published in major journals of architecture and design — residential, educational, commercial, interiors, furniture, lighting and theatrical projects. In 1980 she won first prize in the competition for the interior architecture of Musée d'Orsay du XIXeme Siècle in Paris, scheduled to open in 1986. In Paris, she is also working on the Musée d'Art Moderne at Centre Georges Pompidou. In 1983 she contributed a design for a new use of the FIAT-Lingotto plant in Turin. In 1983 she received the Medal of Architecture from the Academy of Architecture in Paris. In February 1984 she was elected Academic Correspondent of the National Academy of San Luca in Rome. In March 1984 she received the "Josef Hoffmann 1983" award from the School of Applied Art in Vienna. In May 1984 she received the Exploit award for the woman who has contributed most to the evolution of the female condition.

Selected bibliography: 1958 - A. Rossi, "Il passato e il presente nella nuova architettura," *Casabella-Continuità*, no. 219, Milan. ☐ 1963 - E.N. Rogers, "Progetti di architetti italiani,"*Casabella-Continuità*, no. 276, Milan; F. Tentori, "Progetti e problemi," *Casabella-Continuità*, no. 276, Milan. ☐ 1964 - G. Dorfles, "La tredicesima Triennale," *Casabella-Continuità*, no. 290, Milan; E.N. Rogers, "La Triennale uscita dal coma," *Casabella-Continuità*, no. 290, Milan. ☐ 1968 - *Dizionario enciclopedico di architettura e urbanistica*, Roma. ☐ 1969 - F. Correa, "Dottore Architetto Gae Aulenti," *Cuadernos de Arquitectura*, no. 74, Madrid. ☐ 1970 - A. Arbasino, "Gae Aulenti, New Force in Italian Design," *Vogue America*, New York, July; D. Mosconi, *Design Italia '70*, Milan; M. Tafuri, *Progetto e utopia*, Bari. ☐ 1972 -T. Ito, "Creation of Substantive Interior," *Japan Interior Design*, no. 160, Tokyo. ☐ 1973 - D. Maraini, *E tu chi eri?*, Milan. ☐ 1975 - F. Dal Co, M. Manieri Elia, "La génération de l'incertitude," *L'Architecture d'Aujourd'hui*, no. 185, Paris. ☐ 1976 -B. H., "Des images de la production à la production de l'image," *L'Architecture d'Aujourd'hui*, no. 188, Paris; G. Drudi, "The Design of Gae Aulenti," *Craft Horizons*, New York, February. ☐ 1977 -R. Reif, "Home and Office: Bridging The Gap," *The New York Times Magazine*, New York, February; P. Santini, "Gae Aulenti: architetture, scene, design," *Ottagono*, no. 47, Milan. ☐ 1979 - F. Quadri, *Nello spazio dell'ambiguità*, Milan; F. Raggi, "Da grande voglio fare una città," *Modo*, no. 21, Milan; G. Aulenti, "Elementi per una casa," *Lotus*, no. 22, Milan; N.H. Shapira, *Design Process Olivetti 1908-1978*, Los Angeles; F. Tiezzi, "Le ali di Rauschenberg e i passi di Luca," *Magazzini Criminali*, no. 2, Florence; *Gae Aulenti*, Electa, Milan (texts by E. Battisti, V. Gregotti, F. Quadri; the catalogue includes the complete list of texts by G. Aulenti till 1979)*. ☐ 1982 - P. Nicolin, "Museo d'Orsay," *Lotus*, no. 35, Milan; E. Regazzoni, P. A. Croset, "Destinazione Museo," *Casabella*, no. 482, Milan, July. ☐ 1984 - *Venti progetti per il futuro del Lingotto*, Etas Libri, Milan.

Marco Bagnoli

Born 1949 in Empoli. Lives in Florence. One-man exhibitions: 1975 - Milan, Galleria Betti; Milan, Officina di Porta Genova; Pescara, Galleria De Domizio; Turin, Galleria Russo-Marinucci. ☐ 1976 - Pescara, Galleria De Domizio; Rome, private house. ☐ 1978 - Rome, Galleria L'Attico; Naples, Galleria Amelio; Pescara, Galleria De Domizio. ☐ 1979 - Milan, Galleria Ala; New York, Ala Gallery. ☐ 1980 - Perugia, Accademia di Belle Arti Pietro Vannucci; Amsterdam, De Appel Foundation. ☐ 1981 - Genoa, Samangallery; Artimino, Villa dei Cento Camini. ☐ 1983 - Genoa, Galleria Locus Solus; Rome, Galleria Pieroni; Milan, Politecnico. ☐ 1984 - Florence, Cappella de' Pazzi; Amsterdam, De Appel Foundation.

***

I would like to offer the single word *Ali* as a dedication for the brief notes that follow.
This word apophtegmatically defines the spirit of this leisurely amble, since it represents both the primal image of an inaudible sound and sound as *Aleph*, which I always picture as an unattainable and indented halo of light...
These notes refer to a recent work from which I pluck the connection with a different and more remote work...
The ideal bridge is the field that the two define externally, one referring to this side of the painterly and one to that side of the plastic. A field that is to art as, in nature, the spectrum of invisible light is to the spectrum of visible light...

Excerpts from notes of Marco Bagnoli to an edition of forty-nine drawings dated 1975 now being printed.

Anti Hertz, / not every theory of the / rainbow touches on / the decisive argument.
The cone of sight / against the sphere of vision. / This probability is a tendency / it is a field on the passage / it is an elevator on the outline / it is a sphere and a student / and a luminous wave it is transversal / and it propagates at the speed of light in the void sight comes from the earth / whereas vision originates from the cosmos.
They move in respect to each other while they are relatively still. / This powerful uncertainty is purely objective./ It is a horizon on the apparent / it is a rainbow / with North-South poles like Black and White / It breaks its lute naturally. / It is tangent / the cone of sight contains the sphere of vision / a mechanical hypothesis extended to the totality of nature.
In a given situation / and in different aspects / the distinction / between the object and the rest of the world / is not arbitrary; / the device reveals itself. / It is a field on a passage / hysterical nature / it would be the circle / the dead female lion-tamer of the / Wolt Circus.
In truth the vision creates / an ulterior cone certain and / without a doubt / neither light nor dark.

Marco Bagnoli, 1979

***

Selected bibliography: 1976 - M. Bagnoli, *La Città di Riga*, no. 1, Rome, Fall; C. Ferrari, "Paragrafi," *Data*, no. 23, Milan, October-November. ☐ 1978, M. Bagnoli, *Il buon luogo*, Turin; *M.B.*, Collezione del Clavicembalo, De Domizio, Pescara; M. Bagnoli, *Cinque domande ipercritiche*,

Accademia di Belle Arti, Perugia. □ 1980 - B. Corà, "Profili/opere," *AEIUO*, no. 1, Rome, September. □ 1982 - M. Bagnoli, "Orso - Panorama - Vedute intere," *AEIUO*, no. 6, Rome, December. □ 1983 - M. Bagnoli, *Spazio × tempo*, no. 1, Tipografia Giuntina, Florence, June; M. Bagnoli, *Manca una citazione di Seneca*, Pieroni, Rome; M. Bagnoli, "Indice," *AEIUO*, no. 8-9, Rome, December.

Giuseppe Bartolucci

Theatrical critic and essayist, erstwhile theatre reviewer for the newspaper *Avanti!* and co-director for five years of the Teatro Stabile di Torino, has for many years been director of the Teatroscuola del Teatro in Rome. Among his other publications are: *La scrittura scenica* (Lerici, 1969); *Teatro-corpo, teatro-immagine* (Marsilio, 1970); *Il vuoto teatrale* (Marsilio, 1971); *Il Living Theatre* (Savelli, 1972); *Il teatro di Memè Perlini* (Studio Forma, 1979); *Il gesto teatrale* (Electa, 1980); *Paesaggio metropolitano* (Feltrinelli, 1982). He is editor of the theatrical review *La scrittura scenica* and he contributes to the *Drama Review, Alfabeta, Scena* and many other Italian and foreign magazines.

Georg Baselitz

Born 1938 in Deutschbaselitz/Sachen. Lives in Derneburg/Niedersachsen. One-man exhibitions: 1961 - Berlin, First *Pandämonium* (with E. Schönebeck). □ 1962 - Berlin, Second *Pandämonium*. □ 1963 - Berlin, Galerie Werner and Katz. □ 1964 - Berlin, Galerie Werner; Berlin, Freie Galerie; Berlin, Galerie Werner. □ 1965 - Munich, Galerie Friedrich & Dahlem; Badenweiler, Galerie Krohn; Berlin, Galerie Werner. □ 1966 - Berlin, Galerie Springer. □ 1967 - Munich, Galerie Friedrich & Dahlem; Zurich, Galerie Obere Zäune; Erlangen, Galerie Beck. □ 1969 - Erlangen, Galerie Beck. □ 1970 - Basel, Kunstmuseum ; Cologne, Galeriehaus; Antwerp, Wide White Space Gallery; Munich, Galerie Friedrich; Stuttgart, Galerie Berner. □ 1971 - Cologne, Galerie Borgmann; Heidelberg, Galerie Rothe; Cologne, Galerie Tobiès & Silex. □ 1972 - Mannheim, Kunsthalle; Amsterdam, Galerie im Goethe Institut/Provisorium; Karlsruhe, Galerie Graphikmeyer; Hamburg, Kunstverein; Munich, Staatliche Graphische Sammlung; Frankfurt, Galerie Loehr; Munich, Galerie Friedrich; Cologne, Galerie Zwirner. □ 1973 - Munich, Galerie Friedrich; Frankfurt, Galerie Loehr; Vienna, Galerie Grünangergasse; Darmstadt, *Pandämonium I und II,* Hessisches Landesmuseum; Hamburg, Galerie Neuendorf. □ 1974 - Cologne, Galerie Friedrich; Leverkusen, Städtisches Museum; Ravensburg, Städtische Galerie. □ 1975 - Munich, Galerie Friedrich; Cologne, Galerie Werner; Frankfurt, Galerie Loehr. □ 1976 - Bern, Kunsthalle; Munich, Galerieverein München und Staatsgalerie moderner Kunst; Cologne, Galerie Friedrich; Cologne, Kunsthalle. □ 1977 - Cologne, Galerie Friedrich; Munich, Galerie Friedrich. □ 1978 - Amsterdam, Galerie van der Meij; Cologne, Galerie Friedrich. □ 1979 - Eindhoven, Stedelijk van Abbemuseum; Paris, Galerie Gillespie-Laage-Salomon; Munich, Galerie Friedrich; Cologne, Kunsthalle; Groningen, Groninger Museum. □ 1980 - Cologne, Galerie Friedrich; Berlin, Galerie Springer; Paris, Galerie Gillespie-Laage-Salomon; London, Whitechapel Art Gallery. □ 1981 - Cologne, Galerie Werner; Copenhagen, Kastrupgardsammlungen; Eindhoven, Stedelijk van Abbemuseum; Braunschweig, Kunstverein; Amsterdam, Stedelijk Museum; Zurich, Galerie Verna; Munich, Galerie Jahn; New York, Fourcade Gallery; New York, Brooke Alexander Gallery. □ 1982 - New York, Sonnabend Gallery; Vienna, Galerie nächst St. Stephan; Amsterdam, Galerie van der Meij; Cologne, Galerie Werner; London, Waddington Galleries; London, d'Offay Gallery; Munich, Galerie Jahn; Cologne, Galerie Zwirner; Göttingen, Kunstverein; Chicago, Hoffman Gallery. □ 1983 - Cologne, Galerie Werner; Brussels, Galerie Baronian; Berlin, Galerie Springer; Krefeld, Museum Haus Esters (with A.R. Penck); Schwäbisch Hall, Galerie am Markt; Paris, Galerie Gillespie-Laage-Salomon; Bordeaux, Musée d'Art Contemporain; New York, Fourcade Gallery; New York, Sonnabend Gallery; Hamburg, Galerie Neuendorf; Akron/Ohio, Akron Art Museum; London, Whitechapel Art Gallery; Berlin, Galerie Skulima; Munich, Galerie Jahn; Los Angeles, L.A County Museum. □ 1984 - Amsterdam, Stedelijk Museum; Eindhoven, Stedelijk van Abbemuseum; Berkeley, University Art Museum, University of California; Basel, Kunstmuseum; Basel, Kunsthalle; New York, Boone/Werner Gallery; Paris, Galerie Gillespie-Laage-Salomon; Munich, Staatliche Graphische Sammlung, Neue Pinakothek; Cologne, Galerie Borgmann; Bonn, Städtisches Kunstmuseum; Ghent, Cabinet d'Estampes, Musée d'Art et d'Histoire.

Selected bibliography: 1963 - *G.B.*, Werner & Katz, Berlin. □ 1965 - *G.B.*, Friedrich, Munich. □ 1970 - *G.B.: Zeichnungen*, Kunstmuseum, Basel; *G.B.*, Wide White Space, Antwerp. □ 1972 -*G.B.*, Kunsthalle, Mannheim; *G.B.*, Kunstverein, Hamburg. □ 1973 - *G.B., Ein neuer Typ*, Neuendorf, Hamburg. □ 1974 - *G.B., Radierungen 1963-1974/Holzschnitte 1966-1967*, Städtisches Museum, Leverkusen. □ 1975 - *G.B., Zeichnungen 1960-1974*, Michael Werner, Cologne; *G.B., Adler*, Friedrich, Munich. □ 1976 - *G.B. Malerei, Handzeichnungen, Druckgraphik*, Kunsthalle, Bern (text by T. Kneubühler); *G.B., Gemälde, Handzeichnungen und Druckgraphik*, Kunsthalle, Cologne. □ 1970 - *G.B.*, Stedelijk van Abbemuseum, Eindhoven (text by R. Fuchs); *G.B., 32 Linolschnitte aus den Jahren 1976-1979*, Kunsthalle, Cologne; *G.B., Zeichnungen*, Groninger Museum, Groningen (text by J. Gachnang). □ 1980 - *G.B.*, La Biennale, Venice (texts by J. Gachnang, T. Kneubühler, K. Gallwitz). □ 1981 - *G.B., Grafik og malerier*, Kastrupgardsamlingen, Copenhagen; *G.Baselitz/G. Richter*, Kunsthalle, Düsseldorf (text by J. Harten); *G.B.*, Kunstverein, Braunschweig (texts by J. Schilling, G. Gercken, M.G. Buttig, A. Kosegarten, D. Koepplin, H. Pée, R. Fuchs, A.R. Penck, E. Wiess, J. Gachnang, T. Kneubühler, S. Gohr, F. Dahlem, C. Schulz-Hoffmann, K. Gallwitz, P. Kirkeby. G. Baselitz)*; *G.B.*, Stedelijk Museum, Amsterdam. □ 1982 - *G.B.*, Michael Werner, Cologne; *G.B.*, Waddington Galleries, London; G.B., *16 Holzschnitte rot und schwarz 1981-1982*, Fred Jahn, Munich (text by P. Kirkeby). □ 1983 - *Baselitz, Sculptures*, Centre d'Art Plastique Contemporain, Bordeaux; *G.B. Holzplastiken*, Michael Werner, Cologne; *G.B. Zeichnungen 1961-1983*, Neuendorf, Hamburg; *G.B. peintre-graveur*, Verlag Gachnang & Springer, Bern/Berlin (text by J. Gachnang); *G.B., Schilderijen/Paintings 1960-1983*, Whitechapel, London (texts by E. de Wilde, N. Serota, R. Calvocoressi, G. Baselitz). □ 1984 - *G.B., Zeichnungen 1958-1983,* Kunstmuseum, Basel/Stedelijk van Abbemuseum, Eindhoven (texts by R. Fuchs, D. Köpplin); *G.B., Das malerische*

Werk 1960-1983, Linolschnitte 1976-1979, Kunsthalle, Basel (texts by J.C. Ammann, R. Calvocoressi, G. Baselitz); *G.B.*, Boone/Werner, New York; *G.B., Druckgraphik-Prints-Estampes 1963-1983*, Verlag Prestel, Munich (text by S. Gohr); *G.B., Gravures 1963-1983*, Musée d'Art et d'Histoire, Ghent.

Lothar Baumgarten

Born 1944 in Rheinsberg. Lives in Düsseldorf.
One-man exhibitions: 1972 - Düsseldorf, Galerie Fischer. ☐ 1973 - Rome, Galleria Fischer-Sperone. ☐ 1974 - Antwerp and Brussels, Wide White Space; Düsseldorf, Galerie Fischer (with M. Oppitz); Cologne, Botanischer Garten. ☐ 1975 - Düsseldorf, Galerie Fischer; Basel, Galerie Preisig. ☐ 1976 - Bremerhaven, Kabinett für Aktuelle Kunst ; Düsseldorf, Galerie Fischer. ☐ 1977 - Venezuela, South America. ☐ 1978 - Munich, Kunstraum. ☐ 1978-1980 - T.F. Amazonia, Venezuela, South America. ☐ 1979 - Zurich, InK. ☐ 1982 - Eindhoven, Stedelijk van Abbemuseum; Düsseldorf, Galerie Fischer. ☐ 1983 - Mönchengladbach, Museum Abteiberg. ☐ 1984 - Venice, XLI Biennale, German Pavilion (with A.R. Penck); Amsterdam, Stedelijk Museum.

Selected bibliography: 1970 - "L.B.," *Interfunktionen*, no. 5, Cologne. ☐ 1971 -"L.B.," *Interfunktionen*, no. 7, Cologne. ☐ 1973 - "L.B.," *Interfunktionen*, no. 9, Cologne. ☐ 1974 - M. Oppitz, "Kultur -Natur," *Notwendige Beziehungen*, Frankfurt; L. Baumgarten (with M. Oppitz), *T'E - NE' - T'E*, Konrad Fischer, Düsseldorf. ☐ 1982 - R. Flood, "L.B. -Documenta," *Artforum*, New York, October; B. Curiger, "Melancholie im Schollwinkel," *Kunstforum*, no. 53-54, Cologne, September-October; B.H.D. Buchloh, "Documenta 7 - A Dictionary of Received Ideas," *October*, New York, Fall; L. Baumgarten, *Die Namen der Bäume*, Stedelijk van Abbemuseum, Eindhoven. ☐ 1983 - A. Pohlen, "L.B.," *Artforum*, New York, February; L. Baumgarten, *Land of the Spotted Eagle*, Museum Abteiberg, Mönchengladbach. ☐ 1984 -L. Baumgarten, *Amazonas Tapajos Xingu Purus Orinoco Vaupes Tocantins*, La Biennale, Venice.

Joseph Beuys

Born 1921 in Kleve. Lives in Düsseldorf.
One-man exhibitions: 1961 - Kleve, Städtisches Museum Kooekoek. ☐ 1963 - Cologne, Galerie Zwirner. ☐ 1964 - Berlin, Galerie Block. ☐ 1965 - Düsseldorf, Galerie Schmela. ☐ 1966 - Berlin, Galerie Block; Düsseldorf, Staatliche Kunstakademie; Berlin, Galerie Block; Vienna, Galerie nächst St. Stephan (with H. Christiansen); Darmstadt, Galerie Dahlem; Mönchengladbach, Städtisches Museum. ☐ 1968 - Antwerp, Wide White Space Gallery; Eindhoven, Stedelijk van Abbemuseum; Munich, Haus der Kunst; Nuremberg, Künstlerhaus; Hamburg, Kunstverein. ☐ 1969 - Düsseldorf, Galerie Schmela; Berlin, Neue Nationalgalerie; Basel, Kunstmuseum. ☐ 1970 - Darmstadt, Hessisches Landesmuseum; Innsbruck, Galerie am Taxispalais; Braunschweig, Herzog Anton Ulrich-Museum. ☐ 1971 - Vienna, Galerie nächst St. Stephan; Stockholm, Moderna Museet; Wuppertal, von der Heydt Museum; St. Gallen, Kunstverein; Eindhoven, Stedelijk van Abbemuseum; Düsseldorf, Galerie Schmela; Cologne, Galerie Intermedia; Naples, Modern Art Agency; Munich, Galerie Thomas. ☐ 1972 - Düsseldorf, Galerie Schmela; Boston, Harcus Krakow Gallery; Darmstadt, Hessisches Landesmuseum; Rome, Galleria L'Attico. ☐ 1973 - New York, Feldman Gallery; Frankfurt, Galerie Loehr; Hanover, Kunstverein; Bonn, Galerie Magers; Bonn, Galerie Klein; Karlsruhe, Galerie Grafikmeyer; Tübingen, Kunsthalle. ☐ 1974 - Paris, Galerie Bama; Oxford, Museum of Modern Art; Krefeld, Museum Haus Lange; New York, Block Gallery; London, Institute of Contemporary Art. ☐ 1975 - Freiburg, Kunstverein; New York, Feldman Gallery; Hanover, Kestner-Gesellschaft. ☐ 1976 - Basel, Kunstmuseum. ☐ 1977 - Basel, Kunstmuseum; Ghent, Museum van Hedendaagse Kunst; Munich, Galerie Schellmann & Klüser. ☐ 1978 - Basel, Kunstmuseum; Braunschweig, Kunstverein. ☐ 1979 - Lucerne, Kunstmuseum; Golsar, Museum für Moderne Kunst; New York, Guggenheim Museum; Rotterdam, Museum Boymans van Beuningen. ☐ 1980 - Berlin, Nationalgalerie; Bielefeld, Kunsthalle; Düsseldorf, Kunstmuseum; Bonn, Wissenschaftszentrum; Cologne, Galerie Dreiseitel; Karlsruhe, Badischer Kunstverein. ☐ 1981 - Zurich, InK (with B. Nauman); Rotterdam, Museum Boymans van Beuningen; East Berlin, Ständige Vertretung der Bundesrepublik Deutschland; Bonn, Städtische Kunstmuseum; Munich, Städtische Galerie im Lenbachhaus; London, d'Offay Gallery. ☐ 1982 - Paris, Galerie Durand-Dessert; London, d'Offay Gallery; Ulm, Kunstverein; Düsseldorf, Sparkassenhochhaus; Cologne, Galerie Jöllenbeck. ☐ 1983 - Leeds, City Art Gallery; Cambridge, Kettle's Yard Gallery; London, Victoria and Albert Museum; Frankfurt, Städtisches Kunstinstitut; Lausanne, Musée Cantonal des Beaux-Arts. ☐ 1984 - Tokyo, The Seibu Museum of Art; Bonn, Landesvertretung Rheinland-Pfalz; Koblenz, Mittelrhein-Museum; Winterthur, Kunstmuseum; Calais, Musée des Beaux-Arts; St. Etienne, Musée d'Art et d'Industrie; Linz, Neue Galerie der Stadt; Marseille, Musée Cantini; Hovikodden, Sonja Henies og Niels Ostads Stiftelser; Tübingen, Kunsthalle.

Selected bibliography: 1961 - *J.B. Zeichnungen, Aquarelle, Ölbilder, Plastische Bilder aus der Sammlung van der Grinten*, Städtisches Museum Haus Koekkoek, Kleve. ☐ 1963 - *J.B.*, van der Grinten, Kranenburg. ☐ 1965 - R. Schaukal, *Von Tod zu Tod und andere kleine Geschichten, Illustrationen - J.B.*, Brühl. ☐ 1967 - *J.B.*, Städtisches Museum, Mönchengladbach (text by J. Cladders, H. Strelow). ☐ 1968 - *J.B.*, Stedelijk van Abbemuseum, Eindhoven (text by O. Mauer). ☐ 1969 - *J.B., Zeichnungen, Kleine Objekte*, Kunstmuseum, Basel (texts by D. Koepplin, F.J. van der Grinten); *J.B., Zeichnungen von 1949-1969*, Schmela, Düsseldorf; *J.B.*, Kunstmuseum, Basel (text by F. Meyer). ☐ 1970 - *J.B.*, Stadhuis, Middelburg; *J.B., Sammlung Hans und Franz Joseph van der Grinten*, Innsbruck/Vienna; *J.B.*, Kunstverein, Ulm (texts by H. and F.J. van der Grinten). ☐ 1971 - *J.B., Handzeichnungen*, Kunsthalle, Kiel (text by C. Jensen); *J.B., Zeichnungen von 1946-1971*, Schmela, Düsseldorf; *J.B., Aktioner, Aktionen*, Moderna Museet, Stockholm. ☐ 1972 - *J.B., Zeichnungen und andere Blätter aus der Sammlung Karl Stroeher*, Hessisches Landesmuseum, Darmstadt (texts by G. Bott, J.K. Schmidt); H. Bastian, *Tod im Leben, Gedicht für J.B.*, Munich. ☐ 1973 - J. Beuys, *Die Leute sind ganz prima in Foggia*, Staeck, Heidelberg; G. Adriani, W. Konnertz, K. Thomas, *J.B.*, Verlag DuMont Schauberg, Cologne. ☐ 1974 - *J.B., The Secret Block for a Secret Person in Ireland*, Museum of Modern Art, Oxford/Edinburg/Dublin/Belfast; *Some Artists, for Example J.B. Multiples,*

Drawings, Videotapes, University of California, Riverside; *J.B., Zeichnungen 1946-1971*, Museum Haus Lange, Krefeld. □ 1975 - *J.B., Zeichnungen - Zu den beiden 1965 wiederentdeckten Skizzenbücher "Codices Madrid" von Leonardo da Vinci*, Manus Presse, Stuttgart; *J.B.*, Kestner Gesellschaft, Hanover (text by P.Wember). □ 1976 - C. Tisdall, *J.B. Coyote*, Schirmer/Mosel, Munich; *J.B.*, Kaiser Wilhelm Museum, Krefeld (text by G. Storck); *J.B.*, La Biennale, Venice; Harlan, Rappman, Schata, *Soziale Plastik*, Achberg Verlagsanstalt, Achberg. □ 1977 - C.M. Joachimides, *J.B. Richtkräfte*, Nationalgalerie, Berlin; I. Burgbacher-Krupka, *Prophete rechts Prophete links — J.B.*, Stuttgart; *J.B.*, Museum van Hedendaagse Kunst, Ghent. □ 1978 - *J.B. Multiplicerad Konst*, Kulturhuset, Stockholm; G. Celant, *Beuys - Tracce in Italia*, Lucio Amelio, Naples. □ 1979 - C. Tisdall, *J.B.*, The Solomon R. Guggenheim Museum, New York*; J. Stüttgen, *Das Warhol - Beuys - Ereignis*, Gelsenkirchen; A. Murken, *J.B. und die Medizin*, Münster; *J.B., Zeichnungen, Tekeningen, Drawings*, Rotterdam/ Berlin/Bielefeld/Bonn; N. Bentzan, *J.B.*, Arnus. □ 1980 - *J.B., Sandzeichnungen in Diani*, Frankfurt; H. Bastian, *Die Strassenbahnhaltestelle von J.B.*, Berlin; *Beuys in Boymans*, Museum Boymans van Beuningen, Rotterdam; *Werkstattgespräch mit J.B.*, Städtisches Gymnasium, Porz. □ 1981 - J. Stüttgen, *Similia similibus - J.B. zum 60. Geburtstag*, DuMont Buchverlag, Cologne; *J.B. Multiplizierte Kunst 1965-1981*, Berlin; D. Rochtus, J. Beuys, *Sciora* (photos U. Klophaus), Lier; F.J. and H. van der Grinten, *J.B. Ölfarben 1936-1965*, Munich. □ 1982 - C. Tisdall, *J.B., dernier espace avec introspecteur 1964-1982*, London; *Beuys, Rauschenberg, Twombly, Warhol*, Sammlung Marx, Munich; *J.B. Frauen - Zeichnungen von 1947-1961*, Sparkassenhochhaus, Düsseldorf. □ - 1983 - J. Stüttgen, *Professor lag der Länge nach in Margarine*, Düsseldorf; *J.B. Zeichnungen 1949-1969*, Städelsches Kunstinstitut, Frankfurt; T. Vischer, *Beuys und die Romantik*, Cologne; H.Bastian, *J.B. Zeichnungen, Dessins*, Lausanne/Winterthur/Calais/St. Etienne/Linz/Marseille/Oslo; *His Holiness the 14th Dalai Lama of Tibet trifft Prof. Joseph Beuys*, Bonn. □ 1984 - F.J. Verspohl, *J.B., Das Kapital Raum 1970-1977*, Frankfurt; *J.B.*, The Seibu Museum of Art, Tokyo (texts by G. Adriani, N.J. Paik, G. Ulbricht); *J.B. Tiere - Zeichnungen und plastische Beispiele 1948-1961*, Mittelrhein-Museum, Koblenz; *J.B. Ölfarben 1949-1967*, Kunsthalle, Tübingen/Kunstverein, Hamburg/Kunsthaus, Zurich (text by F.J. van der Grinten).

Vittorio Boarini

After graduating in Political Science in 1961 at the "Cesare Alfieri" Institute of Florence University, Vittorio Boarini was appointed in the following year Secretary General of the Teatro Stabile and Secretary of the Municipal Commission for cinematographic activities in Bologna.
In 1967 he became director of the Bologna City Film Library, a position he still holds, while at the same time he continues to edit numerous catalogues and monographs concerning foreign cine-production and Italian film directors.
He has also collaborated to the catalogues of Galleria De' Foscherari with articles on art and on the presentation of exhibitions, after which in 1982 he began to write an art column for the daily *La Repubblica*.
Since 1969 he has been directing the "Mostra internazionale del cinema libero" of Porretta.
Together with Pietro Bonfiglioli, in 1976 he published an exhaustive and complete study on twentieth century culture (*Avanguardia e restaurazione*, Zanichelli, Bologna).
In the same year he was nominated professor for the History of Theater by the Fine Arts Academy of Bologna.
After founding a series of works on the cinema in 1982 (*I Quaderni della Cineteca*), he assumed its editorship. So far, five volumes of this series have been issued by Tipografia Compositori of Bologna, each of them containing one of Boarini's essays. In 1983 he undertook to direct the "Immagine elettronica" exhibition which is held every year in Bologna and is now being presented for the third time.
His most important publications are: *Erotismo, eversione, merce* (Cappelli, Bologna, 1973); "La neoavanguardia cinematografica," in *Storia generale del cinema*, vol. III (Ellemme, Milan, 1977); *La Mostra internazionale del cinema libero*, together with Pietro Bonfiglioli (Marsilio, Venice, 1981); "Cinema e televisione: differenza e serialità," in *Il cinema della televisione* (ERI, Turin, 1983); "Il passato è un'immagine elettronica," in *La Casa di Dedalo*, no. 1, 1983.

Gottfried Böhm

Born 1920 in Offenbach, the son of Prof. Dominikus Böhm and Maria Böhm Schreiber.
In 1939 he left the "Apostel-Gymnasium" of Cologne.
From 1942 to 1947 he studied architecture and sculpture at the Technical High School and Academy of Art in Munich.
In 1948 he married Elisabeth Haggenmuller, an engineer. At that time he was working with his father Dominikus Böhm in Cologne.
In 1950 he worked with Rudolph Schwartz in the "Wiederaufbangesellerschaft" (Association responsible for the rebuilding of Cologne) and in 1951 he collaborated with the architect C. Baumann in New York.
From 1952 till his father's death in 1955, they worked together.
In 1963 he became Professor at RWTH Technical University of Aachen where he taught Urban Planning and use of building materials.
In 1968 he became a member of the Berlin Academy of Arts and in 1976 a member of the German Academy for Urban Planning.
In 1983 he founded the Studio MIT in Boston.
He won various prizes and honours in Germany and other countries, as honorary professor of Lima University and honorary Fellow of AIA, USA.

Selected bibliography: 1949 - G. Böhm, "Die Gewebedecke in H. Hoffmann," *Neue Baummethoden*, no. 1, Stuttgart. □ 1955 - F. Otto, "Rheinische Kirchenbauten und hängendes Dach," *Bauwelt*, no. 51. □ 1968 - *Der Baumeister Gottfried Böhm*, Eduard von der Heydt Prize, Wuppertal. □ 1970 - "Gottfried Böhm: un architecte- sculpteur," *L'Oeil*, no. 182, Paris. □ 1973 - W. Pehnt, *Die Architektur des Expressionismus*, Stuttgart; "Works of Gottfried Böhm," *a+u*, no. 7, Tokyo; B. Zevi, *Spazi dell'architettura moderna*, Turin. □ 1976 - P. Nestler, P. M. Bode, *Deutsche Kunst seit 1960, Architektur*, Munich. □ 1977 - H. Klump, E. Schirmbeck, "Gottfried Böhm" (interview), and Gottfried Böhm, "Anmerkungen zum architektonischen Werk," *Bauen+Wohnen*, no. 11, Munich; U. Kultermann, *Die Architektur im 20. Jahrhundert*, Cologne. □ 1978 - S. Raev, "Zur Technik und Semantik in der Architektur Gottfriend Böhm's," *DAI*

(Deutsche Architekten und Ingenieur), no. 1-2; S. Raev, "Architecture of Synthesis - Remarks on the Architecture of Gottfried Böhm," *a+u*, no. 89, Tokyo; L. Benevolo, *Geschichte der Architekture des 19. und 20. Jahrhunderts*, vol. 2, Munich; P.M. Bode, "Expressive Kraft und schöpferische Humanität der Architekt Gottfried Böhm's," *a+u*, no. 89, Tokyo. □ 1979 - *Fünf Architekten zeichnen für Berlin* (edited by F. Burkhardt), IDZ Symposium, Berlin; *Transformation in Modern Architecture* (edited by A. Drexier), The Museum of Modern Art, New York. □ 1980 - H. Klump, "Der Architekt Gottfried Böhm," *Week, Bauen+Wohnen*, no. 9, Nuremberg. □ 1981 - *Wohnen in der Stadt heute*, Kunsthalle, Bielefeld/Lehrstuhl für Stadtbereichsplanung-RWTH, Aachen. □ 1982 - G. Böhm, *Bauten und Projekte 1950-1980*, Verlag König, Cologne*.

Andrea Branzi

Architect and designer, was a leader of the Italian avant-garde in the sixties, founder of Archizoom Associates and promoter of Global Tools. He has exhibited at the Milan Triennale, the Venice Biennale, the Victoria and Albert Museum, the New York Museum of Modern Art, in Berlin and Rotterdam. In 1977 he coordinated the important exhibition "Italian Design in the Fifties" held in Milan.
In 1979, as a member of CDM (Milan Design Consultants), he won the Golden Compass award for his research in primary design. He has published *Decorativo* (1975-1977), *Colordinamo* (1975-1978), *Moderno, postmoderno, millenario* (1980), *La casa calda* (1984). Monographs on his work have been published by Space Design and Japan Interior Design. He is educational director of Domus Academy, the post-graduate school of studies in New Design and director of *Modo,* the design and architecture magazine.

Nicoletta Branzi

Born in Florence, lives and works in Milan.
She has researched customs, images and trends in the fashion field for industry, magazines and publishing houses.
1973, publication of the book *Vestiti per un anno,* a do-it-yourself manual (AMZ Ed.).
1976, in charge of the fashion sector of the exhibition "Il design italiano degli anni '50" at Centrokappa.
1979, created the multivision *Come leggere la moda* for the Milan Triennale.
1981, in charge of the fashion sector of the exhibition "Il consumo culturale in Italia" for the Venice Biennale.
At present she is designing the "Animali tessili" collection with Cinzia Ruggeri.

Bazon Brock

Born 1936 in West Prussia.
Since 1965 Professor of Aesthetics at the Staatlichehochschule für bildende Kunst in Hamburg; from 1977 to 1979 at the Gesamthochschule in Vienna and since 1979 at the University of Wuppertal. His earliest books were *Kotflügel* and *Das Erschrecken am S.*
In 1959, in collaboration with Hundertwasser, he drew an infinite line non-stop for five days, thus giving rise to a spectacular and theoretical event known as the "Besucherschule." Since then Brock has continued along these lines within the theatre, in teaching, in psychotherapeutical practice and in museums.
Brock has written and directed over twenty television programmes. Articles he has written have been published in the catalogues of "Documenta" and the Paris Biennale as well as in the magazines *Artforum, Kunstforum* and *Die Zeit.* His theoretical writings have been published in the volume *Estetic als Vermittlung* by Dumont Verlag in 1976.
Biographical and bibliographical material on Brock and his work can be found in Bazon Brock, *Was machen Sie jetztso?*, Melzer Verlag, Frankfurt, 1978.

Tilmann Buddensieg

Born 1928.
He studied history of art and archeology at the Universities of Heidelberg, Hamburg, Cologne and Paris. Since 1968 he has held the Chair of History of Art at the Freie Universität in Berlin, and since 1978 in Bonn as well.
Buddensieg has written numerous works on early medieval art, on Renaissance art and architecture, on 19th and 20th century architecture arts and design. He is author of: *Industriekulture Peter Behrens und die AEG, Die nützlichen Künste, Die Weimarer Keramik, Villa Hügel.*
In 1967 he was visiting professor at the University of Harvard, and in 1971 at Stanford and Berkeley. In 1974 he was Professor of Fine Arts at Cambridge in England. In 1984 he taught at the Hebrew University of Jerusalem and in 1985 at Columbia University in New York.

Alberto Burri

Born 1915 in Città di Castello (Perugia). Lives in Città di Castello and Rome. One-man exhibitions: 1947 - Rome, Galleria La Margherita. □ 1948 - Rome, Galleria La Margherita. □ 1952 - Rome, Galleria dell'Obelisco; Florence, Galleria d'Arte Contemporanea. □ 1953 - Rome, Fondazione Origine; Chicago, Frumkin Gallery; New York, Stable Gallery. □ 1954 - Rome, Galleria dell'Obelisco; Chicago, Frumkin Gallery. □ 1955 - New York, Stable Gallery; Colorado Springs, Fine Arts Center; Oakland, Oakland Art Museum; Pasadena, Pasadena Art Museum. □ 1956 - Seattle, Seligman Gallery; Venice, Galleria del Cavallino; Paris, Galerie Rive Droite (with César). □ 1957 - Milan, Galleria del Naviglio; Rome, Galleria dell'Obelisco; Bologna, Galleria La Loggia; Turin, Galleria La Bussola; Pittsburgh, Carnegie Institute. □ 1958 - Chicago, The Arts Club of Chicago; Buffalo, Albright-Knox Art Gallery; San Francisco, San Francisco Museum of Art; Rome, Galleria La Salita; Milan, Galleria Blu; Brescia, Galleria Alberti. □ 1959 - Basel, Galerie M.S. Feigel; Brussels, Palais des Beaux Arts; Basel, Galerie Beyeler (with A. Tapies); Rome, Galleria La Tartaruga; Bologna, Galleria La Loggia; Krefeld, Museum Haus Lange; Vienna, Wiener Secession; Dortmund, Museum am Ostwall. □ 1960 - Venice, XXX Biennale; New York, Jackson Gallery; London, Hanover Gallery; Cologne, Galerie Abels; Buenos Aires, Museo Nacional de Bellas Artes. □ 1961 Rome, Galleria La Medusa; Paris, Galerie de France. □ 1962 - L'Aquila, Castello Cinquecentesco; Rome, Galleria Marlborough. □ 1963 - Houston, The Museum of Fine Arts; London, Marlborough Gallery. □ 1964 - Minneapolis, Walker Art Center; Buffalo, Albright-Knox Art Gallery; Pasadena, Pasadena Art Museum; New York, Marlborough-Gerson Gallery; Milan, Galleria Blu. □ 1965 - Turin, Galleria La Bussola; Sao Paulo, VIII Biennial. □ 1966 - Turin, Galleria La Bussola; Venice, XXXIII Biennale. □ 1967 - Darmstadt,

Kunsthalle; Rotterdam, Museum Boymans van Beuningen; Rome, Galleria La Tartaruga; Città di Castello, Palazzina Vitelli. □ 1968 - Milan, Galleria Blu. □ 1969 - Turin, Galleria Notizie; Bologna, Galleria San Luca. □ 1970 - Brescia, Galleria ACME; Rome, Galleria Qui Arte Contemporanea; Rome, Galleria La Tartaruga; Milan, Galleria Transart. □ 1971 - Turin, Galleria Civica d'Arte Moderna; Naples, Modern Art Agency; Verona, Libreria Galleria Cangrande; Turin, Libreria Stampatori. □ 1972 - Paris, Musée National d'Art Moderne. □ 1973 - Milan, Galleria Grafica Oggi. □ 1974 - Geneva, Galerie Benador; Pesaro, Galleria Il Segnapassi; Assisi, Sacro Convento di San Francesco. □ 1976 - Rome, Galleria Lo Spazio; Rome, Galleria Nazionale d'Arte Moderna; Pesaro, Palazzo Ducale. □ 1977 - Lisbon, Fundacao Calouste Gulbenkian; Bologna, Galleria San Luca; Madrid, Palacio de Velázquez, Parque del Retiro; Rome, Galleria 2RC; Los Angeles, UCLA, Frederick S.Wright Art Gallery; Santa Barbara, The Santa Barbara Museum of Art; San Antonio/Texas, Marion Koogler McNay Art Institute; Milwaukee, Milwaukee Art Center; Naples, Museo di Capodimonte; New York, The Solomon R. Guggenheim Museum. □ 1979 - Milan, Galleria Lorenzelli; Milan, Studio Marconi; Los Angeles, Corcoran Gallery; Rome, Galleria D'Ascanio; Città di Castello, Manifattura Tabacchi. □ 1980 - Perugia, Rocca Paolina (with J. Beuys); Munich, Staatsgalerie Moderne Kunst; New York, Istituto Italiano di Cultura; Madrid, Istituto Italiano di Cultura; Florence, Orsanmichele. □ 1981 - Rome, L'Isola; Siena, Palazzo Comunale; Pesaro, Teatro Rossini, Rossini Opera Festival; Geneva, Galerie Jeanneret; Innsbruck, Galerie Im Taxispalais. □ 1982 - Palm Springs/California, Desert Museum; Salzburg, Salzburger Kunstverein, Künstlerhaus; Bologna, Galleria San Luca; Vienna, Museum Moderne Kunst, Palais Lichtenstein; New York, Brooklyn Museum; Klagenfurt, Kärntner Landesgalerie; Columbus, Museum of Art; San Francisco, San Francisco Museum of Art. □ 1983 - Venice, Ex Cantieri Navali Giudecca. □ 1984 - Nice, Galerie Sapone; Milano, Pinacoteca di Brera, Palazzo Citterio.

Selected bibliography: 1947 - *A.B.*, Galleria La Margherita, Rome (texts by L. De Libero, L. Sinisgalli). □ 1953 -*A.B.*, Fondazione Origine, Rome (text by E. Villa). □ 1955 - *A.B.*, L'Obelisco, Rome (text by J. Sweeney); *The Collages of A.B.*, Fine Arts Center, Colorado Springs (text by J.P. Byrnes). □ 1956 -*Burri et Cesar*, Galerie Rive Droite, Paris (text by M. Tapié). □ 1957 - *A.B.*, Galleria del Naviglio, Milan (text by A. Pieyre de Mandiargues); *Opere di A.B.*, Galleria La Loggia, Bologna (text by F. Arcangeli); *Paintings by A.B.*, Pittsburgh, Carnegie Institute (text by J.J. Sweeney). □ 1959 - *A.B.*, Galerie Feigel, Basel (text by E. Vietta); *A.B.*, Palais des Beaux Arts, Brussels (text by G.C. Argan); *A.B.*, Museum Haus Lange, Krefeld (text by P. Wember). □ 1960 - *A.B.*, Hanover Gallery, London (text by H. Read); *A.B.*, Anne Abels, Cologne (text by P. Wember). □ 1961 - *Mostra antologica 1948-1955*, Galleria La Medusa, Rome (text by E. Crispolti); *A.B.*, Galerie de France, Paris (text by M. Ragon); E. Crispolti, *Burri - Un saggio e tre note*, Scheiwiller, Milan; E. Crispolti, M. Drudi Gambillo, *I ferri di Burri*, Biblioteca di Alternative Attuali, Rome. □ 1962 - *Alternative attuali - Omaggio a Burri*, Castello Cinquecentesco, L'Aquila (text by E. Crispolti); *A.B.*, Galleria Marlborough, Rome (text by C. Brandi). □ 1963 - C. Brandi, *Burri*, Editalia, Rome; *A.B.*, Museum of Fine Arts, Houston (text by J.J. Sweeney). □ 1967 - *A.B.*, Kunsthalle, Darmstadt/Boymans van Beuningen, Rotterdam (texts by H.G. Sperlich, B. Krimmel). □ 1971 - M. Calvesi, *A.B.*, Fabbri, Milan/Abrams Artbooks, New York*; *A.B.*, Galleria Civica d'Arte Moderna, Turin (text by A. Passoni). □ 1972 - *A.B.*, Musée National d'Art Moderne, Paris (text by J. Leymarie). □ 1973 - C. Brandi, *A.B. - Opere grafiche*, Galleria 2RC, Rome/Milan. □ 1975 - *A.B.*, Sacro Convento di S. Francesco, Assisi (text by C. Brandi); V. Rubiu, *A.B.*, Einaudi, Turin. □ 1976 - *A.B.*, Galleria Nazionale d'Arte Moderna, Rome (texts by B. Mantura, G. De Feo). □ 1977 - *A.B.*, Palacio Velázquez, Madrid (texts by G.C. Argan, V. Aguilera Cerni, B. Mantura, G. De Feo); *A.B. - A Retrospective View 1948-1977*, Frederick S. Wright Art Gallery, University of California, Los Angeles (text by G. Nordland). □ 1978 - *A.B.*, Museo di Capodimonte (texts by R. Causa, G.C. Argan). □ 1979 - *A.B. - Recent Works*, J. Corcoran Gallery, Los Angeles (text by R. Houston); *A.B., la misura aurea della materia*, Anna D'Ascanio, Rome (text by A. Bonito Oliva); F. Caroli, *Burri*, Mazzotta, Milan. □ 1980 - *A.B., il viaggio*, Electa, Milan (texts by N. Sarteanesi, E. Steingraber); *A.B.*, Orsanmichele, Florence (text by V. Bramanti). □ 1981 - *A.B. - Teatri e scenografie*, Rossini Opera Festival, Pesaro (text by E. Villa); *Collezione Burri*, Fondazione Palazzo Albizzini, Città di Castello (text by C. Brandi); *A.B. -Cellotex und Multiplex, Material und Magie*, Galerie Taxipalais, Innsbruck (text by D. Ronte). □ 1982 - *A.B.: Echoes and Alchemical Implications*, Desert Museum, Palm Springs (text by J. Butterfield). □ 1983 - *Burri, Sestante*, Electa, Milan (text by G.C. Argan). □ 1984 - *Burri*, Mondadori, Milan (texts by C. Bertelli, C. Pirovano); *A.B.*, Sapone, Nice (text by D. Abadie).

Pier Paolo Calzolari

Born 1943 in Bologna. Lives in Milan and Vienna.
One-man exhibitions: 1965-Bologna, Studio Bentivoglio. □ 1967 - Bologna, Studio Bentivoglio. □ 1969 - Turin, Galleria Sperone. □ 1970 - Turin, Galleria Sperone; Paris, Galerie Sonnabend. □ 1971 - Paris, Galerie Sonnabend; New York, Sonnabend Gallery. □ 1972 -Naples, Modern Art Agency. □ 1973 -Paris, Musée Gallièra, "Festival d'Automne"; Berlin, Galleria Skulima. □ 1974 - Milan, Galleria Toselli. □ 1975 -Turin, Galleria Marinucci/Russo; Milan, Galleria Betti; Pescara, Galleria De Domizio. □ 1976 - Milan, Galleria De Ambrogi/Cavellini; Brescia, Galleria Cavellini; Genoa, Galleria Forma. □ 1977 - Turin, Galleria Russo; Bologna, Studio Bentivoglio; Naples, Museo Diego Aragona Pignatelli Cortes. □ 1978 - Bologna, Galleria Fata; Rome, Galleria Sperone; Milan, Galleria Ala; Athens; Bernier Gallery. □ 1979 - Modena, Galleria Mazzoli; Turin, Galleria Russo; Athens, Bernier Gallery; Cologne, Galerie Bernier-Russo. □ 1980 - Venice, Cantieri Navali (Luigi De Ambrogi); Venice, Galleria il Capricorno; Turin, Galleria LP 220; Rome, Galleria De Crescenzo. □ 1981 - Paris, Galerie Fabre; Stuttgart, Galerie Schurr; Modena, Galleria Mazzoli. □ 1982 - Zurich, Galerie Knoedler. □ 1983 - Milan, Galleria De Ambrogi; Verona, Galleria Ferrari. □ 1984 - Paris, Galerie de France; Athens, Bernier Gallery; Vienna, Galerie Pakesc.

Selected bibliography: 1965 - *P.P.C.*, Studio Bentivoglio, Bologna (text by A. Napolitano). □ 1967 - *P.P.C.*, Studio Bentivoglio, Bologna (texts by A. Boatto,

V. Boarini). □ 1979 - L. Rogozinski, "P.P.C.," *Flash Art*, no. 90-91, Milan, June-July. □ 1980 - L. Rogozinski, "La doppia ombra dell'astrazione - P.P.C. ," *Acrobat Mime Parfait*, no. 0, Bologna; D. Zacharopoulos, "P.P.C.," *Flash Art*, no. 98-99, Milan, Summer. □ 1984 - *P.P.C.*, Galerie de France, Paris (text by D. Zacharopoulos); *P.P.C.*, GaleriePakesc, Vienna (text by D. Ronte).

Vincenzo Castella

Born 1952 in Naples. Lives in Rome. Selected one-man exhibitions: 1980 - Rome, Libreria Vecchia Talpa; Milan, SICOF; Modena, Palazzo Comunale; Treviso, Galleria Nuova Fotografia. □ 1981 - Malmö, Museum of Malmö; Rome, Galleria Rondanini. □ 1982 - Cologne, Kunstmuseum; Antwerp, Galerie Paule Pia; Rimini, Musei Comunali; Milan, Galleria Fotografia Arte; Fusignano, Palazzo Civico. □ 1983 - Graz, Museum of Graz; Bari, Pinacoteca; Rimini, Musei Comunali. □ 1984 - Milan, Galleria Fotografia Arte.

***

Everday topography, objects and the atmospheres that reveal presences appear magically liberated from the forced scheme of the old geography and for a brief moment re- veal a new scheme which, caught in a room, extends in the mental prospect of a little universe.

Vincenzo Castella, 1982

***

Selected bibliography: 1977 - V. Castella, *Documenti del Sud, USA*, Sciascia, Milan. □ 1978 - V. Castella, *Black People USA*, film, color, 16 mm, 38'. □ 1981 - V. Castella, *I castelli romani, fotografia sul territorio*, Rondanini, Rome. □ 1982 - *La fotografia europea*, Jaca Book, Milan. □ 1983 - *Notte e Dì*, Il Quadrante, Alessandria. □ 1984 - V. Castella, "Casa d'anonimo milanese," *Domus*, Milan; V. Castella, *Interni*, Milan; V. Castella, "Spazio della memoria," *Vogue*, Milan; *Viaggio in Italia*, Il Quadrante, Alessandria; *Penisola - Nuova fotografia in Italia*, Camera Austria, Graz; *Rassegna*, Electa, Milan, December, special issue on architectural photography.

Public collections: Paris, Cabinet des Estampes, Bibliothèque Nationale; Frankfurt, Manfred Heiting Konzeptio; Amsterdam, Polaroid Museum; Milan, Graphic Art Collectors; Parma, Centro Studi e Archivio della Comunicazione.

Achille Castiglioni

Born 1918 in Milan.
After graduation from the Milan Polytechnic in 1944 he joined his brothers Livio and Pier Giacomo's architecture firm. In their first few years together, besides their professional and research activity in urban planning and construction, the Castiglionis concentrated on industrial design and when Livio left the firm in 1952 to branch out on his own, Achille and Pier Giacomo continued their experiments especially aimed at creating structures and furnishings for exhibitions. It was in this area more than in construction that the Castiglionis were able to check the validity of their designs having as a reference the general public, its reactions to the objects shown, and its perception of spaces, volumes, colors and lights.
The decade from 1954 to 1964 was very important for Italian design and Achille and Pier Giacomo were protagonists of the major exhibitions — Triennale, Compasso d'Oro, founding of ADI. This lively cultural climate fostered some of their most innovative proposals for living spaces in the form of inventive objects, furniture and lighting fixtures. Their design took on definite lines and when Pier Giacomo died in 1968, Achille carried on the tradition of this very close collaboration.
In 1969 he started his university teaching and until 1977 was professor of Artistic Design for Industry in the Faculty of Architecture at the Turin Polytechnic. In 1978 he was given the chair for interior design at the same university. And in 1981 he began lecturing in interior and industrial design at the Faculty of Architecture at the Milan Polytechnic. Alongside his teaching activity, Castiglioni intensified his participation both as author and as selector and member of the jury in exhibitions and contests, obtaining numerous recognitions and prizes for the objects he designed: Bronze medal VIII Triennale of Milan, 1947; the grand prize at the IX (1951) and X (1954) Triennales; gold prize XI (1957) and XII (1960) Triennales; silver prize XI (1957) and XV (1963) Triennales — at the latter he won two prizes. He has won various Golden Compasses: in 1955, 1960, 1962, 1964, 1967, 1979.
He has had his own section at the following exhibitions: "Colori e forme nella casa d'oggi," Villa Olmo, Como, 1952-54; "La casa abitata," Palazzo Strozzi, Florence, 1965; "Oggetti per la casa," by A. and P.G. Castiglioni, Centro Fly, Milan, 1966; " Fem Italienska Designer i Stockholm," Sweden, 1974; "Originale und Plagiate," A. and P.G. Castiglioni and Tobia Scarpa, Vienna, 1974; "Il design dei Castiglioni," Centro Master's, Lissone, 1978; "Art and Industry," Victoria and Albert Museum, London, 1982; "Exhibition of Italian Design," Tokyo, 1984; European itinerant one-man shows: first city, Vienna, February 1984, followed by Berlin, London, Paris, Milan.
Besides exhibitions which he participates in as artist or as designer of the actual structures, Castiglioni is quite active in industry as a designer of objects, exhibition spaces, shops and interior-design. He has designed industrial design objects and structures for the most prestigious companies such as: Aereotecnica italiana, Alessi, ANIE (Associazione italiana nazionale industrie elettrotecniche), Arnolfo di Cambio, Arteluce, Brionvega, Camera di Commercio di Milano, Cassina, Danese, ENI (Ente italiano idrocarburi), Ferrania, Flos, Gavina, ICE (Istituto del commercio estero), Ideal Standard, Kartell, Knoll, Montedison, Omsa, Phonola Radio, RAI (Radiotelevisione italiana), Siemens, Zanotta.
His objects, shown in the most important international exhibitions, are included in the collections of the Museum of Modern Art, New York; The Victoria and Albert Museum, London; Kunstgewerbe Museum, Zurich; Staatliches Museum für Angewandte Kunst, Munich; Unèleckoprumyslove Museum, Prague; Israel Museum, Jerusalem.

***

Planning and research involve a steady curiosity in verifying whether an object is able to express by way of its own form. The curiosity of everything artificial, hence only a product of the human mind, helps us to see all the reasons for planning and constructing objects.
The unbiased observation of any expression can lead to recovering the rationality of certain forms, which, precisely because they have always been acquired during our upbringing, are ultimately never discussed.

Achille Castiglioni

Selected bibliography: 1961 - A. Castiglioni, "L'industrial design determina le qualità," *Ideal Standard*, no. 3, Milan. □ 1963 - A. Castiglioni, "Le dessin industriel italien," *L'Architecture d'Aujourd'hui*, no. 48, Paris. □ 1965 - A. Castiglioni, "Analisi e giudizi sul design," *Edilizia Moderna*, no. 85, Milan. □ 1970 - G.C. Argan, *L'arte moderna 1770-1970*, Sansoni, Florence; E. Benevolo, *Storia dell'architettura moderna*, Laterza, Bari; G. Dorfles, *Le oscillazioni del gusto*, Einaudi, Turin. □ 1972 - G. Dorfles, *Storia dell'architettura moderna*, Einaudi, Turin. □ 1973 - K. Mang, *Storia del mobile moderno*, Laterza, Bari; L. Rubino, *E quando le sedie avevano le gambe*, Bertani, Verona; P. Fossati, *Il design*, Tattilo, Rome. □ 1977 - G. Massobrio, P. Portoghesi, *Album degli anni cinquanta*, Laterza, Bari. □ 1980 - A. Grassi, A. Pansera, *Atlante del design italiano 1940/1980*, Fabbri, Milan; Centrokappa, *Il design italiano degli anni cinquanta*, Editoriale Domus, Milan; A. Castiglioni, "Progetto e produzione" (interview by E. Bettinelli), *Forum*, Linz. □ 1982 - *Art and Industry - A Century of Design in the Products We Use*, The Conrad Foundation, London; V. Gregotti, *Il disegno del prodotto industriale*, Electa, Milan. □ 1983 - E. Frateili, *Il disegno industriale italiano 1928/1981*, Celid, Turin; A. Castiglioni, *Design since 1945*, Philadelphia Museum of Art, Philadelphia. □ 1984 - *Achille Castiglioni*, Electa, Milan (texts by V. Gregotti, P. Ferrari)*.

Pierluigi Cerri

Born 1939.
Architect, joint founder of the Gregotti partnership. He directed the Biennial Exhibition in Venice 1976, and was art director of Electa Publishers, on the editorial staff of the magazines *Rassegna* and *Casabella*.
He has written for *Lotus International* and has edited numerous books including the Italian edition of *Vers une architecture* by Le Corbusier, Milan, 1972; *Autentico ma contraffatto*, Venice, 1976; *Pubblicità d'autore*, Milan, 1983. Responsible for the chain of graphic design *Pagina*. Planned exhibitions all over the world such as: "Peter Behrens und die AEG," Berlin, 1978; "La carrozzeria italiana," Turin and Rome, 1978; "Identité italienne," Centre Pompidou, Paris, 1981; "Alexander Calder," Turin, 1983; "Italian Design," Stuttgart, 1983 and Tokyo, 1984; "Venti progetti per il futuro del Lingotto," Turin, 1984. Has taken part in international design and architecture exhibitions.

***

The Design of Institutions
Those same problems of identity and image faced by private enterprises must also be tackled by institutions. In reality, in Italy, there is a split between attitudes toward public and private; how else can one explain the accidental nature of graphic design for public clients, while other examples of the artform are often distinguished by their ideological choice? One only has to think of paper currency; what is produced is not only an ugly object, but an inadequate one as well. Once the banks understood that money can "signify" something beyond its banal use, there was a proliferation of colored plastic cards, whose introduction into the electronic machines produced the same sound as a pinball machine. Using these cards is doubtless a more pleasant experience than that produced by studying the rhetorical doodles on an ordinary banknote. And with a little bit of imagination, one might say that the Swiss state entrusts the images on its currency with messages of order, practicality, control, efficiency...
It might be that behind the general disinterest on the part of Italian institutions for their image lies a lazy, pre-industrial attitude. The occasional commissioning of artists to design stamps has the nostalgic aura of nineteenth-century patronage. Or perhaps the lack of a "coordinated image" really denotes a deeply embedded tangle of powers, a multiform, self-absorbed and uncontrollable apparatus. In this case, the idea of furnishing everything with a façade-identity would be as ridiculous as speaking of the "heart" of the state.
The state is without heart, but at the same time it constitutes a "centered" and a centering totality. Perhaps one shouldn't expect the graphic designer to have a real identity, expecting instead mimesis, the foundation of all-efficient bureaucracy — with its deferrral of both confrontation and the assumption of responsability. No "1," but rather the third person, the "non-person," uncommitted to possible identities.
There is both anonymous centralism and a captious refusal to function at the level of imagery, which still constitutes the prevailing mode of communication in our society. Even the political parties, constrained to abandon the hypocritical moralism whereby ideals are cloaked in expressive sadness, so as to be set apart from abrasive cheerfulness, now choose in favor of spectacle. In this sense the case of the Italian Republican Party and Michele Spera is paradigmatic, perhaps also because of the involvement of the higher-ups of the businness world. The transportation sector, local agencies, and cultural demonstrations — these are the institutions that have felt it necessary to make use of the communicative skills of the graphic designer. What we are dealing with is ideology; the search for an identity (including a formal one) on the part of the local agencies bears witness to a desire for decentralization and autonomy in opposition to the centralizing tendencies of the state. And it is without doubt in the realm of cultural demonstrations that a collaborative relationship is clearly achieved among administration, planning and design. In fact, graphic designers would like to be able to do more work on public projects. Their best efforts have been energetically given to the "design" of objects which can furnish identity, an escape from the traditional frustration of being called in by private clients to apply "make-up" to finished products.
And, while it might seem out of fashion, there is also the desire/pitfall of producing *services*, of considering society not as a mass of consumers, but rather as users and citizens. On the other hand perhaps there are few designers today who would "redo the face" of a public administration without having a larger say in the problem of restructuring. To fall into the role of "stylists" would only create problems of collaborationism.

Pierluigi Cerri, 1978

Bruno Corà

Born 1942 in Rome where he still lives and works.
Since 1970 he has been on the board of directors of the International Art Encounters organization as well as doing critical and literary writings many of which have appeared in catalogues and in newspapers and magazines such as *Il Giorno*, *Paese Sera*, *Il Mondo*, *Data*, *Vogue*, *Kunstforum*, *Domus*, *Artistes*. In 1979 he obtained the chair in art history at the Academy of Fine Arts in Perugia. An organizer of exhibitions and conferences, he proposed and coordinated the European conference "The Space for

Art Today"(it had a scientific museographical orientation) for the opening of Perugia's Modern and Contemporary Art Gallery.
In 1980 he founded the art magazine *Anoir, Eblanc, Irouge, Uvert, Obleu,* which he also directs.

Enzo Cucchi

Born 1950 in Morro d'Alba. Lives in Ancona.
One-man exhibitions: 1977 - Rome, Incontri Internazionali d'Arte/Palazzo Taverna; Milan, Galleria De Ambrogi. □ 1978 - Rome, Galleria De Crescenzo. □ 1979 - Rome, Galleria De Crescenzo; Bologna, Galleria Diacono; Turin, Galleria Russo; Modena, Galleria Mazzoli. □ 1980 - Rome, Galleria dell'Oca; Cologne, Galerie Maenz. □ 1981 - New York, Sperone-Westwater-Fischer Gallery; Zurich, Galerie Bischofberger; Rome, Galleria Diacono; Modena, Galleria Mazzoli; Rome, Galleria Sperone; Cologne, Galerie Maenz; Amsterdam, Art & Project. □ 1982 - Zurich, Kunsthaus; Modena, Galleria Mazzoli; Essen, Museum Folkwang. □ 1983 - St. Gallen, Galerie Buchmann; New York, Sperone-Westwater Gallery; Rome, Galleria Diacono; New York, Sperone-Westwater Gallery and Boone-Werner Gallery.

Selected bibliography: 1977 - E. Cucchi, *Il veleno è stato sollevato e trasportato,* La Nuova Foglio, Macerata. □ 1979 - M. Diacono, *E.C. - Disegnoggetto, cosmèdipo,* Mario Diacono, Bologna; A. Bonito Oliva with E. Cucchi, *Canzone,* Emilio Mazzoli, Modena; A. Bonito Oliva, *Tre o quattro artisti secchi,* Emilio Mazzoli, Modena. □ 1980 - *E.C., Diciannove disegni* (text by E. Cucchi), Emilio Mazzoli, Modena; E. Cucchi, *Eroe delle campagne marchigiane,* Kunsthalle, Basel/Museum Folkwang, Essen/Stedelijk Museum, Amsterdam. □ 1981 - M. Diacono, *E.C.,* Mario Diacono, Rome; *E.C.,* Paul Maenz, Cologne (texts by E. Cucchi and D. Cortez). □ 1982 -*Zeichnungen,* Kunsthaus, Zurich/Groninger Museum, Groningen (text by E. Cucchi); *Scultura andata -scultura storna,* Emilio Mazzoli, Modena (texts by E. Cucchi and S. Chia); *E.C. -Un'immagine oscura,* Museum Folkwang, Essen (texts by E. Cucchi and Z. Felix). □ 1983 - *E.C.,* Buchmann Gallery, St. Gallen (text by A. Wildermuth); *E.C. -Giulio Cesare Roma,* Stedelijk Museum, Amsterdam-Kunsthalle, Basel (text by E. Cucchi)*. □ 1984 - E. Cucchi, *Tetto,* Mario Diacono, Rome (texts by E. Cucchi and M. Diacono); E. Cucchi, *Italia,* Anthony d'Offay, London; E. Cucchi, *Vitebsk/Harar* (edited by M. Diacono), Sperone-Westwater, New York.

Francesco Dal Co

Born 1945 in Ferrara,is a professor at the University Institute of Architecture in Venice.
Senior Fellow of the National Gallery, Washington DC, he writes for numerous Italian and foreign publications such as *A+, Casabella, Oppositions.* Some of his books are: *Hannes Meyer, Scritti 1921-1942* (Padua, 1972), *De la vanguardia a la metropoli* (Barcelona, 1972), *La città americana* (Bari, 1973), *Architettura contemporanea* (with Manfredo Tafuri, Milan, 1977), *Teorie del moderno* (Milan, 1982), *Abitare nel moderno* (Milan, 1982), *Carlo Scarpa* (Milan, 1984).

Hanne Darboven

Born 1941 in Munich. Lives in Hamburg.
One-woman exhibitions: 1967 - Düsseldorf, Galerie Fischer. □ 1968 - Düsseldorf, Galerie Fischer. □ 1969 - Mönchengladbach, Städtisches Museum; Munich, Galerie Friedrich. □ 1970 - Cologne, Galerie Werner; Düsseldorf, Galerie Fischer; Amsterdam, Galerie Art & Project; Turin, Galleria Sperone. □ 1971 - Düsseldorf, Galerie Fischer; Münster, Westfälischer Kunstverein; Düsseldorf, Videogalerie Schum. □ 1972 - Cologne, Galerie Friedrich; Bari, Galleria Bonomo; Brussels, Galerie MTL; Milan, Galleria Toselli; Amsterdam, Galerie Art & Project. □ 1973 -New York, Castelli Gallery; Paris, Galerie Lambert. □ 1974 - Bremerhaven, Kabinett für Aktuelle Kunst; Amsterdam, Galerie Art & Project; Brussels, Galerie MTL; Antwerp, Art & Project-MTL; Turin, Galleria Sperone; Oxford, Museum of Modern Art; Brussels, Palais des Beaux Arts; Basel, Kunstmuseum; New York, Castelli-Sonnabend Galleries. □ 1975 - Amsterdam, Stedelijk Museum; Lucerne, Kunstmuseum; Düsseldorf, Galerie Fischer; Bremerhaven, Kabinett für Aktuelle Kunst; Amsterdam, Stedelijk Museum. □ 1976 - Amsterdam, Galerie Art & Project (with R. Colmer); Houston, Cusack Gallery; Paris, Galerie Durand-Dessert; New York, Castelli Gallery. □ 1977 - New York , Castelli Gallery. □ 1978 - New York, Castelli Gallery and Sperone-Westwater-Fischer Gallery. □ 1979 - Bonn, Rheinisches Landesmuseum; Zurich, InK. □ 1980 - Cologne, Galerie Maenz; New York, Castelli Gallery; Cologne, Palais Atelier. □ 1981 - New York, Castelli Gallery. □ 1982 - Bonn, Kunstverein; Zurich, Galerie Fischer. □ 1983 - Hamburg, Kunstverein; Mönchengladbach, Museum Abteiberg; Otterloo, Kröller-Müller Museum; Hamburg, Kunsthalle. □ 1984 - New York, Castelli Gallery.

Selected bibliography: 1969 - *H.D.,* Städtisches Museum, Mönchengladbach (text by J. Cladders); "H.D. - 6 Manuskripte 69," *Kunst Zeitung,* no. 3, Düsseldorf. □ 1971 - *H.D.,* Westfälischer Kunstverein, Münster (texts by J. Cladders and K. Honnef). □ 1973 - H. Darboven, *El Lissitzky, Kunst und Pangeometrie,* Hosmann, Hamburg/Gevaert, Brussels; *H.D.,* Flash Art Editions, Milan. □ 1974 - H. Darboven, *Ein Monat, ein Jahr, ein Jahrhundert - Arbeiten von 1968-1974,* Kunstmuseum, Basel; H. Darboven, *Diary NYC, February 15 until March 4 1974,* Castelli, New York/Sperone, Turin. □ 1975 - H. Darboven, *Textes de Charles Baudelaire, Texte von Heinrich Heine...,* Pour, Brussels; H. Darboven, *60 Arbeiten à 1 Arbeit,* Konrad Fischer, Düsseldorf; H. Darboven, *Een maand, een jaar, een eeuw - Werke von 1968-1974,* Stedelijk Museum, Amsterdam (text by F. Meyer); H. Darboven, *Atta Troll nach Heinrich Heine,* Kunstmuseum, Lucerne (text by J.C. Ammann); H. Darboven, *1975 - Ausgewählte Texte...,* Hamburg; H. Darboven, *00-99 Ein Jahrhundert...,* Hamburg; H. Darboven, *2=1,2; 1+1=2...,* Hamburg. □ 1979 - H. Darboven, *Bismarckzeit,* Rheinisches Landesmuseum, Bonn (text by K. Honnef). □ 1982 - H. Darboven, *Wende 80,* Kunstverein, Bonn; H. Darboven, *Schreibzeit,* La Biennale, Venice (text by J. Cladders).

Paolo Deganello

Born 1940 in Este (Padua).
Graduated in Architecture at Florence in 1966. Between 1963 and 1974 he was town planner for the city of Calenzano (Florence). In 1963 he worked with Massimo Morozzi on the restoration of the halls above the church of Orsanmichele in Florence, for the Superintendence of Florence's Monuments. In 1966 he founded Archizoom Associates with Andrea

Branzi, Gilberto Corretti and Massimo Morozzi.
In *Space Design* (issue 127, 1974) there is a complete documentation of this studio's design activity. Archizoom closed in 1973 and in 1975 Deganello founded "Collettivo Tecnici Progettisti" with Gilberto Corretti, Franco Gatti and Roberto Querci, taking part in many architectural competitions (*L'architettura cronache e storia* no. 2, 1980, and *Modo* no. 29, 33 and 57). He has ectured at the University of Florence and the Architectural Association in London n '71, '72 and '74). In 1975 he and Ennio Chiggio published and edited a series of essays called "Quaderni del progetto." In the second volume he published the essay "Il lavoro di progettazione nel settore dell'arredamento." His articles have appeared in *Casabella*, *In*, *Rassegna*, *Domus*, *Urban Politics Problems*, *Modo*.
He has designed products for Planula, Marcatré, Driade, Cassina and the Ycami Collection.
In 1981 he exhibited three of his architectural projects in the "Design by Circumstance" show held at the Clocktower, New York, organized by PS1 and sponsored by the city's Institute for Art and Urban Resources (the catalogue is published by Arcolade Books Inc., New York).
In 1983 he designed a furniture shop for the Schöner Wohnen AG compagny in the historic center of Zurich including the small square in front of the shop where he created a monument to snow (*Casa Vogue*, January 1984).
He has participated in many architecture and industrial design shows including the XIV through XVII Triennale.
At the 17th Triennale in the exhibition "Dal cucchiaio alla città" he showed a model and pictures of his "Monumento alla neve," and the product *Torso* designed for Cassina.
For the exhibition "La casa della Triennale" he designed *La casa in comune* together with A. Magnaghi (*Domus* no. 645).

Selected bibliography: 1967 - "Gli Archizoom" (edited by E. Sottsass), *Domus*, no. 455, Milan, October. □ 1968 - G. Celant, "Critica come evento," *Casabella*, no. 330, Milan, November. □ 1969 - Archizoom, "Architettonicamente," *Casabella*, no. 334, Milan, March. □ 1972 - A. Bonito Oliva, *Il territorio magico*, Centro Di, Florence; *Italy, New Domestic Landscape*, The Museum of Modern Art, New York. □ 1973 - T. Crosby, *How to Play the Environment Game*, Penguin Books, London; C. Jencks, *Modern Movements in Architecture*, Penguin Books, London; M. Tafuri, *Progetto e utopia*, Laterza, Bari. □ 1974 - J.A. Walker, *Glossary of Art, Architecture and Design since 1945*, Praeger, New York; "Archizoom," *Space Design*, September. □ 1975 - A. Isozaki, *The Destruction of the Canons of the Modern Architecture*, Bijutsu Shuppausha, Tokyo; *Avanguardia e cultura popolare*, Centro Di, Florence. □ 1977 - P. Deganello, "Il lavoro di progettazione nel settore dell'arredamento," *Quaderni del Progetto*, no. 2, Milan; P.C. Santini, *Facendo mobili con...*, Poltronova, Milan. □ 1979 - *Storia e struttura del settore edilizio in Italia dal dopoguerra ad oggi* (edited by A. Sessaro), CLUP, Milan; "Poltrona e divani Oliblit," *Domus*, no. 601, Milan, December; P. Deganello, "La produzione del territorio," CNR. □ 1980 - P. Deganello, "Quando il sole cambia l'architettura," *Modo*, no. 29, Milan. □ 1981 - *Design by Circumstance*, Arcolade Books Inc., New York; C. Jenchs, *Late Modern Architecture*, Academy Edition, London; P. Deganello, "Scenario post-moderno," *Domus*, no. 614, Milan. □ 1982 - P. Deganello, "Il design oggi in Italia," *Quaderno di Domus*, Milan, June. □ 1983 - "I protagonisti" (interview), *Interni*, no. 330, Milan, May; *Le case della Triennale*, XVII Triennale, Milan; R.P. Baacke, U. Brandes, M. Erlhoff, *Design als gegenstand*, Frolich & Kaufmann. □ 1984 - B. Gravagnolo, "Di casa in casa," *Modo*, no. 66, Milan, January; "Paolo Deganello," (interview), *Domus*, no. 655, Milan; A. Branzi, *La casa calda*, Idea Books, Milan.

Michele De Lucchi

Born 1951 in Ferrara.
Lives in Milan.
He studied at Padua and graduated in Architecture at Florence. While still at university he founded the Cavart group operating in the area of avant-garde and radical architecture. In the brief period from 1973 to 1976 the group produced projects, films, documents, happenings, and seminars. The most important one on the theme of "Culturally Impossible Architectures" took place in the quarries of Monselice (Padua).
After graduating he taught as Adolfo Natalini's assistant at the Faculty of Architecture and at the International Art University in Florence.
In 1977 he went to Milan where he helped organize the exhibition and catalogue of "Il disegno italiano degli anni '50." He also began to work with Centrokappa (Noviglio) especially in designing industrial products. 1978 marks De Lucchi's move to Milan. He left teaching and began a close working relationship with Ettore Sottsass. This collaboration still accounts for a large part of his professional activities.
He has designed for Alchymia and took part in its exhibitions and activities until the founding of Memphis in 1981. For Memphis he made a significant contribution in designing single products, creating some of the best known ones, and in organizing the collection.
In 1979 he became design consultant for Olivetti Synthesis at Massa and in 1984 for Olivetti, Ivrea. With Ettore Sottsass he designed the 45CR series and the support system for Modulo informatics as well as the Icarus furnishing system for office automation (1982).
At the same time, with Sottsass Associates he designed the interiors and image of Fiorucci shops in Italy and abroad (1981-1983).
He presented a series of appliances designed for Girmi at the 1979 Triennale in Milan and a plastic prefabricated house at the 1983 Triennale.
He is presently designing for some of the most prestigious Italian furniture and interior design companies (Acerbis, Artemide, Vistosi, Up&Up, RB Rossana, Fontana Arte, Bieffeplast, Thalia, Cleto Munari, etc.). His work is often reviewed in the most widely circulated magazines.

***

Around eight to ten years ago, when I finished school and began working in what is called "the profession," I was very confident. I knew that I had finally become an architect and that I would be designing houses — perhaps small houses (perhaps also large ones if I became successful), perhaps furniture, chairs, sofas, cabinets, tables, perhaps also computers and some other strange machines of the future. I felt confident enough because I thought that these activities would remain sufficiently distinct from one another and that I would be able to call easily upon those rules which I had been taught in school. That was when I really began my life adventure as an architect, and I realized that, in fact, there was nothing to be confident about. Designing was an

extremely complex activity which required total involvement; all those activities I had previously thought about were really not compartmentalized at all, and the rules I had learned were absolutely naive, insubstantial and insufficient.
It was at that point that I understood that designing is a mental condition, an attitude, capable of harnessing and using the boundless energies of countless activities, images, forms, colors.
I understood that the most vivid reality, the most exhaustive and basic idea for explaining the world, and the idea upon which most certainties can be based, is consumerism. This element of our existence is often considered in a negative light and shunned with horror, but in reality it is a condition without which it is impossible to focus upon the future.
I understood that consumerism possesses great potential for communication, that it will prevail for some time to come, and that it is time to come to terms with this extraordinary tool and use it to disseminate new ideas and to communicate more effectively and positively.
I understood that it is through consumerism that architecture and design can possess an enormous communicative force, and that only through industrial production can they participate in the evolution of the image of the world.
I also understood, however, that the image of the contemporary world is not, as is so often assumed, only that of industry and technology and that perhaps it is this very image — of industry and technology — that is undergoing change.
I understood that perhaps the best thing would be to make a break from those things which are closest to us — certain more or less sophisticated (and no longer particularly useful) domestic objects — various appliances, hi-fi equipment, certain types of furniture, chairs, sofas, tables.
I understood that I could wait no longer, and I began immediately.

Michele De Lucchi, 1984

***

Selected bibliography: 1974 - G. de Bure, "La dernière Triennale à Milan," *Cree*, Paris, January. □ 1975 - "Concorso e seminario di architetture culturalmente impossibili," *Casabella*, no. 403, Milan, June; B. Zevi, "Un magnifico tugurio," *L'Espresso*, Rome, September; Cavart, *Architettura impossibile*, Centro Di, Florence. □ 1976 - Cavart, "Seminary -Impossible Architecture," *Interior Design*, no. 203, Tokyo, February; Cavart, "Architetture impossibili -Risposte possibili," *Casabella*, no. 411, Milan, March; M. De Lucchi, "Homo Trahens," *Interior Design*, no. 213, Tokyo, December. □ 1977 - "La portantina abitabile di M. De Lucchi," *Modo*, no. 3, Milan, September-October. □ 1978 - M. De Lucchi, "Cibo italian style" and "Zoomorfia casalinga," *Modo*, no. 6, Milan, January-February; A. Natalini, A. Poli, C. Toraldo di Francia, "Viaggio con la matita tra gli artefatti del mondo contadino," *Modo*, no. 7, Milan, March; M. De Lucchi, "Achille Castiglioni, Gio Ponti, Marco Zanuso," *Laica Journal*, Los Angeles, April-May. □ 1979 - M. De Lucchi, "Io sono un'autarchica, sedia," *Modo*, no. 20, Milan, June; "Activities of the Studio Alchymia," *Interior Design*, no. 249, Tokyo, December; S. Slesin, "Witty Furniture Design from the Milan Avant-garde," *The New York Times*, New York, November. □ 1980 - A. Branzi, "Triennale anno zero," *Domus*, no. 604, Milan, March; Centrokappa, *Il design italiano degli anni '50*, Editoriale Domus, Milan. □ 1981 - B. Radice, *Memphis the New International Style*, Electa, Milan; *The Possibilities of Michele De Lucchi*, Manhattan Catalogue 3, New York, September; J. Wondhnysen, D. Sudjic, "The New International Style," *Design*, no. 395, London, November. □ 1982 - *Vivere architettando* (edited by E. Pasculli, A. Pulga), Mazzotta , Milan; G.K. Koening, "Memphis," *Modo*, no. 45, Milan, January-February; R. Jensen, P. Convay, *Ornamentalism*, Clarkson N. Potter Inc. Publishers, New York. □ 1983 - E. Fratelli, *Il disegno industriale italiano 1928-1981*, Celid, Turin; M. De Lucchi, "La rivoluzione degli accostamenti cromatici," *Interni*, no. 330, Milan. □ 1984 - P. Sparke, "The Man from Memphis," *Blueprint*, no. 5, London; B. Radice, *Memphis*, Electa, Milan; A. Branzi, *La casa calda*, Idea Books, Milan; *Phoenix: New Attitudes in Design*, Queen's Quay Terminal, Toronto.

Nicola De Maria

Born 1954 in Foglianise. Lives in Turin. One-man exhibitions: 1975 - Naples, Villa Volpicelli (Galleria Amelio); Genoa, Galleriaforma. □ 1976 - Naples, Galleria Amelio; Maastricht, Agora Studio; Naples, Galleria Amelio. □ 1977 - Milan, Galleria Toselli. □ 1978 - Cologne, Galerie Maenz; Bari, Galleria Toselli; Milan, Galleria Toselli; Turin, Galleria Persano. □ 1979 - Bologna, Galleria Diacono. □ 1980 - Turin, Galleria Persano; Milan, Galleria Toselli; Zurich, Galerie Verna. □ 1981 - Turin, Galleria Persano; Zurich, Galerie Verna; Venice, Galleria del Capricorno; London, Lisson Gallery. □ 1982 - Rome, Galleria Diacono; Spoleto, Galleria Bonomo; Turin, Galleria Persano Milan, Galleria dell'Ariete. □ 1983 - Krefeld, Museum Haus Lange; Ghent, Vereniging voor het Museum van Hedendaagse Kunst; Milan, Galleria Toselli; Basel, Kunsthalle; Milan, Galleria Toselli; Cologne, Galerie Greve. □ 1984 - Zurich, Galerie Verna; Cologne, Galerie Greve.

***

Sketching throughout the voyage to Olympus, / I revived the legends, I painted the queen Cleopatra.
I was destined to create nostalgia, far and wide. / And after I had touched the animals and prayed to the dead / there were signs that truly, I might move souls / if I threw all of art into the future.

Nicola De Maria, 1978

***

Selected bibliography: 1979 - M. Diacono *Carro che mi porta lontano*, Mario Diacono, Bologna, April. □ 1980 - N. De Maria, *Musica-Occhi*, Kunsthalle, Basel/Museum Folkwang, Essen/Stedelijk Museum, Amsterdam (text by G. Celant) □ 1982 - M. Diacono, *Viento Nicola: la nostalgia della storia e l'inscrizione del nome*, Mario Diacono, Rome, January. □ 1983 - I. Panicelli, "Direzione Nicola — Nicola's Way," *Artforum*, New York, April ; N. De Maria, *EE AA Stop Campane*, Kunstmuseum, Krefeld (texts by J.C. Ammann, "Carissimo Nicola...;" G. Celant, "Una pittura dalle cento braccia;" M. Diacono, "l'Artenicola;" R.H. Fuchs, "Für Nicola;" J. Heynen, "Axeiropointon;" F. Meyer, M. Stockenbrand, "Augentore;" G. Storck), "Fragmente" - "EE AA stop campane" "12 Ottobre 1492" - "Alberi di notte si ribellano alle case")*; N. De Maria, *Libertà segreta segreta*, Kunsthalle, Basel October (text by J.C. Ammann, "Energies that elicit a feeling of happiness"). □ 1984 - N. De Maria, *Respiro del mondo*, Karsten Greve,

Cologne (texts by J. Cladders, "Molti anni per finire un disegno stellato;" F. Meyer, "La scelta che porta al cielo;" A. Pohlen, "In the Kingdom of Nicola De Maria").

Gillo Dorfles

Born 1910 in Trieste.
Art critic and university professor.
After the war he gained recognition as one of the shrewdest analysts of the transformations which were taking place in the production and consumption of aesthetic phenomena. As a militant critic, he made a fundamental contribution to the introduction and establishment of avant-garde art in Italy.
His best books, several of which have been translated abroad, are: *Discorso tecnico delle arti* (Pisa, 1951); *Le oscillazioni del gusto* (Lerici, Milan, 1958); *Il divenire delle arti* (Einaudi, Turin, 1959); *Il Kitsch* (Milan, Mazzotta, 1969); *Le buone maniere* (Milan, Mondadori, 1978); *Mode & Modi* (Milan, Mazzotta, 1979); *L'intervallo perduto* (Turin, Einaudi, 1980); *I fatti loro* (Milan, Feltrinelli, 1983); *La moda della moda* (Costa & Nolan, Genoa, 1984).

Luciano Fabro

Born 1936 in Turin. Lives in Milan.
One-man exhibitions: 1965 - Milan, Galleria Vismara, □ 1967 - Turin, Galleria Notizie. □ 1968 - Turin, Galleria Notizie. □ 1969 - Rome, Galleria La Salita; Milan, Galleria de Nieuborg. □ 1970 - Munich, Aktionsraum 1. □ 1971 - Milan, Galleria Borgogna; Turin, Giardino Galleria Notizie; Rome, Incontri Internazionali d'Arte. □ 1973 - Milan, Galleria Borgogna. □ 1974 - Turin, Galleria Notizie; Rome, Galleria Sperone-Fischer; Rome, Galleria del Cortile; Naples, Modern Art Agency; Geneva, Salle Patino. □ 1975 - Turin, Galleria Stein; Pescara, Galleria Pieroni; Florence, Galleria Area; Rome, Galleria del Cortile. □ 1976 - Rome, Galleria del Cortile. □ 1977 - Naples, Framart Studio. □ 1978 - Rome, Galleria Il Collezionista; Pescara, Liceo Artistico; Cologne, Galerie Maenz. □ 1979 - Rome, Galleria Pieroni. □ 1980 - Milan. PAC; Turin, Galleria Stein; New York, Ala Gallery; Milan, Galleria Toselli. □ 1981 - Essen, Museum Folkwang; Ghent, Museum van Hedendaagse Kunst; Rotterdam, Museum Boymans van Beuningen. □ 1982 - Genoa, Samangallery; Perugia, Accademia di Belle Arti Pietro Vannucci; Brescia, Galleria Banco. □ 1983 - Aachen, Neue Galerie; Ravenna, Pinacoteca Comunale, Loggetta Lombardesca. □ 1984 - Los Angeles, LAICA; Cologne, Galerie Maenz.

***

On the seventh day God rested,
On the eighth day he climbed back down to earth and saw that it was boring.
Then he took some earth and formed it in his image and likeness, he breathed into it, smiled, and called it artist, or accomplice in the creation.
The man saw all this and, tearing up the grass around him, dug up some earth and, forming it in his image and likeness, blew into it; but the earth dried up, it became arid and turned to dust.
Again the man dug up some earth, formed it, and blew into it, but the earth dried up and became arid. But the man continued to form the earth in his image and likeness until everything around him was arid.

Luciano Fabro, 1979

***

Selected bibliography: 1966 - C. Lonzi, "Intervista con Luciano Fabro — Discorsi," *Marcatré*, no. 19-22, Milan, April, 1966. □ 1968 - *Fabro*, Galleria Notizie, Turin (text by M. Vertone). □ 1973 - L. Fabro, *Letture parallele*, Galleria Arte Borgogna, Milan. □ 1974 - L. Fabro, *Lectures parallèles II*, Salle Patino, Geneva. □ 1975 - L. Fabro, *Letture parallele III*, Christian Stein, Turin. □ 1977 - *L.F.: attaccapanni*, Framart Studio, Naples (texts by L. Fabro and A. Izzo). □ 1978 - L. Fabro, *Attaccapanni*, Einaudi, Turin, □ 1980 - L. Fabro, *Letture parallele IV*, Silvana, Milan; L. Fabro, *Regole d'arte*, Casa degli Artisti, Milan; □ 1981 - *L.F.*, Museum Folkwang, Essen/Museum Boymans van Beuningen, Rotterdam (texts by L. Fabro and Z. Felix). □ 1983 - L. Fabro, *Aufhänger*, Walter König, Cologne; B. Corà, "L.F. - Un habitat geometrico," *AEIUO*, no. 7, Rome, March; J. De Sanna, *Fabro*, Essegi, Ravenna*.

A.G. Fronzoni

Born 1923 in Pistoia.
Graduated in Architecture, he opened his first office in Brescia in 1945. In 1955 he transferred his office to Milan and founded and directed the magazine *Punta*. He began to write for *Casabella* and taught design in visual communications at the Umanitaria School in Milan. In 1968 he became a professor at the State Art Institute in Monza (Milan). He designed and set up the exhibitions on the art poster and concrete poetry for the Venice Biennale and later for the "Nouveau Réalisme" show in Milan. He won third prize at the Third International Poster Biennale in Warsaw. He designed the Astori pavilion for the Verona Fair and restored the stables of the Cairoli College in Pavia which were transformed into the University Art Gallery.
From 1975 to 1977 he was a professor of design for visual communications at the Isia University Institute in Urbino. He restored a seventeenth-century house at Alagna Sesia which became the Walser Museum (it won the Zanotti Bianco award in 1980).
In 1978 he founded the Institute for Visual Communications in Milan and coordinated the image for "Arte e città," Genoa. Since 1983 he has worked with C.C. Fronzoni, R, Nava, A.M. Tagliabue on the project *Casa per abitazioni* in Desio.

***

I began working as a designer in 1945, just after the war and at the start of European reconstruction. It was a particularly stimulating period. I wanted to learn. I believed that through my work I could contribute to the transformation of society, that is, that I could reduce objects and facts to their social significance. I had faith in the progressivist function of applied rationalism.
I persevered, working within a design concept of total space intended as a system of information; I sought a world image of contemporary society, using for my model the *Gesammtkunstwerk* of the city. As a result, my critical stance led me to see the design project as a challenge, a transgression. For me, the project exploited technological tools for the sake of cultural priorities. Not to satisfy the needs of the client, but uproot them. To assiduously avoid waste and redundance. To go against the grain, responding to the needs of the social community, which I considered the true client.
I haven't given up, even if my goals remain unattained. In other words, I

don't really know whether, in the end, the innovative autonomy of my work will show itself to be nothing more than an illusion.
Following this route, the designer's task is an arduous one. But this doesn't faze me. The choice to play a civil, progressive role is always a difficult one, especially if one's profession, as in the case of the designer, always forces one to confront the environment. Especially if one's work consists of a continuing design process, that is, something which is intended to evolve in the future.
Since 1967, when I began teaching, I have been increasingly aware that the true task of the designer is that of the educator, more than that of the technician. The designer's true goal is not to create a city, but to educate others to build a city — a city as the perceptible form of civilization.

A.G. Fronzoni, 1983

***

Selected bibliography: 1965 - G. Veronesi, "A.G.F.," *Sipradue*, no. 10, Turin; L. Vinca Masini, "Grafica e design come funzione educativa del gusto," *La Biennale*, no. 56, Venice; G.C. Argan, *A.G. F.*, Galleria La Polena, Genoa. □ 1967 - G. Celant, "A.G.F. ovvero il design forma zero," *E*, no. 2, Milan; "Grafica e allestimenti di A.G.F. a Milano e a Genova," *Domus*, no. 449, Milan. □ 1968 - "Genova, aule nuove a Palazzo Balbi," *Ottagono*, no. 8, Milan. □ 1969 - U. Apollonio, *A.G.F.*, Politecnico, Turin; G. Celant, "Design ideologico," *Casabella*, no. 335, Milan. □ 1970 - "European Designers," *Idea*, special issue, Tokyo. □ 1971 - "Environment Design of the World," *Idea*, special issue, Tokyo. □ 1976 - G. Guarda, "A.G.F. ovvero dell'essenziale," *Parete*, no. 26, Milan. □ 1979 - *Museo Walser*, Museo Walser, Alagna Valsesia (text by L. Mosso). □ 1981 - "Variazioni sul tema," *Rassegna*, no. 6, Milan. □ 1982 - G. Odoni, "Ipotesi per un deserto domestico," *Casa Vogue*, no. 127, Milan. □ 1983 - V. Pasca, "Rigorosa unità di uno spazio elementare," *Manuali d'Arredamento*, no. 4, Milan. □ 1984 - G. Odoni, "Concetto di casa," *Casa Vogue*, no. 150, Milan; A. Colbertaldo, "La casa povera," *Interni*, no. 341, Milan.

Johannes Gachnang

Born 1939 in Zurich.
He was first trained in drawing and collaborated with various architects in Zurich, Paris and Berlin (e.g., with Scharoun).
Since 1969 he has been working as a freelance artist in Istanbul, Rome and Amsterdam.
From 1974 till 1982 he was the director of the Kunsthalle in Bern.
In 1982 he was elected to the artistic committee of Documenta 7 in Kassel.
In 1983 he founded the publishing house Gachnang & Springer, Bern-Berlin. He organized the exhibition "Idee, Prozess, Egebris — Neubangebiete," in 1984.

Verena von Gagern

Born 1946 in Bonn. Lives in Munich.
One-woman exhibitions: 1975 - Milan, Galleria Il Diaframma; Antwerp, Galerie Paule Pia; Amsterdam, Galerie Fiolet. □ 1976 - Salzburg, College Gallery. □ 1977 - Pisa, Galleria Nadar; Salzburg, College Gallery. □ 1978 - Zurich, Work Gallery. □ 1979 - Munich, Die Neue Sammlung. □ 1980 - Salzburg, Salzburg College. □ 1981 - Munich, Galerie Lange Irschl; Cardiff, The Photographic Gallery; Ingolstadt, Kunstverein; Innsbruck, Taxispalais; London, The October Gallery. □ 1982 - Munich, Kunstakademie; Essen, Museum Folkwang; Tarragona, Forum Galleria; Zurich, Work Gallery. □ 1983 - Lisbon, Goethe Institut.

Selected bibliography: 1979 - *V.v.G., Photographien 1975-79*, Die Neue Sammlung, Munich; *Photography as Art, Art as Photography*, DuMont, Cologne. □ 1980 - *Vorstellung und Wirklichkeit*, Wienand Verlag, Munich. □ 1981 -*Internationale Sommerakademie*, Salzburg. □ 1982 - *Erweiterte Photographie*, Secession, Vienna; "Symposion on Photography," *Camera Austria Reader*, Graz; *Polaroids*, Pol Galerie, Munich; *Momentbilder*, Kestner Gesellschaft, Hanover; *DuMont Photo 4: Photographie in Europa heute*, DuMont, Cologne; *21 photographes contemporains in Europe*, Contrejour, Paris; *V.v.G.,*, Museum Folkwang, Essen. □ 1983 - *Festival international de la photographie*, Arles; *Fotografia europea contemporanea*, Jaca Book, Milan; *Photographie in Deutschland: heute*, Credit Communal / Geneentkrediet, Ghent (text by P. Andries). □ 1984 - *Selections 2*, Verlag Photographie, Munich; *Napoli '84. Fasti barocchi* (edited by C. De Seta), Electa, Milan.

Ludger Gerdes

Born 1954 in Lastrup (Linder-Lower Saxony). Lives in Düsseldorf and Munich.
One-man exhibitions: 1982 - Düsseldorf, Galerie Fischer; Munich, Galerie Schöttle. □ 1984 - Hamburg, Produzentengalerie (with T. Schütte).

***

Until the eighteenth century, art was a discipline that developed ways of creating public and private spaces. It was an important aid in molding the human character and shaping the world people lived in and their ways of seeing that world.
Modern art takes place almost exclusively in the museum. Museums present an inflation of changing trends that often amount to no more than changing fashions. Art produces an endless stream of discourses, but these discourses play almost no role at all for and in real life situations. As a result, the further the inflation progresses, the less interesting the discourses become. All it amounts to in the end is proof of the endless possibilities for diversity. More and more, art is becoming the illustration of art theory and the object of market strategies. It abstracts from the world (or is abstracted from the world); art no longer shapes the world.
Modern art has become autonomous in heroic proportions and has withdrawn into a comfortable museum existence. In a parallel development, modern architecture has turned into mere engineering technology. The task of designing living spaces was instantly usurped by crass technology, eye-catching design, throw-away media, traffic planning and other accomplishments of the twentieth century. The face of modern cities is increasingly dictated by a consumerism bent solely on maximizing profits.
I believe art should serve, above all, to shape and to stage the living spaces of human life. I'm interested in the role art can play in public life. I'm interested in models of art that go beyond the boundaries of the museum and the market place. Models of an art that is a public affair, an art that serves as a medium of social communication, and one

that speaks a "normal everyday" (*gewöhnliche*) language.
Art should be an offering. It shouldn't play itself up as an I-know-better-than-you, utopian avant-garde, but ought to make realistic, constructive recommendations for improving the world. Recommendations that can be tested and put into action.
I'm interested in pictures that say something about what pictures could do. We human beings are forced into nominalism. In a sense, we have no choice but to think in pictures. So why not make a virtue out of the vice? Why not live in pictures, too? A bridge as a mere means of transportation is well and good, but a bridge as a symbolic act is richer. A life without symbols is clean — but the poorer for it.
I'm interested in the rediscovery of traditional means and methods in the arts. I believe that many of the old traditions are still relevant to shaping our lives and molding our ways of seeing things. Doubts concerning the absolute validity of modern methods abound. The rediscovery of older and alternative traditions stretches from farming to medicine. I am convinced of the arrogance and falseness of modern art's absolutist claim that all older art is obsolete and passé.
I'm interested in the capacity for integration that exists in much older art: integration of the various genres of art with one another and integration of art with nature. These examples of integration compose a magnificent metaphor for communication, a communication that almost makes us forget the monologues of the modern purists.
I do not believe that art and reason must necessarily contradict one another. The romantic flight of much modern art into the realm of the irrational certainly has not contributed to improving the conditions of human life. I believe that we should find a rational way of trying to continue making art and that we should use art as an aid in the search for values and forms of living that go beyond the hysteria of industrial progress, beyond the exploitation of nature and human lives and beyond the idiotic stupidity of capitalistic consumerism.
In the search for such values and forms, those examples of older art may serve as a leitmotif that touch us in their beauty like a declaration of love to the world.
I am writing this in Venice, a city that bears witness to how paintings can shape and represent everyday life; to how architecture can provide the stages and sets for public life; to how natural settings can contribute to the *genius loci* of a place and how people can integrate artistic sensuality into the forms of their everyday lives. A city that presents itself as a public stage, where the citizen embodies the *res publica*. A city that demonstrates how the arts can be woven into and become a part of the texture of social communication; how they contribute to a magnificent *theatrum mundi*.
As long as the visual images of this city — from Carpaccio to Bellotto — continue to exist, the desire for a public life in which the arts have had a shaping hand will continue to exist as well.

Ludger Gerdes, 1984

***

Selected bibliography: 1983 - *Gerdes, Klingelhöller, Luy, Mucha, Schütte*, Fischer, Düsseldorf (text by U. Loock); L. Gerdes, "Einige Bemerkungen," *Kunstforum*, vol. 65, Cologne, September; L. Gerdes, "Was zeigt diese Arbeit?" *Kunstforum*,vol. 65, Cologne, September; *Konstruierte Orte*, Kunsthalle, Bern (text and interview by J.H. Martin). □ 1984 - *c/o Haus Esters*, Museum Haus Esters, Krefeld (texts by J. Heynen and L. Gerdes); *Der versiegelte Brunnen*, Lijnbaancentrum, Rotterdam; L. Gerdes, T. Schütte, *Weiter - Warten*, Produzentengalerie, Hamburg; *Von hier aus*, DuMont, Cologne.

Luigi Ghirri

Born 1943 in Scandiano, Reggio Emilia. Lives in Formigine, Modena.
Selected one-man exhibitions: 1972 - Modena, Sette Arti Club. □ 1974 - Milan, Galleria Il Diaframma. □ 1975 - Modena, Galleria D'Arte Moderna; Turin, Galleria Documenta; Amsterdam, Canon Gallery. □ 1976 - Graz, Forum StadtPark; Rome, Galleria Rondanini. □ 1978 - Paris, Galerie Contrejour. □ 1979 - Parma, CSAC Università. □ 1980 - Ferrara, Galleria Civica d'Arte Moderna; Rome, Galleria Rondanini; New York, Light Gallery. □ 1981 - Bordeaux, Galerie Arpa; Bari, Spazio Immagine. □ 1982 - Munich, Galerie Pol; Bari, Expo Arte; Paris, Galerie Esders; Milan, Studio Marconi; Cologne, Kunstmuseum, □ 1983 - Charleroi, Musée de la Photographie; Lausanne, Galerie Junod. □ 1984 - Montreal, Optica Gallery; Vienna, Galerie Photo; Toronto, Mercer Gallery; Arles, XV Festival; Rimini, Musei Comunali; Naples, Studio Dieci.

***

Ever since I was a little boy the pictures I always liked the most were those of landscapes inserted among the maps in atlases.
What I found particularly fascinating was the inevitable, motionless little man in the landscape; he was dominated by waterfalls, mountains, rocks, giant trees, grandiose palms or else he contemplated seas, lakes and endless plains. I used to find this little man on postcards of famous squares, and cities, or perched on historic monuments, lost in the Roman forum. That little man was in a state of continuous contemplation of the world and his presence in these pictures gave them a special fascination. Not only was it a yardstick to measure the wonders shown but it also gave me an idea of space. Through this little man I thought I could understand the world and space.
I also liked the idea that the photographer was never alone in these places, that he always had a friend or acquaintance who traveled around the world with him, discovering and portraying it.
I never managed to see this little man's face or give him an identity, but he accompanied me in the most fascinating undiscovered places which he noticed, contemplated, measured. When I began to photograph later on, I kept looking at landscape pictures but I no longer found the little man.
Fabulous scenery, backdrops, ever more deserted and incomprehensible spaces followed one another, split up, increased at dizzying speed, but to me everything seemed unknown and uninhabitable.
The places had disappeared and what remained were beautiful black-and-white or technicolor backgrounds. In disappearing, the little man had taken along depictions of the places and only their shadows were left.
That's why in order to "photograph" I've travelled through dizzying reproduction in its multiplication, its totally perverse simulation into the area of exasperated fragmentation multiplied to the nth degree.
The world, the landscapes seem more and more transitory, places to see quickly or only to catch a small detail of and we no longer understand where the real landscape ends and simulation begins.

Today, I think it is necessary to find in this landscape of the analogous and of the fragment a method and a way so that our gaze doesn't remain inert in the face of an increasingly incomprehensible exterior. The awareness of this state of things pushes me to search for new strategies of depiction so that our landscape can stop being a place of non-history and non-geography.

Luigi Ghirri, 1984

***

Selected bibliography: 1972 - *L.G.*, Sette Arti Club (text by F. Vaccari. □ 1974 - R. Salbitani, "L.G.," *Le Nouveau Cinéma*, no. 27, September; *L.G.*, Il Diaframma, Milan (text by M. Mussini); L. Carluccio, "Paesaggi di cartone," *Panorama*, Milan, February. □ 1975 -"L.G. - Colazione sull'erba," *Panorama*, Milan, February; *L.G.*, Canon Photo Gallery, Amsterdam (text by A.C. Quintavalle). □ 1976 - "L.G.," *Rondanini*, no. 6-7, Rome, October; G. Niccolai, "L.G. - Colazione sull'erba," *Tam Tam*, no. 10-11. □ 1978 - *Kodachrome*, Punto e Virgola, Modena - text by P. Berengo Gardin). □ 1979 - *Enciclopedia pratica per fotografare*, Fabbri, Milan; *L.G.*, CSAC Università, Parma; *L.G.*, Feltrinelli, Milan. □ 1980 - J.C. Le Magny, "Un art trompeur," *Connaissance des Arts*, no. 337, Paris, March. □ 1981 - V. Savi, *Paesaggio urbano*, Electa, Milan; G. Bonini, "L.G.," *Progresso Fotografico*, no. 3, Milan; C.De Seta, *Napoli, una nuova immagine*, Electa, Milan; G. Tatge, "L.G.," *Artforum*, New York. □ 1983 - L. Ghirri, M.Jodice, *Capri*, ERI, Rome; "L.G.," *I Grandi Fotografi*, Fabbri, Milan (text by F. Vaccari).

Public collections: Paris, Cabinet des Estampes, Bibliothèque Nationale; Arles, Musée de la Photographie Reattù; New York, Museum of Modern Art; Parma, Centro Studi e Archivio della Comunicazione; Amsterdam, Stedelijk Museum; Amsterdam, Polaroid Collection; Chalon-sur-Saône, Fondation pour la Photographie; Peking, National Gallery; Tokyo, Museum of Modern Art; Frankfurt, Manfred Heiting Collection.

Vittorio Gregotti

Born 1927 in Novara.
From 1953 to 1968 he worked with Lodovico Meneghetti and Giotto Stoppino.
In 1974 he founded Gregotti Associates with Pierluigi Cerri, Hiromichi Matsui, Pierluigi Nicolin and Bruno Viganò. He is still part of it with Augusto Cagnardi and Pierluigi Cerri.
He is now professor of architectural composition at the University of Venice.
He has taught in the architecture departments of the universities of Milan and Palermo and been a visiting professor at the universities of Tokyo, Buenos Aires, Sao Paulo, Berkeley, Lausanne and Harvard.
For many years he was editor of *Casabella* and subsequently in charge of the monographic issues for *Edilizia Moderna* and the architectural sector for *Il Verri*. He is presently editor in-chief of *Casabella* and *Rassegna*.
Among his books: *Il territorio dell'architettura* (Milan, 1966; Paris, 1982); *New Directions in Italian Architecture* (New York, 1969); *Il disegno del progetto industriale* (Milan, 1982).
He has taken part in numerous international exhibitions and was responsibile for the introductory section of the XIII Triennale (Milan, 1964) for which he won an international award.
From 1974 to 1976 he was director of the Visual Arts/Architecture section of the Venice Biennale.

***

7 Statement
Everything around us, our environment or *Umwelt* as Husserl and phenomenology term it, is in my opinion the physical manifestation of its own memory, i.e., of the way in which the various strata of memory and of the decisions to shape the place are superimposed.
Environment is nature turned culture, not just in external appearance but, more importantly, in the structural features as the real truths of any place.
In contrast to the abstract purity of the idea of space, the concepts of environment and of site always contain a great quantity of physical and historical debris which can become an important source and material for the architectural project, a material which is capable of describing differences and determining the quality of the architectural project.
The worst enemy of the architecture of modernity is that conception of space which is concerned only with its economic and technical qualities, remaining completely oblivious to other values a particular place might possess.
Seen in this light, I believe that geography may be considered to be the description of the vestiges of history that have assumed their particular physical form; thus geography can also provide clues to that which it unshakingly supports.
The architectural project faces the task of revealing the true essence of an environment by changing its form.
This environment is by no means a structural whole in which architecture disappears; on the contrary, it is the most important material for developing an architectural design.
It is in the concepts of the place and of the principle of settlement that the environment becomes the essence of architectural creation.
As a result, new principles and procedures are developed: the relationship between individual objects becomes as important as the linguistic definition of the object itself; in fact the linguistic definition of the context is determined by the knowledge of the specific place, and this hnowledge is gained through the architectural project.
The origin of architecture lies not in the hut or the cave or even the mythical "House of Adam in Paradise": long before he turned pillar into column and roof into gable, before he placed stone upon stone, man put stones on the ground to mark a place in the middle of an unknown universe and to survey and change it. And just as with any other act of measuring, this process requires a distinct and specific method.
When seen in this light, there are but two different ways of establishing a relationship with a place: the first uses mimetic imitation, organic assimilation, and the creation of a conspicuous complexity, the second relies on measurement, distance, definition, and change within the complexity.
We prefer and believe in the second way, for the simple reason that it does not make us strive for the impossible reconciliation of nature and artifice, of the new and the pre-existing; instead, it enables us, with the aid of the particular tools of the craft, to provide it with a new meaning of its own, based on the specific quality of non-coincidence.
This method involves a series of tension-producing subdivisions.
One need only think of erecting a wall, building a fence, or marking off a particular area: on one hand, the creation of a highly articulated interior corresponding with the diversity of human activities; on the other, a simple exterior which serves as a measure for

the totality of the great potential of our architectural environment.
In this context, "great" does not refer to a spatial dimension but instead denotes the "great" capacity for contextual modification. In order to design a project it is necessary to establish a rule. In essence, this rule has to do with the tradition of the style and the practice and with their advancement. Yet what lends truth and architectural reality to the rule is the encounter with the actual site.
It is only from the experience of the place that the characteristic features emerge which pave the way for architecture and determine its form.

Vittorio Gregotti, 1979

***

Selected bibliography: 1953 - "Padiglioni in un parco alla terza fiera mercato di Novara," *Domus*, Milan, December. □ 1957 - V. Gregotti, "Marco Zanuso, un architetto della seconda generazione," *Casabella*, no. 216, Milan. □ 1960 - V. Gregotti, "P. Behrens 1868-1940," *Casabella*,no. 240, Milan. □ 1961 - V. Gregotti, "L'architettura dell'espressionismo," *Casabella*, no. 254, Milan. □ 1964 - "Architettura italiana 1963," *Edilizia Moderna*, special issue, no. 82-83, Milan. □ 1965 - V. Gregotti, "La ricerca storica in architettura," *Edilizia Moderna*, no. 86, Milan; "Contemporary Italian Architects," *L'Architecture d'Aujourd'hui*, no. 48, Paris. □ 1966 - V. Gregotti, *Territorio dell'architettura*, Feltrinelli, Milan. □ 1967 - V. Gregotti,"L'architettura tedesca dal 1900 al 1930," *L'Arte Moderna*, no. 94, Milan. □ 1968 - V. Gregotti, *New Directions in Italian Architecture*, Studio Vista, London (New York, 1969). □ 1969 - "Le cento città d'Italia: Milano," *Controspazio*, Bari, September-October. □ 1971 - "L'architettura interrotta: tre progetti di Vittorio Gregotti," *Controspazio*, Bari, March. □ 1972 - *Italy: The New Domestic Landscape*, Museum of Modern Art, New York (text by V. Gregotti). □ 1974 - V. Gregotti, "Per una storia del design italiano," *Ottagono*, no. 32, 33, 34, 36, Milan. □ 1977 - "Vittorio Gregotti," *Architecture + Urbanism*, Tokyo, July. □ 1978 - V. Gregotti, "Il filo rosso del razionalismo italiano," *Casabella*, no. 440-441, Milan. □ 1980 - "Vittorio Gregotti," *GA Document*, special issue, Tokyo. □ 1981 - V. Gregotti, "La nozione di contesto," *Casabella*, Milan, January; V. Gregotti, "Carlo Scarpa," *Rassegna*, Milan, July; "Variation on a Grid Shape," *Architectural Record*, London, May; "Construire en terre d'Islam," *L'Architecture d'Aujourd'hui*, Paris, September. □ 1982 - M. Tafuri, *Vittorio Gregotti*, Electa, Milan (New York)*; "Gregotti Associati," *SD*, Tokyo, April; V. Gregotti, "Giuseppe Terragni," *Rassegna*, Milan, September. □ 1983 - V. Gregotti, "Die kritische Kontinuität zwischen den Generationen," *Junge Architekten in Europa*, Stuttgart. □ 1984 - "House in Oleggio," *GA Houses*, Tokyo, January; "Bossi Factory's Extension," *GA Document*, Tokyo, February; *Venti progetti per il futuro del Lingotto*, Etas Libri, Milan; V. Gregotti, "The Place in Time," *Daidalos*, no. 12, London, June; "Gregotti Associati 1981-1983," *Process Architecture*, no. 48, New York, June.

Frank Hess

Born 1939. Received his diploma in 1965 from Ulm School of Design.
From 1965-66 awarded a Post Graduate Grant for studies at the Royal College of Art, School of Industrial Design (Engineering), London.
In 1966 he was in Amsterdam for product development and design with Total Design.
From 1967 to 1970 he was with Lella & Massimo Vignelli and Cambridge Seven Associates for Product - Graphic and Architectural Design in New York City, Cambridge, Mass. and Los Angeles.
In 1970 with F. Bilger, an industrialist, he started Ulm design GmbH. Since 1978 he has been a Professor of Design.

Hans Hollein

Born 1934 in Vienna.
He was educated at the Academy of Fine Arts, Vienna, School of Architecture, receiving his diploma in 1956 and continuing graduate studies at Illinois Institute of Technology and the University of California, Berkeley, College of Environmental Design, where he earned a master's degree in 1960. Among his numerous realized projects and buildings are the Retti Candleshop, Vienna (1964-65); the Siemens Headquarters, Munich (1970-75); the Museum for Glass and Ceramics, Teheran (1977-78); the Municipal Museum Abteiberg, Mönchengladbach (1977-82); and the Beck of Munich Department Store Boutique at Trump Tower, New York (1981-83). His competition entry for the Museum of Modern Art in Frankfurt has recently been awarded First Prize, and he has been selected to design projects for IBA in Berlin and the Lingotto Factory of Fiat in Turin. The range of his design activities extends to furniture, objects, corporate identities and exhibitions of art and architecture. Notable among his contributions to these fields are furniture designs for Herman Miller in the United States, Alessi and Memphis in Italy, Knoll International in France, exhibition designs for "MAN transFORMS" at the Cooper-Hewitt Museum, in New York (1974-76) and "1683-1983", the commemorative exhibition (1982-83) of the three hundredth anniversary of the Turkish siege of Vienna. A frequent lecturer and visiting professor at schools in Europe and the United States, he has been professor of architecture at the Academy of Fine Arts in Düsseldorf since 1967 and head of the School and Institute of Design at the Academy of Applied Arts, Vienna, since 1976. His work has been widely exhibited at institutions such as the Museum of Modern Art, New York, the Musée d'Art Moderne, Paris, the Venice Biennale, Documenta, Kassel and a retrospective is being planned for the National Gallery, Berlin. Editor and contributor to many professional journals and books, he has done historical research on the work of R.M. Schindler and the Pueblos of the North American Indians. Among his awards and honors are the Reynolds Memorial Award, United States, given in 1966 and most recently the Austrian State Award for Art in 1983. He is Austrian state commissioner for the Venice Biennale, 1984, a post he has held several times; vice president of the Austrian Architects Association and an Honorary Fellow of the American Institute of Architects.

Selected bibliography: □ 1961 - H. Hollein, "Rudolph M. Schindler, ein Wiener Architekt in Kalifornien," *Der Aufbau*, no. 3, Vienna, March. □ 1963 - J. Esherick, "Forms and Design by H. Hollein and W. Pichler," *Art & Architecture*, Los Angeles, August. □ 1966 - H. Hollein, "Transformations," *Art & Architecture*, Los Angeles, May; "Candleshop by Hans Hollein Architect," *Art & Architecture*, Los Angeles, April; "Keyhole Shop," *The Architectural Forum*, New York, June. □ 1968 -"Austriennale," *The Architectural Forum*, New York, September; H. Hollein, "Edifices publics — L'architecture: image et enveloppe de la communauté?," *L'Architecture d'Aujourd'hui*, Paris, December; H.

Hollein, "Alles ist Architektur," *Bau*, no. 1, Vienna. □ 1969 - H. Hollein, "Neue Konzeptionen aus Wien, Fragmentarische Anmerkungen eines Beteiligten, Vortrag vom 1.2.1962 in der Galerie St. Stephan, Wien," *Bau*, no. 2-3, Vienna. □ 1970 - H. Hollein, "Alles ist Architektur," *Architectural Design*, London, February; J.S. Margolies, "Art Machine for the 70's," *The Architectural Forum*, New York, January-February; D. Raney, "Architectural Fabergé," *Progressive Architecture*, Stanford, Conn., February; J. Fischer, "Closely Observed Curves," *Design*, no. 256, London, April; "Richard Feigen Gallery: Hans Hollein," *L'Architecture d'Aujourd'hui*, no. 151, Paris, August-September. □ 1975 - "Hans Hollein," *Space Design*, no. 5, Tokyo, May; "Furniture Showroom, Vienna," *The Architectural Review*, no. 915, London, May. □ 1975 - "Hans Hollein," *Arquitecturas*, no. 10, Barcelona, November. □ 1976 - "MANtransForm," *Space Design*, no. 12, Tokyo, December; H. Hollein, "Position and Move," *Space Design*, Tokyo, April; H. Hollein, "Messages," *The Japan Architect*, Tokyo, June. □ 1979 - "H. Hollein - Austrian Travel Agency,Vienna, Austria," *a+u*, Tokyo, January; "La Villa Strozzi à Florence, Italie," *Techniques & Architecture*, Paris, September; M. Mack, "Extracting and Recombining Elements," *Progressive Architecture*, Stanford, Conn., December. □ 1980 - "Musée de la céramique et du verre, Téhéran," *L'Architecture d'Aujourd'hui*, no. 212, Paris. □ 1982 - "Hollein Fragmenta 1972-1982: Die Mönchengladbacher Kunstkolonie auf dem Abteiberg," *Domus*, no. 632, Milan, October; "Hans Hollein: il confronto, il museo municipale Abteiberg Mögla," *Gran Bazar*, Milan, November; "Stirling and Hollein," *The Architectural Review*, no. 1030, London, December. □ 1983 - "Hans Hollein, Portrait," *Architecture Intérieure*, Paris, April-May; "A Museum That Is a Cluster of Eclectic Buildings on a Hilltop, A Jewelry Shop That Is a Sumptuous Confection of Rich Ingredients," *AIA Journal*, New York, August.

Rebecca Horn

Born 1944 in Michelstadt. Lives in Berlin and Zell Bad Koenig.
One-woman exhibitions: 1973 - Berlin, Galerie Block; Hanover, Kunstverein. □ 1975 - Genoa, Samangallery; Berlin, Berliner Festwochen (premiere of the film *Berlin*). □ 1976 - New York, Block Gallery; Genoa, Samangallery; Graz, Galerie H. □ 1977 - Cologne, Kunstverein; Berlin, Haus am Waldsee; Milan, Galleria Ala; Baden-Baden, Kunsthalle. □ 1978 - Tokyo, Videosymposium, video film *Der Eintänzer*; Hanover, Kestner-Gesellschaft with the film *Der Eintänzer*; Genoa, Samangallery. □ 1979 - Eindhoven, Stedelijk van Abbemuseum; Münster, Kunstverein; New York, Ala Gallery. □ 1980 - Linz, Forum Design; Florence, Palazzo Frescobaldi. □ 1981 - Baden-Baden, Staatliche Kunsthalle and premiere of the film *La Ferdinanda*; Amsterdam, Stedelijk Museum; Genoa, Samangallery. □ 1982 - Ghent, Gewad. □ 1983 - Geneva, Galerie Franck; Geneva, Centre d'Art Contemporain; Zurich, Kunsthaus; London, Serpentine Gallery; Southampton, John Hansard Gallery/University; Chicago, Museum of Contemporary Art.

Selected bibliography: 1976 - T. Baum, *Rebeccabook 1*, Nadada, New York; R. Horn, *Dialogue of the Paradise Widow*, Samaneditions, Genoa. □ 1977 - R. Horn, *Die chinesische Verlobte*, Staatliche Kunsthalle, Baden-Baden (texts by R.G. Dienst and R. Horn); R. Horn, *Zeichnungen, Objekte, Video, Filme*, Kölnischer Kunstverein, Cologne/Haus am Waldsee, Berlin (texts by T. Baum, Z. Felix, M. Grüterich, L. Lippard and R. Horn). □ 1978 - R. Horn, *Der Eintänzer*, Kestner-Gesellschaft, Hanover (texts by M. Grüterich, C.A. Haenlein, R.H. Wiegenstein and R. Horn). □ 1981 - R. Horn, *La Ferdinanda - Sonata für eine Medici Villa*, Staatliche Kunsthalle, Baden-Baden (texts by G. Celant, K. Schmidt and R. Horn). □ 1984 - *R.H.*, Kunsthaus, Zurich (texts by B. Curiger, T. Stooss and R. Horn) *.

Peter Iden

Born 1938 in Meseritz/Brandenburg.
Gymnasium in Lüneburg and Frankfurt.
1955-56 scholarship student in California.
Studied Philosophy in Frankfurt and Vienna.
Responsible for the Theater-"Experimenta" in Frankfurt.
Staff editor at *Frankfurter Rundschau* (theater and art criticism).
Organized the collection for the Museum für Moderne Kunst (Museum of Modern Art) in Frankurt.
Author of the monograph *Edward Bond* (1973), *Die Schaubühne am Halleschen Ufer 1970-1979* (1979), *Theater als Wiederspruch* (1984), etc.
Since 1980, professor at the Staatliche Hochschule für Musik (Frankfurt Academy of Music).

Jörg Immendorff

Born 1945 in Bleckede-Lüneburg. Lives in Düsseldorf.
One-man exhibitions: 1961 - Bonn, New Orleans Club. □ 1965 - Düsseldorf, Galerie Schmela; Fulda, Galerie Fulda (with C. Reinecke); Aachen, Galerie Aachen. □ 1967 - Cologne, Galerie Art Intermedia. □ 1968 - Frankfurt, Galerie Patio; Düsseldorf, Staatliche Ingenieurschule (with C. Reinecke). □ 1969 - Frankfurt, Galerie Lichter; Antwerp, A 379089; Cologne, Galerie Werner. □ 1971 - Cologne, Galerie Werner; Munich, Galerie Friedrich. □ 1972 - Cologne, Galerie Werner. □ 1973 - Münster, Westfälischer Kunstverein; Cologne, Galerie Werner; Frankfurt, Galerie Loehr; Baden-Baden, Galerie Cornels. □ 1974 - Copenhagen, Daner Galleriet; Cologne, Galerie Werner; Berlin, Galerie am Savignyplatz. □ 1975 - Cologne, Galerie Werner; Vienna, Galerie nächst St. Stephan. □ 1976 - Amsterdam, Galerie van der Meij. □ 1977 - Utrecht, Hedendaagse Kunst; Cologne, Galerie Werner (with Penck). □ 1978 - Düsseldorf, Galerie Maier-Hahn; Cologne, Galerie Werner. □ 1979 - Basel, Kunstmuseum; Amsterdam, Galerie van der Meij; Cologne, Galerie Werner. □ 1980 - Bern, Kunsthalle. □ 1981 - Eindhoven, Stedelijk van Abbemuseum (with J. Kounellis); Eindhoven, Stedelijk van Abbemuseum; Hamburg, Galerie Neuendorf; Madrid, Galerie Ehrhard. □ 1982 - Düsseldorf, Kunsthalle; Cologne, Galerie Werner; Munich, Galerie Jahn; Düsseldorf, Galerie Strelow; Paris, Galerie Templon; New York, Sonnabend Gallery; Berlin, Galerie Springer; Ghent, Verienigung Aktuelle Kunst vzw Gewad. □ 1983 - Kastrup, Kastrupgardsmlingen; Berlin, Galerie Springer; Eindhoven, Stedelijk van Abbemuseum; Düsseldorf, Kunsthalle; Edinburgh, New 57 Gallery; Milan, Studio d'Arte Cannaviello; London, Greenwood Gallery; Düsseldorf, Rattinger Hof; New York, Sonnabend Gallery; Trondheim, Galerie Horneman; Zurich, Kunsthaus; Paris, Galerie Gillespie-Laage-Salomon. □ 1984 - Hamburg, Galerie Crone; Stuttgart, Galerie Schurr; New York, Boone-Werner Gallery; Cologne, Galerie Werner.

Selected bibliography: 1968 - J. Immendorff, *Eine Eisbärensekte im Lidlraum*, Düsseldorf; *Tierlidl. Eine Arbeitswoche von und mit J.I.*, Düsseldorf. 1969 - J. Immendorff, "LIDL als Gäste" and "Die ideale Akademie," Interfunktionen, no. 2, Cologne. □ 1973 - *J.I. - Hier und jetzt: Das tun, was zu tun ist*, Verlag König, Cologne/New York. □ 1974 - J. Immendorff, "An die 'parteilosen' Künstlerkollegen," *Kunstforum*, vol. 8-9, Mainz, January. □ 1977 - *J.I.*, Hedendaagse Kunst, Utrecht (texts by W. Kotte, J. Kramer). □ 1978 - *Café Deutschland - Von J.I.*, Michael Werner, Cologne (texts by R. Fuchs, J. Gachnang, S. Gohr); J. Immendorff, M. Schürmann, "Beuys geht" (interview), *Überblick*, no. 12, Düsseldorf, December. □ 1979 - J. Immendorff, A.R. Penck, *Deutschland mal Deutschland. Ein Deutsch-Deutscher Vertrag* (Immendorff visits Y), Rogner & Bernhard, Munich; *J.I. Café Deutschland*, Kunstmuseum, Basel (text by D. Koepplin); *J.I. - "Position - Situation," Plastiken*, Michael Werner, Cologne (texts by S. Gohr, A.R. Penck). □ 1980 - *J.I. - Malermut rundum*, Kunsthalle, Bern (texts by J. Gachnang, M. Wechsler). □ 1981 - *J.I. - Teilbau*, Neuendorf, Hamburg (texts by R. Fuchs, J. Gachnang); *J.I. Lidl, 1966-1970*, Stedelijk van Abbemuseum, Eindhoven (text by R. Fuchs); *J.I. - Café Deutschland/Adlerhälfte*, Kunsthalle, Düsseldorf (texts by J. Harten, U. Krempel); *J.I. - Kein Licht für wen?*, Michael Werner, Cologne; *J.I. - Sie haben es genommen, ich bring's uns wieder*, Kunstaus, Zurich (texts by D. Diederichsen, J. Gachnang, S. Gohr, J. Huber, T. Stooss, H. Szeemann); J. Immendorff, *Grüsse von der Nordfront* (poem by A.R. Penck), Fred Jahn, Munich; *J.I. - Brandenburger Tor - Weltfrage* (poem by A.R. Penck), The Museum of Modern Art, New York. □ 1983 - "Dieses Heft ist Jörg Immendorff gewidmet!," *Krater und Wolke*, no. 2, Michael Werner, Cologne (edited by A.R. Penck); *Café Deutschland-Gut*, Maximilian Verlag/Knust, Munich and Michael Werner, Cologne: *J.I.*, Kunsthaus, Zurich (texts by J. Gachnang, J. Huber, S. Gohr, D. Diederichsen, T. Stooss, H. Szeemann, J. Immendorff) *. □ 1984 - *J.I.*, Ascan Crone, Hamburg; *J.I. - Beben/Heben*, Michael Werner, Cologne; *J.I.*, Mary Boone/Michael Werner, New York.

Mimmo Jodice

Born 1934 in Naples. Lives in Naples.
Selected one-man exhibitions: 1967 - Naples, Libreria Mandragola. □ 1968 - Urbino, Teatro del Palazzo Ducale. □ 1970 - Milan, Galleria Il Diaframma. □ 1972 - Boston, City Hall. □ 1973 - Milan, SICOF. □ 1974 - Milan, Galleria Il Diaframma. □ 1975 - Naples, Modern Art Agency. □ 1978 - Naples, Studio Trisorio. □ 1980 - Alessandria, Studio Fossati. □ 1981 - Naples, Museo Diego Aragona Pignatelli Cortes; Rome, Galleria Rondanini; San Francisco, Museum of Modern Art; Bari, Spazio Immagine. □ 1982 - Venice, Biblioteca Marciana; Paris, Institut Culturel Italien; Paris, FNAC.

Selected bibliography: 1974 - M. Jodice, *Chi è devoto*, ESI, Naples. □ 1975 - M. Jodice, *Mezzogiorno: questione aperta*, Laterza, Bari. □ 1980 - M. Jodice, *Vedute di Napoli*, Mazzotta, Milan. □ 1982 - M. Jodice, *Teatralità quotidiana a Napoli*, Guida, Naples; M. Jodice, *Naples, une archéologie future*, Institut Culturel Italien, Paris; M. Jodice, *Gibellina*, Electa, Milan; "La Napoli di Mimmo Jodice," *Progresso Fotografico*, special issue, Milan. □ 1983 - "Mimmo Jodice," *I Grandi Fotografi*, Fabbri, Milan; M. Jodice/L. Ghirri, *Capri*, ERI, Rome. □ 1984 - M. Jodice, *Salemi*, Electa, Milan; M. Jodice, *Demoni e santi*, Electa, Milan.
Public collections: Albuquerque, University Art Museum; New Haven, Yale University Art Gallery; Detroit, The Detroit Institute of Modern Art; Paris, Cabinet des Estampes, Bibliothèque Nationale; Parma, Centro Studi e Archivio della Comunicazione; San Francisco, Museum of Modern Art.

Anselm Kiefer

Born 1945 in Donaueschingen. Lives in Hornbach/Odenwald.
One-man exhibitions: 1969 - Karlsruhe, Galerie am Kaiserplatz □ 1973 - Cologne, Galerie Werner; Amsterdam, Galerie im Goethe Institut/Provisorium. □ 1974 - Basel, Galerie Handschin; Rotterdam, Galerie t'Venster; Rotterdam, Arts Foundation; Cologne, Galerie Werner. □ 1975 - Cologne, Galerie Werner. □ 1976 - Cologne, Galerie Werner. □ 1977 - Bonn, Kunstverein; Amsterdam, Galerie van der Meij; Cologne, Galerie Werner. □ 1978 - Düsseldorf, Galerie Meier-Hahn; Bern, Kunsthalle. □ 1979 - Eindhoven, Stedelijk van Abbemuseum; Amsterdam, Galerie van der Meij. □ 1980 - Venice, XXXIX Biennale, German pavilion (with G. Baselitz); Mannheim, Kunstverein; Stuttgart, Kunstverein; Amsterdam, Galerie van der Meij; Munich, Galerie und Edition Friedrich-Knust; Groningen, Groninger Museum. □ 1981 - Cologne, Galerie Maenz; New York, Goodman Gallery; Milan, Galleria Ala; Munich, Galerie und Edition Friedrich-Knust; Freiburg, Kunstverein; Essen, Museum Folkwang. □ 1982 - London, Whitechapel Art Gallery; New York, Goodman Gallery; Amsterdam, Galerie van der Meij; Cologne, Galerie Maenz; New York, Boone Gallery. □ 1983 - Oslo, Henie-Onstad Foundations; London, d'Offay Gallery; Bernau, Hans Thoma-Museum; Los Angeles, Museum of Contemporary Art. □ 1984 - Cologne, Galerie Maenz; Düsseldorf, Stadtische Kunsthalle; Paris, ARC, Musée d'Art Moderne de la Ville; Bordeaux, CAPC, Musée d'Art Contemporain; Jerusalem, The Israel Museum.

Selected bibliography: 1975 - *A.K.*, Galerie t'Venster, Rotterdam Arts Foundation Verlag, Rotterdam (texts by A.van der Staay, G. Oosterhof). □ 1977 - *A.K.*, Kunstverein, Bonn (texts by D.von Stetten, E. Weiss, A. Kiefer). □ 1978 - *A.K.*, Kunsthalle, Bern (text by J. Gachnang, T. Kneubühler, A. Kiefer); A. Kiefer, *Die Donauquelle*, Michael Werner, Cologne. □ 1979 - *A.K.*, Stedelijk van Abbemuseum, Eindhoven (text by R. Fuchs). □ 1980 - *A.K.*, Kunstverein, Stuttgart (text by T. Osterwold); *A.K.*, Groninger Museum, Groningen (texts by C. Blotkamp, G. Gercken, A. Kiefer); *A.K.*, Kunstverein, Mannheim (text by R. Fuchs); A. Kiefer, *Verbrennen, verholzen, versenken, versanden*, La Biennale, Venice (texts by K. Gallwitz, R. Fuchs). □ 1981 -*A.K. - Aquarelle 1970-1980*, Kunstverein, Freiburg (text by R. Fuchs); A. Kiefer, "Gilgamesch und Enkidu im Zedernwald," *Artforum*, New York, Summer. □ 1982 -*A.K.*, Museum Folkwang, Essen/Whitechapel, London (texts by Z. Felix, N. Serota). □ 1983 - A. Kiefer, *Watercolours 1970-1982*, Anthony d'Offay, London (text by A. Seymour); *A.K.*, Hans Thoma Museum, Bernau (text by K. Schmidt). □ 1984 -*A.K.*, Städtische Kunsthalle, Düsseldorf/ARC, Musée d'Art Moderne de la Ville, Paris (texts by R. Fuchs, S. Pagé, J. Harten); *A.K.*, CAPC, Bordeaux (text by R. Denizot); *A.K.*, The Israel Museum, Jerusalem (text by S. Landau) *.

Klaus Kinold

Born 1939 in Essen.
1958-60 studied art (Kunstakademie) and history of art at the University of Munich.

From 1960 till graduating in 1968 he studied architecture at Karlsruhe Technical High School.
In 1969 opened a studio for architectural photography.
Since 1969 he has been editor of the magazine *Stahl & Form*.
Numerous publications of architectural magazines and books.
At present living in Europe.

One-man exhibitions: 1984 - Cologne, Galerie Kicken; Hamburg, PPS Galerie; Stuttgart, Fotogalerie Rössner; Frankfurt, Fotografie Forum; Munich, Fotomuseum; Rimini, Musei Comunali; Hanover, Sprengelmuseum.

Selected bibliography: 1983 - *K. Kinold, Panorama*, Rudolf Kicken, Cologne (text by G. Knapp).

Michael Klar

Born 1943 in Berlin.
Studied photography in Berlin. From 1963 to 1968, studied at the Hochschule für Gestaltung (Academy of Design) in Ulm, Visual Communications Department. Worked as an assistant there for one year.
Collaborated on the "Projekt Weltausstellung" (World Exhibition Project) in Montreal, 1967.
After graduating from the Hochschule für Gestaltung in Ulm, founded and collaborated with the "Holzäpfel Projektinstitut" (Crab-apples Project Institute). Since 1972, professor for visual design in Schwäbisch Gmünd.
Numerous guest presentations and lectures at, among others, the Hochschule für Bildende Künste (Academy of Fine Arts) and Ohio State University in Columbus.

Josef Paul Kleihues

Born 1933 in Rheine an der Ems.
After studying at the Technical University, Stuttgart (1955-1957) and Berlin (1957-59), he received a scholarship to the Ecole Nationale Supérieure des Beaux-Arts in Paris (1959-60).
Since 1962 he works as architect and town planner (in partnership with H.H. Moldenschardt, 1962-67).
In 1963 he planned the later realized pedestrian street in Gropiusstadt for the client DeGeWe (with H.H. Moldenschardt) and benches and tables in black lacquered wood.
In 1965 he took part in the competition for the German Embassy to the Holy See in Rome and worked out some residential buildings in Titus-Weg, Berlin-Reinickendorf (with H.H. Moldenschardt).
The following year he got the commission for the Old People's Club at Berlin-Schäfersee (with H.H. Moldenschardt).
In 1967 he won the "Junge Generation" art prize.
The competition project for the Bielefeld University in 1968 got premiated. In the same year he designed the later realized small studio in Berlin-Schlachtensee and the Conference Centre with hotel and exhibition halls at the Grosse Stern in Berlin, an alternative proposal to the Kongresszentrum.
In 1969 he took part in the competition for the municipal hospital of Ingolstadt. Then he was invited to the competition for the Central Workshop of the Municipal Cleaning Department in Berlin-Tempelhof where he won the first prize.
The Senator for Construction and Housing and private investor Arthur Pfaff commissioned a feasibility study for the urban design of Lewisham Towers.
Sponsored by the Senator for Construction and Housing of Berlin, in 1970 he realized the Atlas of the Berlin townscape: the development of a theoretical basis and graphic system for the assessment of spatial and architectural qualities of historical town areas.
For DeGeWe in 1971 he projected the Charlottenburg Lock, "Living by the Waterside" and the Block 270 in the Wedding renovation area which got to realization during the following years.
In 1972 he took part in the competition for the Sprengel Museum in Hanover and planned houses for Markus Lüpertz and Georg Baselitz. He developed various ceiling lamps, produced in sheet steel and aluminium.
On the behalf of the Senator for Construction and Housing and the Neukölln District Council in 1973 he was invited to the competition for the New Hospital Building in Berlin-Neukölln.
His project was realized.
In 1974, beside the competition project for a school in Borken, he established the "Dortmunder Architekturtage," since 1975 publishing also the *Dortmunder Architekturhefte*.
The second phase of the Central Workshops of the Municipal Cleaning Department in Berlin-Tempelhof was planned in 1975.
Competition projects for the Landesgalerie Düsseldorf and for the Fourth Ring in Berlin, where he won the second prize.
For EWG Wulfen he started the planning work of the residential and shopping centre Wulfen.
In 1976 he organized the first "Dortmunder Architekturausstellung," showing works of van Eyck, Hollein, Isozaki, Kleinhues, Moore, Rossi, Stirling, Ungers, Venturi and Rauch.
He took part in the competition for the School of Finance in Münster and planned the Pavilion for Documenta 1977 in Kassel.
His project Blankenheim Museum, the reconstruction of the former Hotel zur Post has been realized. At the same time he worked on the projects of a praying area for the Kevelaer Shrine on the Lower Rhine and Park Lenné, an inner-city housing concept in Berlin-Charlottenburg.
GeBau Düsseldorf realized the first building phase of the residential and shopping centre Wulfen with shopping arcade.
In 1977 (in conjunction with W.J. Siedler) he introduced the series "Models for a City" in the Berliner Morgenpost newspaper with contributions by Pehnt, Klotz, Stirling, Rossi, Moore and others.
With the competition project of Hotel Budapesterstrasse in Berlin-Schöneberg he won the third prize. As a proposal for the IBA exhibition pavilion he elaborated the feasibility study of Joachimstalplats in Berlin.
In 1979 he was appointed director of planning for the new buildings area of the international Building Exhibition, Berlin.
In the same time he worked on the reconstruction of the Ephraim Palace with an extension for the Jewish Museum in Berlin-Kreuzberg, the training centre and restaurant for the Benedictine Abbey of St. Joseph in Gerleve and the German Blade Museum and Municipal Archives in Solingen-Grafrath.
In 1980 he took part in the competition for the Pre- and Early History Museum in Frankfurt where he won the first prize. The Hochbauamt of the City of Frankfurt started with the preparatory construction work. In the same year he participated in the first Architecture Biennale in Venice, realizing a facade for the "Strada Novissima." In 1982 he developed a proposal project of the port area De Koop van Zuid in Rotterdam.
Since 1983 he has been consultant to the Senator for Construction and Housing. His project Fasanenstrasse in Berlin-Charlottenburg was awarded a prize. He received numerous architectural prizes and participates frequently in architectural exhibitions, symposia and seminars at home and abroad.

elected bibliography: 1968 - "Junge erliner Architekten," *Deutsche auzeitung*, no. 8, Stuttgart. □ 1973 - H. eilmann, J.C. Kirschenmann, H. feiffer, *Wohnungsbau/The Dwelling/ 'Habitat*, Stuttgart. □ 1974 - J.P. leihues, *Berlinatlas zu Stadtbild und tadtraum*, Berlin. □ 1975 - "Milieu, urrogat einer besseren Welt," *Der rchitekt*, no. 9, Stuttgart; Architekturzeichnungen heute," *auwelt*, no. 19, Berlin. □ 1976 - Landesgalerie Düsseldorf," *Domus*, ilan. □ 1977 - "J.P. Kleihues," special sue of *2C Construción de la Ciudad*, arcelona, June-September; Feuerstein, Gestörte Form," *Transparent*, no. 11-2, Vienna; "Hauptwerkstatt der Berliner tadtreinigung," *Bauwelt*, no. 40, Berlin; Work by J.P. Kleihues," *Space Design*, o. 10, Tokyo; "Block 270, Geschichte der lockbebaung," *Baumeister*, no. 12, unich; "J.P. Kleihues: Recent Work," *otus*, no. 15, Milan; J.P. Kleihues, *Park enné: Eine innerstädtische Wohnform*, erlin. □ 1978 - "Apologie für die rchitektur als Kunst...", *Bauwelt*, no. 1, erlin; "5 Arbeitersiedlungen im Revier," *auwelt*, no. 14, Berlin; "Park Lenné e lock 270," *Lotus*, no. 19, Milan; J.P. leihues, "Siedlung Dahlhauser Heide," *ortmunder Architekturhefte*, no. 12, ortmund. □ 1979 - H. Bofinger, H. lotz, "Architektur in Deutschland," *Das unstwerk*, no. 4-6, Baden-Baden.

nnis Kounellis

orn 1936 in Greece. Lives in Rome.
ne-man exhibitions: 1960 - Rome, alleria La Tartaruga. □ 1964 - Rome, alleria La Tartaruga. □ 1966 - Rome, alleria Arco d'Alibert. □ 1967 - Rome, alleria L'Attico; □ 1968 - Milan, Galleria las; Turin, Galleria Sperone. □ 1969 - ome, Galleria L'Attico; Paris, Galerie las; Naples, Modern Art Agency. □ 71 - Rome, Galleria L'Attico; Turin, alleria Sperone. □ 1972 - Naples, odern Art Agency; Berlin, Galerie ulima; New York, Sonnabend Gallery; ome, Galleria La Salita; Rome, Incontri ternazionali d'Arte. □ 1973 - Paris, alerie Sonnabend; Rome, Galleria 'Attico; Naples, Modern Art Agency. □ 74 - Turin, Galleria Stein; New York, nnabend Gallery; Rome, Galleria 'Attico; Berlin, Galerie Skulima. □ 1975 Naples, Modern Art Agency; Cologne, alerie Zwirner; Pescara, Galleria eroni. □ 1976 - Rome, Galleria L'Attico otel Lunetta); Milan, Galleria Ala. □ 1977 - Rotterdam, Museum Boymans van Beuningen; Lucerne, Kunstmuseum; Turin, Galleria Russo; Athens, Galerie Bernier; Naples, Museo Diego Aragona Pignatelli Cortes. □ 1978 - Mönchengladbach, Stadtisches Museum, Bologna, Galleria Diacono. □ 1979 - Düsseldorf, Galerie Fischer; Athens, Galerie Bernier; New York, Ala Gallery; Bari, Pinacoteca; Essen, Museum Folkwang; Turin, Galleria Stein. □ 1980 - Naples, Galleria Amelio; Rome, Galleria Pieroni; Paris, ARC, Musée d'Art Moderne de la Ville; Spoleto, Galleria Bonomo; Rome, Galleria Diacono; New York, Sonnabend Gallery; Düsseldorf, Galerie Fischer; Zurich, Galerie Verna. □ 1981 - Paris, Galerie Durant-Dessert; Cologne, Galerie Karsten Greve; Munich, Galerie Schelmann & Klüser; Eindhoven, Stedelijk van Abbemuseum; Milan, Galleria Ala. □ 1982 - London, Whitechapel Art Gallery; Baden-Baden, Staatliche Kunsthalle; Rome, Galleria D'Ascanio. □ 1983 - New York, Sonnabend Gallery; Düsseldorf, Galerie Fischer; Rimini, Musei Comunali; Paris, Galerie Durant-Dessert. □ 1984 - Munich, Galerie Schellmann & Klüser; Krefeld, Museum Haus Esters; New York, Sonnabend Gallery; Pesaro, Teatro Rossini, Rossini Opera Festival; Rome, Galleria Ferranti.

Selected bibliography: 1964 - *J.K.*, La Tartaruga, Rome (text by C. Vivaldi). □ 1966 - *J.K. Alfabeto*, Arco d'Alibert, Rome (poems by M. Diacono). □ 1967 - *J.K.*, L'Attico, Rome (text by A. Boatto). □ 1973 - J. Kounellis, *La via del sangue*, Collana di Perle, La Salita, Rome. □ 1977 - *J.K.*, Museum Boymans van Beuningen, Rotterdam (text by M. Calvesi). □ 1978 -M. Diacono, *J.K., Al di là del circo, nel quadro*, Mario Diacono, Bologna; *J.K.*, Städtisches Museum, Mönchengladbach (poem by A. Blok). □ 1979 - *J.K.*, Pinacoteca Provinciale, Bari (texts by C. Maltese, B. Mantura, P. Marino, J. Kounellis); *J.K.*, Museum Folkwang, Essen (texts by B. Corà and Z. Felix); R. White, "Interview at Crown Point Press," *View*, Oakland, California. □ 1980 - *J.K.*, Lucio Amelio, Naples; *J.K.*, ARC/Musée d'Art Moderne de la Ville, Paris (texts by B. Corà and S. Pagé). □ 1981 - *J.K.*, Stedelijk van Abbemuseum, Eindhoven (text by R. Fuchs) . □ 1983 - *J.K.*, Mazzotta, Milan (edited by G. Celant, texts by G. Celant, M. Diacono, C. Vivaldi, A. Boatto, T. Trini, C. Cintoli, M. Volpi Orlandini, F. Menna, R. Fuchs, M. Calvesi, J.C. Ammann, Z. Felix, B. Corà); G. Celant, "The Collision and the Cry: J.K.," *Artforum*, New York, October. □ 1984 - *J.K.*, Museum Haus Esters, Krefeld (text by M. Stockebrand); *J.K.*, Rossini Opera Festival, Pesaro (text by R.H. Fuchs).

Karl Heinz Krug

Born 1934.
After a couple of years as carpenter apprentice, he studied at the Hochschule für Gestaltung Ulm/Produktgestaltung (University for Design in Ulm), where he graduated. Editor of *Form - Zeitschrift für Gestaltung*, official magazine of the Verband Deutscher Industrie-Designer (Organisation of Germany Industrial Designers), of the Bund Deutscher Grafik-Designer (Association of German Grafic Designers) and of the Bund Freischaffender Foto-Designer (Association of free-lance photo designers). Design expertice for companies and in competitions: Product and Graphic Design; Conception for exhibitions. President of the Verband Deutscher Industrie-Designer (Association of German Industrial Designers).
Member of the Board of the Deutscher Designertag (German Designer Congress), Rat für Formgebung (Board of Design) and Gute Industrieform Hannover-Messe (Industrial Design for the Hanover Fair).

Herbert Lindinger

Born 1933 in Wels.He went to school in Darmstadt, Wels and in the monastery of Melk. From 1949 to 1953 he studied at the school of Arts and Craft in Linz/Donau. In 1953 he opened his own studio where among other projects he developed parts of the exhibition "10 Jahre Wiederaufbau o.ö. Landesregierung" (he curated the sections trade unions, City of Linz, Public Health). From 1954 to 1958 he studied visual communication and product design at the University of Design in Ulm where he also graduated. In 1956 he collaborated with Otl Aicher. From 1956 to 1960 he worked in the studio of Hans Gugelot. Since 1960 he has been setting up his own Design Development Group in Ulm. In 1968 together with Herbert Ohl and Herbert Kapitzki he founded the Institut für Umweltgestaltung in Frankfurt. Since 1971 he has worked in Hanover.

Markus Lüpertz

Born 1941 in Librec-Böhmen. Lives in Berlin and Karlsruhe.
One-man exhibitions: 1964 - Berlin, Galerie Grossgörschen 35. □ 1966 - Berlin, Galerie Grossgörschen 35; Berlin, Galerie Potsdamer. □ 1968 - Berlin, Galerie Springer; Berlin, Galerie Werner; Cologne, Galerie Hake. □ 1969 - Berlin, Galerie Bassenge; Berlin, Galerie Katz, Maison de France; Cologne, Galerie Hake. □ 1972 - Cologne, Galerie Der Spiegel. □ 1973 - Baden-Baden, Staatliche Kunsthalle; Amsterdam, Galerie im Goethe Institut/Provisorium. □ 1974 - Cologne, Galerie Werner. □ 1975 - Cologne, Galerie Werner; Hamburg, Galerie Neuendorf. □ 1976 - Cologne, Galerie Werner; Cologne, Galerie Zwirner; Amsterdam, Galerie Seriaal. □ 1977 - Hamburg, Galerie Neuendorf; Cologne, Galerie Werner; Hamburg, Kunsthalle; Eindhoven, Stedelijk van Abbemuseum. □ 1978 - Cologne, Galerie Werner; Munich, Galerie Friedrich; Amsterdam, Galerie van der Meij; Paris, Galerie Gillespie-Laage. □ 1979 - London, Whitechapel Art Gallery; London, Barker Gallery; Cologne, Kunsthalle. □ 1980 - Cologne, Galerie Werner; Amsterdam, Galerie van der Meij. □ 1981 - London, Whitechapel Art Gallery; Oslo, Galerie Riis; Cologne, Galerie Werner; Berlin, Galerie Springer; New York, Goodman Gallery; London, Waddington Galleries; Freiburg, Kunstverein. □ 1982 - Munich, Galerie Jahn; Berlin, Galerie Springer; Cologne, Galerie Werner; Berlin, Galerie Onnasch; Paris, Galerie Gillespie-Laage-Salomon; Eindhoven, Stedelijk van Abbemuseum. □ 1983 - Strasbourg, Musée d'Art Moderne; London, Waddington Galleries; Vienna, Galerie Winter; Zurich, Galerie Maeght; Salzburg, Galerie Popac; Hanover, Kestner Gesellschaft; Berlin, Daadgalerie; New York, Goodman Gallery; Berlin, Galerie Springer; Cologne, Galerie Werner; Berlin, Kunstamt Neukölln. □ 1984 - London, Waddington Galleries; Paris, Galerie Gillespie-Laage-Salomon; Munich, Maximilian Verlag; Vienna, Galerie Winter; Zurich, Galerie Maeght.

Selected bibliography: 1965 - M. Lüpertz, *Dithyrambische Malerei*, Galerie Grossgörschen 35, Berlin. □ 1966 - M. Lüpertz, *Frühling, Kunst die im Wege steht, Dithyrambische Manifest, Die Anmut*, Galerie Grossgörschen 35, Berlin. □ 1968 - M. Lüpertz, *Die Anmut des 20 Jahrhunderts wird durch die von mir erfundene Dithyrambe sichtbar gemacht*, Springer, Berlin (text by C.M. Joachimides). □ 1969 - *M.L.*, Hake Verlag, Cologne (texts by E. Ernst, M. Lüpertz); M. Lüpertz, *Dachpfannen dithyrambisch (Es lebe Caspar David Friedrich)*, Hake Verlag, Cologne (texts by C.M. Joachimides, M. Lüpertz). □ 1973 - M. Lüpertz, *Eine Festschrift-Bilder, Gouachen und Zeichnungen 1967-1973*, Staatliche Kunsthalle, Baden-Baden (texts by K. Gallwitz, G. Tabori, M. Lüpertz). □ 1975 - M. Lüpertz, *13 neue Bilder*, Hamburg (text by G. Gerkken); M. Lüpertz, *9 & 9 Gedichte*, Verlag Danckert/Hallwachs, Berlin. □ 1976 - M. Lüpertz, *Bilder 1972-1976*, Rudolf Zwirner, Cologne (texts by R. Speck, M. Lüpertz). □ 1977 - *M.L.*, Kunsthalle, Hamburg (texts by W. Hafmann, S. Holstein); *M.L.*, Kunsthalle, Bern (texts by T. Kneubühler, J. Gachnang); *M.L.*, Stedelijk van Abbemuseum, Eindhoven (text by R. Fuchs). □ 1978 - M. Lüpertz, *Fünf Bilder*, Michael Werner, Cologne (text by S. Gohr.). □ 1979 - M. Lüpertz, *Still Paintings 1977-1979*, Whitechapel, London (text by S. Gohr); M. Lüpertz, *Gemälde und Handzeichnungen 1964-1979*, Kunsthalle, Cologne (text by S. Gohr). □ 1981 - M. Lüpertz, *Und ich, ich spiele*, Springer, Berlin; M. Lüpertz, *Alice in Wonderland*, Waddington Galleries, London. □ 1982 - M. Lüpertz, *8 Plastiken*, Michael Werner, Cologne; M. Lüpertz, *Ich stand vor der Mauer aus Glas*, Springer, Berlin. □ 1983 - M. Lüpertz, *Bilder 1970-1983*, Kestner-Gesellschaft, Hanover *; M. Lüpertz, *Gedichte 1961-1983*, Michael Werner, Cologne; M. Lüpertz, *Die Bürger von Florenz*, Michael Werner, Cologne. □ 1984 - M. Lüpertz, *Sculptures in Bronze*, Waddington Galleries, London; M. Lüpertz, *Skulpturen und Plastiken*, Maeght/Lelong, Zurich (text by J. Gachnang).

Italo Lupi

Born 1934 in Cagliari.
Italian member of the International Graphic Alliance (AGI), degree in architecture at Milan Polytechnic, is currently interested in graphic design and visual communication and in plans for expository preparation. Has a professional studio in Milan. Has been teacher of publishing graphics at ISIA, Urbino and assistant to Pier Giacomo Castiglioni for the Polytechnic's drawing course. Has been art director for the magazines *Abitare, Costruire, Zodiac, Shop,* and *Il Giornale della Lombardia.*

Responsible for the image of the Triennal of Milan, consultant for manufacturing concerns and for political and civil initiative, has edited for Lombardy the new guide to the nineteen parks in Lombardy and in particular that of the Ticino Valley.
First prize for publishing graphics of the Art Directors Club of Milan in 1978. Honorable mention at World Typomundu of Prague. Various recommendations for the Compasso d'Oro Award.

***

For the Toronto exhibition, we have selected four posters, all linked by public commitment, and several posters as examples of a more complex and articulated project: the sign system for the Parco del Ticino.
The posters use letters of the alphabet a communicating signs. These letters express the "incomplete project" in a poster for "Case della Triennale." They express the need for rearrangement and reconstruction in the poster for Belice. And they express the polemical darts in the poster for the debate in architecture. Some further explanation is necessary fo the sign system project for the Parco de Ticino. The primary and political requirement of the project was the need to speak a language that could be understood by a wide range of different people, a language that would not be so blatant as to offend the frequent visitors of their beloved river. At the same time, this language had to transmit firm messages to the citizens coming in large numbers every Sunday. The more specifically technological factor of the graphic translation involved giving up th beggarly Disney-like naiveté of so much symbology used in signs for Italian and foreign parks. On the other hand, the language had to replace the habitual internationalism of a graphic iconograph devoid of any emotional charge or cultural specificity. The language had to be new, risking the loss of the easy deciphering associated with universally accepted symbols.
However, if highway signs require symbols that make them universal and easy to read, the same is not true for signals read mostly at a slow speed, in environments not overladen with signs and in situations of rustic tranquillity. An attempt was therefore made to abandon the mental laziness that desires uniform and ubiquitously equal signs an letters. Ignoring cultural specificity and different traditions, such signs assume once and for all that only the various characters derived from the standard ar

legible and acceptable. Instead, these signs used characters that, like Times Bold, are graceful and historically evocative.
The same approach was taken with the illustration problem of the sign language, which involves a symbology that is ambiguous because it is based not only on illustrations of prohibitions, but also, and above all, on suggestions for behavior. This symbology rejects the normal "Olympionic"pictograms; instead, it uses illustrative and naturalistic symbols. Ferenc Pinter, a renowned illustrator with a fine knack for bringing things together, came up with the symbolic illustrations that accompany the citizen through the park, reminding him of various points in the code of behavior.

Italo Lupi, 1984

***

Selected bibliography: 1965 - "Una casa," *Abitare*, Milan, April. □ 1967 - "Una libreria universitaria a Milano," *Domus*, Milan. □ 1969 - I. Lupi, "Il duomo nello specchio," *Casabella*, Milan, September. □ 1970 - "Spazi settecenteschi o quasi," *Abitare*, Milan. □ 1976 - *Perfect Team Work from Italy*, Novum Gebrauchs Graphic, Munich, March. □ 1980 -*Casabella*, no. 454, Milan; *Graphis Annual*, Zurich. □ 1981 - "Il campo della grafica italiana," *Rassegna*, no. 6, Milan; I. Lupi, "Un contenitore di eventi" and "Le regole del gioco," *Rassegna*, no. 6, Milan; *Atlante del design italiano 1940/1980*, Fabbri, Milan; *Il progetto grafico*, Milan. □ 1982 - *Italian Revolution*, La Jolla Museum, La Jolla; "Exhibit Design," *Rassegna*, no. 10, Milan. □ 1983 - *Visual Design 1933-1983*, Milan; "Nuova sede di un consorzio," *Casabella*, Milan, June; "Graffiti di grafica editoriale," *Ottagono*, Milan, September. □ 1984 - *La prima biennale della grafica*, Cattolica; "Attraverso luce e acqua," *Domus*, Milan, October; "Comunicazione e territorio," *Annuario Docter*, Milan.

Gerhard Merz

Born 1947 in Mammendorf. Lives in Munich.
One-man exhibitions: 1975 - Munich, Kunstraum. □ 1976 - Munich, Galerie Friedrich; Munich, Galerie Schöttle; Düsseldorf, Galerie Fischer. □ 1978 - Düsseldorf, Galerie Fischer; Munich, Kunstforum, Städtische Galerie im Lembachhaus. □ 1979 - Düsseldorf, Galerie Fischer; Munich, Galerie Schellmann & Klüser. □ 1980 - Zurich, InK; New York, Sperone-Westwater-Fischer Gallery. □ 1981 - Zurich, Galerie Fischer; Munich, Galerie Schellman & Klüser. □ 1982 - Zurich, Galerie Fischer; Munich, Galerie Schellmann & Klüser. □ 1983 - Düsseldorf, Galerie Fischer; St. Gallen, Galerie Kulli; Edinburgh, Scottish Arts Council. □ 1984 - Kassel, Kunstverein; Geneva, Galerie Malacorda; Zurich, Galerie Kaufmann.

Selected bibliography: 1975 - *G.M.*, Kunstraum, Munich. □ 1978 - G. Merz, *5 Bilder*, Schellmann & Klüser, Munich. □ 1982 - G. Merz, *Zuschauer, I love my time, Beton*, Kunstraum, Munich; G. Merz, *Peace, Kinfischer blue, Olympia, Geld und Glück, Schwarz-Kupfer-Gold, Kopf hoch, Celebration area, Die Lage ist normal*, Schellmann & Klüser, Munich; G. Merz, *Serengeti darf nicht sterben*, Schellmann & Klüser, Munich. □ 1983 - G. Merz, *Mondo cane*, Galerie Tanit, Munich.

Mario Merz

Born 1925 in Milan. Lives in Turin.
One-man exhibitions: 1954 - Turin, Galleria La Bussola. □ 1962 - Turin, Galleria Notizie. □ 1968 - Turin, Galleria Sperone. □ 1969 - Rome, Galleria L'Attico; Turin, Galleria Sperone; Paris, Galerie Sonnabend. □ 1970 - Düsseldorf, Galerie Fischer; New York, Sonnabend Gallery, and Downtown, Sonnabend Auxiliary Space; Milan, Galleria Lambert; Cologne, Kunstmarket Videogalerie Schum, Galerie Fischer. □ 1971 - Turin, Galleria Sperone; New York, Sonnabend Gallery; New York, Weber Gallery. □ 1972 - Minneapolis, Walker Art Center; London, Wendler Gallery. □ 1973 - New York, Weber Gallery.□ 1974 - Berlin, Haus am Lützowplatz; Tortona, Cascina Ova; London, Wendler Gallery; Florence, Galleria Area. □ 1975 - Basel, Kunsthalle; London, ICA. □ 1976 - Rome, Galleria Sperone; Genoa, Galleriaforma; Turin, Galleria Sperone; Pescara, Galleria Pieroni; Naples, Museo Diego Aragona Pignatelli; Turin, Galleria Russo; Dusseldorf, Galerie Fischer. □ 1977 - Milan, Galleria Ala; Zurich, Galerie Verna; Naples, Galleria Amelio (with Marisa Merz). □ 1978 - Brescia, Via delle Battaglie 55a; Turin, Galleria Russo; Athens, Bernier Gallery. □ 1979 - Essen, Museum Folkwang; New York, Sperone-Westwater-Fischer Gallery; Paris, Galerie Durand-Dessert; Zurich, Galerie Verna; Milan, Galleria Toselli; Rome, Galleria De Crescenzo. □ 1980 - London, Whitechapel Art Gallery; Brussels, Galerie Baronian; Turin, Galleria Stein; Eindhoven, Stedelijk van Abbemuseum; New York, Sperone-Westwater-Fischer Gallery; Milan, Galleria Ala. □ 1981 -Düsseldorf, Galerie Fischer; Paris, ARC, Musée d'Art Moderne de la Ville; Zurich, Galerie Fischer; Basel, Kunsthalle; Turin, Galleria Russo; Turin, Galleria Stein; Naples, Galleria Amelio. □ 1982 - New York, Sperone-Westwater-Fischer Gallery; Rome, Galleria Diacono; Venice, California, Flow Ace Gallery; Hanover, Kestner Gesellschaft; Bari, Galleria Bonomo; Bologna, Galleria Comunale d'Arte Moderna. □ 1983 - Stockholm, Moderna Museet; London, d'Offay Gallery; Rome, Galleria Pieroni; San Marino, Palazzo Congressi ed Esposizioni; Basel, Galerie Buchmann. □ 1984 - Los Angeles, U.C. Irvine Art Gallery; Buffalo-New York, Albright-Knox Art Gallery; New York, Sperone-Westwater Gallery; Düsseldorf, Galerie Fischer; Chagny, Au Fond de la Cour à Droite; Turin, Galleria Stein.

Selected bibliography: 1962 - *Dipinti di Merz*, Notizie, Turin (text by C. Lonzi). □ 1968 - *M.M.*, Sperone, Turin (text by G. Celant). □ 1969 - *M.M.*, Ileana Sonnabend, Paris (text by M. Sonnabend). □ 1970 - M. Merz, *Fibonacci 1202 - Mario Merz 1970*, Sperone, Turin. □ 1972 - *M.M.*, Walker Art Center, Minneapolis (interview by R. Koshaleck). □ 1973 - M. Merz, *It Is Possible to Have a Space with Tables for 88 People as It Is Possible to Have a Space with Tables for No One*, John Weber, New York. □ 1974 - *M.M.*, Haus am Lützowplatz, Berlin (texts by K. Ruhrberg. W. Schmied, M. Merz). □ 1975 - *M.M.*, Kunsthalle, Basel (text by M. Merz). □ 1976 - M. Merz, *987*, Lucio Amelio, Naples. □ 1979 - *M.M.*, Museum Folkwang, Essen (texts by G. Celant, Z. Felix, M. Merz); G. Celant, "The Artist as a Nomad,", *Artforum*, New York, December. □ 1980 - *M.M*, Whitechapel Art Gallery, London (text by G. Celant); *M.M.*, Stedelijk van Abbemuseum, Eindhoven (texts by G. Celant, M. Merz). □ 1981 - *M.M.*, Studio W Kwietniu, Warsaw (text by M. Merz); *M.M.*, ARC/Musée d'Art Moderne de la Ville, Paris/Kunsthalle, Basel (text by M. Merz, interview by J.C. Ammann and S. Pagé). □ 1982 - M. Diacono, *M.M.*, Mario Diacono, Rome; *M.M.*, Kestner-Gesellschaft, Hanover (text by C.A. Haenlein); *M.M.*, Galleria Comunale d'Arte Moderna, Bologna (texts by M. Bandini, M. Merz). □ 1983 - *M.M.*, Moderna Museet, Stockholm (texts by O.

Granath, C.A. Haenlein, M. Merz); *M.M.*, The Israel Museum, Jerusalem (text by J. Fischer); *M.M.*, Mazzotta, Milan (edited by G. Celant) *. □ 1984 - *M.M. -Pittore in Africa*, Sperone-Westwater, New York; *M.M.*, Albright-Knox Art Gallery, Buffalo.

Nino Migliori

Born 1926 in Bologna. Lives in Bologna. One-man exhibitions: 1967 - Montreal, Expo'67. □ 1974 - Milan, Il Diaframma; Varese, Galleria Broletto. □ 1975 - Trieste, Adriaclub Italia; Lodi, Museo Centrocivico; Amsterdam, Canon Photo Gallery; Bologna, Galleria d'Arte Moderna; Parigi, FNAC; Roma, Calcografia Nazionale. □ 1976 - Bologna, Arte Vetrina. □ 1977 - Parma, Centro Studi e Archivio della Comunicazione; Milan, Il Diaframma/Canon. □ 1978 - Arles, Festival; Bologna, Galleria d'Arte Moderna; Francavilla al Mare; Piacenza, S. Agostino. □ 1980 - Bologna, Galleria d'Arte Moderna; Locarno, Galleria Flaviana; Gavirate, Chiostro di Voltorre; Bucharest, Sala Tudor Arzeghi. □ 1981 - Roma, Palazzo delle Esposizioni; Cattolica, Galleria Comunale S. Croce; Ravenna, Pinacoteca Comunale. □ 1982 - Salerno, La Boite.

***

Photoutopia
A worker of images only has to make his own work known if he wants to make its ideology explicit. For this reason, I do not wish to explain my work here; I would rather discuss certain ideas that have been part of my activity for some time now.
Several years ago, I stopped believing in "appended" photography. I no longer thought of the image as something to contemplate with awe and wonder. Instead of favoring "auteur" photo over some sort of "non-auteur" photo, I no longer distinguish between the photo of the "artist" and the photo of the "professional." Certain significant and frequently used terms — artist, art, sublime — are removed from contingency and from everyday life; others — professional, profession, fee — are tied to vulgar marketing. Actually, however, the whole issue boils down to circuits. I refuse to sell my photographs in limited editions, because this goes against the very essence of photography as unlimited reproduction. The original is a *unicum*. It could be given a large space as a new form of photography, linked more to the publishing world than to the gallery system: in editions of books with a lithographic text and photographs printed by the photofinish process. The publisher could specify the number of copies, the type of material. Popular success would lead to new editions retaining the same characteristics. The prices, while leaving room for decent royalties for the photographer, would make these books generally accessible. The photographer would be seen as a writer, and thus photography would be seen as narrative. This would lead to the development of a new kind of library, a "photothèque," allowing us to consult and compare various "authors."
This could help us overcome the ambiguities caused by a misinterpretation of the genres: photographs linked to fleeting moments, reportages, brief sketches, illustrations; all are lumped together with creative photographs — still lifes, studio compositions, architecture. This is tantamount to throwing together and failing to distinguish between an oil painting, an environment, a sculpture, a graphic work. The first group of photographs is tied chiefly to physical efficiency, quick reflexes, all-around adaptability, and being in the right place at the right time. Creative photographs, on the other hand, usually implement a project and are tied to a story board, participating in a larger linguistic discourse.
Even though photography may be articulated in this way, I do not feel that this form is sufficiently expressive. Several years ago, I formulated my opinion provocatively in a work entitled *Photography Is Dead, Long Live Videography*. I felt then, and am even more convinced today, that photography cannot replace words. The swiftly evolving technology has produced high-definition video cameras (perhaps superior to photo cameras) and printing processes that can block the isolated image in real time. Photographers, no longer hampered by the physical limits of the camera, will have greater possibilities of choosing images and organizing them more effectively in terms of their ideologies. The video cassette can be likened to a container of words; different people can use it to express entirely diverse concepts. Video has many different values, one of which, I believe, is that it can be used to replace exhibition catalogues, i.e., as video catalogues, which, beyond their obviously low costs, would allow involvement by more people. These users would be fascinated by the "real" observation of the art works, the possibility of immediately developing photos of interesting images, including text pages (which is enormously important from a pedagogical viewpoint). The video catalogue could be transformed into a video exhibition, from which we would all benefit. Hence: photography as provocation, transcending the limits imposed by conventional codes, as a language and its mass participation in education.

Nino Migliori, 1984

***

Selected bibliography: 1958 - G. Turroni, "Fotografie astratte di A.M.," *Ferrania*, no. 8, Milan, August. □ 1959 - G. Turroni, "Antonio Migliori's Abstract Photos," *Ferrania*, no. 1, Milan; G. Turroni, *Nuova fotografia italiana*, Milan. □ 1961 - "Des photographes de Bologne (Italie) exposent au Musée Municipal," *L'Echo du Centre*, Paris, June. □ 1972 - G. Ruggeri, "M.," *Progresso Fotografico*, no. 11, Milan, November. □ 1973 - "A.M.," *Tutti Fotografi*, no. 2, February. □ 1974 - A.C. Quintavalle, "I muri di A.M.," *Il Diaframma/Fotografia Italiana*, no. 191, Milan, April; *Progresso Fotografico*, no. 4, Milan, April; G. Turroni, "I Migliori," *Il Diaframma/Fotografia Italiana*, no. 5, Milan, May; G. Ruggeri, "I muri di A.M.," *Il Diaframma/Fotografia Italiana*, no. 195, Milan, September. □ 1975 - E.L. Basaldella, "A.M.," *Speciale Nordest*, no. 28, Milan, May; R. Salbitani, "Fotografia artistica in Italia 1947-1960," *Progresso Fotografico*, no. 9, Milan, September; G. Boudaille, "Photographes italiens à Paris," *L'Oeil*, Paris, October; *A.M.*, Canon photo Gallery, Amsterdam (text by L. Merlo). □ 1977 - *A.M.*, (edited by A.C. Quintavalle), CSAC Università, Parma *; S. Dahò, "A.M., foto d'artista," *Il Fotografo*, September; "Omaggio a M.," *Progresso Fotografico*, Milan, September; A. Colombo, "A.M.," *Progresso Fotografico*, Milan, November; M.G. Guglielmi, "La Fotografia analitica di N.M.," *Art Dimension*, no. 11-12, Rome. □ 1978 - H. Schöttle, *Lexicon der Fotografie*, Cologne. □ 1979 - C. Gentili, "Fotografia gestuale di N.M.," *Quaderni del Verri*, Bologna*; A.C. Quintavalle, "N.M.," *Enciclopedia pratica per fotografare*, Fabbri, Milan. □ 1980 - "N.M.," *Progresso Fotografico*, Milan, May. □ 1982 - "N.M.," *I Grandi Fotografi*, Fabbri, Milan (text by G. Celli).

Reinhard Mucha

Born 1950 in Düsseldorf. Lives in Düsseldorf.

Mimmo Paladino

Born 1948 in Paduli, Benevento. Lives in Paduli and Milan.
One-man exhibitions: 1976 - Brescia, Nuovi Strumenti; Bologna - Galleria d'Arte Duemila. ☐ 1977 - Milan, Galleria De Ambrogi-Cavellini; Naples, Galleria Amelio; Milan, Galleria dell'Ariete. ☐ 1978 - Turin, Galleria Persano; Cologne, Galerie Maenz; Milan, Galleria Toselli; Munich, Galerie Tanit. ☐ 1979 - Geneva, Centre d'Art Contemporain; Naples, Galleria Amelio; Rotterdam, Galerie t'Venster; Modena, Galleria Mazzoli; Amsterdam, Art & Project. ☐ 1980 - Cologne, Galerie Maenz; Turin, Galleria Persano; Zurich, Galerie Verna; Karlsruhe, Badischer Kunstverein; New York, Goodman Gallery; New York, Nosei Gallery; Milan, Galleria dell'Ariete; Munich, Galerie Tanit. ☐ 1981 - Naples, Galleria Amelio; Rome, Galleria Diacono; Basel, Kunstmuseum; Hanover, Kestner Gesellschaft; Mannheim, Kunstverein; Groningen, Groninger Museum; Bologna, Galleria d'Arte Moderna; Milan, Galleria Toselli; Munich, Schellmann & Klüser; Zurich, Bischofberger. ☐ 1982 - St. Gallen, Galerie Buchmann; London, Waddington Galleries; Humlebaek, Louisiana Museum of Modern Art; Wuppertal, Museumverein; Erlangen, Städtische Galerie; Munich, Schellmann & Klüser; Naples, Galleria Amelio; New York, Goodman Gallery. ☐ 1983 - Capodistria, Galerija Meduza; Stockholm, Galerie Engström; Modena, Galleria Mazzoli; New York, Sperone-Westwater Gallery; Rome, Galleria Sperone; Munich, Galerie Thomas; Newport, Los Angeles, Newport Harbor Art Museum; Milan, Galleria Toselli. ☐ 1984 - London, Waddington Galleries; Lyon, Musée St. Pierre.

Selected bibliography: 1968 - A. Bonito Oliva, *M.P.*, Di Portici, Naples. ☐ 1975 - "M.P.," *L'Arte Moderna*, n. 111, Fabbri, Milan. ☐ 1976 - F. Menna, *Le immagini sono riflessi bruciati*, Cavellini, Brescia. ☐ 1978 - B. Radice, "L'arte non serve e io sono un antieroe" (interview), *Modo*, n. 14, Milan, November. ☐ 1980 - J.C. Ammann, *M.P.*, Skira Annuel, Geneva; A. Bonito Oliva, *EN DE RE*, Emilio Mazzoli, Modena; *M.P.*, Kunsthalle, Basel/Museum Folkwang, Essen/Stedelijk Museum, Amsterdam; M. Piller, "M.P.," *Artforum*, New York, April; *M.P.*, Kunstverein, Karlsruhe (texts by M. Schwarz. A. Franke, W.M. Faust); A. Bonito Oliva, *La transavanguardia italiana*, Giancarlo Politi, Milan; "M.P.," *Spazio Umano*, no. 0, Milan, December; I. Puliafito, M. Paladino, *Ore solari, l'intensità del personale*. ☐ 1981 - *M.P.*, Mario Diacono, Rome (text by M. Diacono); "M.P.," *The Print Collector's Newsletter*, New York, April; *M.P.: Zeichnungen 1976-1981*, Groninger Museum, Groningen/ Kunstmuseum, Basel (texts by J.C. Ammann, D. Köpplin, A. Wildermuth); *M.P.*, Galleria d'Arte Moderna, Bologna (text by A. Bonito Oliva). ☐ 1982 - *M.P. - Bilder und Zeichnungen 1981-1982*, Verlag Schellmann & Klüser, Munich (text by A. Pohlen); *M.P.*, Buchmann, St. Gallen (texts by A. Bonito Oliva, A. Wildermuth); *M.P. - Neue Mappenwerke der Edition*, Verlag Shellmann & Klüser, Munich; M. Paladino, R. Comi, "Sul nichilismo dell'uomo contemporaneo," *Spazio Umano*, no. 4, Milan, July-September; M. Paladino, "Una piccola storia," *Tau/ma*, no. 7, Bologna. ☐ 1983 - *Paladino by Thomas*, Thomas, Munich; M. Paladino, *Giardino chiuso*, Emilio Mazzoli, Modena; D. Berger, "M.P. - Interview," *The Print Collector's Newsletter*, no. 2, New York, May-June; M. Paladino, *Groups VI*, Waddington Galleries, London; *M.P.*, Sperone-Westwater, New York. ☐ 1984 -G. Dorfles, *M.P.*, Mazzotta, Milan *; *M.P.*, Waddington Galleries, London.

Giulio Paolini

Born 1940 in Genoa. Lives in Turin.
One-man exhibitions: 1964 - Rome, Galleria La Salita. ☐ 1965 - Turin, Galleria Notizie. ☐ 1966 - Milan, Galleria dell'Ariete. ☐ 1967 - Turin, Teatro Stabile, Sala delle Colonne; Turin, Libreria Stampatori; Venice, Galleria del Leone; Turin, Galleria Stein. ☐ 1968 - Rome, Libreria dell'Oca; Turin, Galleria Notizie. ☐ 1969 - Milan, Galleria De Nieubourg; Rome, Galleria La Tartaruga; Venice, Galleria del Leone. ☐ 1970 - Rome, Qui Arte Contemporanea; Turin, Galleria Notizie. ☐ 1971 - Milan, Galleria dell'Ariete; Rome, Galleria La Salita; Turin, Galleria Notizie; Turin, Libreria Stampatori; Brescia, Studio C; Cologne, Galerie Maenz; Rome, Incontri Internazionali d'Arte. ☐ 1972 - Turin, Galleria Notizie; New York, Sonnabend Gallery; Bari, Galleria Bonomo; Naples, Modern Art Agency. ☐ 1973 -Turin, Galleria Notizie; Milan, Galleria Toselli; Milan, Galleria Lambert; Rome, Galleria L'Attico; Rome, Galleria Sperone Fischer; London, Royal College of Art; Zurich, Galerie Verna; Milan, Studio Marconi. ☐ 1974 - Naples, Modern Art Agency; New York, Museum of Modern Art; Genoa, Galleriaforma; Cologne, Galerie Maenz; Bari, Galleria Bonomo; Bolzano, Galleria Il Sole. ☐ 1975 - Turin, Galleria Notizie; Zurich, Galerie Verna; Munich, Galerie Art in Progress; Cologne, Galerie Maenz; Rome, Galleria D'Alessandro-Ferranti; Bologna, Studio G7; Verona, Galleria Ferrari. ☐ 1976 - Genoa, Samangallery; Turin, Multipli; Milan, Studio Marconi; Paris, Galerie Lambert; Parma, Università degli Studi, Istituto di Storia dell'Arte; Florence, Galleria Area; Rome, Incontri Internazionali d'Arte; Cologne, Galerie Maenz; Brescia, Galleria Banco. ☐ 1977 - New York, Sperone-Westwater-Fischer Gallery; Zurich, Galerie Verna; Mönchengladbach, Städtisches Museum; London, Lisson Gallery; Mannheim, Kunstverein; Rome, Galleria Ferranti; Cologne, Galerie Maenz. ☐ 1978 - Naples, Museo Diego Aragona Pignatelli Cortes; Paris, Galerie Lambert; Turin, Galleria Stein; Spoleto, Galleria Bonomo; Brussels, Galerie Baronian; Bologna, Galleria Diacono; Paris, ARC/Musée d'Art Moderne de la Ville; Cologne, Galerie Maenz. ☐ 1979 - Rome, Galleria dell'Oca; London, Lisson Gallery; Athens, Galerie Bernier; Milan, Studio Marconi. ☐ 1980 - Zurich, Galerie Verna; Amsterdam, Stedelijk Museum; Oxford, Museum of Modern Art; Rome, Galleria Ferranti. ☐ 1981 - Turin, Galleria Stein; Lucerne, Kunstmuseum; Cologne, Galerie Maenz; Brescia, Galleria Banco; Rome, Galleria Nazionale d'Arte Moderna. ☐ 1982 - Milan, Padiglione d'Arte Contemporanea; Bielfeld, Kunsthalle; Wuppertal, von der Heydt Museum; Berlin, Neuer Berliner Kunstverein; Milan, Galleria Lambert; Bari, Galleria Bonomo; Hamburg, Raum für Kunst; Lyon-Villeurbanne, Le Nouveau Musée; Tokyo, The Japan Foundation, Laforet Museum; Paris, Galerie Lambert. ☐ 1983 - Turin, Galleria Stein; Cologne, Galerie Maenz; Pescara, Galleria De Domizio. ☐ 1984 - Los Angeles, Los Angeles Institute of Contemporary Art; Lyon-Villeurbanne, Le Nouveau Musée; Milan, Studio Marconi; Spoleto, XXVII Festival dei Due Mondi.

Selected bibliography: 1965 - *G.P.*, Notizie, Turin (text by C. Lonzi). ☐ 1966 - *G.P.*, L'Ariete, Milan (text by C. Lonzi). ☐ 1967 - *G.P.*, Galleria del Leone, Venice (text by G. Celant). ☐ 1968 - G. Paolini, *Ciò che non ha limiti e che per sua stessa natura non ammette limitazioni di sorta*, Turin. ☐ 1970 - *G.P.*, Notizie, Turin (text by M. Volpi Orlandini). ☐ 1972 - G. Celant, *G.P.*, Sonnabend Press, New York/Paris. ☐ 1973 - *G.P.*, Studio Marconi, Milan (texts by A. Bonito Oliva, G. Paolini). ☐ 1974 - *G.P.*, Museum of Modern Art, New York (text by

C. Rosevear). □ 1975 - G. Paolini, *Idem*, Einaudi, Turin (text by I. Calvino); G. Paolini, *Ennesima*, Yvon Lambert, Paris. □ 1976 - *G.P.*, Studio Marconi, Milan (texts by T. Trini, G. Paolini); *G.P.*, (edited by A.C. Quintavalle), Istituto di Storia dell'Arte, Parma. □ 1977 - *G.P.*, Städtisches Museum, Mönchengladbach (text by J. Cladders); G. Paolini, *Sei illustrazioni per gli scritti sull'arte antica di Johann J. Winckelmann*, Mello/Persano, Turin; *G.P.*, G. de Vries, Cologne (texts by J. Cladders and others). □ 1978 - G. Paolini, *Del bello intelligibile*, ARC/Musée d'Art Moderne de la Ville, Paris (texts by S. Pagé, G. Paolini); *G.P.*, Mario Diacono, Bologna (text by M. Diacono). □ 1979 - G. Paolini, *Atto unico in tre quadri*, Mazzotta/Studio Marconi (texts by C. Bertelli, G. Vattimo); G. Paolini, *Statements*, Verna, Zurich. □ 1980 - *G.P. - Premio Bolaffi 1980*, Bolaffi, Turin (text by F. Menna); *G.P.*, Stedelijk Museum, Amsterdam/Museum of Modern Art, Oxford (texts by H. Szeemann, D. Elliott). □ 1981 - G. Paolini, *Hortus Clausus/Wewrke und Schriften 1960-1980*, Kunstmuseum, Lucerne (texts by M. Kunz, M. Wechsler). □ 1982 - G. Paolini, *Del bello intelligibile*, Kunsthalle, Bielefeld (texts by E. Franz, W.M. Faust); R. Denizot, G. Paolini, *De bouche à oreille*, Yvon Lambert, Paris; G. Paolini, *Questo disegno, questo testo*, Pozzilli, Rome. □ 1983 - G. Paolini, *L'Arte e lo spazio*, Noire, Turin (text by G. Vattimo). □ 1984 - G. Paolini, *L'exil du cygne*, Fratelli Alinari Stamperia d'Arte, Florence (text by G. Celant); G. Paolini, *Figures - Images (1960-1983)*, 2 volumes, Le Nouveau Musée, Lyon (project, selection, lay-out, and texts by the artist; interviews by A. Bonito Oliva, F. Minervino, N. Orengo, P. Tortonese, M. Volpi Orlandini) *; G. Paolini, *La casa di Lucrezio*, Festival dei Due Mondi, Spoleto (texts by B. Mantura, I. Panicelli).

A.R. Penck (Ralf Winller)

Born 1939 in Dresden. Lives in London. One-man exhibitions: 1969 - Cologne, Galerie Werner. □ 1971 - Munich, Galerie Friedrich; Cologne, Galerie Werner; Krefeld, Museum Haus Lange. □ 1972 - Antwerp, Wide White Space Gallery; Basel, Kunstmuseum. □ 1973 - Frankfurt, Galerie Loehn; Milan, L'Uomo e l'Arte; Halifax, Leonowens Gallery, Nova Scotia, College of Art & Design; Copenhagen, Daner Galleriet. □ 1974 - Cologne, Galerie Werner; Vienna, Galerie nächst St. Stephan; Antwerp, Wide White Space Gallery. □ 1975 - Hamburg, Galerie Neuendorf; Bern, Kunsthalle; Eindhoven, Stedelijk van Abbemuseum; Cologne, Galerie Werner. □ 1977 - Amsterdam, Galerie Seriaal. □ 1978 - Basel, Kunstmuseum; Mannheim, Kunstverein; Cologne, Museum Ludwig; Amsterdam, Galerie van der Meij; Berlin, Galerie Springer. □ 1979 - Cologne, Galerie Werner; Rotterdam, Museum Boymans van Beuningen. 1980 - Munich, Galerie Jahn; Leverkusen, Stadtisches Museum, Schloss Morsbroich; Cologne, Galerie Werner. □ 1981 - Basel, Kunstmuseum; Amsterdam, Galerie van der Meij; Ghent, GEWAD; Hamburg, Galerie Neuendorf; Cologne, Josef Haubrick-Kunsthalle. □ 1982 - Cologne, Galerie Werner; New York, Sonnabend Gallery; Naples, Galleria Amelio; Milan, Galleria Toselli; Milan, Studio d'Arte Cannaviello; Paris, Galerie Gillespie-Laage-Salomon; London, Waddington Galleries. □ 1983 - Naples, Galleria Amelio; Toronto, Yarlow-Salzman Gallery; Cologne, Galerie Werner; Berlin, Galerie Springer; Paris, Galerie Gillespie-Laage-Salomon; Rome, Galleria Sprovieri. □ 1984 - New York, Boone-Werner Gallery; Milan, Studio d'Arte Cannaviello; Berlin, Galerie Springer; Zurich, Galerie Maeght-Lelong; London, Waddington Galleries; Tokyo, Akira Ikeda Gallery; Venice, XLI Biennale, German Pavilion (with L. Baumgarten); Munich, Galerie Knust.

***

The principles which have led me to this point have now become the object of critical interest.
The methods I used are becoming comprehensible. In the shadow of two towers, the quality of decisiveness becomes testable. The extent to which the work is really a kind of model, the extent to which the work now truly establishes a criterion can also be clarified.
What is patriotism?
Hager and Sitte didn't want dialogue. They wanted the techniques of the power structure instead.
Kettner said: They took it out of my hands!
Don't FREUD yourself too soon! [*In German Freud is a homonym of "freut": i.e., "Don't get too excited too soon!"*]
Sitte gives *Stern* an interview! What arrogance of power. You've locked yourselves out of the doors you said were garbage!
My foot's in the trap and your head's in the noose.
But what's the point. When philosophy sinks to the niveau of *Schrebergarten* (a weekend garden), the weekend garden becomes the main contents of philosophy. This is the point you've brought things to! We're still talking to each other, even when you're silent. Walesa showed us. There must be a corrective to the moods and whims of authority.
My old friends: The West isn't the way you thought it was.
My old enemies: The West isn't the way you think it is.
Where should German culture, German art go from here?
You're not so different from us.
If the West gets stuck half way on the road to civilization like the East has got stuck half way on the road to revolution, every step forward, burdened with a counterimage, will lose its momentum and its force until at last the old ways will join with the tradition of irrationalism and take over. The most extreme irrationalism, however, is war.
What is the future of the new German Expressionism?

alpha ypsilon (a.r. penck), 1981

***

Selected bibliography: 1970 - A.R. Penck, *Standart Making*, Verlag Jahn and Klüser, Munich; A.R. Penck, *Was ist Standart*, Verlag König, Cologne/New York. □ 1971 - A.R. Penck, *Ich-Standart Literatur*, Edition Agentzia, Paris; *A.R.P. - Zeichen als Verständigung*, Museum Haus Lange, Krefeld. □ 1973 - A.R. Penck, "Standart-Deskriptive Einführung 1 + 2," *L'Uomo e l'arte*, Milan. □ 1974 - A.R. Penck, *Europäisches Sonett*, Wide White Space, Antwerp. □ 1975 - *P mal TM*, Kunsthalle, Bern/Stedelijk van Abbemuseum, Eindhoven (texts by D. Köpplin, A.R. Penck). □ 1976 - A.R. Penck, *Ich bin ein Buch, Kaufe mich jetzt*, Verlagsgesellschaft, Greno. □ 1978 - *A.R.P.Y. - Zeichnungen bis 1975*, Kunstmuseum, Basel (texts by D. Köpplin, J. Gachnang, A.R. Penck); A.R. Penck, *Der Begriff Modell-Erinnerungen an 1973*, Michael Werner, Cologne; Y. (A.R. Penck), *Vierzehnteilige Arbeit 1977*, Jahn, Munich/Werner, Cologne. □ 1979 - *Concept-Conceptruimte*, Museum Boymans van Beuningen, Rotterdam (texts by P. Groot, J. Gachnang, M. Visser, A.R. Penck); *Y. Rot-Grün/Grün-Rot*, Michael Werner, Cologne; A.R. Penck, *Sanfte Theorie über Arsch, Asche und Vegetation*, Groninger Museum, Groningen; J. Immendorff, A.R. Penck, *Deutschland mal Deutschland*, Verlag Rogner & Bernhard, Munich. □ 1980 - *Bilder 1967-1977*, Jahn, Munich;

A.R.P. - Zeichnungen und Aquarelle, Städtisches Museum, Leverkusen. □ 1981 - A.R. Penck, *Ende im Osten*, Rainer Verlag, Berlin; *A.R.P.*, Kunsthalle, Cologne (texts by S. Gohr, A.R. Penck); A.R. Penck, *Je suis un livre, achète-moi maintenant*, Gillespie/Laage/Salomon, Paris. □ 1982 - *A.R.P.*, Gillespie/Laage/Salomon, Paris; *A.R.P.*, Waddington Galleries, London. □ 1983 - *A.R.P. - Skulpturen*, Michael Werner, Cologne. □ 1984 - *A.R.P.*, Galerie Maeght/Lelong, Zurich; *A.R.P.*, Galerie Beveler, Basel; *A.R.P.*, Boone/Werner, New York (text by A.R. Penck); *A.R.P.*, La Biennale, Venice (texts by J. Cladders, A.R. Penck) *; A.R. Penck, *Männer*, Michael Werner, Cologne; *A.R.P.*, Akira Ikeda, Tokyo (text by R. Colvocoressi).

Giuseppe Penone

Born 1947 in Garessio. Lives in Turin. One-man exhibitions: 1968 - Turin, Deposito d'Arte Presente. □ 1969 - Turin, Galleria Sperone. □ 1970 - Munich, Aktionsraum I; Milan, Galleria Toselli. □ 1972 - Cologne, Galerie Maenz. □ 1973 - Turin, Multipli; Turin, Galleria Sperone; Milan, Galleria Toselli; Frankfurt, Galerie Lüpke; Cologne, Galerie Maenz; Rome, Galleria Sperone Fischer. □ 1974 - Rotterdam, Galerie 't Venster; Florence, Galleria Schema. □ 1975 - Cologne, Galerie Maenz; Genoa, Samangallery; Turin, Galleria Sperone; New York, Sperone Gallery. □ 1976 - Brescia, Galleria Nuovi Strumenti; Milan, Studio De Ambrogi. □ 1977 - Lucerne, Kunstmuseum. □ 1978 - Cologne, Galerie Maenz; Cologne, Galerie Zwirner; Baden-Baden, Staatliche Kunsthalle; Milan, Galleria Ala; Essen, Museum Folkwang; Rome, Galleria De Crescenzo. □ 1979 - Paris, Galerie Durand-Dessert; Bologna, Studio G7; Zurich, Halle für Internationale Neue Kunst. □ 1980 - Zurich, Halle für Internationale Neue Kunst; Amsterdam, Galerie van der Meij; Amsterdam, Stedelijk Museum; Bremerhaven, Kabinett für Aktuelle Kunst; Mönchengladbach, Ausstellungsstudio; Turin, Galleria Stein; London, Lisson Gallery; Ghent, Gewad. □ 1981 - New York, Ala Gallery; Düsseldorf, Galerie Fischer. □ 1982 - Mönchengladbach, Museum Abteiberg; New York, Ala Gallery; Zurich, Galerie Fischer; Milan, Galleria Ala. □ 1983 - Milan, Galleria Ala; Turin, Galleria Stein; Paris, Galerie Durand-Dessert; Ottawa, The National Gallery of Canada. □ 1984 - Los Angeles, Fisher Gallery, University of Southern California; Fort Worth, Fort Worth Art Museum; Chicago, Museum of Contemporary Art; Paris, ARC/Musée d'Art Moderne de la Ville.

Selected bibliography: 1971 - G. Penone, *Svolgere la propria pelle*, Sperone, Turin. □ 1973 - T. Trini "Anselmo, Penone, Zorio e le nuove fonti d'energia per il deserto dell'arte," *Data*, no. 9, Milan, Fall. □ 1977 - *G.P.*, Kunstmuseum, Lucerne (texts by J.C. Ammann and G. Penone); G. Penone, J.C. Ammann, *Rovesciare gli occhi*, Einaudi, Turin. □ 1978 - *G.P.*, Staatliche Kunsthalle, Baden-Baden (texts by J.C. Ammann, R. Barilli, H.A. Peters, G. Penone); *G.P.*, Museum Folkwang, Essen (texts by G. Celant, Z. Felix, G. Penone). □ 1980 - G. Celant, "G.P.," *Parachute*, no. 18, Montreal, Spring; *G.P.*, Stedelijk Museum, Amsterdam (texts by G. Celant, G. Penone). □ 1982 - *G.P.*, Museum Abteiberg, Mönchengladbach (texts by J. Cladders, G. Penone). □ 1983 - *G.P.*, National Gallery of Canada, Ottawa (texts by J. Bradley, G. Penone) *. □ 1984 - *G.P.*, ARC/Musée d'Art Moderne de la Ville, Paris (texts by J.Bradley and G. Penone, interview by G. Cerruti).

Renzo Piano

Born 1937 in Genoa. Lives in Paris.
He graduated from School of Architecture, Milan Polytechnic in 1964, and subsequently worked with his father in Genoa. He worked under the design guidance of Franco Albini from 1962 to 1964. Between the years 1965 and 1970 Piano worked with Z.S. Makowsky in London. His collaboration with Richard Rogers dates from 1971 (Piano & Rogers), from 1977 with Peter Rice (Atelier Piano & Rice) and from 1980 with Richard Fitzgerald in Houston. His work is currently divided between London, Genoa, Paris and Houston.
He has been a visiting professor at Columbia University, New York; University of Pennsylvania, Philadelphia; the Oslo School of Architecture; the Central London Polytechnic; the Architectural Association School of London and has lectured in London, Delft, Bucharest, Paris, Milan, Rome, Tokyo, Venice and Houston.
Piano has won recognition in various national and international architectural competitions. In 1978 he was awarded the Union Internationale des Architectes prize in Mexico City, and in 1981 he was awarded the Compasso d'Oro.
He has been awarded the AIA Honorary Fellowship.
Exhibitions devoted to his work have been mounted by the Architectural Association, London; the Musée des Arts Décoratifs, Paris; the Milan Triennale; the RIBA, London; the Paris Biennale; IN-ARC, Rome; the Tre Oci, Venice; the Palazzo Bianco, Genoa; the Sottochiesa di San Francesco, Arezzo; the Convention Center of Bologna; Castello Svevo, Bari; Museo di Capodimonte, Naples; the Architectural Museum, Helsinki; MASP of S. Paulo and Columbia University in New York.

***

A Relationship with Nature
The relationship to natural environment in my work comes to fulfillment through three different experiences. First, a direct, physical relationship to nature, of which the building sometimes becomes a part. Second, to view nature as language reference; recently some structural elements, such as casting pieces and lamellar-wood structures, conform to natural organic elements. Third, to conceive the space not only as a phenomenon realized through physical building elements, i.e., floors, walls and ceilings, but also through those intangible elements of the space: light, air, colour, transparencies and noise.
The Menil Collection Museum under construction in Houston, Texas, is in a natural environment in the center of the city. A spacious exhibition hall is on the ground floor. The first floor we have entitled our Treasure House, since it contains about 10,000 works in a variety of media kept in a state of ideal preservation. We decided to make the best use of available natural light to articulate space. The building is a large platform, about 10,000 m^2 erected five meters above the level of the park. Inside are a number of small gardens. The light enters through the transparent roof of the building and is refracted through a series of "leaves." These leaves of ferro-cement set up a double refraction between themselves as the light enters the building. The central part of the building is serviced by an internal promenade along its 120-meter length. The lighting continuously changes. Light is here the real protagonist of the space. We decided to construct the leaves in ferro-cement because it would permit us to create more organic shapes. The profile was derived from computer analysis and by experimenting with scale and full-size models. The ductile iron castings which collaborate structurally with the leaves were also developed

through similar stages. The final result seems in many ways inspired by nature itself.
The exhibition pavilion for IBM will travel to twenty European cities in the next two years. We used a polycarbonate structure with steel castings and lamellar woods. The building was conceived as a large greenhouse, its transparency allowing it to appear and disappear in the parks and gardens it will be erected in.
The exhibition of five hundred Calder sculptures in Turin during summer 1983 was in the sport centre: a building 15,000 m^2 with a thirty-meter-high ceiling and no intermediate supports. The sunlight was completely obscured and objects were directly illuminated by small halogen lamps. The light created a sort of magical space. We developed a system to generate breezes to move the Calder mobiles. The breezes, sounds coming from the sonorous Calders, and the light and the color of the works themselves, were all intangible elements that developed and manipulated the space.
In 1982 we began the restoration and redesigning of the new Schlumberger head office in Paris. We decided to replace the old courtyards which the buildings surround with an "urban park" two hundred meters on each side. Nature is seen as a winner: it penetrates buildings, not stopping in front of the walls, but passing through them. Nature is the means for eliminating some of the sternness of this industrial complex and so create a pleasant work place.
With UNESCO in 1978 we worked on the restoration of Otranto in the south of Italy and Burano, one of the small Venetian islands. These historical centers are the result of a stratification of ages and cultures, whose unity and articulation are well structured. In both locations we constructed local workshops to aid artisans and inhabitants in the preservation and restoration of local building projects, using the most modern technology and instruments and sharing our knowledge with the people to activate their creative capacities.
The present crisis of the profession is due to an incompetence which hides the architect in a golden, pseudo-artistic world. This mystification leads the architect to take on a marginal role, abrogating the role of builder. There is, as well, often a total lack of sensitivity on the part of the architect towards his client, with the architect seeing the creative experience as the fundamental objective of his work — rather than doing a service for the client. Understanding participation would be extremely useful.
All these examples have one thing in common: a refusal to separate the project from the construction — this is of great cultural importance. Unfortunately in our society there is always the one who thinks and the one who performs, the one who plans and the one who constructs: it is impossible to separate the two if we want to assure creative continuity in the architectural profession.

Renzo Piano, 1984

***

Selected bibliography: 1966 - Piano, Foni, Garbugli, Tirelli, Filocco, "Una struttura ad elementi standard, per la copertura di medie e grandi luci," *La Prefabbricazione*, January. □ 1969 - R. Piano, "Experiments and Projects with Industrialized Structures in Plastic Material," *PDOB*, no. 16-17, October; R. Piano, "Nasce con le materie plastiche un nuovo modo di progettare architettura," *Materie Plastiche e Elastometri*, no. 1.; R. Piano, "Italie recherche de structures," *Techniques & Architecture*, no. 5, Paris. □ 1970 - R. Piano, "Architecture and Technology," *A.A. Quarterly*. no. 3, London; "Italian Industry Pavilion, Expo 70, Osaka," *Architectural Design*, no. 8, London. □ 1971 - R. Piano, "Per un'edilizia industrializzata," *Domus*, no. 495, Milan, February. □ 1974 - Piano & Rogers, "B&B Italia Factory," *Architectural Design*, no. 4, London; Piano & Rogers, "Le Centre Beaubourg," *Chantiers de France*, no. 68, Paris. □ 1975 - Piano & Rogers, "Piano + Rogers," *Architectural Design*, no. XLV, London, May. □ 1976 - "Piano + Rogers," *a + u*, no. 66, Tokyo. □ 1977 - "Centre National d'Art et de Culture Georges Pompidou Paris," *Domus*, no. 566, special issue, Milan, January; Y. Futgawa, "Centre Beaubourg,Piano + Rogers," *GA*, no. 44, Tokyo; J. Bub, W. Messing, "Centre National d'Art et de Culture Georges Pompidou ein Arbeitsbericht von zwei Architekturstudenten," *Bauen + Wohnen*, no. 4, Munich, April. □ 1978 - "Esperienze di cantiere - Tre domande a R. Piano," *Casabella*, no. 439, Milan, September. □ 1979 - L. Rossi, "Piano + Rice + Ass. - Il laboratorio di quartiere," *Spazio & Società*, no. 8, December. □ 1980 - A. Fils, *Das Centre Pompidou in Paris*, Heinz Moos Verlag, Munich; R, Piano, M. Arduino, M. Fazio, *Antico è bello*, Laterza, Bari. □ 1981 - P. Santini, "Colloquio con R.P.," *Ottagono*, no. 61, Milan; R. Pedio, "R.P., itinerario e un primo bilancio," *L'Architettura*, no. 11, November. □ 1982 - "Piano in Houston," *Skyline*, New York, January; "R.P., monografia," *A.A.*, no. 219, special issue, February; "R.P.," *The Architectural Review*, no. 1028, London, October; *R.P., pezzo per pezzo*, (edited by G. Donin), Casa del Libro, Rome; *La modernité un projet inachevé*, Le Moniteur, Paris. □ 1983 - "R.P., artisan du futur," *Technique & Architecture*, no. 350, Paris. □ 1984 -"Exposition itinerante de technologie informatique," *Techniques & Architecture*, no. 354, Paris; R. Piano, *Projects and Buildings 1964-1983*, Electa, Milan/Rizzoli, New York *; *Storia di una mostra, Torino 1983*, Fabbri, Milan; *Venti progetti per il futuro del Lingotto*, Etas Libri, Milan.

Michelangelo Pistoletto

Born 1933 in Biella. Lives in Turin.
One-man exhibitions: 1960 - Turin, Galleria Galatea. □ 1963 - Turin, Galleria Galatea. □ 1964 - Paris, Galerie Sonnabend; Venice, Galleria del Leone; Turin, Galleria Sperone. □ 1965 - Milan, Sala Espressioni-Ideal Standard. □ 1966 Turin, Studio of Pistoletto; Minneapolis, Walker Art Center; Venice, Galleria del Leone; Genoa, Galleria La Bertesca. □ 1967 - Cologne, Galerie Zwirner; Detroit, Hudson Gallery; Milan, Galleria del Naviglio; Brussels, Palais des Beaux Arts; New York, Kornblee Gallery; Paris, Galerie Sonnabend; Turin, Galleria Sperone. □ 1968 - Knokke, Festival of New Cinema; Turin, Galleria Stein; Rome, Galleria L'Attico. □ 1969 - New York, Kornblee Gallery; Buffalo, New York, Albright-Knox Art Gallery. □ 1970 - Naples, Modern Art Agency; Milan, Galleria dell'Ariete. □ 1971 - Cologne, Galerie M.E. Thelen; Milan, Studio Sant'Andrea. □ 1972 - Rome, Galleria Toninelli. □ 1973 - Milan, Galleria dell'Ariete; Milan, Galleria Sperone; Hanover, Kestner Gesellschaft. □ 1974 - Hamburg, Galerie Sachs; Darmstadt, Mathildenhöhe; New York, Janis Gallery. □ 1975 - Roma, Galleria Sperone; Tokyo, Art Agency; Turin, Galleria Stein; Turin, Galleria Multipli. □ 1976 - Milan, Galleria Ala; Genoa, Samangallery; Venice, Palazzo Grassi; Turin, Galleria Persano; Rome, Il Collezionista. □ 1977 - Geneva, Galerie Jeanneret; Naples, Museo Diego Aragona Pignatelli. □ 1978 - Aalborg, Nordiyllands Kunstmuseum; Berlin, Nationalgalerie; Turin, Galleria Persano; Turin, Studio of Pistoletto; East Berlin, Galerie Schweinebraden; Bologna,

Galleria Diacono. □ 1979 - Houston, Rice Museum; Atlanta, High Museum of Art; Athens, Georgia Museum of Art; Antwerp, International Cultureel Centrum; Turin, Galleria Persano; Los Angeles, LAICA. □ 1980 - Berkeley, University Art Museum; Palo Alto, Mayfield Mall; San Francisco, Hansen Fuller Goldeen Gallery; San Francisco, Museum of Modern Art; New York, The Clocktower; Pistoia, Studio La Torre; Turin, Galleria Persano; Pescara, Galleria De Domizio; Rome, Galleria De Crescenzo; Turin, Galleria Persano. □ 1981 - Münster, Westfälisches Landesmuseum; Alternbergen, Museum Dobermann; New York, Ala Gallery. □ 1982 - Rome, Galleria Pieroni; Milan, Galleria Toselli; Munich, Galerie Tanit. □ 1983 - Turin, Galleria Persano; Genoa, Galleria La Polena; Münster, Westfälischer Kunstverein; Madrid, Palacio de Cristal, Parque del Retiro; Madrid, Instituto Italiano de Cultura. □ 1984 - Geneva, Centre d'Art Contemporain; Siracusa, Centro d'Arte Contemporanea; Florence, Forte di Belvedere.

***

There are many kinds of lamps, just as there are many kinds of painting. I wanted the pigment, while remaining part of the painting, to be something more, something magic, like when Aladdin wanted a lamp different from all others, that is, magic. Thus my painting became so clear that it was able to act like a mirror; it was as if I had magically stolen the pigment's porous quality. It is no accident that Aladdin stole the lamp in order to make it become miracoulous. Today's sculptures are, in fact, the embodiment of the Genie who emerges from the reflective painting.

Michelangelo Pistoletto, 1983

***

Selected bibliography: 1960 - *M.P.*, Galatea, Turin (text by L. Carluccio). □ 1963 - *M.P.*, Galatea, Turin (text by L. Carluccio). □ 1964 - *M.P.*, Sonnabend, Paris (texts by A. Jouffroy, M. Sonnabend, T. Trini); *M. Pistoletto - I plexiglas*, Sperone, Turin. □ 1965 - *M.P.*, Ideal Standard, Milan (text by E. Sottsass jr.). □ 1966 - *M.P.: A Reflected World*, Walker Art Center, Minneapolis (text by M. Friedman); *M.P.*, La Bertesca, Genoa (texts by L. Carluccio, J. Ashbery, M. Fagiolo, M. Friedman, A. Jouffroy, S. Simmon, M. Sonnabend, T. Trini, M. Pistoletto). □ 1967 – M. Pistoletto, *Le ultime parole famose*, Turin; *M.P.*, Palais des Beaux Arts, Brussels (texts by J. Dypréau, H. Martin, M. Pistoletto). □ 1968 - *M.P.*, L'Attico, Rome (texts by G.C. Argan, M. Pistoletto). □ 1969 - *M.P.*, Museum Boymans van Beuningen, Rotterdam (texts by H. Martin, M. Pistoletto); *M.P.*, Albright Knox Art Gallery, Buffalo/New York (text by R.M. Murdock). □ 1970 - M. Pistoletto, *L'uomo nero il lato insopportabile*, Rumma, Salerno; *M.P.*, L'Ariete, Milan (text by T. Trini). □ 1973 - *M.P.*, L'Ariete, Milan (text by M. Pistoletto); *M.P.*, Kestner Gesellschaft, Hanover (texts by M. Bandini, A. Boatto, J. Dypréau, M. Friedman, H. Martin, R.M. Murdock, W. Schmied, M. Pistoletto). □ 1974 - *M.P.*, Mathildenhöhe, Darmstadt (text by B. Krimmel); *M.P.*, Janis, New York (text by T. Trini). □ 1975 - M. Pistoletto, *Le stanze*, Stein, Turin. □ 1976 - *M.P.*, Electa, Milan (edited by G. Celant, text by M. Pistoletto); M. Pistoletto, *Cento mostre del mese di ottobre*, Persano, Turin. □ 1978 - *M.P.*, Nordilyllands Kunstmuseum, Aalborg (texts by M. Bandini, G. Celant, J.O.H., T. Trini, M. Pistoletto); *Pistoletto in Berlin*, DAAD, Berlin (texts by H. Ohff, W. Schmied, M. Pistoletto). □ 1979 - *M.P.*, Rice Museum, Houston (texts by M. Jackson, W. Paul, H. Rosenstein, M. Pistoletto). □ 1980 - *M.P.*, University Art Museum, Berkeley (text by G. Celant). □ 1982 - *M.P.*, Pieroni, Rome (interview by B. Corà); *M.P.*, Tanit, Munich (text by R. Comi). □ 1983 - *M.P.*, Persano, Turin (text by M. Pistoletto); *M.P.*, Westfälischer Kunstverein, Münster (text by T. Deecke, interview by B. Corà); *M.P.*, Palacio de Cristal-Parque del Retiro, Madrid (edited by A. Garcia, texts by A. Garcia, G. Celant, L. Carluccio, A. Jouffroy, M. Friedman, A. Boatto, W. Schmied, T. Trini, M. Welish. C, Ferrari, B. Corà. A. Bonito Oliva, E.R. Comi, M. Pistoletto); *M.P.*, Centre d'Art Contemporain, Geneva (text by F. Salvadori); *M.P.*, Fratelli Alinari Stamperia d'Arte, Florence (text by G. Celant); K. Baker, "Interview to M.P.," *The Print Collector's Newsletter*, New York. □ 1984 - *M.P.*, Electa, Milan (edited by G. Celant, texts by G. Celant, L. Carluccio, A. Jouffroy, T. Trini, M. Sonnabend, M. Friedman, A. Nosei, E. Sottsass jr, H. Martin, G.C. Argan, W. Schmied, M. Calvesi, A. Boatto, U. Mulas, M. Diacono, H. Rosenstein, M. Castello, N. Fano, C. Ferrari, A. Bonito Oliva, F. Calvo Serraller, G. Ficara, M. Pistoletto) *.

Sigmar Polke

Born 1942 in Oles (Silesia). Lives in Cologne.
One-man exhibitions: 1966 - Hanover, Galerie H (with G. Richter); Berlin, Galerie Block; Düsseldorf, Galerie Schmela. □ 1967 - Munich, Galerie Friedrich. □ 1968 - Berlin, Galerie Block; Cologne, Kunstmarkt. □ 1969 - Berlin, Galerie Block; Cologne, Galerie Zwirner. □ 1970 - Munich, Galerie Friedrich (with C. Kohlhöfer); Düsseldorf, Galerie Fischer; Bremerhaven, Kabinett für Aktuelle Kunst; Bern, Galerie Gerber; Cologne, Galerie Borgham; Cologne, Galerie Werner. □ 1971 - Hanover, Galerie Ernst; Düsseldorf, Galerie Fischer. □ 1972 - Frankfurt, Galerie Kowallek; Bern, Galerie Gerber; Cologne, Galerie Werner; Karlsruhe, Galerie Grafikmeyer; Amsterdam, Galerie im Goethe Institut,Provisorium. □ 1973 - Düsseldorf, Galerie Fischer; Münster, Westfälischer Kunstverein (with A. Duchow). □ 1974 - Frankfurt, Galerie Loehr; Baden-Baden, Galerie Cornels; Zurich, Galerie Gerber-Hegnauer; Cologne, Galerie Werner; Cologne, Galerie Zwirner; Bonn, Galerie Klein; Berlin, Galerie Springer; Bonn, Städtisches Kunstmuseum (with A. Duchow). □ 1975 - Bonn, Galerie Klein; Kiel, Kunsthalle zu Kiel und Schleswig-Holstein Kunstverein (with A. Duchow); Cologne, Galerie Werner; Sao Paulo, XIII Biennal (with G. Baselitz and Palermo). □ 1976 - Amsterdam, Galerie van der Meij; Düsseldorf, Kunsthalle; Tübingen, Kunsthalle; Eindhoven, Stedelijk van Abbemuseum; Bern, Galerie Gerber. □ 1977 - Kassel, Kunstverein (with A. Duchow); Bonn, Galerie Klein. □ 1978 - Oldenberg, Galerie Centro; Munich, Galerie Grolitsch; Zurich, InK. □ 1979 - Paris, Galerie Bama; Bonn, Galerie Klein. □ 1980 - Bonn, Galerie Klein; Cologne, Galerie Zwirner. □ 1981 - Bern, Galerie Gerber. □ 1982 - Paris, Galerie Bama; New York, Solomon Gallery. □ 1983 - Cologne, Galerie Werner; Mönchengladbach, Städtisches Museum Abtenberg; Milan, Studio d'Arte Cannaviello; Cologne, Galerie Borgmann; Rotterdam, Museum Boymans van Beuningen. □ 1984 - Bonn, Stäatisches Kunstmuseum; Bonn, Galerie Klein; Vienna, Galerie nächst St. Stephan; Zurich, Kunsthaus; Cologne, Josef Haubrich-Kunsthalle.

Selected bibliography: 1966 - *S. Polke/G. Richter*, Galerie h, Hanover (texts by S.

Polke and G. Richter). □ 1972 - S. Polke, *Bizarre*, Staeck, Heidelberg; S. Polke, "Ohne Titel" (photographs), *Interfunktionen*, no. 8, Cologne, January; S. Polke, "Eine Bildgeschichte," *Interfunktionen*, no. 9, Cologne (text by A. Duchow). □ 1973 - S. Polke, *Pappologie...*, Städtische Galerie im Lenbachhaus, Munich; S. Polke, A. Duchow, *Franz Liszt kommt gern zu mir zum Fernsehen*, Westfälischer Kunstverein, Münster; S. Polke, "Registro," *Interfunktionen*, no. 10, Cologne. □ 1974 -S. Polke; A. Duchow, *Original + Fälschung*, Städtisches Kunstmuseum, Bonn. □ 1975 - S. Polke, *Day by Day They Take Some Brain Away*, XIII Biennale, Sao Paulo (texts by E. Weiss, K. Steffen); S. Polke, A. Duchow, *Mu Nieltnam Netorruprup*, Kunsthalle and Kunstverein, Kiel (texts by J.C. Jensen, E. Freitag, C. Vogel). □ 1976 - *S.P. - Bilder, Tücher, Objekte, Werkauswahl 1962-1972*, Cologne (texts by F.W. Heubach, B.H.D. Buchloh); *S. Polke/G. Richter*, Kunsthalle, Tübingen/Kunsthalle, Düsseldorf/Stedelijk van Abbemuseum, Eindhoven. □ 1977 -*Sigmar Polke: Fotos; Achim Duchow: Projektionen*, Kunstverein, Kassel (text by P. Breslaw). □ 1979 - "S.P.," Ink, Zurich (text by C. Saurer). □ 1983 - *S.K.*, Museum Abteiberg, Mönchengladbach (texts by J. Cladders, S. Kimpel); *S.P. - Zeichnungen 1963-1968*, Michael Werner, Cologne (text by A.R. Penck); *S.P.*, Museum Boymans van Beuningen, Rotterdam/Kunstmuseum, Bonn. □ 1984 - *S.P.*, Kunsthaus, Zurich/Kunsthalle, Cologne (texts by S. Gohr, D. Helms, B. Reise, R. Speck, H. Szeemann) *.

Arturo Carlo Quintavalle

Holds the Chair of History of Art at the University of Parma where he also directs the Communications Study Center and Archive that comprises a Photography Department containing the largest public collection of photographs in Italy (five hundred thousand counting negatives and prints). He has also organized and directed a number of exhibitions dedicated to various high points in the history of photography. Among his publications mention should be made of: *Pubblicità, modello, sistema, storia* (Milan, 1977); *Messa a fuoco - Studi sulla fotografia* (Milan, 1984).

Dieter Rams

Born 1932 in Wiesbaden.

At an early age through his grandfather, who had a carpentry shop, he came into contact with carpentry.
In 1947 he took up architecture and interior decorating at the School of Art in Wiesbaden.
From 1948 to 1951 he interrupted his studies to gain practical experience. He concluded an apprenticeship as a carpenter in Kelkheim County, champion in a handicraft competition.
In 1953 he graduated at the School of Art in Wiesbaden. Then he started to work in the office of the architect Otto Apel; he also collaborated with the architects Skidmore, Owings and Merrill (US Consulate building in West Germany).
In 1955 he joined Braun as an architect and interior designer. In 1957 he realized his first furniture designs for Otto Zapf, later on Vitsoe + Zapf, now Wiese Vitsoe. Participated in "Grand Prix Triennale" for the entire production of the Braun AG.
In 1959 a considerable part of Braun program was accepted for the permanent Design Collection of the Museum of Modern Art in New York. One year later Rams became director of the Braun Design Department. In 1961 the Phono-Transistor-Combination of the Braun AG won the International Design Award "Interplast" in London.
In 1963 the Electronic Flash of Braun won the international design award "Interplast" in London and in 1964 the Phono-Radio-Combination Audio I of Braun won the gold medal at the Triennale and the Braun Slide Projector won the gold medal at the first Biennale of Industrial Design in Ljublijana. The following year Rams received the art award "Junge Generation" in Berlin.
In 1968 he was named Hon. Royal Designer for Industry by the Royal Society of Arts, London, for this distinguished design in furniture and light engineering products.
For the 606 Universal Shelving System and the 620 Lounge Chair Program of Vitsoe in Frankfurt, in 1969 he won the gold medals at the international "Wiener Möbelsalon". In the same year he received for the first time the German design award "Gute Form" for the HiFi-Studio Set and the Phono-Radio-Combination Audio 250 of Braun AG, which he won again in 1970 for the table lighter TFG 2 and in participation for the handmixer M 140 with accessories, the electric shaver Sixtant 6006 and the desk fan HL 1 of the Braun AG.
In 1974 at the Salone Internazionale della Musica e dell'HiFidelity, Milan, he won the Award of Public "Gold Sim 72" and the Award of the design jury "Top Form 74" for the Audio 400 of Braun AG.
In 1975 his table lighter "Cylindric" was accepted for the permanent Design Collection of the Museum of Modern Art in New York.
He became a member of the jury committee for the German design award "Gute Form" and in 1976 a member of the executive board of the German Design Council.
In 1978 he won the SIAD Medal of the Society of Industrial Artists and Designers, London, and the Rosenthal Studio Award for the 690 Sliding Door System of Vitsoe in Frankfurt.
The same system in 1979 won the Design Center Stuttgart Award.
In the same year the 601 Chair and the 622 Side Chair were shown at the "Werkbund" Exhibition in Hamburg. The exhibits were donated to the "Werkbund" for further exhibitions: "Badischer Kunstverein," Karlsruhe; "Kunstmuseum," Dusseldorf; "Künstlerhaus," Vienna. Then they were accepted for the collection of the "Werkbundarchiv" in Berlin.
In 1980 the 720 Round/Oval Table of Vitsoe, Frankfurt, won the Design Center Stuttgart Award. In 1981 he became a member of the Braun Management and he was appointed professor at the Hochschule für Bildende Künste in Hamburg.
In 1982 the calculator "Control ET 55" was accepted for the permanent Design Collection of the Museum of Modern Art in New York.
In 1983 he received the German design award "Gute Form" for the Universal Shelving System — a further development with solid wood edges as room-divider program for executive offices (also for residential use), realized at Vitsoe in Frankfurt.

Selected bibliography: 1959 - H. Schwippert, W. Fischer, F. Bode, R. d'Hooghe, R. Müller, A. Schultz, "Braun," *Werk und Zeit*, no. 11, Darmstadt. □ 1962 - R. Moss, *Max Braun*, Whitney Publication, New York, November. □ 1963 - C. Enevoldsen, "Möbel von Dieter Rams," *Spatium*, no. 6, Copenhagen. □ 1964 - G. Dorfles, "Gute Industrieform und ihre Ästethik," *Moderne Industrie*, Munich. □ 1966 - M. Katszumie, "Creativity in Braun's Style," *Graphic Design*, Tokyo, October. □ 1967 - J. Klöckner, H. Dieckman, I. Klöckner, H. Lindiger, D. Skerutsch, M.

Staber, *Zeitgemässe Form*, Süddeutscher Verlag, Munich. □ 1970 - D. Rams, *Design? Umwel wird in Frage gestellt*, IDZ Berlin, Berlin; H. Wichmann, *Made in Germany*, Peter Winkler, Munich; G. Frey, *Das moderne Sitzmöbel von 1850 bis heute*, Arthur Niggli Ltd., Teufen. □ 1973 - H. Wichmann, *Kultur ist unteilbar*, Josef Keller, Starnberg. □ 1974 - *Introduction à l'histoire de l'évolution des formes industrielles de 1820 à aujourd'hui*, Design Editions Stock, Paris; D. Beisel, "Das Firmenportrait," *Werk und Zeit*, no. 5, Darmstadt; F. Eichler, D. Rams, "Now, What Is Design - Design Policy of Braun," *The Management*, Tokyo, March. □ 1976 - D. Rams, "Protokoll aus der Praxis," *Form*, Seeheim; B. Löbach, H. Schmidt, *Was ist Industrial Design?*, IDZ Berlin, Berlin. □ 1977 - D. Rams, "Design ist eine verantwortliche Aufgabe der Industrie," *Format*, Karlsruhe, May; D. Rams, "Kann Design zum Erfol eines Unternehmens beitragen?," *Werk und Archithese*, no. 4, Stuttgart; "To Bauhaus with Love from Dieter Rams," *Interiors*, New York, May. □ 1978 - G. Selle, *Die Geschichte des Design in Deutschland*, Dumont Buchverlag, Cologne; G. Selle, "Ein neuer Beginn? Das Design der 50er Jahre in Deutschland," *Form*, no. 82, Seeheim, February; S. Mukei, "Braun's Convictions," *The Management*, Tokyo, January. □ 1979 - S. Bayley, "In Good Shape," *Design Council*, London; D. Rams, M. Umeda, "On the Design-Development," *Design Age 54*, Tokyo, November; "D.R. Interview," Werk und Zeit, no. 4, Berlin. □ 1981 - *Design D.R.* (edited by F. Burkhardt, I. Franksen), Gerhardt Verlag, Berlin *.

Gerhard Richter

Born 1932 in Dresden. Lives in Cologne. One-man exhibitions: 1963 - Düsseldorf, Demonstration für den Kapitalistischen Realismus, Möbel Haus Berges (with K. Lueg). □ 1964 - Munich, Galerie Friedrich; Düsseldorf, Galerie Schmela; Berlin, Galerie Block. □ 1966 - Rome, Galleria la Tartaruga; Hanover, Galerie H (with S. Polke); Zurich, Galerie Bischofberger; Frankfurt, Galerie Patio; Venice, Galleria del Leone; Munich, Galerie Friedrich; Düsseldorf, Galerie Schmela; Berlin, Galerie Block. □ 1967 - Munich, Galerie Friedrich; Antwerp, Wide White Space. □ 1968 - Kassel, Galerie Ricke; Cologne, Galerie Zwirner. □ 1969 - Milan, Galleria del Naviglio; Berlin, Galerie Block; Aachen, Gegenverkehr e. V. □ 1970 - Brussels, Palais des Beaux Arts; Düsseldorf, Galerie Fischer; Munich, Galerie Friedrich; Hanover, Galerie Ernst (with Palermo); Essen, Museum Folkwang. □ 1971 - Cologne, Galerie Friedrich (with Palermo); Düsseldorf, Kunstverein; Cologne, Galerie Borgmann; Bremerhaven, Kabinett für Aktuelle Kunst. □ 1972 - Cologne, Galerie Friedrich; Venice, XXXVI Biennale, German Pavilion; Cologne, Galerie Zwirner; Düsseldorf, Galerie Fischer; Utrecht, Hedendaages Kunst; Naples, Galleria Amelio; Amsterdam, Galerie Seriaal; Lucerne, Kunstmuseum; Munich, Städtische Galerie im Lembachhaus; Bremerhaven, Kunstverein; Genoa , Galleria La Bertesca; Vienna, Galerie nächst St. Stephan; Munich, Galerie Friedrich; Aachen, Suermondt Museum. □ 1973 - New York, Onnasch Gallery. □ 1974 - Cologne, Galerie Zwirner; Berlin, Galerie Block; Munich, Galerie Friedrich; Mönchengladbach, Städtisches Museum. □ 1975 - Basel, Galerie Preisig; Düsseldorf, Galerie Fischer; Braunschweig, Kunsteverein. □ 1976 - Bremen, Kunsthalle; Brussels, Palais des Beaux Arts; Krefeld, Museum Haus Lange; Naples, Galleria Amelio; Paris, Galerie Durand-Dessert; Genoa, Galleria La Bertesca. □ 1977 - Paris, Centre Georges Pompidou. □ 1978 - New York, Sperone-Westwater-Fischer Gallery; Halifax, Leonowens Gallery; Halifax, Nova Scotia College of Art and Design; Eindhoven, Stedelijk van Abbemuseum. □ 1979 - London, Whitechapel Art Gallery; Isernhagen, Galerie Isernhagen. □ 1980 - New York, Sperone-Westwater-Fischer Gallery; Rome, Galleria Pieroni; Essen, Folkwang Museum; Eindhoven, Stedelijk van Abbemuseum. □ 1981 - Düsseldorf, Kunsthalle (with Baselitz); Cologne,Galerie Fischer. □ 1982 - Bielefeld, Kunsthalle; Mannheim, Kunstverein; Munich, Galerie Jahn; Zurich, Galerie Fischer; Stuttgart, Galerie Hetzler. □ 1983 - New York, Sperone-Westwater-Fischer Gallery; Naples, Galleria Amelio; Rome, Galleria Pieroni (with Isa Genzken); Düsseldorf, Galerie Fischer; Chicago, Deson Gallery. □ 1984 - St. Etienne, Musée D'Art Moderne et d'Industrie; Cologne, Galerie Borgmann; Paris, Galerie Durand-Dessert; Cologne, Galerie Wilkens-Jacobs.

***

Every time we describe an event, add up a column of figures or take a photograph of a tree, we create a model; without models we would know nothing about reality and would be like animals.
Abstract paintings are fictitious models because they visualize a reality which we can neither see nor describe but which we may nevertheless conclude exist. We attach negative names to this reality; the un-known, the un-graspable, the in-finite, and for thousands of years we have depicted it in terms of substitute images like heaven and hell, gods and devils.
With abstract painting we create a better means of approaching what can be neither seen nor understood because abstract painting illustrates with the greatest clarity, that is to say with all the means at the disposal of art, "nothing."
Accustomed to recognizing real things in paintings we refuse, justifiably, to consider color alone (in all its variation) as what the painting reveals, and instead allow ourselves to see the unseeable, that which has never before been seen and indeed is not visible. This is not an artful game, it is a necessity; since everything unknown frightens us and fills us with hope at the same time, we take these images as a possible explanation of the inexplicable or at least as a way of dealing with it. Of course even representative paintings have this transcendental aspect; since every object, being part of a world whose last and first causes are finally unfathomable, embodies that world, the image of such an object in a painting evokes the general mystery more compellingly the less "function" the representation has. This is the source of the continually increasing fascination, for example, that so many old and beautiful portraits exert upon us. Thus paintings are all the better, the more beautiful, intelligent, crazy and extreme, the more clearly perceptible and the less they are decipherable metaphors for this incomprehensible reality.
Art is the highest form of hope.

Gerhard Richter, 1979

***

Selected bibliography: 1963 - G. Richter, "Bericht über eine Demonstration," *Demonstration für den Kapitalistischen Realismus*, Düsseldorf. □ 1965 - *G. Richter, S. Polke*, Galerie h, Hanover (texts by S. Polke and G. Richter). □ 1969 - E.F. Fry, "G.R., German Illusionist," *Art in America*, New York, November-December; *G.R.*, Kunsthalle, Lucerne (text by J.C. Ammann); *G.R., Gegenverhehr, Aachen (text by K. Honnef).* □ *1970 - G.R., Graphik 1965-1970*, Museum Folkwang, Essen (text by D. Honisch). □ 1971 - *G.R.*, Kunstverein,

Düsseldorf (text by D. Helms). □ 1972 - *G.R.*, La Biennale, Venice (text by D. Honisch, interview by R. Schön). □ 1973 - *G.R.*, Städtische Galerie im Lehnbachhaus, Munich (text by J.C. Ammann). □ 1974 - *G.R.*, Städtisches Museum, Mönchengladbach (text by J. Cladders). □ 1975 - *G.R.*, Kunsthalle, Bremen (text by M. Grüterich, M. Schneckenburger); *G.R.*, Kunstverein, Braunschweig (text by H. Heinz). □ 1976 - K. Honnef, *G.R.*, Recklinghausen; *G.R. - Atlas der Fotos, Collagen und Skizzen*, Museum Haus Lange, Krefeld. □ 1977 - *G.R.*, Centre National d'Art et Culture Georges Pompidou, Paris (text by B.H.D. Buchloh). □ 1978 - *G.R.*, Stedelijk van Abbemuseum, Eindhoven (text by R. Fuchs). □ 1981 - *Baselitz, Richter*, Kunsthalle, Düsseldorf (text by J. Harten); *G.R.*, Padiglione d'Arte Contemporanea, Milan (text by B. Corà). □ 1982 - G.R., *Abstrakte Bilder 1976 bis 1981*, Kunsthalle, Bielefeld (texts by R. Fuchs, H. Heere). □ 1984 - J. Harten, "G.R.,"*Von hier aus*, DuMont, Cologne; *G.R.*, Musée d'Art et d'Industrie, St. Etienne (text by B. Blistène) *.

Aldo Rossi

Born 1931 in Milan.
He studied architecture at Milan Polytechnic, receiving his degree in 1959. In his student days he worked on the architectural review *Casabella-Continuità* directed by Ernesto Nathan Rogers during the period in which this publication played a determining role in Italian culture. Rossi was first associated as a writer (1955-60) and later as editor (1961-64) until Rogers left the direction of the journal.
He began his academic activity as assistant to the courses taught by Ludovico Quaroni in Arezzo in 1963 and by Carlo Aymonino in Venice (1963-65). In 1965 he was named to the Faculty of Architecture in Milan, where he involved himself in the process of experimentation begun by the student movement to which he brought a significant cultural contribution.
The principal work of Aldo Rossi is *L'architettura della città*, which was first published in 1966 (Marsilio, Padua) and translated into various languages, and which has since become one of the primary references from new tendencies in architecture. Among his other writings are those contained in the collective volume *L'analisi urbana e la progettazione architettonica* (Clup, Milan, 1970) which assembles material elaborated by the research group led by Rossi at the Faculty of Architecture in Milan, the volume *Scritti scelti sull'architettura e la città, 1956-72* (Clup, Milan, 1st ed. 1975, 2nd ed. 1978), and finally the many essays and articles published in Italy and abroad.
The writings of Rossi are bound to his work as an architectural planner in a relation that combines scientific analysis, theory and planning. He has participated in many design competitions; among his principal constructions are the residential complex in the Gallaratese 2 section of Milan (1969-74) and the elementary school of Fagnano Olona in the province of Varese (1972-77).
From 1972-77 Rossi taught at the Federal Polytechnical Institute of Zurich. Since 1975, reinstated as professor in Italy, he holds the chair of composition at the University Institute of Architecture in Venice. In 1977 he was named Professor at the Cooper Union School of Architecture where since 1979 he teaches an annual course in architectural planning.
In 1973 he directed a section of the XV Triennale of Milan (the International Section of Architecture) in conjunction with which was published the collective volume *Architettura razionale,* with an introduction by Aldo Rossi (Franco Angeli Editore, Milan, 1973). Exhibitions of his work have been held in many European and American cities; he has held lecture series and given conferences for various universities and associations in Europe, the US and in Latin America. He directed the First International Seminar of Architecture at Santiago de Compostela, Spain, in September-October 1976, and the second of these seminars in Seville in 1978.
In 1979 he became Accademico di San Luca. The following year he was invited to Hong Kong and China and as professor of planning to Yale University. He published *A Scientific Autobiography* by Boston Press. In 1982 he became Professor at Cambridge, Mass. and at Texas A&M University, Texas. He is also honorary member of the BDA (Association of German architects) in Bonn.
In 1983 he became director of the architecture department of the Venice Biennale.

Selected bibliography: 1956-1972 - A. Rossi, *Scritti scelti sull'architettura e la città* (anthology edited by R. Bonicalzi, CLUP, Milan, 1974). □ 1959 - E.N. Rogers, "L'evoluzione dell'architettura, risposta al custode del frigidaire," *Cbc*, no. 228, Turin. □ 1966 - C. Aymonino, "L'architettura della città," *Rinascita*, no. 27, Rome; A. Rossi, *L'architettura della città*, Padua (*The Architecture of the City*, The MIT Press, Cambridge, Mass., 1982). □ 1967 - A.R., Centro Arte Viva, Trieste (text by L. Semerani). □ 1968 - M. Tafuri, *Teorie e storia dell'architettura*, Bari. □ 1969 - L. Patetta, "A.R.," *Dizionario enciclopedico di architettura e urbanistica*, Rome; V. Gregotti, *New Directions in Italian Architecture*, New York. □ 1970 - E. Bonfanti, "Elementi e costruzione - Note sull'architettura di A.R.," *Controspazio*, no. 10, Bari; B. Reichlin, F. Reinhart, "Zu einer Ausstellung der Projekte von A.R. an der ETH, Zürich," *Werk*, no. 4, Nuremberg. □ 1973 - *Architettura razionale*, XV Triennale Milan (texts by R. Bonicalzi, M. Scolari, A. Rossi); *A.R. - Bauten, Projekte*, Zurich (text by M. Steinmann). □ 1974 - R. Nicolin, "Note su A.R.," *Controspazio*, no. 4, Rome; A. Rossi, "L'habitation et la ville," *L'Architecture d'Aujourd'hui*, no. 174, Paris. □ 1975 - M. Tafuri, "L'Architecture dans le Boudoir: the Language of Criticism and the Criticism of Language," *Oppositions*, no. 3, New York; V. Savi, *L'architettura di A.R.*, Angeli, Milan. □ 1976 - "A.R.," *a+u*, special issue, no. 65, Tokyo (texts by V. Savi, D. Stewart); *A.R.*, Galleria Solferino, Milan (text by G. Contessi, M. Tafuri); F. Dal Co, *Architettura contemporanea*, Electa, Milan; R. Moneo, "A.R.: the Idea of Architecture and the Modena Cemetery," *Oppositions*, no. 5, New York. □ 1977 - J. Silvetti, "The Beauty of Shadows," *Oppositions*, no. 9, New York. □ 1979 - P. Eisenmann, The House of Dead as the City of Survival," *IAUS*, New York; *A.R.: progetti e disegni 1962-1979*, Centro Di, Florence (text by F. Moschini). □ 1980 - M. Filler, "Rossi Secco and Rossi Dolce," *Art in America*, no. 3, New York; F. Dal Co, "A.R. - Teatro del mondo," *a+u*, no. 3, Tokyo; P. Portoghesi, "Il teatro del mondo," *Controspazio*, no. 5-6, Bari; M. Tafuri, *La sfera e il labirinto*, Turin; P. Portoghesi, *Dopo l'architettura moderna*, Bari; A. Rossi, "Il progetto per il Teatro del mondo," *Venezia e lo spazio scenico*, La Biennale, Venice; A. Rossi, "Lavori costruiti o progetti,', *La presenza del passato - Prima mostra internazionale di architettura*, La Biennale, Venice. □ 1981 - A. Rossi, *A Scientific Autobiography*, The MIT Press, Cambridge, Mass. *; *A.R.* (edited by G. Braghieri), Zanichelli, Bologna.

Salomé (Wolfgang Cilarz)

Born 1954 in Karlsruhe. Lives in Berlin and New York.
One-man exhibitions: 1977 - Berlin, Galerie am Moritzplatz; Berlin, Galerie Petersen. ☐ 1978 - Berlin, Galerie am Moritzplatz; Berlin, Galerie Anderes Ufer; Berlin, *Für meine Schwestern in Österreich* (performance); New York, *Bodyworks* (performance). ☐ 1979 -Berlin, Realismusstudio der Neuen Gesellschaft für Bildende Kunst; Berlin, Galerie Interni. ☐ 1980 - Berlin, *Pink and Blue* (performance); Munich, Galerie Hermeyer; Berlin, Emilia Galotti; Berlin, Theater Freie Volksbühne. ☐ 1981 - Berlin, Galerie am Moritzplatz; Berlin, Galerie Lietzow; New York, Nosei Gallery. ☐ 1982 - Zurich, Galerie Bischofberger; Cologne, Galerie Zwirner; Berlin, Galerie Interni; Munich, Galerie Hermeyer. ☐ 1983 - Paris, Galerie Cadot; Bordeaux, CAPC (with Castella and Fetting); Venice, Galleria Il Capricorno; Nagoya, Akira Ikeda Gallery; Zurich, Galerie Bischofberger. ☐ 1984 - Berlin, Raab Galerie; Kassel, Kunstverein; Munich, Galerie Thomas.

***

I didn't want to call myself Wolfgang Ludwig Goethe
Ant: Why do you call yourself Salomé?
S.: What are we gonna answer now? Years ago I came to this town as a poor child. The city was rich and free and glistening. It attracted me. Soon I became acquainted with a group of colorful friends. Their names were Klara Bella Kuh, Baby Jane Hudson, Anna Boleyn, Claire Walldorf, Rosa Luxemburg and others with liberated names. I needed a name. I didn't want to call myself Wolfang Ludwig Goethe. After selected research in literature and political discussions which lasted for weeks I knew that it could only be a revolutionary name: the one who loves and kills in the name of love and revolution — Salomé!
Ant.: And then you started to paint?
S.: Everybody must do something when you are not born as a poet. In those days I learned to know the — at this time — unknown Rainer Fetting. He was excited by my slim and tender body. He immediately signed me up for modelling and not only for that. I started to get involved with art. It was a lot of fun for me. But then the problem with the money came. I worked as a technical draftsman which became harder and harder for me because I was always surrounded by artists because of my body. I started to draw mostly myself and with increasing fascination, so that in 1974 under strong approval, I was accepted at the Hochschule der Künste, Berlin. The time of masquerade began. I only painted what in any kind of way had to do with myself: foam rubber, underwear, shoes, screens, and myself. At the same time I worked as a barmaid in a Faschingskneipe.
Ant.: What is a Faschingskneipe?
S.: A Faschingskneipe is a bar where carnival is celebrated all the year round. Through tips I could afford to found the Galerie am Moritzplatz with the other guys.
Ant.: Tell us about the gallery.
S.: Yes. The gallery was cold. A bad stove and in winter I can remember you could not come without a fur coat. Also, I had the honor of having the first exhibition. The gallery became a smash hit because there were always such wonderful parties. There were not many sales, very few, except beer of course. But there were always a lot of interested people. It became a kind of Mecca, not only because the police were alarmed, but there were also mistreatments of artists. Next to painting, photography, sculpture, performances, there was a lot of drinking. The gallery had up to fourteen artists periodically.
Ant.: And what happened then with your success?
S.: After a while everyone had solo exhibitions in galleries; 1980 was the exhibition "Heftige Malerei." In 1980 I finished my studies with K. H. Hödicke. Since then I've toured around the world. I saw Japan but no cherry trees, I was in Hawaii but I had no time for waterskiing, I was in Los Angeles but I didn't choke from the smog! I've had lots of television appearances and have made many friends. Now I live in America and Berlin.
Ant.: And your paintings?
S.: They are spread all over the world. Museums, big collections, private collectors.
Ant.: And you haven't earned enough yet?
S.: Not really. No. Everything has become so expensive.
Ant.: Why are you making a kind of "retrospective" now at Galerie Thomas in Munich?
S.: Because I want to show my "old pictures." I also want to celebrate my tenth anniversary as an artist.
Ant.: Salomé, thank you very much for the interview, the cake and the coffee.

Extract from an interview with Salomé by Elke Sonntag (Ant.), 1984

***

Selected bibliography: 1979 - *S. Selbstdarstellung*, Katalogmappe, Berlin. ☐ 1980 - W.M. Faust, "Heftige Malerei," *Kunstforum* vol. 38, Mainz. ☐ 1981 - E. Sommer, "Erotische Kunst - Erotische Wahrnehmung," *Das Kunstwerk*, vol. 5, Stuttgart. ☐ 1982 - J.C. Ammann, "Im Gespräch: die jungen Deutschen," *Kunstforum*, vol. 47, Cologne; H.P. Schwerfel, "S., Wild Boy," *Art Press*, no. 59, Paris, Summer; D.P. Kuspit, "Acts of Aggression: German Painting Today," *Art in America*, New York, September; K. Honnef, "Der neue Manierismus," *Kunstforum*, vol. 56, Cologne, October; W.M. Faust, G. de Vries, *Hunger nach Bildern*, Cologne; J. Russell, "A Big Berlin Show That Misses the Mark," *The New York Times*, New York, December. ☐ 1983 - Z. Felix, "S. 1982, 1983...," *Domus*, no. 639, Milan, May; R. Smith, "Germanations," *Village Voice*, New York, June; *S.*, Akira Ikeda, Nagoya (text by M. Kuwayama). ☐ 1984 - H. Ohff, "Der Ring des S.," *Tagesspiel*, Berlin, February; J.C. Ammann, "S.," *Von hier aus*, DuMont, Cologne; *S. bei Thomas - Bilder und Zeichnungen*, Thomas, Munich (interview by E. Sonntag) *.

Remo Salvadori

Born 1947 in Cerreto Guidi. Lives in Milan.
One-man exhibitions: 1971 - Turin, Galleria LP 220. ☐ 1973 - Milan, Galleria Toselli. ☐ 1975 - Münster, December Gallery. ☐ 1976 - Turin, Galleria Tucci-Marinucci; Pescara, Galleria De Domizio. ☐ 1978 - Bologna, Galleria Fata. ☐ 1979 - Milan, Galleria Betti; Naples, Galleria Amelio; Pescara, Galleria De Domizio. ☐ 1980 - New York, Ala Gallery; Milan, Galleria Ala. ☐ 1981 - Rome, Galleria Pieroni. ☐ 1982 - Milan, Galleria Ala; New York, Ala Gallery.

Selected bibliography: 1971 - M. Bandini, "R.S.," *Nac*, no. 3, Bari, March. ☐ 1973 -R. Salvadori, I. Nagasawa, A. Trotta, *Libro come luogo di ricerca*, Toselli, Venice; R. Salvadori, *Janus*, Milan. ☐ 1975 - R. Salvadori, *Il tiro strabico dell'attenzione*, Russo/Marinucci, Turin. ☐ 1976 - R. Salvadori, *La capriola nella stanza*, De Domizio, Pescara; "R.S.," *La Città di Riga*, no. 1, La Nuova Foglio, Macerata; C.

Ferrari, "Paragrafi," *Data*, no. 23, Milan, October-November; "Italian Art Now," *Studio International*, special issue, London, January-February. □ 1979 -A. Bonito Oliva, "La transavanguardia italiana," *Flash Art*, no. 92-93, Milan October-November. □ 1980 - *R.S.*, Collezione del Clavicembalo, De Domizio, Pescara; B. Corà, "Profili, opere," *AEIUO*, no. 1, Rome, September and *Kunstforum*, vol. 39, Mainz, March; C. Ferrari, "Gravità zero - R.S.," *Domus*, no. 606, Milan, May; B. Corà, "R.S., musiche ampie," *AEIUO*, no. 2, Rome, December. □ 1981 - R. Salvadori, *Gennaio 1981*, Pieroni, Rome. □ 1982 - R. Salvadori, "senza titolo," *AEIUO*, no. 5, Rome, January-July; N. Ciardi, "R.S.,"*Modo*, Milan, November.

Philipp Scholz Rittermann

Born 1955 in Lima, Peru. Lives in San Diego, USA.
One-man exhibitions: 1981 - Hamburg, Landesbildstelle. □ 1982 - Barcelona, Fotomania Gallery; Zaragoza, Galeria Canon-Spectrum; Stuttgart, Galerie Jutta Roessner; Paris, Studio 666. □ 1983 -Providence, Providence College Art Department, Los Angeles, Arco Center for Visual Arts . □ 1984 - San Diego, Galerie 5; Schaffhausen, Kunstverein; Seattle, Equivalente Gallery.

Selected bibliography: 1981 - "A New German Vision," *Camera*, no. 8, Luzern. □ 1982 - *Photographie Ouverte*, spring issue, Charleroi; "Young European Photographers II," *European Photography*, no. 12, Göttingen; "Poetica de la noche," *Photovision*, no. 5, Madrid. □ 1983 -*Photometro*, vol. 2, no. 8, San Francisco; *Photometro*, vol 2, no. 12, San Francisco; "P.S.R.," *L'architecture: sujet, objet ou pretexte?*, Aquitaine; "P.S.R.," *Allemagne années 80*, First International Art, Photography and Cinema Festival, Quimper; *P.S.R.*, Kunstverein, Schaffhausen; *Aperture*, no. 92, Millerton, Fall.

Public collections: Arles, RIP (Rencontres Internationales de la Photographie); Mexico City, Televisiva; Hamburg, Museum für Kunst und Gewerbe; Hanover, Kunstmuseum mit Sammlung Sprengel; Paris, Bibliothèque Nationale; New York, Metropolitan Museum; New York, Museum of Modern Art.

Wilhelm Schurmann

Born 1946 in Dortmund. Lives in Herzogenrath.

Thomas Schütte

Born 1954 in Oldenburg. Lives in Düsseldorf.
One-man exhibitions: 1979 - Paris, La Vitrine; Düsseldorf, Galerie Kohnen. □ 1980 - Munich, Galerie Schöttle. □ 1981 - Düsseldorf, Galerie Fischer. □ 1982 - Munich, Galerie Schöttle. □ 1983 - Zurich, Galerie Fischer. □ 1984 - Lyon, Galerie Nelson; Hamburg, Produzentengalerie (with L. Gerdes); Cologne, Galerie Johnen; Athens, Bernier Gallery.

Selected bibliography: 1983 - *Gerdes, Klingelhöller, Luy, Mucha, Schütte*, Fischer, Düsseldorf (text by U. Loock); V. Horndash, "Föhn," *Kunstforum*, vol. 65, Cologne, September; L. Krier, "Architektur, Bildhauerei, Malerei," *Kunstforum* vol. 65, Cologne, September; *Kostruierte Orte*, Kunsthalle, Bern (text by J.H. Martin, T. Schütte). □ 1984 - *c/o Haus Esters*, Museum Haus Esters, Krefeld (text by J. Heynen); L. Gerdes, T. Schütte, *Weiter - Warten*, Produzentengalerie, Hamburg; T. Schütte, *Fifteen Monuments*, Philip/Nelson, Villeurbanne (texts by J.H. Martin, D. Zacharopoulos); L. Gerdes, "T.S.," *Von hier aus*, DuMont, Cologne.

Wolfram Schütte

Born 1939 in Frankfurt am Main. Studied German, Philosophy and Sociology at the Frankfurt University; since 1967 editor in the German newspaper *Frankfurter Rundschau;* editor of *Reihe Film* (30 volumes). Author of several essays on Fassbinder, Godard, Visconti, Pasolini, Keaton, Achternbusch, Herzog, Kluge, Straub, Rosi.

Ettore Sottsass jr.

Born 1917 in Innsbruck.
Graduated from Turin Polytechnic in 1939. Sottsass began his professional life in 1947 when he opened an office in Milan where he designed, participated in numerous competitions and built a number of residential buildings, hotels and schools in Italy.
He collaborated in several "Triennale" shows and appeared in personal and collective exhibitions in Italy and abroad. Sottsass is internationally known as an upholder of innovation in design and architecture beyond the functional approach which prevailed before and after World War II. He especially strove to find a more stimulating way to define form and space in everyday life. His designs are greatly dependent upon color as a source of potential energy and as a symbol of liveliness as opposed to the intellectual rigidity of a structure.
Since 1959 Sottsass has been working as a design consultant for Olivetti. After a long tour of conferences in British universities, he was awarded an honorary degree from the Royal College of Art, London.
Sottsass participated in the exhibition held at New York's Museum of Modern Art entitled "Italy: A Domestic Landscape."
In 1976 Sottsass was invited to participate in the opening of the Cooper-Hewitt Museum of Design in New York with a personal exhibition. Upon that occasion, he put together his considerations on design and architecture with a series of photographs of buildings erected in deserts and mountains. Also in 1976, Berlin's Internationales Design Zentrum organized an exhibition of Sottsass's work from the last twenty years; this exhibition later moved to the Biennale of Venice, the Musée des Arts Décoratifs of Paris, the Centro de Diseno Industrial of Barcelona, the Israel Museum of Jerusalem, and the Visual Arts Board of Sydney.
In 1977, jointly with other professionals (CDM) he developed a traffic sign and road system, advertising board system, chromatic scheme and logotype for Rome's Fiumicino airport.
In 1978, the government of the city of Berlin invited Sottsass to submit a project for the reorganization of the city's Museum of Modern Art.
In 1980, Sottsass formed a partnership (Sottsass Associati) with three architects — A. Cibic, M. Thun, M. Zanini — with whom he continues his design activity. Lately, he designed several pieces of furniture for the Memphis collection, of which he is also a promoter.

***

I have designed a number of pieces of furniture which, in my personal history, imagined or not, represent (for the moment) the final point of thoughts and actions, experienced either alone or with friends, in a period of at least ten and perhaps fifteen years and which, for want of a better name, we called radical design or sometimes counterdesign or things like that. Certainly, this furniture that I have designed represents (as far as I am concerned) an attempt to get out of, or rather an attempt to re-enter the crux of

the matter. It is an attempt to get back into design, bringing with me everything that has happened and maybe also everything that has not.
I have tried again to design objects, things, furniture, and to have them made. I have made them big and heavy, with pedestals and bases to save them from the kitsch of bourgeois and petty bourgeois décor. There's almost nowhere you can put them and in any case they don't "match" and they can't even produce sets. They only go by themselves, like monuments in squares, and they don't even manage to create style (in fact nobody buys them, apart from the odd collector or desultory Hollywood film star).
They are also decorated, because in this way I can convey different cultural states (in an anthropological sense), according to situations and real functional necessities. In the case of this exhibition I have chosen for the drawing of the decorations (plastic laminate designed and especially produced by Abet Laminati in Italy), extracts from a figurative iconography found in spaces uncorrupted by the sophistication of the standard culture of private interior design. I have chosen textures from those cultural areas that do not by any means represent poverty but which are untouched by kitsch, whatever their origin happens to be.
They are areas abandoned, that is, by any intellectual intent or expectation; a kind of no-man's-land, an extra-human cultural wasteland. So I have chosen texture like the grit and the mosaics of public conveniences in the underground stations of big cities, like the tight wire netting of suburban fences, or like the spongy paper of government account books, and detective stories, and then I have chosen colors like those of the chair in the dairy shop under my house where they sell eggs, margarine, bottles of mineral water, miscellaneous detergents, spaghetti and liquorice and, naturally, soft cheeses and milk. In the dairy shop you can even sit down and have a coffee. And I have chosen the plastic laminate which is in itself a material with no uncertainties; and I have chosen metal plate used for trams, containers and the like; I have chosen layers of airport floor rubber and layers of artificial lawn used at Texan filling stations; and I have also chosen the galvanized sheet used on electrical appliances which are normally hidden. I should like to have been able to propose some sort of iconography of non-culture, of no-man's-culture (and not to the culture of the anonymous) — the iconography of a culture of an unused and unusable culture, not because it does not exist or even because it is not used, but because it is not looked at, because it is not taken into consideration, because it's got nothing to do with the question, because it does not seem to exist in known culture and perhaps does not even produce culture.
These zones of non-culture, of no-man's-culture do exist. But on this plane, I have not — for the moment — succeeded in getting much farther. In fact, everything has maybe turned out differently from what I had expected.

Ettore Sottsass jr., 1980

***

Selected bibliography: 1940 - E. Sottsass jr., *Le camere*, Lambello, Turin. □ 1946 - E. Sottsass, "Europa e America," *Architettura in America*, Turin. □ 1947 - E. Sottsass jr., "Architettura e pittura," *Numero Pittura*, Turin, 15 March; E. Sottsass jr., "Le case camminano," *Sempre Avanti*, Milan, 10 April. □ 1951 - A. Gatto, "Architettura di E.S. jr.," *Spazio*, Milan, December. □ 1954 - E. Sottsass jr., "Lussuoso e finito," *Domus*, no. 301, Milan, May. □ 1957 - E. Sottsass jr., "Struttura e colore," *Domus*, no. 327, February. □ 1960 - B. Zevi, "L'architetto in Italia, l'artigianato di lusso," *L'Espresso*, Rome, 26 June. □ 1962 - E. Sottsass jr., "Automatizzazione e design," *Stile Industria*, no. 37, Milan, April. □ 1963 - P.C. Santini, "Introduzione a Ettore Sottsass jr.," *Zodiac*, no. 11, Milan, February; B. Alfieri, "Ettore Sottsass jr.," *Pagina*, no. 2, Milan, June. □ 1964 - E. Sottsass jr., "Pop e non Pop," *Domus*, no. 414, Milan, May. □ 1965 - E. Sottsass jr., "Offerta a Siva," *Domus*, no. 422, Milan, January. □ 1966 - A.D., "Cahier di Ettore Sottsass jr. 1966," *Lotus*, Milan; E. Sottsass jr., F. Pivano, "Viaggio a Occidente, che cosa fanno lì dentro," *Domus*, no. 436, Milan, March. □ 1967 - T. Trini, "E.S. jr.," *Domus*, no. 449, Milan, July; E. Sottsass jr. "Come proteggere la bellezza dalla polvere e dai piranhas," *Almanacco letterario Bompiani*, Milan. □ 1968 - G. Celant, "E.S. jr. - Design," *Flash Art*, no. 8, Rome, September. □ 1969 - E. Fratelli, "Olivetti Juke-box," *Form*, no. 46, Munich, May; "Poetic Sottsass," *The Times*, London, 26 September; *Dizionario enciclopedico di architettura e urbanistica*, Rome. □ 1970 - E. Sottsass jr.,"Esperienze con la ceramica," *Domus*, no. 489, Milan, August; E. Sottsass jr.,"Could Anything be More Ridiculous?," *Design*, no. 262, London, October. □ 1971 - E. Sottsass jr., "Proposta di comportamento," *Nac*, no. 8-9, Milan, September. □ 1972 - G. Bossi, "S.," *Rassegna*, no. 21, Milan, April; G. Celant, "Monsù Travet si colora, ovvero S. con ironia in ufficio," *Casabella*, no. 365, Milan, May; A. Natalini, "Italy: The New Domestic Landscape," *Architectural Design*, London, August; P. Fossati, *Il design in Italia 1945-1972*, Einaudi, Turin. □ 1973 - E. Sottsass jr., "Creatività pubblica," *Casabella*, no. 378, Milan, June. □ 1975 - E. Sottsass jr., *Ukyo-é Haiku & Suspence*, Quadragono Libri, Conegliano Veneto; E. Sottsass jr., "Voglio risolvere per sempre il problema mondiale dell'architettura," *Casabella*, no. 408, Milan, December. □ 1976 - F. Di Castro, *Sottsass Scrap-Book*, Documenti di Casabella, Milan *. □ 1977 - P.C. Santini, *Facendo mobili con...*, Poltronova, Firenze; M. De Lucchi, P. Bulletti, "Ettore Sottsass," *Eco d'Arte Moderna*, Firenze, May-June. □ 1980 - E. Sottsass jr., *Catalogue for decorative furniture in modern style*, Studio Forma/Alchimia, Milan. □ 1982 - V. Gregotti, *Il disegno del prodotto industriale*, Electa, Milan. □ 1983 - Design since 1945 (edited by C. Hiesinger, G. Markus), Philadelphia Museum, Philadelphia. □ 1984 - B. Radice, *Memphis*, Electa, Milan; A. Branzi, *La casa calda*, Idea Books, Milan; R.P. Baacke, U. Brandes, M. Erlhoff, *Design als Gegenstand*, Frölich & Kaufmann, Berlin; *Phoenix: New Attitudes in Design*, Queen's Quay Terminal, Toronto.

Ettore Spalletti

Born 1940 in Cappelle sul Tavo (Pescara). Lives in Capelle sul Tavo.
One-man exhibitions: 1975 - Rome, Galleria La Tartaruga. □ 1976 - Rome, Galleria Mario Pieroni. □ 1977 - Milan, Galleria Betti. □ 1978 - Bologna, Galleria Fata. □ 1979 - Rome, Galleria Pieroni. □ 1981 - Rome, Galleria Pieroni. □ 1982 - Pescara, Galleria De Domizio; Essen, Museum Folkwang; Ghent, Museum van Hedendaagse Kunst. □ 1984 - Rome, Galleria Pieroni; Villeurbanne-Lyon, Nelson Gallery.

Selected bibliography: 1975 - T. Trini, "E.S.," *Data*, no. 19, Milan, September-October. □ 1978 - B. Corà, "Contatto." *Domus*, Milan, August. □ 1980 - A. Izzo, "Colonna di colore," *Domus*, Milan, March; B. Corà, "Profili," *AEIUO*, no. 1, Rome; E. Spalletti, "Panneggio," *AEIUO*, no. 1, Rome; *E.S.*, Collezione del Clavicembalo, De Domizio, Pescara. □ 1981 - E. Spalletti,

"Gruppo della fonte," *AEIUO*, no. 2, Rome. □ 1982 - B. Corà, "Silenziose regioni del colore di E.S.," *AEIUO*, no. 5, Rome, January-July; *E.S.*, Museum Folkwang, Essen/Museum van Hedendaagse Kunst, Ghent (text by B. Corà) *. □ 1983 - E. Spalletti, "Le radiazioni azzurre...," *AEIUO*, no. 7, Rome, March. □ 1984 - J. De Sanna, "E.S.," *ArteFactum*, no. 5, Antwerp; E. Spalletti, "Monte, Collina sopra Cappelle," *AEIUO*, no. 10-11, Rome, July.

Gino Valle

Born 1923 in Udine.
Early experience in painting: two works accepted at the "Premio Bergamo" 1943. After graduating from the University Institute of Architecture, Venice 1948, he joined the studio of his father Provino.
Fullbright grant for Town planning at the Harvard Graduate School of Design 1951. BCPHGSD 1952. Travel grant to USA from the Institute of International Education, visited the works of F.L. Wright. Teacher at the CIAM International Summer School, Venice 1952-54.
Lecturer University Institute of Architecture, Venice, 1954-55.
Compasso d'Oro Award: Electric clock "Cifra 5" Solari, 1956. Compasso d'Oro Award: Kitchen Rex Zanussi, 1962.
Exhibitions: VI Biennial, Museum of Modern Art, Sao Paulo, 1956; "Form and Technique of Contemporary Architecture," Gallery of Modern Art, 1959; Exhibition of Italian industrial design, Illinois Institute of Technology, Chicago, 1959.
Academic co-ordinator and teacher of product design, advanced class of industrial design, Venice.
Member of the Education working group of ICSID, 1963-67; vice-president of ICSID, 1967-71.
Member of Unimark International, New York, Chicago, 1965-68. Annual lectureship for Royal Institute of British Architects, London: lectures at Nottingham, Preston, Glasgow, Liverpool, 1965. Visiting professor, University of Natal winter school, Durban, South Africa, 1967.
Exhibition "Ten Italian Architects," County Museum of Art, Los Angeles; Lectures at County Museum of Art, Los Angeles, Columbia University, New York, 1967. Visiting critic, Harvard Graduate School of Design, Masters program of advanced architectural design, 1970-71.
Lecturer IV course of composition for the University Institute of Architecture, Venice, 1972-76.
National member of Accademia di San Luca, 1975.
Lecturer Composition, 1-5 University Institute of Architecture, Venice, from 1977.
Exhibition "Neues Bauen in alter Umgebung," Bavarian Chamber of Architecture and New Collection, Munich, 1978. Conference at the Akademie der Bildenden Kunste, Vienna, 8 May, 1979.
Personal "Gino Valle Architect 1950-78," PAC, Milan, May/June 1979.
Conference at ETH Honggerberg, Zurich, 13 December, 1979.
Conference "Oppositions 15/16," The Institute for Architecture and Urban Studies, New York, 15 October 1980.
Conference "On my work (but gently)," The Cooper Union for the advancement of Science and Art — School of architecture, New York, 16 October, 1980.
Exhibitions: "Zgraf" International Exhibition of Graphic Design, Zagabria, 5/25 November, 1981; "Architecture in the Seventies," Gallery of Modern Art, Rome, 1981.
Visiting critic, International Summer Academy of Art, Salzburg, 1981-82.
Member of the "Creative Committee," Salzburg, 1983-84.
Guest professor, Academy of Art, Vienna, 1985.

Selected bibliography: 1955 - G. Samonà, "Architettura di giovani," *Casabella*, no. 205, Milan. □ 1958 - J. Rykwert, "L'opera dello Studio architetti Valle," *Architecture and Building*, London, April; R. Banhan, "Condominio a Trieste," *The Architectural Review*, no. 742, London, November. □ 1959 - F. Tentori, "Tre opere ed un progetto dello Studio Valle," *Casabella*, no. 226, Milan, April; B. Zevi, "Monumento alla Resistenza di Udine," *L'Architettura*, no. 46, Rome, August. □ 1960 - F. Tentori, "Dieci anni di attività dello Studio Valle," *Casabella*, no. 246, Milan, December. □ 1961 - R. Banhan, "World Studio Valle," *The Architectural Review*, no. 772, London, June. □ 1962 - G. Dorfles, *Il disegno industriale e la sua estetica*, Cappelli, Milan. □ 1964 - J. Rykwert, "Il lavoro di G.V.," *Architectural Design*, London, March; E.L. Smith, "Things Seen - The Architectural Imagination," *Times*, New York, April. □ 1965 - J. Rykwert, "Architetture di G.V.," *Domus*, no. 426, Milan. □ 1970 - J. Rykwert, G.V., edifici industriali," *Domus*, no. 429, Milan, November; "G.V.," *Zodiac*, no. 20, Milan, December. □ 1975 - F. Dal Co, "La necessità dell'architettura," *Lotus International*, no. 11., Milan. □ 1978 - "Büro und Geschaftshaus, Udine, Italien, 1966," *Neues Bauen in alter Umgebung*, Die Neue Sammlung Staatliches Museum für angewandte Kunst, Munich. □ 1979 - *G.V. architetto 1950-1978*, Padiglione d'Arte Contemporanea/Idea Editions, Milan (text by G. Celant, J. Rykwert) *; J. Glancey, "Factory, Udine, Italy," *The Architectural Review*, no. 992, London, October. □ 1981 - C. Santini, "G.V.," *Il materiale delle arti*, Punto e Linea, Milan; C. De Seta, *Storia dell'arte in Italia - L'architettura del novecento*, UTET, Turin. □ 1982 - V. Gregotti, *Il disegno del prodotto industriale - Italia 1860-1980*, Electa, Milan; M. Tafuri, *Storia dell'arte italiana - Il novecento*, Einaudi, Turin; K. Frampton, "The Ism of Contemporary Architecture," *Architectural Design*, no. 52, London, July,-August; "Gino Valle, Banca Commerciale Italiana," *Skyline*, New York, November. □ 1983 - "Gino Valle," *Wege oder Irrwege der Architektur*, Internationale Sommerakademie Salzburg/Tusch, Vienna.

Emilio Vedova

Born 1919 in Venice. Lives in Venice. One-man exhibitions: 1942 - Milan, Galleria La Spiga e Corrente. □ 1945 - Mantua, Galleria del Pioppo; Venice, Galleria Venezia; Venice, Piccola Galleria. □ 1946 - Rome, Galleria dell'Art Club; Rome, Galleria dello Scorpione; Turin, Galleria del Bosco; Venice, Piccola Galleria. □ 1947 - Venice, Galleria del Cavallino. □ 1951 - New York, Viviano Gallery. □ 1952 - Venice, XXVI Biennale. □ 1953 - Modena, Saletta degli Amici dell'Arte. □ 1954 - Venice, Galleria del Cavallino. □ 1956 - Munich, Galerie Franke; Venice, XXVIII Biennale; Vienna, Galerie Würthle. □ 1957 - Berlin, Galerie Springer. □ 1958 - Warsaw, Palais Zachenta; Poznan, Museum Narodowe. □ 1959 - Munich, Galerie Franke; Rome, Galleria Il Segno; Milan, Galleria Blu; Milan, Galleria del Disegno; Palermo, Galleria Tindari; Kassel, Documenta III, Museum Fridericianum and Alte Galerie. □ 1960 - Venice, XXX Biennale. □ 1961 - Verona, Galleria Civica d'Arte Moderna, Palazzo della Gran Guardia; Bologna, Galleria Il Cancello; Naples, Galleria San Carlo; Copenhagen, Galerie M 59; Madrid, Atheneum; Barcelona, Sala Gaspar; Cordoba, Galeria Liceo; Florence, Galleria Quadrante. □ 1962 - Munich, Galerie Franke; Freiburg im Breisgau,

Kunstverein; Rome, Libreria Einaudi; Copenhagen, Galerie Haghfelt. □ 1963 - Stockholm, Galerie Pierre; Rome, Galleria Marlborough. □ 1964 - Kassel, Museum Fridericianum and Alte Galerie; Soest, Kunstpavillon; Munich, Galerie Franke and Galerie Franke Arco Palais; Baden-Baden, Staatliche Kunsthalle. □ - Washington, Institute of Contemporary Art; Salzburg, Künstlerhaus. □ 1967 - Prague, Galerie Hollaru; Padua, Galleria La Chiocciola. □ 1968 - Salzburg, Palais Residenz; Ferrara, Galleria Civica d'Arte Moderna, Palazzo dei Diamanti. □ 1969 - Vicenza, Galleria Ghelfi; Salsburg, Schloss Mirabell. □ 1970 - Trieste, Galleria Torbandena; Havana (Cuba), Museo de L'Habana; Heidelberg, Galerie Rothe. □ 1971 - Bolzano, Studio 3B; Zagreb, Galerie Forum; Munich, Galerie Franzius. □ 1972 - Milano, Galleria Falchi; Saciletto, Centro Internazionale Grafico. □ 1973 - Rome, Galleria Lo Spazio. □ 1974 - Verona, Galleria Linea 70; Trieste, Galleria Forum; Milan, Galleria Rizzardi. □ 1975 - Turin, Galleria 3A; Aosta, Tour Fromage Teatro Romano; Vigevano, Galleria Il Nome; Pavia, Civici Musei, Castello Visconteo. □ 1976 - Ravenna, Galleria Mariani; Verona, Galleria Nuova Scaligera; Rome, Galleria Incontro d'Arte. □ 1977 - Florence, Galleria 4 Emme; Varese, Galleria Bluart; Naples, Galleria Lo Spazio. □ 1978 - Portofino, Galleria Civica d'Arte Moderna, Castello di Portofino. □ 1979 - Prato, Sala Medievale di San Jacopo; Sidney, The Art Gallery of Western Australia; Brisbane, National Gallery; Adelaide, National Gallery; Mexico City, Museo Carillo Gill; Innsbruck, Galerie im Taxispalais. □ 1980 - Bregenz, Künstlerhaus, Palais Thurn und Taxis; Vienna, Museum für Moderne Kunst, Palais Lichtenstein; Trieste, Galleria Planetario. □ 1981 - Leverkusen, Städtisches Museum Schloss Morsbroich; San Marino, Palazzo dei Congressi; Braunschweig, Kunstverein. □ 1982 - Eindhoven, Stedelijk van Abbemuseum; Bologna, Galleria d'Arte Moderna; Zurich, Galerie Verna. □ 1983 - Zurich, Galerie Verna; Venice, Università, Facoltà di Lettere e Filosofia, Istituto di Discipline Artistiche; Cologne, Galerie Borgmann; Munich, Galerie Jahn; Padua, Galleria Stevens; Milan, Studio Marconi; Belgrade, Galerie Sebastian. □ 1984 - Capo d'Istria, Galerie Loza and Galeria Meduza; Basel, Galerie Buchmann; Turin, Galleria Giorgio Persano.

***

...There are messages, in the "Plurimi", in the "Pages," in the "Binari", in the "fragments" — there among the things that are hidden, thrown away; there in the attempts where discovery places you "at the mercy" of everyone, buffeted by the wind.

The greatest work, after having "understood" infinite freedom, is work that delves. Putting out constant antennae of free exploration, open to everything. To penetrate secret, not readily identified territory — I repeat — to be tied down to no place, to possess without categorizing, is a dramatic gymnastic feat, meant to recreate — in the territories of equivalence, of metaphor, of sign, of scribbling — subtle, deep stratifications, and also equivalents of possible rarefications... The stronger the delving, the greater one's chance of locating the equivalent — in this sense the gymnastics, the means, the materials... We will not deck ourselves out in "tinsel"... In these "other" realms, feelings/facts are nude.

Experimentation... "to no purpose"... one begins by chance, "as if according to a game," I wrote (1967) "and then you are *inside,* initiations exist side by side, one after the other... the material hones you, it realizes you."

How many times, recently too, yesterday in the studio, that work which you pull off, which you don't pull off, becomes "magic," it becomes a person, a dialogue, until it finally becomes the equivalent of your feelings, of yourself.

In this way one might recuperate fragments, technical attempts, automatic truths, first confessions — wild, unbridled, flailing... without prefabrication or mental control, without being ritualized or swathed in the robes of the painter/pontiff... Defenceless fragments, to be called defenceless, begin thus.

Unsayable words, difficulties. The uncommunicable, the relentless, tense attempts at equivalences. The extremely fragile, disquieting terrain of equivalence. The stratified initiations to the "afterward," the possible verifications which then, sometimes, really aren't there.

"Abstract" — ? — My attachments delve into the "real," but where does reality begin and end? Life, in a continuum, with its infinite and never resolved experimentation, carries you to extreme realizations, in open articulation. "Confrontations"..., "lacerations"... "No"...? "...the complexity is also made up of sex, of blue, of love (but in my case, I was writing this in 1962)... confronted, lacerated... by barriers, by rhythms, by injustice."

The coherence is this propulsion of yourself into the realm of interests, life, behavior, your whole being. This final accounting of the overall: events (inner ones, as well), confrontations, choices, dramatic choices...But also "secret" portions of yourself that are not always recognized by the "clear conscience." For me, tension exists in not wanting to lose my perception of — my plumbing the depths of — the possibility of coming into contact with that interception. No style is imposed, there are no set rules.

One adopts the word "coherence" in blundering fashion; at times it is a question of maniacal faith — a wedding to a style; I have never worked with this type of prefabrication. I am too churning with life, with recklessness, with curiosity, with questions, to travel to the realm of doubt and contradiction.

As early as 1946 I wrote:"I am not afraid of contradictions, they offer me extreme evidence". What are the real implications of the question, "what party do you belong to: minimal, gestural, arte povera, land art, conceptual, etc."? And they talk about the avant-garde, the "end" of art, etc. Art: it's always something else, when it's not an acrobatic feat. Art, man, they both have secret aspects, not easily identified — just as well!

Yes, to reclaim the artist's initiation, the "mysterious" part opposed to everything that can be explained (so dear to the critic who knows everything and who lends himself to generalizations and demagogical theorizings, certainties, and sectarian divisions with ritualized expiration dates.

Going my own way, I have established the difficulty of this "mirror" work = question/identification — to reveal myself to myself, to astonish myself. That which remains non-identifiable, that which continues to be delved into, grows, proliferates, invades your knowledge of yourself.

"Complex stratifications," I wrote in 1953... In this perennial, extended investigation one more often than not interjects the question, "the avant-garde?" The *Truth* is not that we're a pile of old bones (that's a self-perpetuating argument), but that we can "touch extreme truths, moments, flashes, of truth..." (I wrote in 1962)... Artistic pratice lies in one's reckless entry into new territory, one's pushing, one's contradictions, one's betrayals. In this sense I am against styles. I want to break them, destroy them, in the peremptory verification of feeling, in every choice I make, from yesterday to today... It requires more strength for me to let go of the document I have produced, with all my existential errors, in a "wild state" — I/text, you/text.

Emilio Vedova, 1980

***

Selected bibliography: 1942 - *E.V.*, Galleria La Spiga e Corrente, Milan (text by D. Morosini). □ 1945 - *E.V.*, Galleria del Pioppo, Mantua (text by G. Marchiori). □ 1946 - *E.V.*, Piccola Galleria, Venice (text by E. Vedova). □ 1951 - *E.V.*, Viviano Gallery, New York (text by R. Pallucchini). □ 1956 - *E.V.*, Günther Franke, Munich (text G.C. Argan). □ 1957 - *E.V.*, Springer, Berlin (text by W. Haftmann). □ 1958 - *E.V.*, Zachenta, Warsaw (texts by G.C. Argan, G. Marchiori, J. Starzynski); *E.V.*, Muzeum Naradowe, Poznan (text by Z. Kepinski). □ 1959 - *E.V.*, Günther Franke, Munich (text by W. Haftmann). □ 1960 - E. Vedova, *Blätter aus dem Tagebuch*, Prestel Verlag, Munich. □ 1961 - *E.V.*, Galleria Civica d'Arte Moderna, Verona (texts by G.C. Argan, V. Aguilera Cerni, U. Apollonio, S. Branzi, M. Calvesi, W. Haftmann, Z. Kepinski, J. Leymarie, L. Magagnato, G. Marchiori, G. Mazzariol, N. Ponente, C.L. Ragghianti, F. Russoli, M. Valsecchi, L. Venturi, C. Vivaldi); *E.V.*, Galerie M 59, Copenhagen (text by M. Calvesi); *E.V.*, Ateneo, Madrid (texts by G.C. Argan, V. Aguilera Cerni, U. Apollonio, W. Haftmann, J. Leymarie, Z. Kejanski, G. Marchiori, M. Pedrosa); *E.V.*, Sala Gaspar, Barcelona (texts by G.C. Argan. V. Aguilera Cerni). □ 1962 - *E.V.*, Kunstverein, Freiburg (text by F. Bayl); *Papeles de son Armadans*, special issue on Vedova, n. LXXX, Palma de Mallorca. □ 1963 - E. Vedova, *Scontro di situazioni*, Pesce d'Oro, Milan; *E.V.*, Galleria Marlborough, Rome. □ 1964 - *E.V.*, Staatliche Kunsthalle, Baden-Baden (text by W. Haftmann, D. Mahlow, W. Sandberg, E. Vedova). □ 1968 - *E.V.*, Galleria Civica d'Arte Moderna, Ferrara (texts by G. Montana, E. Vedova). □ 1974 - *E.V.*, Tour Fromage, Aosta (texts by G.C. Argan, Z. Birolli, F. Bayl, J. Leymarie, E. Vedova); *E.V.*, Civici Musei, Pavia (texts by R. Alberti, V. Aguilera Cerni, G.C. Argan, V. Fagone, A. Tapies, E. Vedova). □ 1978 - *E.V.*, Galleria Civica d'Arte Moderna, Portofino (texts by G.C. Argan, V. Fagone. E. Vedova). □ 1979 - *E.V.*, Sala San Jacopo, Prato (texts by G.C. Argan, Z. Birolli, A. Bonito Oliva, V. Fagone, A. Ginsberg, G. Marchiori, N. Ponente, E. Sanguineti, L. Vinca Masini, E. Vedova); *E.V.*, Galerie im Taxispalais, Innsbruck (texts by G.C. Argan, U. Apollonio, F. Bayl, M. Fagiolo, W. Haftmann, J. Leymarie, G. Marchiori, E. Vedova). □ 1980 - *E.V.*, Galleria Planetario, Trieste (texts by P. Restany, E. Vedova). □ 1981 - *E.V.*, Städtisches Museum, Leverkusen (text by R. Wedewer); *Vedova -Compresenze 1946-1981*, Electa, Milan (texts by G.C. Argan, M. Calvesi); *E.V.*, Kunstverein, Braunschweig (texts by J. Schilling, E. Vedova). □ 1982 - *E.V.*, Stedelijk van Abbemuseum, Eindhoven (texts by R. Fuchs, E. Vedova); F. Menna, *Vedova*, Vanessa Edizioni d'Arte, Milan. □ 1984 - *E.V.*, Bachmann, Basel (texts by P. Guyer, M. Kunz, E. Vedova); *Vedova 1935-1984*, Electa, Milan (edited by G. Celant, texts by G.C. Argan, U. Apollonio, D. Ashton, P. Bucarelli, F. Bayl, C. Brandi, A. Bonito Oliva, M. Cacciari, M. Calvesi, G. Celant, A. Coliva, M. Fagiolo, V. Fagone, R. Fuchs, J. Gachnang, P. Hulten, W. Haftmann, G. Marchiori, G. Mazzariol, L. Magagnato, F. Menna, R. Pallucchini, N. Ponente, G. Romanelli, F. Russoli, H. Read, P. Restany, E. Sanguineti, C. Spadoni, W. Sandberg, A. Tapies, B. Zevi) *.

Massimo Vignelli

Born 1931 in Milan.
Studied architecture in Milan and Venice. Since then he has worked with his wife, Lella, an architect, involved with the design of corporate identity and graphic programs; transportation and architectural graphics; books, magazines and newspapers; exhibitions and interiors, and through Vignelli Designs, furniture and a variety of products.
Originally based in Milan, the firm has been working for major American and European companies and institutions. Based in the USA since 1965, the Vignellis have had their work exhibited throughout the world and entered in the permanent collections of several museum. Mr. Vignelli has taught and lectured on design in the major cities and universities in the USA and abroad.
Among the Vignellis' many awards: Gran Premio Triennale di Milano 1964; Compasso d'oro, ADI 1964; the 1973 Industrial Arts Medal of the American Institute of Architects; Honorary Doctorate from the Parsons School of Design, NY; the Art Directors Club 1982 Hall of Fame; the 1983 Gold Medal of the American Institute of Graphic Arts.

Selected bibliography: *Design: Vignelli*, Rizzoli, New York, 1981.

Finito di stampare nel gennaio 1985
presso le Arti Grafiche Leva A & G di Sesto S. Giovanni (MI)
per conto delle Nuove Edizioni Gabriele Mazzotta srl